AF718471

The Fall and Rise of Keynesian Economics

Finance and the Economy

A CERF Series edited by John Eatwell

The Cambridge Endowment for Research in Finance (CERF) was founded in 2001 as an independent resource at the University of Cambridge. It is dedicated to developing an enhanced understanding of the evolution and behaviour of financial markets and institutions, notably in their role as major determinants of economic behaviour and performance. CERF promotes theoretical, quantitative and historical studies, crossing conventional disciplinary boundaries to bring together research groups of economists, mathematicians, lawyers, historians, computer scientists and market practitioners. Particular attention is paid to the analysis of the impact of financial market activity on the formulation of public policy. As well as individual research projects, CERF funds *Cambridge Finance*, the organisation that brings together researchers in finance from all departments of Cambridge University. The CERF series of publications on *Finance and the Economy* embodies new research in these areas.

Global Governance of Financial Systems: The International Regulation of Systemic Risk
Edited by Kern Alexander, Rahul Dhumale, and John Eatwell

Identifying International Financial Contagion: Progress and Challenges
Edited by Mardi Dungey and Demosthenes N. Tambakis

Transmission of Financial Crises and Contagion: A Latent Factor Approach
Edited by Mardi Dungey, Renée A. Fry, Brenda González-Hermosillo, and Vance L. Martin

The Fall and Rise of Keynesian Economics
John Eatwell and Murray Milgate

The Fall and Rise of Keynesian Economics

JOHN EATWELL AND MURRAY MILGATE

OXFORD
UNIVERSITY PRESS

OXFORD
UNIVERSITY PRESS

Oxford University Press, Inc., publishes works that further
Oxford University's objective of excellence
in research, scholarship, and education.

Oxford New York
Auckland Cape Town Dar es Salaam Hong Kong Karachi
Kuala Lumpur Madrid Melbourne Mexico City Nairobi
New Delhi Shanghai Taipei Toronto

With offices in
Argentina Austria Brazil Chile Czech Republic France Greece
Guatemala Hungary Italy Japan Poland Portugal Singapore
South Korea Switzerland Thailand Turkey Ukraine Vietnam

Copyright © 2011 by Oxford University Press, Inc.

Published by Oxford University Press, Inc.
198 Madison Avenue, New York, New York 10016

www.oup.com

Oxford is a registered trademark of Oxford University Press

All rights reserved. No part of this publication may be reproduced,
stored in a retrieval system, or transmitted, in any form or by any means,
electronic, mechanical, photocopying, recording, or otherwise,
without the prior permission of Oxford University Press.

Library of Congress Cataloging-in-Publication Data

Eatwell, John.
The fall and rise of keynesian economics /
John Eatwell and Murray Milgate.
p. cm.
Includes bibliographical references and index.
ISBN 978-0-19-977769-3 (cloth. : alk. paper)
1. Keynesian economics. 2. Economic history—1918–1945.
3. Economic history—1945– I. Milgate, Murray. II. Title.
HB99.7.E26 2011
330.15'6—dc22 2010032103

3 5 7 9 8 6 4

Printed in the United States of America
on acid-free paper

Contents

Part Three: Critical

Part Four: Historical

Preface

The global financial crisis and the world recession it produced were the latest in a series of crises that have come to plague the international economy. Such crises have become increasingly frequent and more intense as the liberalization of financial markets accelerated after the collapse of the Bretton Woods system some forty years ago. That each of them cannot be treated as an isolated event with solitary causes, but were instead events that shared common origins, has become clear to us all. Their origins, we now find, reside in part in the consequences of a process of financial liberalization that was allowed to proceed without sufficient consideration being given to the magnification of systemic risk it entailed, and in part in the consequences of the neoliberal dogmas that came to dominate practical policymaking during those same years.

The almost hypnotic power of these failed dogmas should not be underestimated. There are grown men and women—some even among professional economists—who continue to maintain that there are no multiplier effects to be had from loan expenditure undertaken by governments during a slump. It is still possible to hear the wrong-headed opinion that while an increase in public indebtedness during a recession is to be avoided at all costs, an increase in the aggregate of private indebtedness on a similar scale (supposedly easily engineered simply by getting credit channels flowing) offers an entirely unproblematic solution to our present problems.

There remain a few academic economists continuing to promote the perverse idea that in times of actual or threatened deflation, widespread spare capacity, and involuntary unemployment—with world growth, effective demand, and investor and consumer confidence all fragile—we should focus all our attention on the remote possibility of inflation "down the line." There are politicians who warn us that by borrowing for current spending we are transferring the burden of repayment to future generations, apparently not noticing that if we actually had such magical powers, future generations would simply use them to do the same thing when the time came.

There are authorities and policymakers urging us to do something about "the huge" budget deficit; and there are not a few European governments actually instituting swinging cuts in public spending to reduce the ratio of the deficit to GDP (some of them, admittedly, against their will)—seemingly without any discernable concern for the economic consequences of what they are saying and doing. Even when schoolchildren begin to learn about fractions, one of the first things they are taught is that a fraction can be lowered either by reducing its numerator or increasing its denominator (or by doing a bit of both). But when that fraction is the ratio of the budget deficit to GDP, it is surprising how many seem to forget entirely their elementary arithmetic and proceed to speak as if the only way to reduce that ratio is to cut the deficit. This would be misleading enough—since the objective might just as well be achieved by thinking of ways of increasing GDP—but it is positively crazy if cutting expenditure may *decrease* GDP. This is a lesson that the European Union has chosen to learn the hard way—as governments from Greece and Ireland, through to Italy, Spain, Portugal, Germany, and Britain, are slashing public expenditures to reduce "the deficit." The U.S. administration is understandably concerned.

Then there is the national debt to be considered. Should this be as worrying a thing in our present circumstances as we are led to believe it is? Those who urge us to think so, often speak of it as a "mountain of debt." They mention, for example, that in the United States during 2010 it was increasing by $3.8 billion every day—not noticing that without some point of reference, this number on its own is completely meaningless. Or they talk about the ratio of debt to GDP and "the mess we are in" because of it—forgetting that "the mess we are in" is the result of a global recession (caused by a financial crisis) from which recovery appears to be slow at best. Moreover, just what this particular ratio actually tells us about how vulnerable we are, since it is the ratio of a stock to a flow, is difficult to say. If we imagine that it has reached, say, one to one (100%), what would that mean? Before answering, it is well to remember that for most ordinary citizens with a mortgage, the ratio of their *stock* of debt to their *flow* of income ratio is usually about two or three to one (200–300%)—and for some corporations it can be several hundreds to one. Yet they are all perfectly solvent. Our vulnerability might, therefore, be more meaningfully captured by looking at the ratio of a stock to a stock—say, public debt to private net wealth. In the United States in 2009, for example, this was a little under a rather more prudent 23%. Or one might look at the ratio of a flow to a flow—say, the ratio of annual debt servicing charges to GDP. In Britain in 2010, for example, this was just over a rather insignificant 2%. In the United States in 2010, it was a little less than this. Even if we add a charge against current income to allow for the retirement of existing debt, that figure goes up only slightly.

The only thing that the public debt to GDP ratio actually tells us at a glance is roughly how many years (and what average annual tax revenue) would be needed to redeem it—and the answer is "not many" (and "not too much"). Furthermore, even a quick glance at the level this misleading ratio for the last hundred years in the UK, for example, reveals that current-level debt to GDP looks rather more like a molehill than a mountain. It moved above one to one (100%) in 1918, peaked at above two to one (237%) in 1947, and did not again fall below one to one until 1962. The reality is that the truly alpine levels of UK public debt persisted for the better part of half a century, during which governments were following exactly the wrong-headed fiscal policies recommended by the purveyors of debt-crisis talk of today. The mountainous regions were left behind only once the economic policies of the Keynesian Consensus took full effect over fifty years ago. The message of experience is simple and compelling: reduce public spending and one thing is bound to follow—effective demand will fall and exert a dampening effect on growth. If the economy is operating with spare capacity and unemployment, as it normally is, this in turn will lead inevitably to more unemployment, more business failures, and possibly even *higher* ratios of deficit and debt to GDP in the medium term, not lower ones.

Nevertheless there are powerful vested interests, economic and political, devoted to preserving these and other failed dogmas. The facts of experience are not allowed to stand in the way of their propagation. Contrary evidence is either ignored or taken as providing exceptions that prove the rule. But sometimes when things sound like nonsense, they are just that.

A tendency just as unhelpful was going on in the tabloid press: to go after the culprits. They demand to know *who* was to blame—and given the widely reported size of bankers' bonuses, it was hardly surprising to find a strong public sentiment, coupled with a remarkable political consensus, ready to blame greedy bankers for all that they are going through. The unedifying spectacle of bankers (whose annual bonuses often exceeded the prospective lifetime earnings of ordinary citizens) defending obscenely large bonuses was not well designed to win favor in the public eye. When the public was told by those very bankers that, without such mammoth bonuses the world as they knew it would come to an end, the public had apparently not forgotten that the world almost *did* come to an end when those very bonuses (and the kind of incentives they created) went unquestioned. When bankers warned that they might pack their bags and leave town if their bonuses were curtailed, the numbers who might have joined a line at the airport to wave them goodbye would likely have stretched for miles. In these circumstances, the public disgust at the money-grubbing behavior of bankers, the vilification and sense of moral outrage that accompanied it, was understandable. But while many individuals certainly behaved recklessly, and many were driven by raw greed, an explanation of the crisis based on that fact is not at all satisfactory. Nor is it a sound starting point from which to draw any moral, social, or economic lessons from what has happened.

Fortunately, however, there are wiser and more considered voices to be heard. They can be heard in business, in government, in finance, and in academia—all advocating a return to a sounder, tried-and-tested set of ideas. They have exerted a salutary influence on the framing of policy responses to the global financial crisis, recession, and recovery that may just save the day. But the climate of opinion is in a state of flux in more ways than one. Politicians are listening increasingly to the sectional interests when they would be better advised to focus on targets for growth and jobs rather than targets for borrowing and the debt. Unlike growth and unemployment, the levels of borrowing and the debt can be left to take care of themselves if economic growth picks up. Hitting ill-judged targets for borrowing and the debt is likely to leave growth and unemployment either unchanged or permanently worsened. The one thing we have learned from our experience is that it is an error to think that growth and unemployment can be left to "take care of themselves" if deficit targets are actually achieved.

There is also another danger with this perverse but growing fashion for fiscal austerity—namely, that we will overlook the fact that what is urgently needed is reform of the international financial system, which delivered us into the recession, rather than the immediate downsizing of public finances. That recession has taught us nothing if not that the idea that real economy invariably takes care of itself, and that markets for financial assets (money and securities) merely reflect those real "fundamentals," needs modifying. What economists call "the neutrality of money" and "the classical dichotomy" are dangerous doctrines—something John Maynard Keynes pointed out many years ago. It always comes as something of a shock to think that many apparently sensible people believed in these fictions. In the 1980s, central bankers believed them when they convinced themselves that by restricting monetary growth and creating independent central banks they had brought oil-shock inflation down to single digits—when inflation was actually halted by the crash in the real economy that their monetary policies induced. In the 1990s, subscribers to the efficient-markets hypothesis continued to believed them even in the face of the collapse of Japanese asset markets and the bursting of the dot-com bubble. That the idea still has adherents, even after the global financial crisis of 2008 produced the biggest collapse in real economic activity across the world since the Great Depression, is positively mind-boggling.

In this volume, we have brought together in one place some of our own attempts to understand what has gone wrong, why we have regularly found ourselves in such predicaments, and how the situation might begin to be remedied. Some of these essays are newly written and are published here for the first time, while others are newly revised versions of previously published work. A few appear as originally written. The central theme of all of them, collectively, is not only that it is time to act boldly but that it is time to think boldly as well. Acting boldly in the face of a crisis is admirable and to be welcomed. But without thinking boldly too, we may well find ourselves, in not too many years from now, being seduced by the same old and failed economic dogmas that landed us in the mess in the first place.

We have organized the chapters that follow under four themes. The first theme is practical: the role of liquidity in financial crisis; the problem of systemic risk and its regulatory implications; the framing of appropriate fiscal and monetary policies in the face of recession and a fragile recovery; the consequences of financial liberalization on world development; and the effectiveness of the various policy responses to the financial crisis and world recession that have been tried so far, and some suggestions for reform. The second theme is analytical: the foundations of both the theoretical ideas that appear to inform past dogmas and those of an alternative framework that seems to offer a more solid analytical basis from which to proceed. The third theme is critical of the orthodox approaches to theory and practice that have contributed to our current difficulties. The last theme is historical. With the name of Keynes now appearing with greater frequency in the media than at any other time in the last forty years, we must ask not only what we might and might not have to learn from Keynes but also how his legacy has been transformed in the process of attempting to accommodate some of his more challenging analytical innovations within the mainstream of economic thinking. Whether and how what Keynes had to say in the context of the interwar economic crisis might apply to us today is an important question to be answered. The answer is not straightforward.

Some of these chapters focus on a range of issues that have arisen since the fall of Keynesian economics—but they do so from a consistently Keynesian perspective. We seek to highlight the possibility that different and compelling interpretations are available to explain what were, and are, often believed to be anti-Keynesian "facts." Different national experiences of unemployment (and the phenomenon of jobless recovery), for example, may be better understood by reference to a slackening of global effective demand, and as a consequent increase in disguised unemployment, than by reference to the operation of labor-market inflexibilities. Or, to take another example, the poor macroeconomic performance of certain economies after the imposition of externally formulated crisis-resolution measures (usually by the IMF) may similarly be better understood as a consequence of the negative impact on aggregate demand (and growth) of those very measures than by reference to incomplete or inadequate structural reform. Other chapters attempt to show how Keynesian ideas might fruitfully be applied to a variety of contemporary economic problems to yield not only a better understanding or their nature and causes but also a better guide to the remedies we might seek to apply in our efforts to solve them. However, together with the welcome rise of Keynesian economics in the face of the global financial crisis and world recession, where its practical insights have saved us much pain and suffering, has come a potential threat to its persistence. The danger is that Keynesian economics may yet come to be viewed as nothing more than the "economics of crises"—to be put aside "when things get better." It is our contention that there is (and was) much more to it than that.

The chapters attempt to illustrate how powerful Keynesian ideas can be when applied to our past and present economic and financial predicaments, and how helpful they are in explaining how we came to be in the mess we are in; they seek to reveal the analytical and methodological foundations of the conventional macroeconomic wisdom and to highlight where and how they may be wanting; they discuss an alternative analytical and conceptual framework drawing on the original Keynesian theoretical insights; and they highlight some of the interpretative weaknesses that have come to characterize Keynesian scholarship itself.

Taken together, these chapters suggest some of the concrete ways in which Keynesian economics might have much more to offer, both practically and analytically, to the serious study of the global economy. If these suggestions do no more than induce the reader to think again, we should regard our efforts as worthwhile. Acknowledgment is due to Academic Press, Duckworth, Elsevier, M.E Sharpe, Macmillan, Oxford University Press, Polity Press, the UNDP/ODS, and the editors of the *Cambridge Journal of Economics, Contributions to Political Economy* and the *History of European Ideas* for permission to use material by us previously published.

John Eatwell and Murray Milgate
Cambridge
July 2010

Preamble

The fall of the Keynesian Consensus may be dated from Milton Friedman's Presidential Address to the 1967 meeting of the American Economic Association. The main target of Friedman's critique was an adaptation of the Phillips Curve, which began as an empirical observation but had by then been transformed into an analytical function—a precise and stable trade-off between inflation and unemployment that served to close the familiar four-quadrant relationship among money markets, investment and output, and output and employment. It completed the Keynesian model, creating a satisfying closed system within which the impact of the levers of monetary and fiscal policy on output, employment, and inflation might be analyzed.

Friedman argued that the trade-off could only be a short-run phenomenon. In the longer run, once actors in the economy had fully absorbed and could anticipate the rate of inflation, the Phillips Curve would be vertical at a given level of employment—the natural rate. Hence, monetary policy might affect the employment–inflation trade-off in the short run, but in the long run it could not influence the level of employment that is "ground out by the Walrasian system of general equilibrium equations" (Friedman, 1968, p. 8). Similarly, fiscal policy could have no permanent effect on output. An increase in government spending would result in a higher rate of interest, "crowding out" private-sector investment.

The events of the 1970s, in particular the coexistence of high rates of inflation and rising unemployment following the oil crisis of 1974, suggested that Friedman's critique of the Phillips Curve was well founded and that expansionary fiscal policy was not effective as a means of increasing output and employment. The simple verities of the era of Keynesian demand management had gone. Attention switched to the monetarist approach advocated by Friedman: free markets would ensure that the Walrasian equations had full scope to grind out the long-run equilibrium, and monetary policy would determine the rate of inflation. The financial liberalization that followed the collapse of the Bretton Woods system in 1971 reinforced the emphasis that policymakers now placed on financial stability ("sound monetary policies").

A wide variety of analytical developments followed. These ranged from real-business-cycle models that attributed fluctuations in economic activity to real shocks to the rise of New Keynesian Economics—models that studied the impact of market rigidities on macroeconomic outcomes. In real-business-cycle theory, recessions are the outcome of changes in the real economy, not the result of "sticky" nominal variables. Business cycles are "real" in that they do not represent a failure of markets to clear, but instead reflect the most efficient possible operation of the economy, given its structure. Governments should therefore concentrate on the long-run structural policy changes and not intervene actively to smooth short-term fluctuations.

What is remarkable is that all these models, from that embodied in Friedman's address to all the models that have followed, presume that the economy has a tendency to operate at a position in which all markets clear at full employment. Equilibrium prices and equilibrium quantities are determined simultaneously. What differentiate the models are the assumptions made about the formation of expectations (rational or otherwise), the nature of nominal and/or real shocks, and the modeling of price and quantity rigidities. Macroeconomic models are therefore catalogues of imperfections and shocks.

Nonetheless, all of these models assume that the economy tends to exhibit a market-clearing equilibrium. Without this assumption, none of them have analytical substance; yet few of them bother to consider whether that assumption is valid.

Market-Clearing Equilibrium and Macroeconomic Models

The only proof of market-clearing equilibrium is that provided by Arrow and Debreu (1954), and it is therefore on that analysis that macroeconomic modeling rests. However, no such link can be shown to exist. The so-called Sonnenschein-Mantel-Debreu theorem demonstrates that well-behaved microfoundations may be associated with *any* arbitrary market aggregate excess-demand function, thus effectively ruling out the possibility of uniqueness and stability. Equilibria exist, but they are totally arbitrary. As Mas-Collell, Whinston, and Green put it, "Anything goes" (1995, p. 598). This result is robust even in the face of major simplifications, such as the assumption of homothetic utility functions. Therefore, "every theorist who wants to argue that a change in some price variable (a wage, interest or exchange rate, for example) affects a corresponding quantity aggregate in a definite direction cannot base this argument on general equilibrium theory" (Rizvi, 1994, p. 363).

These results are devastating for any macroeconomic theory based on the presumption of a market-clearing equilibrium, since no such presumption can be made. In fact, all models based either on imperfections and rigidities or on shocks, financial or real, are otiose. Given that Sonnenschein-Mantel-Debreu results were developed by distinguished analysts working within the core of neoclassical theory, the systematic neglect of their implications is, to put the matter politely, extraordinary.

It worth emphasizing that the Sonnenschein-Mantel-Debreu results exist for an exchange economy. They derive essentially from the implications of wealth effects on the aggregation of individual excess-demand functions. The extension of the model to production from nonreproducible factors (land and labor, say) does not introduce any further complications (as if any were necessary), but removes any sense from the assumption of gross substitutability—one of the mathematical "escape routes" with, even in the pure exchange case, negligible economic rationale.

The further extension of the analysis to include reproducible means of production—that is, the extension to some relevance to real economic problems—creates yet more problems. As is now well known, it is not possible to prove an existence theorem for the long-run equilibrium of an economy that includes reproducible means of production. In this case, the problem arises from the fact that it is not possible to specify the endowment of reproducible means of production in a manner that is compatible with the determination of an equilibrium in which there is a uniform rate of profit on the value of each set of capital goods. The association of the uniform rate of profit with long-run equilibrium is exactly the same as the proposition that, in equilibrium, the supply of reproducible commodities (whether consumer goods or capital goods) will be adjusted to the demand for them. This conception of equilibrium is inherited from Adam Smith's definition of "natural price" and Marshall's "long-run"; it is intuitively powerful as a "centre of gravitation" of the economy, whether in prices or quantities.[1] The idea of long-run equilibrium is therefore unavailable to neoclassical analysis.

The Arrow-Debreu equilibrium is different. Each potentially producible commodity is listed in the endowment as a fixed quantity, and prices clear markets for those quantities. Suppose, then, that there is a relatively large quantity of capital good *A* in the endowment. Its price will tend to be low relative to its cost of reproduction (its production would result in a return lower than that on other capital goods), and instead of being produced, the stock will be run down. But this below-"normal" price is the equilibrium market price. And for each arbitrary set of initial endowments there will be a different set of market-clearing prices. The whole idea of equilibrium being associated with the *adjustment* of supply to demand is lost, as is any meaningful sense of a center of gravitation.

These overwhelmingly negative results suggest that it is not possible to construct macroeconomic analysis on neoclassical microeconomic foundations. In particular, the assumption that the normal position of the economy may be characterized as a market-clearing, and hence full-employment, equilibrium is totally unwarranted. A different approach is needed.

The Rise (Again) of Keynesian Analysis

At first sight, Keynes's analysis of effective demand eschews any consideration of the theory of value and distribution. But given that the essence of the principle of effective demand involves a link between monetary expenditures and the determination of levels of real output and employment, prices must be a necessary component of the analysis—including the relative prices of commodities and labor. This, then, poses the question of what the relationship is, if any, between the determination of relative prices and the determination of the level of effective demand. Simply taking prices as given opens the theory to criticism that the role of prices in a market economy has simply been assumed away.

However, an alternative approach to price determination is available. Piero Sraffa presented an analysis of the relationship between the distribution of income and the conditions of production of commodities in the determination of normal prices that is totally different from neoclassical theory. Instead, his analysis is akin to the classical theory of price associated with Ricardo. In classical theory, the question of the relationship between aggregate capacity and demand is subsumed in the *assertion* that saving is investment. Demand could not set a permanent limit to production or, as Ricardo put it, "demand is only limited by production" (Ricardo, 1951–1973, vol. 1). The link to the demand for individual commodities is characterized as an adjustment of supply to the given "effectual demand." There was, of course, no presumption of full employment of labor.

In contrast to this assertion of normal equality between capacity and demand, neoclassical writers presented a *theory* to explain how the balance of capacity and demand is established in the long run. The demand for factors is equated to the given quantities of factors of production as the counterpart of the determination of prices by supply and demand. The competitive tendency of prices to gravitate to normal levels determined by utility maximization subject to the constraints of technology and endowments would be accompanied by a tendency toward levels of output consistent with the full utilization of all factors of production (other than free goods). The aggregate adjustment of capacity to demand is the summation of the general equilibrium adjustment of the demand for individual goods and services to the capacity available to produce them. Unfortunately, as already explained, the summation does not result in a credible analysis.

Keynes also presented a *theory* of output. In the simplest version of Keynes's analysis, the level of aggregate demand is determined by investment and the multiplier. What is the relationship between demand and capacity? It might be argued that Keynes's theory is essentially a theory of capacity *utilization*—capacity is simply given by history, and the level of effective demand determines the level of utilization, including, of course, the level of employment. As such, Keynes's theory is susceptible to interpretation as a short-run version of neoclassical theory, with the long-run tendency to full-capacity utilization being inhibited by imperfections—sticky wages, sticky prices, inappropriate monetary policies, or the impact of uncertainty disarming the price mechanism. Indeed, that is the direction that the Neoclassical Synthesis and various versions of New Keynesian Economics have taken.

Yet Keynes presented his theory as something more—as a theory of output determining a center of gravitation: "we oscillate, avoiding the gravest extremes of fluctuations in employment and prices in both directions, round an intermediate position appreciably below full employment and appreciably above the minimum employment a decline below which would endanger life" (Keynes, 1936, p. 254). The language is clearly reminiscent of Smith's "centre of gravitation." Keynes is suggesting that his theory defines the normal positions of the economy: "the mean position determined by "natural" tendencies, namely by those tendencies which are likely to persist" (Keynes, 1936, p. 254).

Two important points should be noted. First, if Keynes has indeed established a long-run or normal theory of output in which labor, and perhaps other means of production, are not fully utilized, and not free goods, then that theory would necessarily be incompatible with neoclassical analysis. Second, if the classical approach to the determination of normal prices is to be relevant within the Keynesian context of a less-than-full-employment "equilibrium," then to what extent is it presumed that productive capacity is adjusted to demand—that is, fully utilized? The answer to the conundrum rests in two empirical characteristics of price formation.

The first characteristic is that changes in the forces that determine normal prices "if continuous, would be sufficiently slow as to not endanger the gravitation toward the (slowly moving) long-period values. That same persistence would ensure that, should the changes be rapid, they would be once-for-all changes, and that, after a period of transition, gravitation to the new long-period values would again assert itself" (Garegnani, 1976, p. 28). The forces determining normal prices in the classical approach are the conditions of production of commodities and the distribution of income.

It might be reasonably assumed that the conditions of production change relatively slowly in so far as those conditions are not themselves functions of capacity utilization. Changes in demand are likely to result not only in changes in unit inputs associated with one technology as it is used more or less intensively but also in the use of different vintages of technologies (fossils) that co-exist with the competitively dominant technique. Moreover, in a dynamic setting, the dominant technique may co-exist with new, technically and economically more efficient techniques that, for the moment, earn super-normal profits. But the key to price determination is the notion that there will be a dominant or normal technique that is the determinant of normal price in competitive markets.

The second characteristic is that such a normal technique might be reasonably presumed to exist, as suggested by the study of price formation in industrial economies. It is found that normal capacity utilization does not involve the total utilization of capacity but, instead, is a level of utilization that is less than 100% and around which output will fluctuate. Prices are determined by the conditions of production at this normal level of (less-than-full) capacity utilization:

> [P]rices are determined by normal (or standard) costs, and... they do not react to temporary or cyclically reversible, changes in either demand or cost. This is what we shall call the *normal price hypothesis*. According to this view, the firm calculates the level of costs at a normal level of output, and sets prices as a mark up on normal costs without reference to temporary variations in demand. (Coutts, Godley, and Nordhaus, 1978, pp. 1–2)

In an earlier study, Godley and Nordhaus (1972) had recognized that changes in the distribution of income would impinge on their prediction of movements in normal prices:

> It must be stressed that the assumptions on which the prediction is based do not correspond completely to the authors' views of industrial price behaviour. We know, for example, that the markup on cost has declined considerably over the decade of the 'sixties. We also have reservations about the omission of capital costs and the extreme assumption relating to historical cost pricing. Despite these reservations, we do not think that any of the assumptions or procedures would contaminate the prediction by introducing a bogus cyclical element, or by removing a genuine association between the mark-up and demand. (Godley and Nordhaus, 1972, p. 855)

Taking these two points together, we find that the normal conditions of production are those around which cyclical changes in capacity utilization occur, and empirical evidence suggests that these normal conditions play the dominant role in the determination of prices.

It might then be concluded that Keynes theory of normal output is complementary to Sraffa's analysis of normal prices. But one further analytical difficulty remains: the two-sided nature of investment (determining demand and determining the growth of capacity) that was discussed by Roy Harrod (1948) in his examination of the characteristics of the warranted rate of growth. The process of adjustment of sectoral capacity to effectual demand must involve changes in investment—the independent variable in Keynes's theory of demand. At the aggregate level, this difficulty is manifest in the instability of Harrod's warranted rate of growth.

The solution that Keynes proposes to the dilemma that investment is, on the one hand, the independent variable and, on the other hand, the means of adjustment of capacity to demand is to suggest that it is not ultimately investment that is the independent variable; instead, "the state of long-term expectations" fulfills that role:

> If we suppose a state of expectations to continue for a sufficient length of time for the effect on employment to have worked itself out so completely that there is, broadly speaking, no piece of employment going on which would not take place if the new state of expectation had always existed, the steady level of employment thus attained may be called the long period employment corresponding to that state of expectation. (Keynes, 1936, p. 48)

So there will be a level and composition of capacity corresponding to any given level of long-term expectation. If existing capacity is above or below this level, then the prospect of profit will induce investment to change the level of composition of capacity to that appropriate to the state of expectation. The process may overshoot. But as long as the state of expectation may be supposed to be given, then competition will tend to push capacity toward that which is appropriate to sustain the long-term level of employment *at normal prices.*

An immediate reaction to this might be to say that far too much weight is being placed on the idea of a given state of long-term expectations. The approach encourages an individualistic interpretation. However, Keynes embeds the formation of long-term expectations in social and economic convention. In other words, long-term expectations are themselves the product of industrial structure, the relationship between finance and industry, the recent history of competitiveness and technological change, the state of industrial relations, and so on—all factors that define the institutional environment within which economic activity takes place. It is these factors that stabilize or destabilize convention—and that can, on occasion, break down catastrophically.

Finance and Other Institutions

Keynes's principle of effective demand, in its most simple form the determination of output and savings by the level of investment, is inconceivable in an economy without a fully developed financial sector. It is the availability of finance that sets investment free from dependence on savings. Without money and finance, investment (or the state of long-term expectations) could not be the independent variable in the model. Thus, the development of financial products and the interaction of finance and the real economy are integral components of the analysis of output.

This fact has been eminently clear in the recent financial crisis. The growth of liquidity—that is, spending power—in the financial sector was a function of a number of financial innovations, notably the growth of the repo market and the interaction between securitization and the newly developed credit derivatives. The expansion of liquidity was further enhanced by higher and higher leverage in financial institutions. The result was a prolonged boom in the real economy and growing financial imbalances, internationally and domestically. The withdrawal of credit following the financial crisis has created severe difficulties, particularly to over-indebted households and to small and medium enterprises that do not have direct access to the bond market, with consequent falls in output and employment.

Without the neoclassical faith in automatic adjustment of demand to capacity, the Keynesian approach to the crisis is to examine where demand might come from—whether from government expenditure, a recovery of household spending, increased spending by firms, or the growth of net exports. Each of these components and their interactions must be modeled within a consistent accounting framework that ensures consistency in sectoral financial balances. In each case, economic analysis must interact with institutional factors. For example, the scale and liquidity of international bond markets have changed the nature of the constraints facing borrowers, including sovereign borrowers. Similarly, the financial possibilities open to households by way of secured mortgages and unsecured credit card debt have significantly increased the potential contribution of consumers to overall volatility.

The stark choices exposed since 2007 have forced Keynesian issues into the consciousness of policymakers. However, it is not clear how durable the rise of Keynesian ideas will be. The reaction of governments to the uncertainties of sovereign bond markets has been to implement potentially deflationary measures, without spelling out clearly where demand is to come from. Old beliefs in automatic stabilizing mechanisms, clearing markets, linger long after they have been disproved theoretically and by events.

Consider, for example, the argument that sustaining demand by means of government deficits is "imposing a burden on our children." If the economy is always in market-clearing equilibrium and, consequentially, the growth path of the economy is unaffected by fiscal policy, then this proposition has some (though not much) merit. An increase in government expenditure, financed by borrowing or by printing money (quantitative easing), will, via higher interest rates and increased inflation, transfer resources from households and firms to the public sector. The net deficit could then be paid off at a future date by increasing taxation to reduce the real income of the private sector, thus validating the transfer. At all times, the output per head in the economy as a whole is always the same, unless, of course, the transfer of resources to the public sector changes the dynamics of the full-employment growth path.

Consider now, the same argument when there is no presumption that the economy is always at a market-clearing equilibrium. If there is surplus capacity in the economy, the increase in government net spending will increase real output. Future taxation to pay interest or pay back the principal of any borrowing will simply be a transfer payment between taxpayers and lenders, unless the shift to net surplus results in a slowdown in activity. Hence, the question of "burdens on our children" requires consideration of the impact of government's net position on the level of activity and thus of the growth path of the economy as a whole.

The Rise of Keynesian Economics

The core contention of this book is that the attempt to build macroeconomic analysis on neoclassical foundations is fatally flawed, from both an analytical and an empirical point of view.[2] Throughout the years of fall and rise of Keynesian economics, we have maintained a (hopefully) consistently Keynesian position. The empirical chapters in this volume deal with policy issues raised by the neoclassical ascendancy, demonstrating that Keynesian interpretations of the various problems are both credible and have distinctive policy implications. The theoretical chapters offer our attempt to reinforce this position.

As to the prospects for the future of Keynesian economics, the situation is hopeful and more precarious at the same time. The analytical structure of Keynesian analysis is necessarily a developing task. Markets for goods and for finance display significant changes over time, driven by technological change and other innovations. So the analysis of those markets must also develop, and the Keynesian theory of output, together with the classical approach to price determination, provides a firm foundation upon which discussion can proceed. But the zeitgeist must also be right. Economic policy debate has always been remarkably impervious to analytical deficiencies in the contending arguments. The welcome return to more Keynesian ways of thinking that the global financial crisis and recession have engendered is already being undermined by misguided policy efforts, especially in Europe, to reassert the old orthodoxy.

Notes

1. Given that all economic models are abstractions, the very act of constructing a model embodies the implicit assumption that the results generated by the model will be "centers of gravitation" for the determined variables, be they prices or quantities, with factors excluded by abstraction constituting the "noise" around those centers. No model is all-encompassing—or a map on the scale of one to one!

2. For a thought-provoking empirical critique of the notion of market-clearing equilibrium, consider Reinhart and Rogoff (2009).

The Fall and Rise of Keynesian Economics

1

The Fall and Rise of Keynesian Economics

Towards the end of 2008, with the world economy in the grip of an unprecedented financial crisis and entering into a deep recession, the name of John Maynard Keynes began to crop up with a frequency that would have been completely unimaginable only a decade or two earlier. The parallels with the economic circumstances of the 1930s—financial crisis, recession, and the threat of deflation—had apparently been lost on no one. But not since an image of Keynes had adorned the front cover of *Time* magazine in December 1965 was "Keynes" a name on everyone's lips.[1] Things had changed. In October 2008, the *Financial Times* carried an image with a column by Ed Crooks; on November 8, *The Independent* of London did the same with a Nick Fraser article; and on November 30, the *New York Times* carried yet another image, this time attached to an article by Greg Mankiw. Even Keynes's face was popping up everywhere. Whether it was Richard Nixon or Milton Friedman who said, "We are all Keynesians now" (or, indeed, whether it was actually either of them), something like it could surely be said today of a raft of politicians, policy-makers, financial journalists, opinion leaders, and even economists. They were all dusting the cobwebs off their old copies of his books.

Consider the changes that had taken place. Only a year or two after we learned of the death of Milton Friedman, whose name had been better known than that of almost any other economist for most of the last quarter of the twentieth century—and whose ideas had become the basis of the neoliberal consensus that swept to dominance in economic circles during those same years—the name of his arch adversary was back in fashion with a vengeance. Just a few years after Robert Lucas (who did so much to carry forward the banner of new classical macroeconomics) had assured the American Economic Association that "for all practical purposes" the "central problem of depression prevention has been solved"—and that while there remained "important gains in welfare" to be had "from better fiscal policies" these were gains to be had "from providing people with better incentives to work and to save" rather than from a "better fine tuning of spending flows" (2003, p. 1)—it seemed that experience had taught us that we should draw the very opposite conclusions.

What had happened? Why were we witnessing such a turn around in ideas and practice? What are we to make of it? How useful might Keynesian ideas actually prove to us today? Will this new enthusiasm for Keynesian ideas last? These are a few of the questions that need an answer. These answers lead to the story of the fall and rise of Keynesian economics, not only because is it a story that has often been inaccurately recounted but also because it is one that whispers not a few important messages concerning how we might (or might not) usefully deploy Keynesian ideas to address some of our most pressing contemporary problems.

The Keynes Problem

Keynes was already an international figure of some renown when his *General Theory of Employment, Interest and Money* appeared in February 1936. He had been an uncompromising critic of the Treaty of Versailles, which had levied a preposterous and dangerous bill for reparations payments on Germany. He had been a lone voice against the decision of the British government to return to the gold standard in 1925 at the pre-World War I parity. He had been a vocal supporter of public-works programs in Britain during the 1929 general-election campaign. He had never tired of reminding those who were willing to listen that it was of little help in the short run to focus on possible salvation in the long run, when in the long run we are all dead. He had always been, as he often said, like Cassandra in the Greek myths—usually right, usually ignored, and often thought to be quite mad.

But with the *General Theory* in 1936 came a new and fundamental challenge to prevailing economic thinking. It was not now just that economic policies were misguided, or that they had been inadequately thought through, or that too much weight had been given to long-run outcomes at the expense of leaving short-run problems untouched but, rather, that some of the most basic understandings of how market economies actually worked, understandings upon which generations of economists had been brought up, were fatally flawed. As Keynes put it: "the orthodox equilibrium theory of economics has assumed ... that there are natural forces tending to bring the volume of ... output ... back to the optimum level whenever temporary forces have led it to depart from this level. But ... the equilibrium level towards which output tends to return after temporary disturbances is not necessarily the optimum level" (Keynes, 1973–1983, 13:406). The significance of this claim should not be underestimated. If this new argument were to prove to be true, then even if we reached the long run there would be absolutely nothing to hope for there.

If markets really were mechanisms that could be relied upon to allocate scarce resources in the most efficient manner, as Lionel Robbins had incautiously proclaimed in the middle of the Great Depression, then persistent and sustained underutilization of those resources would be a virtual impossibility. But there it was, said Keynes—in the form of mass involuntary unemployment and enormous levels of spare industrial capacity—right before everyone's very eyes. In Britain, unemployment never dropped much below 10% in any one of the years between 1919 and 1939. In America, while unemployment rates in the 1920s were somewhat better than in Britain, the rates in the 1930s were if anything a little worse, averaging out at more than 15% per year over the whole decade. These facts of economic life, Keynes now said, had to be addressed not just with the right economic policies but also with a wholesale reconstruction of economic thinking. But just how was this to be achieved?

"The Keynes Problem" was thus born: did Keynes's new ideas truly require the reconstruction of economic thinking from the ground up, or was it possible to reconcile his new theory with the old ways of economic thinking? As it turned out, the first task proved too much of a challenge to almost everyone; and instead of attempting to develop the profound analytical reach of the theory of effective demand that Keynes had suggested, mainstream thinking opted instead to find ways of putting the new wine into old bottles.[2]

Two broad approaches emerged very quickly in an attempt to do just that—they mark the beginning of the fall of Keynesian economics. One involved the suggestion that the new results came from working, as Keynes had done, with economic aggregates rather than with the decisions of individual agents, as older ways of thinking had been more accustomed to doing. In short, it was suggested that the reconciliation might be brought about by thinking in terms of macroeconomics rather than microeconomics. The other was to seek an analytical basis for Keynes's new conclusions in the operation of frictions and rigidities—market imperfections—that might prevent prices from fully adjusting to their equilibrium levels, as traditional economic thinking maintained would happen in the long run. This second line of argument proved to be hugely influential—and unstoppable. It swept the board. Not without a trace of irony, friend and foe alike grounded their suggested interpretations of the *General Theory* upon it.

Outside of his immediate Cambridge colleagues, Keynes had no greater friend than Roy Harrod. The two had a lengthy correspondence while Keynes was writing the *General Theory,* and Harrod had commented extensively on its many draft versions. And what did Harrod think? Here is what he said back then: "Mr Keynes' conclusions need not be deemed to make a vast difference to the general theory, but they do make a vast difference to a number of short-cut conclusions of leading importance" (1937, p. 75). And why? Essentially, said Harrod, for two reasons. First, because the short-run rate of interest was a monetary phenomenon determined by liquidity preference rather than the underlying real forces of productivity and thrift (p. 79). Second, because "the contracts or bargains of the entrepreneurs with prime factors [workers] are normally *fixed* in money" (p. 80, italics added). The upshot of all of this, according to Harrod, was that while Keynes "had not affected a revolution in fundamental economic theory," he had made important improvements in the sphere of "short cuts, which are of the greatest concern for the ordinary working economist" (p. 85).

Among his immediate Cambridge colleagues, Keynes found in Arthur Cecil Pigou no greater intellectual foe. Pigou and Keynes had been at loggerheads on economic-policy matters throughout most of the 1920s, and it would be fair to say that Pigou was outraged at the *General Theory.* Here is what Pigou had to say: "Einstein actually did for Physics what Mr Keynes believes himself to have done for Economics" (1936, p. 115). And why? Because Pigou thought that Keynes's analysis did "not differ from what is commonly maintained" since it was only due to the fact that money wages were not "permitted to move freely" that full employment was not maintained (p. 128). At least as Pigou saw it in 1936, all Keynes had really done was to present the existing analysis of unemployment—based on the presence of sticky wages—and then he had had the audacity to over-egg his own originality.

Disciples and dissenters, then, were at one. Keynes's idea that even in the long run all would not be for the best in the best of all possible worlds was dropped entirely. The debate was translated back into more familiar terms—whether we might or might not all be dead when we got there. How long was the short run? Were prices quick or slow to adjust to temporary disturbances? Was the market near or far from the perfectly competitive benchmark? This response was no more than a testimony to just how right Keynes had been when he said how difficult it would be (and had been for him) to escape from habitual modes of thought. It had proved impossible. The consequence of choosing to think within the old-fashioned box was the beginning of the end for Keynesian economics. Keynes himself had predicted that his readers might fluctuate "between a belief that I am quite wrong and a belief that I am saying nothing new" (1936, p. 1)—he was right. But the challenge laid down by Keynes still remains an open question: "it is for others to determine if either of these or the third alternative is right" (p. 1).

At stake in any response to the Keynes problem, then, was the most fundamental tenet of the economic thinking of Keynes's day and of ours—namely, that the market mechanism has a tendency to ensure the full employment and full-capacity utilization of all resources in the long run. Do we live in a world where if we just waited long enough things would fix themselves or do we not? Have we somehow discovered in the workings of uncoordinated market forces a permanent solution to all of the economic problems we might ever face or have we not? Is it the case that any collective effort that we might make to secure greater economic efficiency or equity is doomed ultimately to be self-defeating or is it not? Is Keynesian economics just the economics of depression—better, to be sure, than anything found in Friedman or Lucas, but the economics of crisis nonetheless? Or is there more to it than that?

The Neoclassical Synthesis and the Keynesian Consensus

In the first textbook of the immediate postwar years, Paul Samuelson set out the analytical foundations of what was to become the Keynesian Consensus. Building on interpretations suggested by Hansen, Hicks, Meade, Modigliani, and others, Samuelson outlined an analytical framework (the so-called Keynesian-Cross Diagram) that could be used to build a simple macroeconomic model where an intersection of aggregate demand and aggregate supply curves embodied the possibility of an outcome that might, or might not, entail full employment. He called it a Neoclassical Synthesis. Here is how he described it: "In recent years 90 percent of American Economists have stopped being 'Keynesian economists' or 'anti-Keynesian economists.'. Instead they have worked toward a synthesis of whatever is valuable in older economics and in modern theories of income determination" (1955, p. 212).

To a whole new generation of economists, Samuelson had bequeathed a model in which, depending on the shapes of the curves involved, one could be, by turns, either classical or Keynesian, as the case required. As Samuelson put it in the very first edition of his *Economics*, the "analysis here described is itself neutral: it can be used as well to defend private enterprise as to limit it, as well to attack as defend government fiscal intervention (1948, p. 233).[3] Sixty years later this is still one of the first bits of macroeconomics that every schoolchild is taught.

As to what determines the shapes of the curves, just ask any schoolgirl. They will tell you that if the prices of some goods or services are not fully flexible, then the curves will have "Keynesian" shapes. If not, then the old story is true. Actually, the really well-drilled ones will even be able to sketch for you an aggregate supply curve on which the elasticity of output varies from infinity to zero—from Keynes to the classics all on one curve.

It was this agreement as to how one should render Keynesian economic analysis that formed the essential ingredient of the Keynesian Consensus. The other ingredient was how one should conduct domestic economic policy. Here, another curve, one that could likewise take on different shapes, came in handy. This was the celebrated Phillips Curve—appropriated from A. W. H. Phillips's classic empirical study of the relation between money wages and inflation in Britain between 1861 and 1957. Translated into a functional trade-off between inflation and unemployment, and shown to be analytically deducible from the aggregate demand and aggregate supply model in the presence of sticky wages, it suggested that governments could trade off lower unemployment against inflation in the short run.

Almost every policy conclusion drawn from it sounded truly Keynesian: deficit spending could revive a failing economy without necessarily causing too much inflation, fine-tuning could be used to iron out fluctuations in the business cycle, automatic stabilizers could be put in place to keep the economy at or near full employment, and flows of expenditure on aggregate consumption and aggregate investment could be managed through an active fiscal policy. It seemed that every practical domestic-policy measure suggested by Keynes could be integrated into the Keynesian Consensus. High economic growth, full employment, and price stability were all achievable with the help of the government. But what about external balance?

Fortunately, the Keynesian Consensus had an international dimension, too. This took concrete form in what was to become known as the Bretton Woods system. Keynes, of course, had been instrumental in its creation in 1944. His principal concern had been to build a new international payments order that might obviate the need for individual economies facing current-account deficits to have resort to contractionary domestic policies to solve their individual balance-of-payments problems whenever they arose. That response, he was all too aware, had had disastrous consequences for world employment and growth between the wars. Contractionary policies to solve individual balance-of-payments difficulties were contagious. What was essential, he recognized, was a mechanism that might ensure that current-account surpluses could be redistributed to those facing deficits. Without that, he felt sure, a contractionary bias would be built into the world economy and the growth of trade and employment in the world economy would suffer—just as it had in the 1930s.

To achieve this, and to lock in an expansionary basis for global effective demand, Keynes proposed an international clearing union in which member states would agree to hold credit/debit balances equal to their respective current-account surpluses/deficits. These balances were to be denominated in a unit of account that would have a fixed exchange rate against their individual national currencies. In this system, the mechanism whereby current-account surpluses/deficits are matched by the sum of capital outflows/inflows and changes in foreign-exchange reserves would have been replaced by one linking those surpluses/deficits to accumulated credit/debit balances held by the international clearing union. A complicated set of financial penalties for both creditor and debtor economies, which need not detain us here, was envisaged—along with the possibility of imposed revaluations or devaluations, as the case required, and even resort to import controls or other forms of protectionism—to back up the system. In his superb account of this whole episode, Robert Skidelsky concluded that it showed Keynes "doing best what he was best at: constructing realisable utopias" (2000, p. 208).

But at Bretton Woods, another compromise emerged—one that in a sense paralleled the analytical compromise that was at the heart of the

Neoclassical Synthesis. There was to be no international clearing union; instead, we had the International Monetary Fund, which would deal with payment problems (but with depository resources far more limited than the Keynes plan had envisaged).[4] There was to be no resort to currency realignments, except *in extremis*, and instead we had the system of adjustable pegs. There was to be no resort to import controls; instead, we had the scarce-currency clause. Capital flight was to be reigned in with the help of capital controls.

As it stood on paper, however, the Bretton Woods system embodied no sustainable way of redistributing the burden of adjustment to balance-of-payments surpluses/deficits of the kind Keynes had envisaged. On paper, the burden of adjustment would continue to fall on deficit nations, not creditors. But what things looked like on paper turned out to work very differently in practice: the architectural flaws in the Bretton Woods system were not to be exposed for nearly twenty years.

The absence of a sustainable mechanism for redistributing surpluses did not turn out to matter because U.S. capital outflows stepped in to substitute for it. The vast U.S. programs of postwar reconstruction aid, and subsequent U.S. private lending and private investment abroad, did the job instead. The scarce-currency clause became irrelevant. Europe and Japan proceeded to erect protectionist barriers to sustain growth and full employment at home—without U.S. retaliation. Even Britain's system of Imperial Preference faded away only slowly. And all the time, capital controls succeeded in insulating economies from the threat of capital flight by limiting cross-border speculative transactions.

Despite all the compromises, Keynesianism seemed to be working on both a domestic and an international scale. In its relation to Keynes, the Keynesian Consensus had both preservative and destructive tendencies. As long as its policies were working, everything was to the good. Economies enjoyed high growth, low inflation, and low unemployment, without periodic balance-of-payments crises.

But the good times could last only so long. When the U.S. economy began to see its current-account position with respect the rest of the industrialized world turn from semi-permanent surplus into semi-permanent deficit during the 1960s—as Japan, Germany, and others began to catch up—the U.S. capital-account deficit that had so effectively financed the growth of world trade and employment for the best part of twenty years was no longer sustainable. And there was nothing to take its place.[5] When stagflation emerged in the late 1960s, the domestic policy agenda of the Keynesian Consensus was likewise called into question.

The Fall of the Keynesian Consensus

From an analytical point of view, the fall of Keynesian economics had begun almost the day copies of the *General Theory* reached the shelves of bookshops in 1936. But the late 1960s and early 1970s marked a decisive moment for the Keynesian Consensus. By the end of the 1960s, the fault lines in that consensus were becoming increasingly apparent to all. In domestic affairs, the problem of stagflation seemed to call into question its simple messages about the nature of the trade-offs between output and inflation that confronted policymakers. In international affairs, the appearance of persistent U.S. current-account deficits posed a mortal threat to the very survival of the Bretton Woods system itself—and so to the continuance of the high and stable growth of trade and employment that the international economy had enjoyed under its auspices.

It was perilous enough to the survival of the Keynesian Consensus for the whole domestic and international policy order to have come under threat from these turns in economic conditions; but the coup de grâce was the almost simultaneous collapse of its whole analytical edifice.

Milton Friedman led the way. He took on the Phillips Curve. This, he argued, needed to be specified in terms of changes in inflation—and it would take on the shape imagined by the Keynesian Consensus only when some of those changes were unanticipated. His statement of this proposition is as famous as it is important:

> there is always a *temporary* trade-off between inflation and unemployment; there is no permanent trade-off. The *temporary* trade-off comes not from inflation per se, but from *unanticipated* inflation, which generally means, from a rising rate of inflation. The widespread belief that there is a permanent trade-off is a sophisticated version of the confusion between "high" and "rising" that we all recognize in simpler forms. (1968, p. 11, italics added)

The expectations-augmented Phillips Curve, as it came to be known, focused attention on the key analytical weakness of the Keynesian Consensus: only in the face of expectational errors, of inertia in the response of prices of goods and/or services to changing inflation in the short run, could its policy conclusions be allowed to stand. Behind the scenes there had always been a position of the economy where involuntary unemployment would eventually vanish—the natural rate of unemployment, as Friedman called it. And Friedman also argued that the natural rate itself could be increased by man-made and policy-made changes to the structure of labor markets.[6]

By foolishly trying to exploit what was thought to be a permanent trade-off between inflation and unemployment, Friedman argued that all those twenty years of the Keynesian Consensus had actually achieved was a permanent increase in core inflation *and* an increase in the natural rate of unemployment. The outstanding feature of the economic landscape of the late 1960s and early 1970s, a stagflation involving high unemployment (now thought of as entirely voluntary in nature) and high inflation, was thereby explained—and the Keynesian Consensus was to blame.

But Friedman had left a glimmer of light for the Keynesians of the day: just how long was temporary? If it was long enough to outlive a man, then the Keynesian Consensus might yet find a way to fight back. This all depended on how long it took firms and workers to correct the errors in their expectations.

Enter Robert Lucas, who took on the aggregate supply curve. The Keynesian Consensus had this wrong, too. Aggregate supply was a not a relation between the price level and output, but a relation that shows the amount of output firms are collectively willing to supply at different price levels, *given their expectations about inflation*. This became known as the Lucas Supply Curve. If those expectations were wrong, the aggregate supply curve would have the shape imagined by the Keynesian Consensus in the short run. But what about those expectations? How were they formed? Why might they be wrong? Friedman had used a simple adaptive rule when he had talked about expectations: inflation today was expected to be connected to what it had been in the past—and such expectations could be wrong if inflation was changing.

But what if, said Lucas, expectations were formed *rationally*? By this he meant that agents would use all of the market information available to them, together with the "true" model of the market, to form their expectations of inflation. As long as the "true" model of the market was the long-run analysis of employment underlying traditional economic thinking—and the Keynesian Consensus had already accepted this to be the case when it had dropped Keynes's more far-reaching suggestion that it was not—then expectations of inflation formed rationally could differ from actual inflation (that is, could be wrong) only randomly. The short-run and the long-run aggregate supply curves would be the same. The elasticity of output would be zero in all imaginable cases. The manipulation of aggregate demand to improve unemployment would be a fruitless exercise—and it would be inflationary, to boot.

It has to be said that the Keynesians of the day were left almost speechless in the face of this two-pronged attack on all that they had stood for. Their only policy response to stagflation was to argue for more of the same at the level of fiscal policy (which Friedman was saying had got us into the mess in the first place), plus the hugely unpopular introduction of wage and price controls. Their only analytical response was to argue among themselves. The details of those arguments need not detain us here. For just as in the 1930s, when a clash between prevailing economic circumstances and existing economic thinking generated a crisis that allowed Keynes to suggest a new way forward, in the 1970s something happened. The incongruity between prevailing economic circumstances and the existing economic thinking of the Keynesian Consensus generated another crisis, and Friedman and Lucas carried the day. Monetarism and New Classical Macroeconomics now took center stage, not only in the analysis of inflation and unemployment but also in the design of economic policy. Of course, this was not so much a new way forward as it was going back to the old ways of economic thinking.

As to the collapse of the international dimension of the Keynesian Consensus that was unfolding at the very same time, Friedman had a similarly convenient explanation. By thinking in old-fashioned ways he was able to show that the demise of the Bretton Woods system was both inevitable and easily understood. Friedman had long argued that flexible exchange rates were to be preferred to adjustable pegs. Fixed rates, he claimed, led to the build-up of underlying pressure for adjustment, and so to large and violent changes when things finally came to a head. Flexible rates, on the other hand, were supposed to be capable of quick change and so of ensuring smooth and small adjustments as the need arose.[7] Not only would they promote greater stability, they would underwrite a better and more efficient allocation of global resources, and they would guarantee the automatic correction of any payments imbalances immediately they arose. The idea of an *optimally* self-adjusting market mechanism, to which Keynes had taken exception in the 1930s, was at work at home and abroad—and was back. In fact, it had never really gone away.

This is not the place to discuss just how far the new world thus ushered in actually failed entirely to live up to this promise: productivity growth slowed, the trend rate of unemployment rose permanently, the rate of growth of world trade slowed from its Bretton Woods rates, exchange rates became more volatile and not less, and financial crises became more frequent and contagious than they had been since before the war—that is clear enough. For now, the point is rather different: since the Keynesian Consensus retained at its core the old ways of economic thinking, when things went wrong in the late 1960s and early 1970s, it was no surprise that those old ideas reemerged. Back-to-basics carried the day.

The Return of Keynesian Economics

It is sometimes said that these days you know when someone or something is back in vogue if you can find it on YouTube. Sure enough, Keynes and Keynesian economics are right there. But the question is not whether Keynesian economics is back—that may be taken as given; the question is, What is the analytical content and policy content it is supposed to bring back with it, and will it last?

To answer this question, it is tempting simply to turn to Keynes's distinguished biographer, Robert Skidlesky. But while Skidelsky's biographical skills are considerable, his rendition of how to reconstruct a more Keynesian economics is far less satisfactory. Skidelsky does not like mathematics, mechanical analogies, or microeconomics, so he calls in the name of Keynes to reject all of them as being parts of a "regressive research programme" (2009a, p. 3). Skidelsky wants economics to be designed "to protect macroeconomics from the methods and habits of the mathematician"; he wants it to be about the "art of government." This is all well and good, and some of Skidelsky's own proposals for the reform of economics teaching are even appealing; but is it how to finish the job? What Keynes had objected to was empty formalism, not the formal methods of thought "without which we would be lost in the woods." It was the economic assumptions of most mathematical economists to which he objected, not the mathematics itself (except in so far as their romance with technique often made them forget those assumptions). Theory without fact is a problem—but so is fact without theory. It was not that Keynes insisted that there were no "natural forces" at work in the economy, or that the economy might not be usefully imagined to resemble "a machine," but that those "natural forces" (that "economic machine") did not have a tendency to produce the beneficial outcomes his predecessors had proposed. It was not that one could do without a theory of price determination (microeconomics, as we now call it), but that supply did not create its own demand, that decisions to investment and decisions to save were not rendered mutually compatible by the operation of the market mechanism, as the neoclassical theory of value had claimed. If there was to be a new theoretical basis for employment policy, the whole rational of the *General Theory*, what had to go was this particular rendition of the operation of the price mechanism. In short, what Keynes dubbed "Say's Law" had to go. Skidelsky is of little help here.

A better place to start, however, is at Paul Krugman's door. In recognizing that Skidelsky's version of Keynes largely misses the key analytical point, Krugman identifies the true problem: "the current disputes over economic policy, above all about the usefulness of government to promote employment, seem to be primarily about Say's Law —that is Keynes 1936" (2009a, p. 3). To understand the analytical content of the Keynesian economics to which he urges us to return, his *Return of Depression Economics and the Crisis of 2008* (2008) seems to be is a good place to start. Krugman has been among the strongest and most vocal advocates of a return to Keynesian ideas and policies—and he also makes his case clearly and simply. That case, however, is not as different from the old ways of thinking as one might have hoped.

Going on what Krugman says, it seems that the Keynesian ideas to which we are being urged to return are effectively those embodied in the Keynesian Consensus of so many decades ago. It seems that the only problem Krugman sees with Say's Law is that the market mechanism does not render plans mutually compatible because there are some sticky prices. Here is how Krugman puts it: "shortfalls in overall demand would cure themselves if only wages and prices fell rapidly in the face of unemployment [but] in reality prices don't fall quickly" (2008, p. 183). To be sure, there have been changes in the way sticky wages and prices might be explained—ways now associated with a New Keynesian Macroeconomics that had emerged during the 1980s, but these continue to be seen as the central cause of the problem of unemployment in the mind's eye of contemporary Keynesians like Krugman.[8]

At a commonsense level, Say's Law involves a simple enough error. Its mistake is to forget that for businesses to make any kind of profit at all, or to be induced to produce more than they already are doing, there needs to be a demand for their goods or services (or they need to create one). Manipulating the supply side of their activities may increase their profits, but it will be of little avail from an output and employment point of view if there is no (or there is stagnant) demand for what they bring to market. This is precisely the situation that prevails in Krugman's sticky-wage economy: there is a demand deficiency. But, as Keynes recognized in the *General Theory*, there is a little more to Say's Law than this. It is not so much that situations of deficient demand cannot exist but, rather, that when they do, the consumption plans (savings) and the production plans (investment) of households and firms are mutually incompatible *because* prices are fixed (and that they would be rendered compatible *if* prices were flexible). Say's Law in this more formal sense is, therefore, still in place in Krugman's sticky-wage economy.

What is required to expose the formal error in Say's Law is a recognition that it is the level of output that changes, not prices, to restore the macroeconomic balance between plans to save and plans to invest whenever they vary. In short, whenever price flexibility bears no systematic relationship to excess supplies, possibly because the relative prices of goods and services are determined by factors other than those which determine the quantities of them produced, then Say's Law has no place in the story—namely, the situation that Keynes outlined in the *General Theory*.

If the analytical content of Krugman-style arguments differs little from the old Keynesian Consensus, the policy content of these contemporary arguments is also roughly the same as that of the old Keynesian Consensus. Despite Krugman's skepticism about the likely success of the present policies in the United States and elsewhere—a skepticism that arises more from his view that more may be needed, and that the Obama administration might find it politically difficult to make the kind of radical break from Bush administration dogma than it suspects—he seems to be in basic accord with its general thrust.

However, the deepest flaws in the Keynesian Consensus were never really to be found in its practical message but, rather, in its neoclassical foundations—namely, the Neoclassical Synthesis. This became very apparent when circumstances conspired to facilitate the immensely successful Friedman-Phelps-Lucas "back to basics" campaign of the 1970s. That campaign ushered in an era of neoliberal economic policy that has only recently begun to show signs of subsiding. Unfortunately, however, the weaknesses of the New Neoclassical Synthesis are the same as those of its predecessor, and its fate may yet prove to be the same. There is no debate in mainstream Keynesian circles today over this common foundation in neoclassical theory. Indeed, far from its being seen as a potential shortcoming, just the opposite is the case.

The conventional macroeconomic wisdom sees great virtue in what it characterizes as a "convergence" of approach to underlying economic theory in contemporary macroeconomics. It is true that there tends to be some excessive product differentiation when it comes to how all this is said to stand in relation to the old Neoclassical Synthesis. After all, the only difference between the old and the new Keynesians is that the imperfections required to give the underlying neoclassical model its distinctive Keynesian flavor emerge from the optimizing behavior of individual agents in the presence of asymmetric information, rather than from the ad hoc imposition of certain features of the real world thought to have been left out by the benchmark neoclassical model of markets.

Despite deep differences when it comes to policy advice, then, the shared foundations of opposing policy camps are presented by today's practitioners to illustrate the "coherence" and "scientific" character of modern macroeconomic thinking, rather than its vulnerability. Nowhere is this vulnerability better illustrated than in the current fashion for the use of dynamic stochastic general-equilibrium (DSGE) models in macroeconomics.

Of course, the limitations of DSGE models have not entirely escaped the notice of some of the best-known names in the macroeconomic establishment. They feel that little practical insight has been added by their development and that a great cost in terms of technically complicated modeling (and simplifying assumptions) has been imposed. They contrast pretensions to scientific precision of DSGE with the practical art of policy making. They worry about assuming away incomplete markets and nonlinear dynamics. They are uneasy about being able to think only in terms of exogenous shocks rather than endogenously generated crises. They wonder just how complicated a macroeconomic model really needs to be; and they sometimes yearn for a return to the old-fashioned simplicities of Marshalian partial-equilibrium analysis. They note the patent absurdity of assuming that representative agent models can capture the complicated interactions of very many heterogeneous agents. And they are right to do so.[9]

But what if the problems of the general-equilibrium foundations of the New Neoclassical Synthesis are not in its simplifying assumptions? Macroeconomists talk a lot about their microeconomic foundations, but perhaps they do not talk enough to their microeconomics colleagues? If they did a little more of that, they might hear it said that even with quite general assumptions about preferences, technology, and endowments, it is not possible to think in terms of the unique or stable equilibrium that their DSGE models presuppose. Instead, when it comes to uniqueness, stability, and sustainability of equilibrium, everything is up in the air. If it is not possible to be confident that there exist unique and stable equilibria—ones to which the economy will either return after a shock or which will be determined anew if the data change in the face of a stochastic shock—then adding additional constraints to the basic general-equilibrium model (often called "institutional features" by DSGE modelers), does not really recommend itself as an especially "coherent" or "scientific" practice.

Just as in the past, then, contemporary critics and converts to Keynesian ideas seem to be navigating in the same direction as led inexorably to their demise. The Keynesian Consensus contained the seeds of its own destruction, as does its contemporary reincarnation. Its policies may be the ones that are called for. All of our experience suggests that they are likely to work if applied with consistency of purpose. But without a change in the economic thinking that still lurks behind the scenes, we shall find that when new circumstances present a challenge, and when the policies that were right for today are in need of modification and adjustment—and it can be guaranteed that this will take place—it is likely that old ways of thinking will simply reassert themselves, as they did in the past. If the fall of Keynesian economics was inevitable the first time around, to allow the same thing to happen again would certainly amount to foolishness. The world is different now, and we have come a long way in our understanding of what works and what does not; and a return to the Keynesian Consensus not only will no longer do but would also be positively dangerous.

We have become accustomed to thinking and speaking of our economic difficulties as arising from imperfections, market failures, irrationalities, bubbles, inflexibilities, instabilities, externalities, and the like—as events that are somehow abnormal, singular, or even pathological. This kind of thinking and language is profoundly misleading. It suggests that, in the normal course of things, markets would not produce such unfriendly outcomes. But nothing could be further from the truth. The whole history of capitalist society reveals nothing if not the unwelcome *normalcy* of such events. If anything, the good times are the exceptions that prove the rule.

It is time to translate these outstanding features of our actual experience into new ways of thinking about the economy—and not just from a practical point of view but from an analytical point of view as well.

Keynes once quipped that it would be no bad thing if economists could be thought of in the same way as we think of dentists—an analogy well worth thinking about. The normal course of life involves tooth decay and disease. These situations may, of course, "correct" themselves, but they will do so only after extreme discomfort and pain followed by permanent tooth loss. Cavities do not magically reseal themselves. When dentistry recognized this, it became a science as well as an art—an analytical understanding of a process as well as a practical approach to treatment.

The operation of economic processes is rather like this. In the normal course of things, markets will give us all kinds of problems—some big, some small. As with tooth decay, given enough time these economic things will "correct" themselves—but at the short-run cost of considerable pain and at the long-run cost of a permanent reduction in our economic potential and productive capacity. Just as we expect and demand dental intervention in the normal course of life, we should expect and demand economic intervention in the normal course of economic activity.

Our predicament, therefore, is not how to choose a point on some fictional trade-off between short-run pain and long-run gain—and to manage, or not to manage, the economy depending on that choice. Our only option is to manage economic activity in a purposeful way. Our predicament is to find that improved analytical understanding of the operation of the market mechanism that is capable of giving full weight to this practical necessity. We shall not reach that objective until we cease to view as imperfections what are, in fact, events and characteristics that are part and parcel of the normal operation of the economic machine.

Effective economic management on a domestic and an international scale over the long run requires not only consistency of purpose but also a willingness to adapt policies to changing needs and problems. The world does not stand still. There is no once-for-all solution to economic problems, and we can be sure that we will face new and different challenges in the future. When we are called upon to find new polices, when today's remedies no longer seem to suffice, we need to be sure that we do not again fall back on ways of thinking about the economy as a beneficent, self-adjusting mechanism—that will only lead us astray.

Notes

This is a newly revised version of a lecture delivered by Murray Milgate at Osaka Gakuin University, Japan, in July 2009.

1. So long had it been since this was the case that it was not uncommon today to hear his name mispronounced.

2. It should be remembered that Keynes's younger collaborators in Cambridge, and we speak here of Joan Robinson and Richard Kahn in particular, continued to build on his progressive suggestion as, later, did others in Cambridge. See Dutt and Amadeo (1990).

3. To a few, however, especially those who had worked closely with Keynes on the *General Theory*, it seemed that at a stroke, wine had been turned into water, gold had been transformed into base metal. This is what Joan Robinson used to call "Bastard Keynesianism"—strong language to be sure, but razor-sharp insight into what had happened.

4. To appreciate the scale of the depository resources that might be needed to do this effectively, it is worth remembering that at the Bretton Woods Conference, Keynes had proposed that the United States contribute what amounted to $23 billion to his international clearing union. The U.S. negotiators took fright. In the end, the maximum U.S. contribution to the IMF was set at $2.75 billion. But, as Barry Eichengreen has noted, in the first four years of the Marshall Plan, "the United States extended some $13 billion in intergovernmental aid to finance Europe's deficits" (1996, p. 98). It is apparent that what the IMF lacked in resources was made up for in other ways.

5. The global imbalances that we still see today testify to the good sense of Keynes's original proposals.

6. Friedman mentions minimum-wage legislation, the strength of labor unions, legislation on minimum working hours, and health and safety provisions as all being measures that would increase the natural rate of unemployment.

7. Nicholas Kaldor had shown convincingly back in 1939 that speculative behavior was actually destabilizing, but no one seemed to remember—it was left to the painful actual experience of exchange-rate volatility after 1974 to prove him right.

8. Even Joseph Stiglitz, who like Krugman has been an unstinting advocate of more sensible practical policies along Keynesian lines, is willing to go only as far as deferring to "imperfect information and asymmetric information" to dispute the principal implication of Say's Law—namely, that free markets are efficient (2010b, p. 1).

9. In no particular order, see Blanchard (2008), Buiter (2010), Krugman (2000), Mankiw (2006), Solow (2008), Stiglitz (2010b), and Woodford (2009).

Part One

Practical

2

Liquidity and Financial Crises

Liquidity is an elusive concept. On the one hand, an asset is liquid if it can be immediately exchanged for money without any significant change in price (a fire sale is not a manifestation of liquidity). Financial assets command a liquidity premium determined by their market relationship to cash. So *liquidity* is an adjective, not a noun. On the other hand, aggregate liquidity is often characterized as if it were a measurable quantity. Adrian and Shin (2008, p. 1) cite popular phrases such as "a flood of global liquidity" and "excess liquidity" as metaphors embodying this quantitative image. *Liquidity* is a noun.

It is this latter characterization of liquidity that is at the heart of financial turmoil. Adrian and Shin define *aggregate liquidity* as "the growth rate of financial intermediaries' balance sheets," and they relate that growth to the development of the repo market. This amounts to defining *liquidity* as "the ability of agents to command purchasing power by acquiring liquid liabilities," an ability in turn dependent on the willingness of others to supply purchasing power against the issuance of liabilities. An economy "awash with liquidity" is then an economy in which the financial system becomes, as Shin argued in his Clarendon Lectures (2008), an "inflating balloon" looking for assets to fill up its expanding balance sheets. Conversely, that balloon may deflate when the ability to issue liabilities disappears and balance sheets shrink.

The history of financial bubbles (see Kindleberger and Aliber, 2005) demonstrates that all bubbles require two components: First, an asset or set of assets that becomes the focus of speculation, in the sense that it is purchased purely as a financial placement, not for its intrinsic characteristics, whether it be tulip bulbs, railway shares, dotcom companies, or securitized mortgages. In particular, the price of the financial placement becomes divorced from any likely return from the underlying asset. Second, the rising value of the financial placement requires a continuous expansion of purchasing power. This is often a stimulus to financial innovation to provide the wherewithal. The Dutch tulip mania of 1637 is famously associated with the introduction of trading on the margin (Posthumus, 1929). The railway bubbles of the early and mid-nineteenth century saw the development of the joint stock company to something approximating its modern form.

The relationship between the innovation that enhances liquidity and the rising value of placements that demand liquidity is a complex one: does the growth of liquidity set off the spiraling value of placements, or does the growth of the value of placements stimulate the innovation necessary to the expansion of liquidity?

The assets that were the focus of the recent boom in the United States were provided by the development of securitization,[1] enabling mortgages (and other assets) to be packaged into tradable bundles, allied with the tranching of risks characteristic of credit derivative markets from the mid-1990s onward. The liquidity was provided by the expansion of the repo and reverse repo market.[2]

Shin (2008) has argued that the interaction of securitization and the growth of the repo market stimulated and fueled the growth of liquidity, and that led to the development of a "shadow banking system" that became an "inflating balloon." The system comprised an interdependent chain: subprime borrower ⇔ mortgage broker ⇔ originating bank ⇔ mortgage pools ⇔ commercial and investment banks ⇔ rating agency ⇔ SPV ⇔ final investors (see Alexander, Eatwell, Persaud, and Reoch, 2007).

Historically, financial innovation has been fundamental to the ability of financial institutions to acquire purchasing power by growing their liabilities and hence growing liquidity. Changes to the structure of the financial markets, and the inter-relationships between changing financial institutions and monetary policy, have presented a challenge to the development of monetary theory and have been a fertile source of controversy.

This chapter attempts to clarify exactly what liquidity is, what constitutes a liquid market, how liquidity expands and contracts, and the relationship between liquidity and monetary and financial policy. We shall find that a liquid market is a market in which there is both "adjective" liquidity and "noun" liquidity in evidence, and that financial innovation is the driving force behind the expansion of liquidity.

Liquidity and Systemic Risks

In the past three decades, innovations in data-analysis capability, in statistical theory, and in the theory of finance have transformed risk management and pricing and, in the range of financial products, have transformed the liquidity of financial markets. Efficient risk management by firms is a fundamental component of competitive success in today's financial markets. It also makes an important contribution to general market stability—in normal times. However, in the face of extreme events (even "moderately" extreme events), rational risk management by individual firms may precipitate a macroeconomic reaction that is destabilizing, can place those firms in jeopardy, and can result in a loss in general welfare.

The classic example is a bank run. A depositor at a particular bank would be willing to leave funds on deposit, but he or she believes that other depositors are likely to react to an adverse event by withdrawing their funds, forcing the bank to call in loans or sell securities and suffer losses, perhaps even suspend payments. Consequently, a rational investor will seek to be the first to withdraw funds at the first sign of serious trouble. Hence, all depositors withdraw their funds as rapidly as possible when there are adverse developments, resulting in a "run." A run on one particular bank necessarily effects perceptions of the liquidity of other banks, and the run spreads to other, nominally solvent, banks.[3] More formally, while a depositor may be certain about the probability of suffering a liquidity shock, the depositor cannot be certain about the probability that his or her shock will occur early or late relative to others. In other words, the depositor cannot be sure where he or she will be in the line to withdraw funds. The result is the rush to withdraw (Caballero and Krishnamurthy, 2006, p. 8).

However, in recent decades the structure of financial markets has changed, shifting from a bank-based to a market-based financial system (Hendricks, Kambhu, and Mosser, 2006), with banking now following an Originate, Rate, and Relocate model. Financial intermediation has moved from banks into markets, and as a consequence of this disintermediation, financial crises are now manifest in markets rather than at institutions. Accordingly, analytical interest has moved from bank runs to "market gridlock" as a source of systemic risk.[4] A market-oriented systemic crisis is a breakdown in the functioning of markets for traded assets. It may be triggered, for example, by a sharp decline in the price of one asset that sparks a widespread sell-off in the general rush for liquidity. Again, in more formal terms, the individual agent knows the probability of a shock, but does not know the probability of being able to trade with the market counterparties on whom his or her liquidity depends. Not knowing, and being averse to uncertainty, the agent, and all other agents, has a collective bias toward liquidity (Caballero and Krishnamurthy, 2006, p. 15). The collective rush for liquidity produces the market gridlock characteristic of market-based systemic crises. It is important to note that a relatively small event can produce this gridlock in very large markets. The market for subprime mortgages was a relatively small part of the credit market. Yet failure in that sector precipitated an almost total gridlock.

Externalities and the Macroeconomics of Systemic Risk

Financial risk-taking is a concern of public policy because associated with the risk-taking actions of individuals are externalities—that is, costs and benefits accruing to the society that are *external* to the calculations of the individual investor and not accounted for in the marketplace.[5] A major financial failure imposes costs on society going far beyond the losses suffered by the immediate investors. In an economy where there are important externalities, competitive markets will be socially inefficient. The task of public policy—in this case, of financial regulation—is to attempt to mitigate these market failures.

Financial externalities are particularly potent because they are transmitted *macroeconomically*. Financial markets are markets for stocks of current and future assets, the value of which today is dependent on the expectation of their future value. To the extent that expectations are shared, any factor that leads to a general shift in expected future values will have an immediate impact on financial markets, and on the major macro-financial variables, such as the interest rate and the exchange rate. So the failure of a single firm can, by influencing expectations, have an influence not only on its immediate counterparties, or even just on firms dealing in similar products, but also, through its impact on expectations, on financial markets as a whole; and then, via the interest rate or the exchange rate, the contagion may spread to the whole economy.

Yet despite the presence of externalities and potential contagion, a peculiarity of market expectations is that they can be remarkably stable (or tranquil) for substantial periods of time, even when underlying real circumstances might be decidedly unpropitious. Periods of tranquillity defined by stable expectations and stable market confidence may sustain the illusion that, despite evidence to the contrary, financial markets are truly reflecting a strong and balanced real economy. The shattering of that illusion can be catastrophic. In consequence, the financial markets can resemble the cartoon character who, having run off the edge of the cliff, remains suspended for some time in the midair, with no visible (or rational) means of support, before suddenly plunging into the abyss.

One of the tasks of financial regulation, then, is to keep markets away from the cliff edge, but when they rush over, to ensure that the damage to the economy as a whole is minimized.

The Analysis of Liquidity (Adjective)

If markets are to be liquid and reasonably stable, then as Avinash Persaud has emphasized (2000, 2003), it is not enough that markets should be large; it is also a fundamental requirement that they be characterized by a wide range of participants with heterogeneous objectives and methods *and* with confident expectations that markets will be relatively stable. A market is liquid when buyers are broadly balanced by sellers. Markets become illiquid when actions become homogeneous—especially when everyone wants to sell.

A number of factors contribute to the relative heterogeneity of actors in financial markets:

1. Individual investors and traders must be highly heterogeneous with regards to their objectives, risk preferences, time horizons, market valuations, structures, and infrastructures. In economics, this was traditionally described as the difference between those seeking income certainty and those seeking wealth certainty, with the implied different patterns of risk aversion, time horizons, and so on (Robinson, 1951).
2. Investors may have differing access to information, so even if their goals might be the same, they will behave differently.
3. When the general opinion is that markets are stable, then stability becomes a convention. Convention (meaning belief in stability) is vital in financial markets because convention *creates* and *sustains*

heterogeneity. This power of stable expectations should not be underestimated; by defining the *expected* range of movements in asset prices, convention fixes (at least for a while) the *actual* range of fluctuations in current asset prices. But of course once convention is breached, then the flood will follow.[6]

4. Investors may be forced, by government regulation, into segmented markets, where heterogeneity is effectively imposed by the authorities. For example, the UK mortgage, insurance, and cash-deposit markets used to be legally separated. Part of this separation was achieved through nonprice mechanisms such as credit rationing and queuing, as was common in the hire purchase and mortgage markets in Europe. Similarly, the Glass-Stegall Act (1932) segmented U.S. financial markets. Exchange and capital account controls segmented national financial markets.

Taking these four dimensions as a starting point, we see that it is clear the liberalization, and hence internationalization, of financial markets that has taken place over the past three decades has inevitably reduced heterogeneity in financial markets. By definition, liberalization and internationalization have broken down market segmentation—allowing cross-market correlations to rise sharply at times, in a way that would not have been possible before.

With liberalization has come a growing professionalization of financial management (BIS, 1998, ch. 5) and extensive conglomeration of financial institutions (Group of Ten, 2001; IMF 2004a, 2004b). Most investments are now managed by mutual funds, pension funds, insurance companies, and so on; and these funds are themselves locked into sophisticated wholesale money markets, securitizing and packaging, and hence homogenizing, funds from previously segmented markets. Professionalization has reduced the heterogeneity of investor preferences as expressed in the marketplace. The professional investor is subject to a continual competitive pressure to maximize (short-term[7]) returns, and is constrained by the well-known institutional dilemma that "it is better for reputation to fail conventionally than to succeed unconventionally" (Keynes, 1936, p. 158). So whatever the preferences of the private investor might be, convergence on "professional" or "conventional" strategies by institutional investors are homogenizing the market. And with professional investment go professional information services—both in sources and in processing—again making for a more homogeneous environment.

Conglomeration is clearly a major homogenizing force, too. As conglomeration proceeds, risk-management procedures acquire common characteristics throughout the financial sector, whether in banking, securities, fund management, or insurance. Where once management techniques were sector specific, they are now becoming firm specific, applied across all sectors of the firm's activities.

In addition, increased credit-risk transfer (CRT; through credit derivatives and other forms of securitization) may be another homogenizing force. In principle, risk transfer can enhance the heterogeneity of risk bearing, transferring risks from those without an adequate capacity for it to those who have. But risk transfers do not inherently do this, and a number of questions arise from any risk transfer: Has risk been better spread or has it been concentrated, either through a small number of intermediaries or through a large number of investors with homogenous behavior? Has risk been transferred to those institutions with a greater capacity for the risk in question, or merely to those with a greater appetite for risk premiums? When a risk erupts, has the transfer of risk made it easier or harder for central banks to mitigate the wider, systemic impact? How does the CRT change the risk-taking, risk-absorption, and risk-monitoring capacity of both buyers and sellers of risk? These questions are as yet unresolved, with only tentative answers on offer.[8] However, what does seem clear is that risk transfers were a powerful homogenizing force across financial institutions.[9]

Regulation and Homogeneity

Financial-sector regulators are tending to reinforce the homogenizing process. The most important reaction to the recurring crises that have followed the process of liberalization since the 1970s has been the development of international regulatory standards and procedures. In this context, the International Monetary Fund–World Bank Financial Sector Assessment Program (FSAP) is of particular note since it locates regulation within a treaty framework under Article IV of the IMF Articles of Association. The FSAP surveillance concentrates on the adherence of national regulation and practices to core principles developed by the Basel Committee, together with the International Organization of Securities Commissions (IOSCO) and the International Association of Insurance Supervisors (see IMF, 2004a, 2004b). But it is in the principles underlying Basel 2 that the most important intellectual foundations of the new international financial architecture are revealed.

These principles are expressed through the three pillars of Basel 2: Pillar One, the determination of regulatory capital now heavily weighted toward use of banks' internal risk-weighting models, as well as the views of ratings agencies; Pillar Two, supervision; and Pillar Three, market discipline enforced by greater disclosure of banks' financial status, as well as their internal risk-management procedures.

What is particularly noticeable is the emphasis on the role of firms' own risk-management procedures and on market discipline. This is a rather odd way to confront systemic risk, which is by definition an externality that internal procedures do not encompass and is not accounted for in the marketplace. But perhaps of even greater importance is that Pillar One and Pillar Three will tend to increase the homogeneity of financial markets, as follows:

1. There is the emphasis on the use of firms' internal risk-management systems, systems that are by definition market sensitive. While firms' models may differ in detail, they are constructed on similar analytical principles, estimated on similar historical data, and sensitive to the same market information.

   Modern risk-management practices will result in firms' holding a portfolio of assets that in quiet times exhibit high expected returns, low price volatility, and low price correlation with other instruments and assets. The composition of the set of assets that exhibit these characteristics will, therefore, be shared by many investors. Suppose, however, that the volatility of a given asset rises sharply. The rise in volatility will cause the risk models to signal that a reduction in risk is required and best achieved by selling those assets where volatility has recently risen. As all those investors who share similar assets try to sell the same assets at the same time, volatility will rise further, spilling over to other instruments, leading to a rise in correlation, causing risk models to signal that further selling is required. Previously uncorrelated assets are now correlated in the general sell-off, enhanced by the model-driven behavior of other institutions caught up in the contagion.[10] The attempt to reduce risk augments its rise. While in normal times such models may encompass a wide range of behavior, in extreme circumstances the models will encourage firms to act as a herd, charging toward the cliff edge together (Persaud, 2000).
2. The emphasis on disclosure reduces the diversity of information that has in the past created diversity of views. Today, information is

> ever more readily available, and disclosure of price-sensitive information is legally required before it can be traded upon. Insider dealing on private information is, rightly, characterized as market abuse. But the attainment of equal information is bought at a cost—increased homogeneity and hence potentially reduced liquidity.
>
> In the light of the enforcement of greater homogeneity by Pillars One and Three, considerable weight is placed on Pillar Two (enhanced supervision) to inhibit the behavior that generates systemic risk. Unfortunately, it is not at all clear that an essentially subjective, personal interaction between bureaucrat and risk taker can be either consistent or effective, particularly on an international scale (Ward, 2002; IMF 2004a).

The drive toward homogeneity is not confined to the Basel 2 banking proposals. Regulators are responding to the creation of seamless financial markets, spanning banks, securities firms, insurance companies, pension funds, and so on, by requiring that they all follow the same regulatory regime. For example, in considering the relationship between banking and insurance, Sir Howard Davies, then chairman of the UK Financial Services Authority, argued "Our general view is that the capital treatment should in principle be the same, where the risks are the same" (Davies, 2002). The homogenizing pressure exerted by the regulators was evident in the UK Financial Services Authority's (FSA) Consultation Paper 142, on operational risk systems and controls (which enunciates policies that apply to all regulated firms) and is a defining theme of the European Union Capital Requirements Directive (CRD) and the Market in Financial Instruments Directive.

More generally, the Financial Stability Forum Report on Enhancing Market and Institutional Resilience (2008), while recommending a number of detailed specific measures, had at its core the familiar homogeneity-enhancing trio of greater transparency, more disclosure, and yet more rigorous risk management by firms.

Strategic Behavior

To the increased homogenization of financial markets must be added a further, potentially yet more destabilizing phenomenon: strategic behavior by market participants.

The essence of strategic behavior in financial markets was captured by Keynes in his famous analogy of a "beauty contest." In Keynes's contest, beauty is not in the eye of the beholder; instead, the game is won by those who can accurately assess what others think is beautiful. In financial markets, it is knowing what others believe to be true that is the key to knowing how markets will behave. The market is driven by participants' belief about what average opinion believes average opinion believes, and so on (Keynes, 1936, ch. 12; Eatwell and Taylor, 2000, chs.1 and 3; Morris and Shin, 2002).

Such strategic behavior is notable by its absence from the predominant models of asset pricing, whether Black-Scholes or later variations on the theme. In these models, the individual agent is portrayed as an independent atom, unheeding of the actions of others. Once strategic behavior is taken into account, then, even in quite simple models, prices can be shown to deviate systematically from what might be deemed to be competitive market prices (Persaud, 2003). Bubbles are generated by the same behavior (Allen, Morris, and Shin, 2006).

It is not hard to see that homogenization will interact with and encourage strategic behavior. As markets become more homogeneous, agents will become increasingly aware of the interdependence of their actions. The changing character of financial markets has resulted in greater homogenization and a greater tendency toward strategic behavior, especially in the face of extreme events.

Financial Structure and the Expansion of Liquidity (Noun)

A very simple monetary structure (perhaps representative of the early stages of the development of market economies, or of some developing countries today) is presented in table 2.1.

In normal times (one historically significant sort of "abnormality" is considered below), the only private assets are the value of tangible capital $p_k K$, with K as the existing stock at historical or replacement cost and p_k as its asset price. "Money" (broadly construed) Z is the sole liability of the banking system.[11] There is no significant market in bonds, so private holdings of government securities are negligible. On the liability side, private business may borrow L_p from the banks. Loans from abroad are negligible, and both private housing and the value of equity outstanding are effectively nontraded.

The system's assets are loans (at this stage only L_p to the private sector), bonds B_b, which the government has placed with the banks, and

Table 2.1 Stage one

Sector Assets	Private	Banks	Government	RoW	– Real Assets	Σ
Tangible capital	$+ p_k \cdot K$				$- p_k \cdot K$	0
Govt Bonds		$+ B_b$	$- B$		0	0
Loans	$- L_p$	$+ L$			0	0
Foreign reserves		$+ e \cdot F^*$		$- e \cdot F^*$	0	0
"Money"	$+ Z$	$- Z$			0	0
– Net worth	$- NW_p$	0	$+ \Gamma$	$+ e \cdot F^*$	$+ p_k \cdot K$	0
Σ	0	0	0	0	0	0

international reserves of the central bank eF^*, with F^* as the value of reserves in foreign currency and e as the exchange rate (units of local currency per unit of foreign currency). The sum of bank assets determines the money supply Z. The government's total borrowing, which at this stage is only from the banking system, is $B = B_b$. The corresponding asset is the "full faith and credit" of the State, Γ.

Table 2.1 is a matrix that describes the interlocking system of balance sheets within the economy. Symbols with a plus sign describe assets and negative signs indicate liabilities. The sum of each row must be zero, since (a) every financial asset of a given sector is a liability of another one, and (b) there is a column allowing every real asset to appear as a double entry. The last row presents the sum of each column—zero other than the final entry representing national net worth. The entries in this table represent values of *stocks* of assets. They change in two ways. One is through flow accumulation or decumulation over time. The other is the capital gains and losses consequent upon changes in asset prices p_k or e. For the private sector, liquidity takes the form of one *asset*, namely money. Nothing else is at hand.[12]

The accounting framework just sketched puts strict limitations on policy options. Suppose that money demand is described by the equation of exchange $Zv = PX$, with P the price level, X output, and v the velocity of circulation of money. If X is set by "full employment" as determined by the Walrasian equations of exchange, P comes from an inflation forecast or target, and v is determined "institutionally," then money demand must follow. This is in accordance with the basic closed-economy monetarist inflation model, set out by Wicksell (1935) and developed by Friedman (1968). A higher fiscal deficit, B, is "monetized" because the government cannot easily place debt obligations other than with the banks. The resulting increase in Z forces P up.

If loans L_p to the private sector are set by needs of production, the sum of bank loans to the government and international reserves is determined from the consolidated banking system's balance sheet: $B_b + eF^* = Z - L_p$. If reserves are targeted to increase as the current account improves, then government debt B_B must fall via a larger fiscal surplus. This is the basis of the "twin" fiscal/foreign deficits that have been at the heart of IMF financial programming for more than half-a-century.

Because liquidity in many economies now comprises a spectrum of financial assets and liabilities far wider than just money, such monetarist inflation models are anachronistic. However, the inflation in Zimbabwe that took off in the mid-2000s can be interpreted along these monetarist lines (including the fact that money creation was mostly in the form of cash).

Even in this simple structure, financial manias can appear. One familiar scenario is based on government assets that have been privatized and sold through a dealer to the public.[13] If the dealer happens to have a captive bank at his disposal, he can lend money to himself to bid up the share price leading to a capital gain (or ongoing inflation). Others may then start borrowing from the captive and other banks to try to buy shares, setting off a boom that ends inevitably in a crash. Famous examples are the Mississippi and South Sea crises early in the eighteenth century, in which John Law's Banque Générale in Paris and the Swordblade Bank in London issued the loans. These examples illustrate what was to become a recurring theme in financial instability. Capital gains are financed by liquidity in the form of *liabilities* assumed by financial actors to buy the appreciating assets. Many possibilities along these lines exist in more complicated financial systems.

In table 2.2, the model is extended by incorporating a domestic market in government debt. The banks and the nonbank private sector now have substantial holdings of government bonds (B_b and B_p, respectively). Keynes (1936) thought in terms of this sort of financial system, with the significant extension of having markets in corporate debt instruments as well. Primary liquidity is still money. Keynesian ideas about liquidity preference come into play, with the interest rate mediating portfolio choices between more liquid money and less liquid bonds (with government bonds being more liquid than corporates, which are subject to interest-rate spreads associated with both liquidity and solvency risks). Financial instability takes the form of shifts in liquidity preference, mixed with overborrowing (high leverage), such shifts provide the foundation for Minsky's financial instability hypothesis (Minsky, 1975).

The potential for the use of liabilities as a source of liquidity is expanded in table 2.3 (the foreign sector is dropped to simplify the exposition). A local market for equity issued by the private sector can provide the dynamic. In the table, the value of private-sector shares outstanding is $p_v V$, with p_v as a price index and V a measure of outstanding volume.[14] The use of liabilities (and derivatives built around them) as sources of liquidity is illustrated in the table's Finance sector that holds shares $p_v V_f$ financed by borrowing from banks and abroad. The sector's net worth is NW_f, held by the private sector as an asset. Within the Finance sector, there are offsetting asset and liability entries R. Individual financial

Table 2.2 Stage two

Sector Assets	Private	Banks	Government	RoW	– Real Assets	Σ
Tangible capital	$+ p_k \cdot K$				$- p_k \cdot K$	0
Govt Bonds	$+ B_p$	$+ B_b$	$- B$		0	0
Loans	$- L_p$	$+ L$			0	0
Foreign reserves		$+ e \cdot F^*$		$- e \cdot F^*$	0	0
"Money"	$+ Z$	$- Z$			0	0
– Net worth	$- NW_p$	0	$+ \Gamma$	$+ e \cdot F^*$	$+ p_k \cdot K$	0
Σ	0	0	0	0	0	0

Table 2.3 Stage three

Sector Assets	Private	Banks	Finance	Government	– Real Assets	Σ
Tangible capital	$+ p_k \cdot K$				$- p_k \cdot K$	0
Govt Bonds	$+ B_p$	$+ B_b$		$- B$	0	0
Loans	$- L_p$	$+ L$	$\mathbf{- L_f}$		0	0
Repos			**+/– R**		0	0
Equities	$\mathbf{- p_v \cdot V}$		$\mathbf{+ p_v \cdot V_f}$		0	0
"Money"	$+ Z$	$- Z$			0	0
– Net Worth (financial sector)	$+ NW_f$		$- NW_f$		0	0
– Net worth (others)	$- NW_p$	0	0	$+ \Gamma$	$+ p_k \cdot K$	0
Σ	0	0	0	0	0	0

actors such as broker-dealers and hedge funds can borrow from one another, but for their "leveraged" subsystem as a whole, many of these transactions will be mutually offsetting.[15] By increasing transactions R, financial institutions can add to cash flow as they build up their leverage ratios $(p_v V_f + R)/NW_f$. The liabilities $(L_f + R + eL^*_f)$ underlying total assets $(p_v V_f + R)$ can support imposing structures of leverage and liquidity.[16] So long as p_v continues to rise, for example, then growing intra-financial sector claims make it possible to mobilize large sums of liquidity to buy stock. This is exactly how the repo and reverse repo markets have worked to the size of balance sheets in the Finance sector.

The use of repos and reverse repos by financial institutions as a source of liquidity was analyzed by Minsky (1957), who demonstrated that the tight U.S. monetary policy of the mid-1950s led government bond houses to develop repurchase agreements in order to finance the expansion of their balance sheets, despite the rise in short-term interest rates.[17] Repos can be depicted as a financial innovation that makes "idle" liquidity circulate; for instance, repos can allow a financial institution to obtain funds from another financial institution whose lending capacity has not reached its regulatory maximum. In addition, repos can result in an increase in the velocity of circulation by shortening the time intervals between overlapping transactions and so increase the liquidity of the economy.[18]

Nowadays, apart from repos, the potential expansion of liquidity has been further enhanced by the development of asset securitization (see table 2.4). Suppose that, as well as capital, the private sector holds a tangible asset, residential housing H, with price p_h. It borrows M (mortgages) from banks, using $p_h H$ as collateral. The banks in turn bundle the mortgages into a security S with price p_s that is then sold on to other financial actors. This makes it possible to borrow large sums and increase leverage by increasing claims on the nonfinancial sector. It is also potential collateral for repo or short-term commercial paper borrowing.

The combination of securitization and the growth of the repo market have greatly expanded the potential for the growth of liquidity by the expansion of the balance sheets of financial intermediaries. Indeed, Adrian and Shin (2008, p. 12) have argued that not only are repos and reverse repos important financing activities for investment banks but that "the margin of adjustment in the expansion and contraction of balance sheets is through repos and reverse repos."

Given that liquidity is defined as "the growth of the balance sheets of financial intermediaries," it is instructive to examine the composition

Table 2.4 Securitization

Sector Assets	Private	Banks	Finance	Government	– Real Assets	Σ
Tangible capital	$+p_k \cdot K$				$-p_k \cdot K$	0
Real estate	$+p_h \cdot H$				$-p_h \cdot H$	0
Govt Bonds	$+B_p$	$+B_b$		$-B$	0	0
Loans	$-L_p$	$+L$	$-L_f$		0	0
Mortgages	$-M$	$+M_b$			0	0
MBS		$-p_s \cdot S$	$+p_s \cdot S$		0	0
Repos			$+/-R$		0	0
Equities	$-p_v \cdot V$		$+p_f \cdot V_f$		0	0
"Money"	$+Z$	$-Z$			0	0
– Net Worth (financial sector)	$+NW_f$		$-NW_f$		0	0
– Net worth (others)	$-NW_p$	0	0	$+\Gamma$	$+p_k \cdot K$ $+p_h \cdot H$	0
Σ	0	0	0	0	0	0

of balance-sheet growth in different sectors of the economy (see Adrian and Shin, 2007). In the household sector, the growth of assets is associated with a decline in leverage (see figure 2.1). Among commercial banks, there is a very weak relationship between the growth of assets and the growth of leverage (hardly surprising, since capital ratios in commercial banks are regulated).

However, in the case of the (former) investment banks, there was a strong positive relationship between the growth of assets and the growth of leverage. In other words, as asset values increased, the investment banks increased their leverage, further bidding up asset values. The system also worked in reverse. When asset values fell sharply in 1998 following the long term capital management (LTCM) crisis (see figure 2.2), the investment banks cut leverage sharply, precipitating further falls in asset prices and adding an additional twist to the vicious downward spiral.

"The Innovation that Failed": The Originate, Rate, and Relocate Model of Banking

Regulatory incentives played an important role in the evolution of the credit crunch. In early 2007, according to the regulatory-prescribed

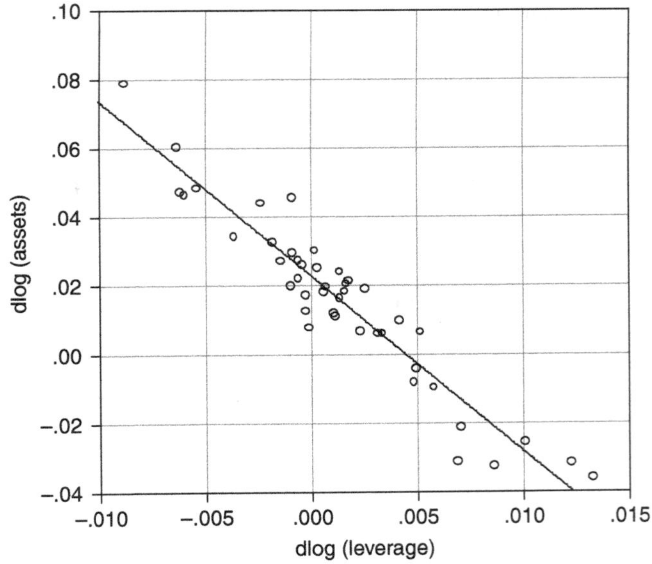

Figure 2.1 Assets and leverage growth rates of households, 1992–2006
Source: U.S. Federal Reserve.

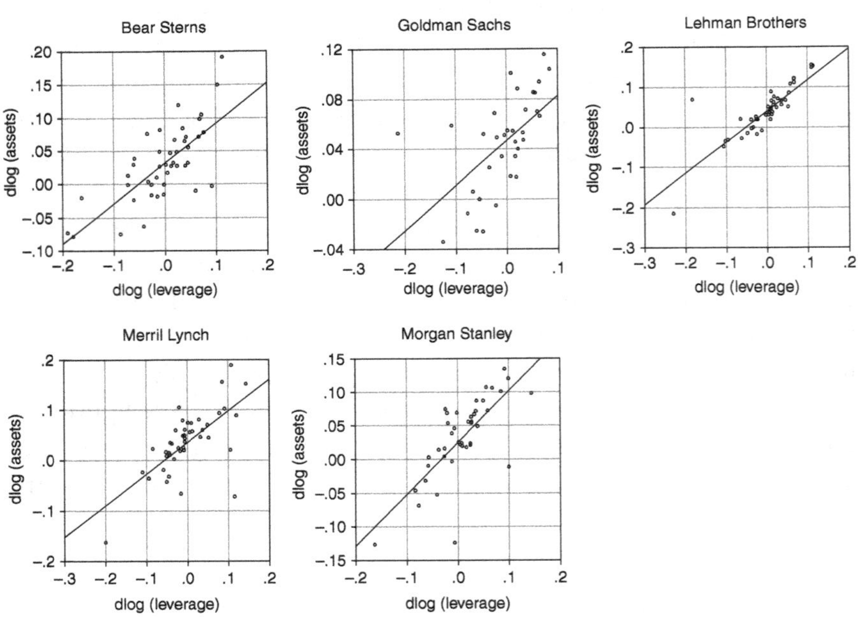

Figure 2.2 Assets and leverage growth rates of five investment banks, 1992–2006
Source: U.S. Securities Exchange Commission; Adrian and Shin, 2007. Liquidity and leverage. Working Paper. Federal Reserve Bank and Princeton University.

models of their "riskiness," banks had a safe buffer above their capital requirements.[19] In some systemically important banks, this was to diminish dramatically.[20] One of the recent puzzles of banking was the contrast between the risky activities they were increasingly associated with, such as prime-brokerage and credit derivatives, and the increasingly healthy ratio of their regulatory capital to the risk that they reported. Banking appeared riskier, but capital ratios declared them safe. In the run-up to the credit crunch, this apparent safety encouraged banks to do more of the same: to originate more debt with the intention of relocating it. It also made regulators generally comfortable that they were doing so.

Many bank regulators portrayed the rapid growth of securitization as a welcome way of bankers spreading risks more evenly.[21] Regulatory-prescribed risk models, such as those embedded in the EU Capital Requirements Directive (CRD), not only failed to provide an early warning signal but also signaled the "all clear." Moreover, they contributed to the homogenizing of financial participants' behavior that significantly worsened the crisis.

Moreover, recent experience casts doubt on the efficacy of markets as a means of "disciplining" financial institutions. Market discipline is a critical component of Pillar Three of Basel 2. But prior to the collapse of Northern Rock, the UK stock market "rewarded" its management and praised its risk-management strategy.[22] Elsewhere, any bank with a high degree of capital that was not showing a competitive growth in earnings would have been considered by stock markets to be wasting shareholders' capital. They would have paid a stock-market penalty that, through share-ownership incentives, would have hit the pockets of their management. This was what Chuck Prince, then CEO of Citigroup was intimating when he commented, notoriously, on July 10, 2007, "When the music stops, in terms of liquidity, things will be complicated. But as long as the music is playing, you've got to get up and dance. We're still dancing." Just as Mr. Prince was taking time out from dancing to make his comments, the music stopped.[23]

While the music was playing, banks were incentivized by bank regulation to earn fees for originating debt and for relocating the debt elsewhere. As a result of capital adequacy requirements, the cost of keeping a loan on the balance sheet made banks uncompetitive providers of capital to the most creditworthy borrowers; especially when liquidity was high, nonbanks were providing cheap consumer debt (e.g., auto loans) and the banks' best clients could go straight to the capital markets.

It is often said that investors were to blame for not knowing what they were buying, and more investor knowledge, transparency, and disclosure—the perennial response to all crises—will solve the problem. To an extent, this reflects a misunderstanding of the nature of the market for securitized bank loans and other debt instruments. It is a market where investors, almost by definition, know less detail than normal of the instruments they own.

A stylistic characterization of modern banking is that borrowers who can go directly to investors do so, as it is cheaper. Hence, the bank-loan books of today generally represent borrowers or instruments to which investors do not want direct exposure. The borrower may be small or an infrequent borrower, the borrower's business may be hard for investors to understand or monitor, or maybe the risks are just too great. Loans also carry interest-rate and liquidity risks, as well as credit risks. To attract investors, banks have to persuade them, with some reasonableness, that a portfolio of idiosyncratic credit risks will yield substantial diversification benefits: lower risk for a given yield (or equivalently, higher yields for a given risk). This is why the ratings agencies are so important to structured finance.

Investors using statistical models to optimize the risk and return of their credit portfolios find these credit instruments highly attractive. They provide an attractive yield, not just because of the diversification of credit risks but also because they offer a liquidity premium—a higher return because they are illiquid, a premium paid on assets that are *liquid*—and therefore should attract only those investors who do not need liquidity.

Up to two years ago, they represented an ideal investment for German Landesbanks, which enjoyed a state guarantee that virtually ensured they would have fail-safe access to liquidity. Landesbanks were, therefore, incentivized through that guarantee to seek out investments that offered an extra liquidity premium in their choice of assets, like private equity and CDOs. However, two years ago, the European Commission, in the interests of fostering fairer competition, removed these credit guarantees. This was the right thing to do from a competition perspective, and inevitably it introduced a risk to the existing asset holdings of the Landesbanks that had not been there originally—the risk that access to liquidity would be denied. This was a risk that was not in the living memory of the Landesbanks' managements, and according to statistical models of the past five years, was considered a very low risk. At the same time, these illiquid credit instruments were delivering good returns, while the removal of the guarantee was hurting margins. These returns would have been largely lost if the funding for the assets was maturity matched to the asset (i.e., funding ten-year assets by raising a ten-year loan). Armed with their risk-sensitive models for assurance, the Landesbanks held on.

Other buyers who were incentivized to buy these assets were investors not required to observe capital-adequacy or solvency requirements for owning illiquid loans: investors who were acting like banks and insurance companies but without the regulatory requirements. No one was more aware of this than the banks themselves, and they often organized investors into structure investment vehicles (SIVs) that owned the assets and leveraged the funding through short-term debt. Like any bank, SIVs had an inherent liquidity problem in that they were buying illiquid long-term assets using short-term borrowing; and so to allay the fears of investors and rating agencies, the banks often provided a liquidity "backstop." According to the banks' risk-sensitive models—measured over a period of calm in the credit markets—the probability of having to employ the backstop was small.

It is interesting to note that under the risk-sensitivity approach of Basel 2 and the CRD, these contingent liabilities would have required the banks to put aside more capital than they did. It is argued by some that this would have tempered their use and is an argument for the CRD. While this appears so from a static perspective, it is worth considering the dynamic implications of risk-sensitive provisioning for contingent liabilities. When liquidity is high, and it might be hoped that banks would apply discretion, risk-sensitivity models would indicate that these liabilities were not risky and so they would have been acquired with relative ease. When the credit cycle turns, volatility and correlation rise, so risk-sensitive models would indicate that these liabilities had become extremely risky, requiring the banks to set aside substantial amounts of capital at a time when such capital was in scarce supply. This pushes up money-market rates, and when capital is hard to find, it will lead to a fire sale of assets to generate liquidity. The static position looks prudent, but the dynamic is dangerous. The dynamic aspects of these risk-sensitive models are discussed further below.

Risk Traders versus Risk Absorbers

It is important to note that many of the investors who hold assets in SIVs or as an investment in CDOs/CDS are set up as "traders." Their risk-management systems assume that if they cannot fund the assets for whatever reason, they will be able to sell them. They trade and treat the assets as ratings with yields. They "outsource" the monitoring and understanding of the risks to the rating agencies, so they have no independent view of the risks. They are not risk absorbers.

A risk absorber needs to have the capacity to take a different view of the risks than the marketplace. To do this, they would not depend on market liquidity, and they would have a credit-monitoring capacity that was independent of market prices. The stylized characterization of Warren Buffet's insurance company, Berkshire Hathaway, is a risk absorber: prepared to buy assets that have been beaten down in the marketplace, in calculated anticipation that while they may not appreciate shortly, they will do so in a time horizon shorter than its liabilities.

Investors with long-term liabilities, like pensions funds and insurance companies, are natural risk absorbers. Their ability to be risk absorbers, however, has been curtailed by regulations that require or encourage pension funds and insurance companies to mark-to-market their assets and respond to short-term changes in asset prices.

Risk-Sensitive Models and Liquidity

Before we consider risk models in greater detail, it is important to emphasize that the Originate, Rate, and Relocate model is a direct by-product of the incentives facing financial institutions. It is arguable that greater individual and institutional responsibility should have tempered the impact of these incentives. But it is unlikely that there will be any lasting change unless incentives are changed. Regulatory requirements encourage the banks to originate but quickly relocate loans to investors that do not have those regulatory obligations. The direction of this flow of credit risk, from banks to investors, is not always wrong from a systemic-risk perspective. But the size and concentration of the flow to risk traders has proved destabilizing. This is due in part to risk-sensitive models that, in the dynamic of the crisis, turned out to be part of the problem rather than of the solution.

The statistical-risk models used by banks, credit-rating agencies, and investors have differences, but at their core lies the modern portfolio theory developed by Harry Markovitz and further extended by Robert Merton. That theory presumes that instruments have inherent risk and return characteristics. There is a frontier of portfolios of instruments that maximize returns for a given average level of risk, and the ones that investors pick relates to their own investor risk aversion. Risk and return of instruments and portfolios of instruments are not fixed points, but are distributions. Using a model that optimizes this mean-variance relationship, an investor can estimate the probability of a loss of a specific cash level. Equivalently, an investor can infer the loss he or she would suffer at a given probability level. For example, an investor may say of his portfolio, based on past distributions of risk and correlation, that there is a 2.0% probability that his loss tomorrow is greater than 1 million euro. This is referred to as a DEAR limit (daily earnings at risk). Risk management using DEAR limits was developed by banks in the late 1980s.[24]

Risk is a subject that generates much concern, uncertainty, and confusion. It is a subject for which people seek confidence and convention. These risk-sensitive models have become the convention, for three broad reasons. First, they had academic credibility. The models were based on the work of distinguished professors of finance, notably H. M. Markovitz (1952), R. C. Merton (1973), and William Sharpe (1963). Second, regulators had approved their specific use for the evaluation of market risks held by banks in the 1996 amendment to the Basel Accord (Basel 1). Today, the approach to modeling risks based on distributions of past risk is the lynchpin of the risk-sensitive approach to risk in Basel 2 and the CRD. Third, "everybody" uses these models. Uncertainty leads to herding. The fact that many are using a similar risk model lends confidence to many more to follow suit. Paradoxically, their widespread use lies at the heart of why these models fail (see Persaud, 2000).

The modern statistical versions of the Markovitz and Merton models were developed to help banks measure their private risks. Banks are commonly assumed to have short-term liabilities. Consequently, risk was defined as the probability of a loss occurring "tomorrow" based on past distribution of volatility and correlations. If volatility or correlation rises, increasing the probability of a loss above the bank's DEAR limit, it reduces its exposure to return within its DEAR limit. Implicit in the drawing of inference from the past distribution of volatility and correlation to tomorrow is the assumption of statistical independence. Specifically, the process of selling risk return into the DEAR limit, or the period in which DEAR limits are hit, is assumed to be independent of the previously observed volatilities and correlations.

Risk Models and Strategic Behavior

This all made sense in the 1950s, when Markovitz was developing modern portfolio theory, and even in the 1970s, when Merton was developing the Merton model. In those days, investors were "segmented" behind country and regulatory borders. The supply of capital was relatively inelastic. Information was sparse. Investment management was less professionalized, and computing power limited. Cross-border financial flows were a tiny fraction of the levels they are today. For example, the stock of international bank lending rose from $265 billion in 1975, to $42,000 billion twenty years later (Eatwell, 1997, pp. 4–5). If a single, small investor were to construct a portfolio that maximized his or her expected return for a given level of short-term risk based on past observations, he or she could reasonably assume statistical independence. Accordingly it would be supposed that measures of volatility, correlation, and returns reflected inherent characteristics. Risk models today are essentially the same, but the world has changed in such a way as to undermine the assumptions that make these models work. These models systematically underestimate risk in "quiet" times and overestimate risk in "stressed" times.

Today's world is flat in terms of information and investment flow. When an asset or portfolio of assets offers a higher yield than its historic risk based on databases of five or more years, investors are aware of it globally, and they begin to add these assets to their portfolios. The response of global capital changes the characteristic of the asset into an increasingly overpriced instrument that is vulnerable to the herd exiting.

This vulnerability is not picked up in the five-year average of short-term volatility until the herd has assembled and there is a bump in the night.[25] When the price volatility of an asset rises following some bump, and the DEAR limits of the herd of investors invested in the asset are in danger of being breached, the investors try to reduce their risk exposures. However, because they are all doing so at the same time, and the wider set of instruments that looked attractive on a risk-return basis to one investor looked so to all other investors, the investors are selling a similar set of instruments. Correlation as well as volatility rise further, which causes the DEAR limits to be hit again and forces the holders to sell more. This dangerous circularity has been described as a liquidity black hole (Persaud, 2003, 2004).

The essential problem with the traditional models is that, in assuming statistical independence, they also assume away the strategic behavior that is the hallmark of investing today. They assume that when individual investors use a readily available database of market prices and a common risk model to identify markets with better risk-return characteristics, they are the only ones to react to what they see.

And when investors see risk-return characteristics changing and want to reduce risk to back below some level, that they again are the only ones doing so. In today's more fluid markets, where the supply curve of capital is almost horizontal, the observation of statistical characteristics triggers an investor response that is large enough—over time—to change these statistical characteristics. The implication is that, at a time of stress, the probability distribution of future price is unstable. This instability cannot be addressed simply by assuming fatter tails of the historic distribution. A good analogy is that Markovitz- and Merton-derived risk models are like seat belts in a car that lock when you are at standstill and unlock when you start moving. Adjusting the inertia settings will not help.

In normal times, price declines bring out buyers looking for bargains; in a liquidity black hole, falling prices, by triggering some risk limit, lead to more sellers, more price declines, and more selling. There is growing evidence for these risk-model-induced liquidity crises (see Cohen and Shin, 2003).

Risk models attract herds of investors, and then use adverse movements in price measures to signal to the herd that it is time to reduce risk by "hitting" the same prices. This is why when a bank or fund finds itself in a liquidity black hole, a harried risk manager is often seen explaining that, according to the risk model, it was a "once in a thousand-year" event. Those who recall the 1987 problem of "portfolio insurance," the 1994/95 Tequila crisis, the 1997 Asian financial crisis, the 1998 LTCM debacle, and today's credit crunch would observe that these "once in a thousand-year" events occur every five years or so.

The problem is not caused solely by an overly static measurement of risk, but also by mechanistic reaction to these faulty measures of risk. In the case of banks and insurance companies, these mechanistic rules to "sell risk when it appears high" are often part of regulation. Even where they are not part of formal regulation, mechanistic rules are used by a great many other investors, in part to reassure and signal to regulators and clients that they are applying commonly accepted risk-management practices. While it would be impossible to put the genie back into the bottle and request that market participants not look at mark-to-market measures or market-price measures of risk, the systemically dangerous degree of responsiveness of market participants to contemporaneous measures of risk could be lowered.

For example, many prudential regulations require investors to only hold assets of a minimum credit rating. This leads to the mechanistic selling of assets that have been downgraded below this level, even though the price of the assets has already discounted the news that subsequently led to its downgrading. The herd selling leads to a disproportionate response to the rating change, causing a valuation hit in portfolios that triggers further selling of risk. It has been suggested that it would be better to require that investors not purchase assets below a certain credit rating, and give the managers some freedom as to whether to hold on to the assets that have been downgraded or determine when to sell them.

Risk modeling in this form also amplifies the credit cycle, with potentially systemic implications. In economic good times, when credit defaults and market volatility is low, historic measures of risk are low, encouraging more risk-taking. Continuing along the economic up cycle, historic price measures suggest that this increased risk-taking is "safe" and emboldens further risk-taking. Risk-taking grows ever more aggressive until the peak of the credit cycle, when some bump causes the herd to rush for the exit, forcing up volatility and correlation measures. Risk models encourage more risk-taking at the height of the boom, when we would rather greater circumspection, and discourage lending as the boom collapses, just when the economy would benefit from some forbearance. Although the primary purpose of banking regulation should be to avoid the undesirable systemic implications just discussed, Basel 2 and the CRD place these pro-cyclical risk models at the heart of capital-adequacy requirements. It is not surprising that, despite substantial investment in risk management using these models, they have failed to protect the financial system. Financial market crises occur as a result of market failure to fully recognize risks. If the markets completely anticipated risks, they would not materialize. But if market pricing is the problem, using risk models that rely on market prices is very unlikely to prove a defense against market failure. Nonmarket price measures of risk, such as measures of concentration or measures of the economic cycle, are more likely to anticipate a market failure than are market prices.

What is surprising is that these models of private risk should have been adopted as the measure of choice by regulators. The models are measuring the sensitivity of individual bank profitability to risks. The issue regulators should be addressing is the sensitivity of systemic risks to banks' pursuing their individual profitability. This is clearly not the same thing, and where the use of these faulty models of individual risks generates systemic selling or buying, as described above, it is almost the opposite of how regulators should be tempering private behavior.

The prescriptive reliance on these market-price, risk-sensitivity models at the heart of the CRD appears, at best, tangential to the objective of regulation and, at worse, dangerous.

Systemic Liquidity and Search Liquidity

As noted above, and contrary to common belief, the liquidity of a market today rests not so much on its size (as measured by market capitalization or turnover) as in the diversity of its participants. It is easier for observers to see this distinction in the midst of a crisis than during the quiet time before a crisis, when liquidity appears high and capitalization is galloping ahead. The global corporate credit market is hardly small.[26]

In several markets, there are many different types of market participants, like hedge funds or pension funds, and within each type there are many different investment strategies. But diversity is often richer in appearance than in the reality of behavior. A key measure of the critical degree of diversity required for liquid markets is how differently market participants respond at times of stress to short-term price declines. A market where, for whatever reason, falling prices trigger selling by most players and generate few buyers is one that may be large and appear liquid in quiet times, but will be fragile and illiquid in stressful times. This is a stylized description of what has occurred in the global credit markets.

Many investors have long-term liabilities that do not require sensitivity to daily market moves. Examples would be pension funds, insurance companies, Sovereign Wealth Funds (SWFs), or any other investor type where funding or liabilities are long term. These investors can earn a liquidity premium versus other investors who require short-term liquidity. From a systemic point of view, these investors act as a liquidity absorber during time of stress.

For example, if the Abu Dhabi Investment Authority (ADIA) were constrained by a tight DEAR limit, it would not have been able to purchase 4.9% of Citibank shares in November 2007, just as the market was anticipating the bank to be forced to raise fresh capital. But ADIA is a SWF, investing for when Abu Dhabi runs out of oil in several decades. On this long view, it was buying Citibank shares at a bargain-basement price. ADIA's presence and behavior countered the likelihood of a steep price fall in Citibank shares that could have developed into a vicious cycle. European pension funds and insurance companies should have been vying with ADIA to buy Citibank shares. These investors would be ideal candidates for holding illiquid but good credit-quality packages of debt instruments, or for buying them from investors who are forced to sell them during a time of stress. But they cannot do so if they are required to behave in the same way as liquidity-hungry investors, as a result of inappropriately applied mark-to-market accounting of assets, Solvency II,[27] or risk-management fashion.

Investors who have short-term funding, or who are forced to follow short-term solvency or stop-loss rules, or who intended to trade an asset and so are not incentivized to understand it sufficiently to hold on to losing positions, will be forced to sell assets when they fall sharply in price. Indeed, they are incentivized to try to be the first to sell the assets before other investors do. Liquidity disappears in this rush for the exit. These liquidity-hungry investors act not as risk absorbers but as risk amplifiers.

Many regulators used to argue that the transfer of risk from one bank's balance sheet to several investors was a desirable spreading of risk. But what matters is not the number of or names of those that risk is transferred to but their behavior. The transfer of risk from banks was a transfer from a risk absorber to entities that acted as risk traders or amplifiers. This did not spread risk—it concentrated it. Supervisors ignored or misunderstood the distinction between risk traders and risk absorbers, and the need for heterogeneity.

It may appear from this analysis that the most liquid markets are those where there are only risk absorbers. But an efficient market requires both risk absorbers and risk traders. This is because there are at least two types of liquidity, and different players serve different type (see Lagana, Peoina, von Koppen-Mertes, and Persaud, 2006). Risk absorbers improve *systemic liquidity*—the liquidity available under times of market stress. A world full of Warren Buffets would suffer fewer liquidity crises.

But there is another kind of liquidity: *search liquidity*. This is the cost and time required to find securities that don't trade often during less stressful times. Search liquidity is important for the efficiency of markets in the quiet times—that is, most of the time. This type of liquidity is best served by risk traders who are trading assets on a continuous basis, repeatedly turning them over and checking their prices. Markets require a balance between risk traders and risk absorbers, and regulators must ensure that their regulation does not cut across this balance and does not artificially suppress one type of risk taker for the other. In the recent past, regulators focused on supporting risk traders at the expense of risk absorbers. This is a little odd, given that financial markets have demonstrated that, via innovation, they can support search liquidity themselves, while regulators are the key defense against a worsening of systemic liquidity.

Summing Up

We began the chapter by identifying two different uses of the term "liquidity," as adjective and as noun. The two uses come together in the characterization of a liquid market, in which the expansion of liquidity is driven by financial innovation. Financial innovation both induces the expansion of liquidity and, by its very novelty, creates entirely new risks that are often not well understood until they are manifest in a sudden loss of liquidity.

This situation poses a dilemma for financial policy. Innovation can be an important element in the enhanced efficiency of a financial system, and stifling innovation by excessive regulation may reduce significantly the growth of real income. Dealing with externalities is never a precise science (as environmental legislation demonstrates), and achieving a balance between systemic risk and financial innovation poses difficult choices. However, the starting point must be the recognition that the task of regulation is to reduce systemic risk, and this cannot be achieved through reliance on market forces or market driven processes such as risk management by firms.

For example, it is often said that "greater transparency" should be a dominant theme of any regulatory reform package. Precisely what is meant by "greater transparency" is not made clear: does this refer to improved availability of market information or to enhanced understanding of the structure of complex instruments? Unfortunately, in neither case will "greater transparency" reduce systemic risk in financial markets. Indeed, in some cases, greater transparency could make things worse.

Events in financial markets have demonstrated beyond all reasonable doubt that the sophisticated market-sensitive risk models deployed by banks and other financial firms, and espoused so enthusiastically by the regulators, have totally failed to ensure stability in financial markets. On the contrary, to the extent that anyone believes them anymore, the models have been a major factor in the failure of credit markets since, in the face of extreme events, they all tended to endorse the same actions at the same time, guaranteeing widespread illiquidity. One of the drivers of the consequent lemming-like behavior has been the greater transparency that regulators have campaigned for over the past twenty years or so. Greater transparency meant that more firms shared the same information, had access to the same procedural knowledge, and even followed the same modeling—so it is hardly surprising that they all behaved in the same way.

But the risk modelers should not be blamed. Their models are not capable of measuring market liquidity risk, nor are they intended for that task. A firm's risk model seeks to price the risks that are the result of its actions in the marketplace. They are necessarily market sensitive, and greater transparency will tend to increase that sensitivity. But it is not just that market sensitivity may increase the likelihood of stampedes. In the presence of the systemic externalities, such as liquidity risk, even the most transparent competitive market will be inefficient, and therefore risk will be mispriced. Financial turmoil is clearly a systemic event. There is no way it could have been accurately priced by an individual firm. Greater transparency will only add to the illusion of accuracy, and by reinforcing herd behavior, it may well make things worse. Indeed, a number of writers have suggested that the requirement to mark complex investments to market, hence increasing transparency, has been an important element in rapid deleveraging and subsequent financial collapse.

The second interpretation of the case for "greater transparency" rests on frequent references to securitized market instruments that "no one understands" and "no one knows how to price." Once again, the call for greater transparency is misconceived. What is at issue is not the transparency of such instruments but their complexity and the controls employed by buyers and sellers. Firms have bought complex instruments without understanding the risk, often relying exclusively on rating agencies to assess the risk, and in most cases have relied on valuations provided by sellers. Banks have sold complex products to unsophisticated investors with little attention to whether the investment is appropriate or whether the risks are understood, and have provided valuations using models that cannot price liquidity risk accurately. Where all parties involved believe in a particular asset class and in the rating of such assets, and where both sides of a transaction are financially motivated to see the transaction completed, then no amount of transparency will result in greater stability.

But transparency has nothing to do with the systemic risk that is the proper object of regulation. Indeed, the persistent emphasis on transparency is a dangerous diversion from the massive task of regulatory reform that is now required. Unfortunately, for the past twenty years or so, the regulators have swallowed the argument that superior market-sensitive risk management by firms would result in greater overall stability. They must abandon their belief in the tired trinity of greater transparency, more disclosure, and better risk management by firms. It must be recognized that that regulatory model has failed. Instead, regulators should turn to finding ways to develop a systemic approach to regulation, including pro-cyclical provisioning and system-wide stress testing, and confront the vicious market cycle of rising asset prices accompanied by rising leverage, and the even more vicious cycle running in reverse.

The need for systemic regulation is not confined to the financial systems of the United States and the United Kingdom. It is a quite general requirement of all financial and monetary structures. All financial systems are risky, since all financial systems rely ultimately on confidence and trust. Maintaining that confidence and trust is the first task of the financial regulator, and the basis of the maintenance of liquidity—and of liquid markets.

Notes

This is a newly revised text of a lecture delivered by John Eatwell at the Egyptian Centre for Economic Studies, in Cairo, on October 19, 2008 the section from pages 30 to 36 is based on work by Tarik Mouakil and Lance Taylor.

1. In the United States, mortgage-backed securities began to be significant in the 1930s, with the creation of Fannie Mae.

2. A repurchase agreement (or repo) is an agreement between two parties whereby one party sells the other a security at a specified price with a commitment to buy the security back at a later date for another specified price. While a repo is legally the sale and subsequent repurchase of a security, its economic effect is that of a secured loan—the party purchasing the security makes funds available to the seller and holds the security as collateral.

3. Before the introduction of deposit insurance in the twentieth century, bank runs were common in Europe, UK, and the United States. In the late nineteenth century, there was approximately one major bank run every decade. During the national banking era in the United States (1863–1914), there were five major bank runs: 1873, 1884, 1890, 1893, and 1907.

4. The crises at IKB and at Northern Rock are examples of market gridlock, not of a bank run. In the case of Northern Rock, the bank run was not a cause of Northern Rock's difficulties but a result of the crisis and of the preliminary response of the authorities.

5. There are a number of other important market failures in the financial sector that attract the concerns of public policy, most notably the asymmetry

of information between individual savers and market professionals, that is the motivation for consumer-protection legislation. This chapter deals solely with the market failure manifest in systemic risk and the implications for risk management by the authorities.

6. The most powerful convention of all is that imposed by governments. When the exchange rates of the future Eurozone currencies were declared prior to being irrevocably fixed on January 1, 1999, the markets rapidly converged on those rates.

7. "There is a peculiar zest in making money quickly, and remoter gains are discounted by the average man at a very high rate.... It is the long-term investor...who will in practice come in for most criticism, wherever investment funds are managed by committees or boards or banks" (Keynes, 1936, p.157).

8. See also Bank of England, 2001; FSA, 2002; IAIS, 2004; BIS, 2004; BCBS, 2004; Wagner and Marsh, 2004.

9. "With higher activity in risk transfer markets, financial market participants with traditional business lines could assume completely different roles as 'virtual insurers' or 'virtual bankers'" (OECD, 2002, p. 2).

10. The change in correlation is a market manifestation of what the individual agent cannot know prior to an "abnormal" event.

11. As is often the case in macroeconomic modeling, bank equity held as an asset by the private sector is omitted from the table. It is introduced and discussed in connection with financial regulation below.

12. To limit the number of symbols in the balance sheets, government liabilities to the private sector in the form of coin and currency are omitted from the present discussion. They were key components of the rich countries' financial systems well into the nineteenth century and remain important in many developing economies today.

13. The "assets" might be claims on hypothetical future revenue streams (the South Sea and Mississippi examples) or equity of former state enterprises.

14. For the private nonfinancial sector, table 2.4 follows the accounting convention of the flow of funds by treating equity outstanding as a "liability" and allowing nonzero net worth. So, for example, in flow of funds terms, Google has highly negative net worth because its stock-market valuation vastly exceeds its tangible capital and financial assets. On a balance sheet set up to follow accountants' conventions, Google—like all other corporations—would have zero net worth.

15. In available U.S. flow-of-funds data, they do not offset completely—leveraged financial institutions typically have negative net positions in fed funds and security repurchase (repo) agreements. Gross repo asset and liability positions are not reported.

16. In the United States at the end of 2007, leverage for households was around 1.2, for commercial banks it was about 10, and for investment banks it was over 30.

17. "If the institutional framework is stable, a tight monetary policy will be effective and the interest rate will rise to whatever extent is necessary in order to restrict the demand for financing to the essentially inelastic supply. However, the rise in interest rates feeds back upon the institutional framework. With rising interest rates the incentives to find new ways to finance operations and new substitutes for cash assets increase.... Hence there is a favourable environment for financial innovations. Since the significant institutional innovations during

a period of monetary policy will be those which tend to increase velocity, they can be represented as shifting the [supply of money]-interest rate relation to the right" (Minsky, 1957, p. 182).

18. Suppose initial repo contracts are for two weeks. Then, after receiving liquid funds, the issuer can buy a further asset, using that asset as collateral in a second repo to raise the funds to conclude (or roll over) the first contract. The original asset may then be used to raise funds to settle (or roll over) the second contract, and so on. The average length of a repo contract is now one week and the velocity of circulation has doubled, as has the liquidity generated by the repo contracts. As the average length of repo contracts shortens, the velocity of circulation accelerates.

19. At the end of 2006, the ratio of regulatory capital to risk-weighted assets was 13% in the United States, 12.9% in the UK, 12.2% in Germany, 10.7% in Italy, significantly above the 8.0% minimum.

20. In the third quarter of 2007, Citigroup reported that its Tier 1 capital fell below its 7.5% target, below the 8.0% standard of Basel 1 and close to its 6.0% regulatory minimum.

21. For example, as late as November 23, 2007, Mr. Patrick Neary, chief executive of the Irish Financial Services Regulatory Authority, said "All of us would probably agree that the spreading of risk via new and sophisticated financial techniques and instruments is, in principle, positive for the financial system, insofar as it reduces the likelihood that such risk would be concentrated in one or more financial institutions."

22. A little over twelve months before its collapse, on March 31, 2006, Northern Rock's shares hit a price-earnings-ratio high of 17.78, significantly ahead of its peer group that averaged a price-earnings-ratio of round 11.5 in 2006.

23. It stopped for Mr. Prince on November 2, 2007, when he was released from his position as CEO of Citibank.

24. JP Morgan was one of the first banks to develop a bank-wide "daily-earnings-at-risk" model under Till Guilderman in 1987. JP Morgan's approach was seen by many at the time as industry "best practice" and later a division selling market risk management knowhow, called Riskmetrics, was spun out.

25. *The Financial Times* (August 27, 2005) described this as the Persaud Paradox: "the observation of safety creates risk and the observation of risk creates safety."

26. The nongovernment bond market makes up almost 50% of daily turnover of fixed-income instruments.

27. Solvency II is a fundamental review of the capital adequacy regime for the EU insurance industry. It mirrors Basel 2 and aims to establish a revised set of EU-wide capital requirements and risk-management standards to replace Solvency I.

3

A Practical Approach to the Regulation of Risk

A peculiar characteristic of financial regulation today, and one of the causes of its failure, has been the divergence of theory and practice.[1] Recent proposals by regulatory and banking lobbies appear to be continuing this divergence. In theory, it is generally accepted that the core purpose of financial regulation is to mitigate systemic risks, such as a global credit crunch. In practice, however, the regulatory rules are focused entirely on risk-taking by individual firms.

It is a fallacy of composition to think that if good behavior is encouraged at the company level, the system will inevitably look after itself. One of the striking things about the report requested by the Swiss Federal Banking Commission into the facts leading to UBS's subprime losses is that much of what UBS did to get into difficulty was considered to be best practice for individual firms. Banks put their resources in places where their risk-management systems, using publicly available data, told them it was safe, generating systemically large concentrations.

As environmental regulators have found, formulating practical "systemic" policies is far from easy. But giving up is not an option. When confronted with this point, regulators have asked us, "What would systemic regulation look like?" The following three proposals provide a flavor.

- While financial institutions are encouraged by supervisors to conduct thousands of stress tests, few are conducted by the regulators on a systemwide scale. If it is possible to have systemwide stress tests on the impact of Y2K, or on avian flu, why not on liquidity? The regulator should conduct systemwide stress tests of those scenarios most likely to produce systemic stress—such as a 40% drop in house prices. Fears of a meltdown in global house prices were not rare before the crisis. These tests will probably underestimate spill-over effects, but the information gleaned from them would help regulators estimate these effects and consider mitigating action.

- The proposal by Willem Buiter, of the London School of Economics, that regulation be targeted at highly leveraged institutions, whatever their legal status, is an important step toward a comprehensive regulatory framework. We would add the distinction of leverage with short-term funding. Many years ago, the only significant highly leveraged institutions were commercial banks. Today, leverage is a characteristic of companies throughout the financial system. It is this leverage—when coupled with short-term funding liquidity—that threatens market gridlock in a disintermediated financial system. The attention of the central bank and the regulators needs to be switched from an institutionally defined approach to a functionally defined approach. Institutions are not born with original sin or original virtue; it is their behavior that can have potentially damaging systemic implications. It is the spread of pollution that matters, not the legal entity of the polluter.
- A clear distinction must be made between a capital charge *à la* Basel and provisioning that is available to cover losses in a downturn. One of the main problems is that a minimum capital requirement is a charge, not a buffer. If resources are to be available in the downturn, then they must be freely released as necessarily as they have been compulsorily accumulated. Because the economic cycle is the big source of systemic risks, Charles Goodhart and Avinash Persaud (2008) have suggested that capital charges be raised in a boom and relaxed in a slump. There are complicating issues with this proposal, but the point is that countercyclical charges should be based as much as possible on systemic phenomena and less on the characteristics of individual firms.

These three measures are practical steps toward the regulation of systemic risk. But there remains the cross-border problem. Many sensible proposals are wrecked on this rock. However, if widespread improvement is to be achieved, the Basel committees and the Financial Stability Forum must shift away from sole reliance on the new Basel consensus of regulation—greater transparency, more disclosure, and more market-sensitive risk management at the company level—and instead develop practical systemic proposals.

Coordination Failure in Financial Markets

At the height of the credit crunch in 2008, the complete seizure of the wholesale financial markets, the distress of retail borrowers, and the seeming immunity of the financial sector to all remedial measures produced an air of desperation among policymakers.[2] Yet the problem was one that would have been familiar to John Maynard Keynes. His name has been bandied about in the debate over appropriate fiscal and monetary policy. But insufficient attention has been paid to the core insight in Keynes's analysis: that recession is essentially the consequence of coordination failure.

The textbook example of a coordination failure is that of an individual industrialist who, confronting an uncertain and potentially unprofitable future, decides to postpone an investment. If all others do the same, aggregate investment will decline and their pessimism will be self-fulfilling, as profits and incomes fall. A similar tale can be told of families postponing their expenditure and precipitating unemployment. If only all could be persuaded to spend, then all would be better off, with demand and profits sustained and jobs preserved. The state should, therefore, undertake monetary loosening (to encourage expenditure) and fiscal expansion (to prime the pump and encourage others to spend) in order to overcome coordination failure. Most policymakers have taken this idea on board.

A second coordination failure can exist between nation-states. A country that expands alone during a worldwide downturn will find itself the repository of the world's deficits. The expansionary plans of the Obama administration are more in tune with UK goals. But the unwillingness of Germany to adopt similar expansionary measures seriously threatens the UK's recovery, as export markets weaken. The G20 negotiations are an attempt to address this coordination failure.

However, little seemed to have been done about the coordination failure in financial markets. Individual financial institutions would not lend to each other because they were concerned about whether they, in turn, would be able to borrow cash when they needed it. Every institution's board of directors was faced with pressures to maintain high levels of solvency. In these circumstances, there was little incentive for them to be the first to resume normal money-market operations; it was much safer to wait for others to act. If they were to be persuaded to lend, they needed to know that others would do so, too.

In the past, such coordination was achieved in the old-fashioned way. Bankers and fund managers were approached by the Bank of England,

and they were persuaded to act together to restore life to failing money markets. It was a meeting of the institutional investors hosted by the Bank of England in the early 1970s that called the bottom of the stock-market crash. Today, such coordination is made more difficult by the globalization of finance and the many institutions involved in disintermediated capital markets. And the primary problem is in credit rather than equity markets. However, there is little evidence that the Bank of England had in train any sustained effort to coordinate the banks and the institutions in a return to normal lending. Hence, the appeal by Peter Sands, CEO of Standard Chartered, for politicians and regulators to engage directly with institutional investors to break the paralysis in the banking sector.

Neither threats by the governor of the Bank of England nor the Treasury's Lending Panel, announced in the Pre-Budget Report, was likely to achieve this goal. This stands in contrast to the coordinating central-bank activism evident in the secondary banking crisis of the early 1970s, and in the American LTCM crisis of 1998—although, admittedly, these difficulties were rather small compared with the problems of the credit crunch.

More promising was the UK government's acquisition of equity stakes in the banks. But in contrast to similar U.S. measures that were cheap and compulsory, the British scheme was expensive and voluntary. Britain's refinanced banks argued that they were being encouraged to pay off the expensive capital that the government had subscribed, rather than to use it to expand their lending. For those banks that were not refinanced, it was all too easy to wait and see while the government exerted its shareholder influence to make others do all the heavy lifting. In the meantime, the system as a whole was left in doubt. In the week before Christmas 2008, two months after the government's refinancing, the deputy governor of the Bank of England criticized banking analysts for being "mistaken in thinking the authorities are insisting on higher capital ratios." This left open the urgent need to explain clearly just what the banks were expected to do.

The authorities addressed Keynes's insights into the coordination of goods markets and the need to stimulate the international economy. One lesson of the credit crunch is that the coordination of financial markets must be taken equally seriously. The financial institutions and the relevant authorities need collective huddles in smoke-free rooms, with coordination the agenda and agreement on the actions necessary to attain a coordinated expansion of wholesale and retail lending the goal. Urgent and sustained effort is required. As Keynes observed, acting alone results in self-fulfilling misery. Acting together can result in self-fulfilling recovery.

Transparency Is Not the Answer

A head of steam is building beneath the proposition that "greater transparency" should be a dominant theme of the reform package.[3] Precisely what is meant by "greater transparency" is clear; does this refer to improved availability of market information or to enhanced understanding of the structure of complex instruments? Unfortunately, in neither case will "greater transparency" reduce systemic risk in financial markets. Indeed, in some cases greater transparency could make things worse.

As events in financial markets have demonstrated beyond all reasonable doubt, the sophisticated market-sensitive risk models deployed by banks and other financial firms, and espoused so enthusiastically by the regulators, totally failed to ensure stability in financial markets. On the contrary, to the extent that anyone believes them any more, the models have been a major factor in the failure of credit markets since, in the face of extreme events, they all tended to endorse the same actions at the same time, guaranteeing widespread illiquidity. One of the drivers of the consequent lemming-like behavior was the greater transparency that regulators had campaigned for over the past twenty years or so. Greater transparency meant that more firms shared the same information, had access to the same procedural knowledge, and even used the same modeling—so it is hardly surprising that they all behaved in the same way.

Yet the risk modelers should not be blamed. Their models are not capable of measuring market-liquidity risk, nor are they intended for that task. A firm's risk model seeks to price the risks that are the result of its actions in the marketplace. They are necessarily market sensitive, and greater transparency will tend to increase that sensitivity. But it is not just that market sensitivity may increase the likelihood of stampedes. In the presence of the systemic externalities, such as liquidity risk, even the most transparent competitive market will be inefficient, and therefore risk will be mispriced. The financial turmoil of 2008 was clearly a systemic event; there is no way it could have been accurately priced by an individual firm. Greater transparency will only add to the illusion of accuracy, and by reinforcing herd behavior, may well make things worse. Indeed, a number of writers have suggested that the requirement to mark complex investments to market, hence increasing transparency, has been an important element in rapid deleveraging and subsequent financial collapse.

The second interpretation of the case for "greater transparency" rests on frequent references to securitized market instruments that "no one understands" and "no one knows how to price." Once again, the call for greater transparency is misconceived. What is at issue is not the transparency of such instruments but, rather, their complexity and the controls employed by buyers and sellers. Firms have bought complex instruments without understanding the risk, often relying exclusively on rating agencies to assess the risk; and in most cases they have relied on valuations provided by sellers. Banks have sold complex products to unsophisticated investors with little attention to whether the investment is appropriate or whether the risks are understood; and they have provided valuations using models that cannot price liquidity risk accurately. Where all parties involved believe in a particular asset class and in the rating of such assets, and where both sides of a transaction are financially motivated to see the transaction completed, then no amount of transparency will result in greater stability.

Of course, reducing informational inefficiencies can often be worthwhile and may result in greater market efficiency. Ensuring that complex instruments come with "full disclosure" at least places some responsibility on buyers to understand what they are buying. But transparency has nothing to do with the systemic risk that is the proper object of regulation.

The persistent emphasis on transparency is a dangerous diversion from the massive task of regulatory reform that is required in the United States and the United Kingdom. Unfortunately, for the past twenty years or so, the regulators have swallowed the argument that superior market-sensitive risk management by firms would result in greater overall stability. They must abandon their belief in the tired trinity of greater transparency, more disclosure, and better risk management by firms. It must be acknowledged that that regulatory model has failed. Instead, regulators should turn their attention to finding ways to develop a systemic approach to regulation, including pro-cyclical provisioning and systemwide stress testing, and they need to confront the vicious market cycle of rising asset prices accompanied by rising leverage, and the even more vicious cycle running in reverse.

Those who argue that greater transparency is the answer, do not understand the question.

Notes

1. The opening section of this chapter was written by John Eatwell and Avinash Persaud and originally appeared in the *Financial Times*, August 25, 2008.

2. This section was originally written by John Eatwell and David Pitt-Watson.

3. This section was written by John Eatwell and Robert Reoch.

4

Can Barack Obama Do It?

Speaking at the Yale commencement nearly fifty years ago, President John F. Kennedy said that what was at stake in making economic decisions was "not some grand warfare of rival ideologies...but the practical management of a modern economy" (1962). What was needed, he said, was "not labels and clichés but more basic discussion of the sophisticated and technical questions involved in keeping a great economic machinery moving ahead." Much the same could be said of our current predicament—and much the same was indeed said by President Barack Obama in his Inaugural Address back in 2009. He told those listening that "the stale political arguments that have consumed us for so long no longer apply" and that "the question we ask today is not whether our government is too big or too small, but whether it works." He went on to say that the "state of the economy calls for action, bold and swift, and we will act—not only to create new jobs, but to lay a new foundation for growth."[1]

The question on everyone's lips, however, was Can Barack Obama do it? Even now one is tempted to answer with a slight variation on his campaign theme: Yes he can. But overcoming the legacies of those stale political arguments may prove harder to achieve, and creating the jobs and laying the foundation for growth may require not just bold action but also more lasting measures of reform than the initial enthusiasm of Inauguration Day might lead one to hope. Undoing the mistakes of the past, finding the appropriate fiscal and monetary policies to combat recession and ensure recovery, together with designing a regulatory framework within which systemic risk can be managed and minimized, will require not only arduous and purposeful effort and clear thinking but also coordinated action on an international scale.

Almost as important as the need to have the Obama administration work more effectively and forcefully toward securing a coordinated international response to financial crisis and recession is the need for it to be clear about just what policy measures are best suited to produce what results. The three tasks to be confronted—rescue, recovery, and reform—need to be addressed systematically. They are interrelated but partially separable in crucial ways. Not only does a coherent policy mix need to be found, but the appropriateness of the various policy instruments available for achieving any one of these tasks needs to be properly understood. Some immediate rescue measures to shore up financial firms were introduced. Although acting largely independently of each other, most national monetary authorities tried similar things on this front. Approaches to recovery, however, or medium-term measures to ease and reverse recession, were more varied, especially in the arena of fiscal policy. Longer-term reform of the international financial system has, even now, hardly begun.

Rescue Measures

The speed of the decline of major international financial institutions into insolvency at the onset of the global financial crisis was nothing if not breathtaking.[2] The rescue measures introduced by the relevant authorities certainly went some way toward forestalling the danger of complete collapse. Table 4.1 summarizes some of the things that have been done so far. But it is clear that further emergency measures may yet be needed, especially if there are significant negative-feedback effects in financial markets from the deep recession in the macro economy. These are not at all unlikely.

For example, markets for mortgage-backed securities, which still make up a substantial proportion of the balance sheets of the U.S. banking sector, are in a very fragile state. With effective demand still falling precipitously, property prices apparently not yet at their lowest turning point, and unemployment continuing to rise, it seems quite likely that default and delinquency rates on both commercial and residential loans will continue to rise as well. Any general weakening of the asset side of the banking sector's balance sheets that went along with this situation might well find expression in equity markets—and perhaps be magnified. And even

Table 4.1 Financial-sector rescue measures: Selected national responses, 2008–10*

	Recapitalization	Nationalization	"Troubled" Asset Schemes	Guarantee & Insurance Schemes
USA	*$425b*	*($200b)#*	*$100b*	*$429b*
Japan	*¥12,000b*	–	*n.a.*	*¥40,000b*
United Kingdom	*£50b*	*£50b*	*n.a.*	*£268b*
Germany	*€80b*	–	–	*€400b*
France	*€22b*	–	–	*€13b*

Source: OECD, 2009b. *Fiscal packages across OECD countries: Overview and country details.* Paris: OECD.
* In billions of national currency as announced up to the end of the first quarter of 2009.
# This figure is an estimate of the cost incurred by U.S. authorities in the takeovers of Fannie Mae and Freddie Mac, and in the disposal of Washington Mutual.

if equity markets had already accurately priced-in this risk (and there is no reason to believe this to be the case), an unexpected failure of another major lender or sovereign borrower (or of any large financial services firm) would certainly have ramifications in equity and bond markets.[3]

The approach taken by the U.S. authorities to rescuing the financial sector involved a combination of recapitalization, introduction of asset-guarantee schemes through the quarantining of so-called troubled assets, enhanced depositor protection, and a touch of nationalization (table 4.1). The effect was certainly to reestablish a measure of order in the financial sector. But there remains considerable downside risk even there, and work has yet to begin on an overhaul of the financial system itself. So long as unmarketable (illiquid) asset-backed securities remained on the balance sheets of private-sector financial institutions—even if they were ring-fenced and subject to all sorts of government guarantees (as they were in the United States and in the UK)—there was both a low probability that those assets would be managed efficiently (so as to recover any value that they may retain) and a high probability that whatever fillip ring-fencing them may give to a bank's reputation, it would be tenuous and temporary. It is no accident that talk of "zombie banks" began to catch on at the time.

Much of this response was reminiscent of what went on in Japan during its lost decade. Faced with the collapse of property prices in the early 1990s, and the accompanying dramatic rise in the number of nonperforming loans on the banking sector's balance sheets, together with widespread insolvency among financial institutions, Japanese authorities tried almost everything: greater deposit protection, capital injections, the encouragement of mergers between larger and smaller financial institutions, the purchase of "bad debt" by especially established (private-public) asset-management firms, and a touch of nationalization. It is widely agreed that in Japan it was a failure to deal with the "bad debt," and the authorities' reluctance to oversee the euthanasia of failed financial institutions were two factors that ensured the pain would be prolonged.[4] More was needed in the way of financial rescue measures then—as it probably was in the United States. The U.S. Troubled Asset Recovery Program (TARP) went some way toward providing what was needed, and the funds devoted to the Public-Private Investment initiative for the purchase of "troubled" assets was large; but there was an reluctance to allow for the euthanasia of failing financial institutions.

It is well to remember that the task of the "rescue team" is to get the patient to the hospital alive; once the patient is in their hands, it is not the task of the authorities to keep the life-support machines running indefinitely. If there are some individual financial institutions that need to pass into insolvency, they should be allowed to do so, quietly and in a managed way. The rescue measures are taken for the benefit of the financial system, not for the benefit of every institution that is a part of that system. This is where a measure of nationalization can come in handy. Even the customarily cautious OECD has advised the U.S. authorities in no uncertain terms on this subject. According to the OECD, they should have made it clear that they would not "not hesitate to restructure systemically important but fragile financial institutions, even if that entails taking control of them, putting them into receivership, and recapitalizing the remaining "good bank" with public funds" (OECD, 2009a, p. 70).

Transferring the ownership and control of insolvent financial firms to the state opens up the possibility either of engineering their quiet demise (as is often needed) or of managing the orderly realignment of their balance sheets so as to return those institutions to commercial viability. The response of Swedish authorities to their 1990s banking crisis illustrated what might have been achieved. In that case, "bad assets" were transferred to state-owned entities ("bad banks") at book value; and the state recapitalized participating financial institutions and nationalized them. The OECD reckoned that the front-end costs of this exercise amounted to about 4% of Swedish GDP (2009a, p. 50), but that by the time the "bad assets" had been liquidated in 1997, the net cost was only around 2% of GDP. Of course, the problems of the international financial system during the global financial crisis were on a much larger scale than was seen in Sweden in the 1990s, and the feedback effects between the nation's money and the real economy were far more direct and powerful than they were in the Swedish case, but the experience is worth revisiting.

Recovery Measures

Some combination of monetary and fiscal policy was the preferred option when it came to medium-term recovery measures. Within the OECD, however, the weighting given to each has been markedly uneven. The Obama administration was most active—boldly so—on the domestic fiscal front (as were Japan, Canada, Spain, and Australia).[5] Japan's willingness to give greater weight to fiscal stimulus than it had done in the past perhaps reflected the lessons learned from its failure to do so in the 1990s. Table 4.2a summarizes some of the variations as they existed at the end of the first quarter of 2009. Table 4.2b and 4.2c outline some of the actual and projected fiscal consequences (public debt and fiscal deficit) of these actions in selected economies.

Table 4.2a Discretionary fiscal responses in selected economies, 2008–2010*

	Net Fiscal-Balance Effect (% of GDP)	% of Fiscal-Balance Effect due to Expenditure Measures
USA	*–5.6*	*57*
Japan	*–2.0*	*20*
United Kingdom#	*–1.4*	*0*
France	*–0.6*	*33*
Germany	*–3.0*	*53*
Australia	*–4.6*	*71*
Canada	*–4.1*	*58*
Spain	*–3.5*	*48*
Hungary	*4.4*	*100*
Iceland	*9.4*	*n.a.*
Ireland	*4.4*	*21*

Source: OECD, 2009b. *Fiscal packages across OECD countries: Overview and country details.* Paris: OECD, p. 4.
* Estimates do not include the potential impact of financial-system rescue measures or changes in the timing of tax payments or government disbursements for expenditure purposes.
# These figures do not include the £179 billion borrowing requirement announced in the April 2009 budget.

Table 4.2b General government gross debt: Selected economies, 2007–2015 (*Percentage of GDP in descending order by 2015*)

Country	2007	2008	2009	2010	2011	2012	2013	2014	2015
Japan	187.7	198.8	*217.6*	*227.3*	*234.1*	*240.1*	*244.0*	*246.7*	*248.8*
Italy	103.4	106.0	115.8	*118.6*	*120.5*	*121.6*	*122.8*	*123.9*	*124.7*
United States	62.1	70.6	83.2	*92.6*	*97.4*	*100.7*	*103.5*	*106.4*	*109.7*
France	63.8	67.5	77.4	*84.2*	*88.6*	*91.6*	*93.2*	*94.3*	*94.8*
United Kingdom	44.1	52.0	68.2	*78.2*	*84.9*	*88.6*	*90.2*	*90.7*	*90.6*
Germany	65.0	65.9	*72.5*	*76.7*	*79.6*	*81.4*	*82.1*	*82.0*	*81.5*
Canada	64.2	70.4	81.6	*82.3*	*80.9*	*78.7*	*76.2*	*73.4*	*70.5*

Source: IMF, 2010. *World economic outlook*. Washington, DC: International Monetary Fund.
Note: Figures in italics are estimates.

Table 4.2c General government net lending/borrowing: Selected economies, 2007–2015 (+/– *Percentage of GDP in ascending order by 2015*)

Country	2007	2008	2009	2010	2011	2012	2013	2014	2015
Japan	–2.4	–4.2	*–10.3*	*–9.8*	*–9.1*	*–8.5*	*–8.1*	*–7.6*	*–7.3*
United States	–2.7	–6.6	–12.5	*–11.0*	*–8.2*	*–5.9*	*–5.7*	*–6.0*	*–6.5*
Italy	–1.5	–2.7	–5.3	*–5.2*	*–4.9*	*–4.9*	*–4.8*	*–4.7*	*–4.6*
United Kingdom	–2.7	–4.8	–10.9	*–11.4*	*–9.4*	*–7.6*	*–6.2*	*–5.2*	*–4.3*
France	–2.7	–3.4	–7.9	*–8.2*	*–7.0*	*–6.1*	*–5.1*	*–4.6*	*–4.1*
Germany	0.2	*0.0*	*–3.3*	*–5.7*	*–5.1*	*–4.0*	*–3.0*	*–2.3*	*–1.7*
Canada	1.6	0.1	–5.0	*–5.1*	*–2.8*	*–1.7*	*–1.0*	*–0.4*	*0.01*

Source: IMF, 2010. *World economic outlook*. Washington, DC: International Monetary Fund.
Note: Figures in italics are estimates.

Leaving aside the positive stimulus that this level of fiscal expansion entailed, the budgetary consequences meant that governments faced difficult political challenges as well as economic ones. It was a relatively easy matter for opposition parties to scare the electorate with talk of massive deficits and huge debts, and it required both a strong will and consistency of purpose by governing administrations to remain on the road to recovery in the face of such talk. This has not always been forthcoming. Policymakers were also constrained by the fact that financial markets, too, responded badly to deficits—the more so when they had been shaken to the core by a financial crisis of the magnitude of the 2008 collateralized-debt-obligation collapse. Toward the end of his life, J. K. Galbraith told an interviewer (when speaking of the Roosevelt expansionary fiscal programs of the 1930s) that "the basic Keynesian idea... resisted conservative finance, borrowed money, and hired people across the country, rescuing them from unemployment... and... you didn't worry about accumulating debt, or, more precisely, you worried about it but did it anyway" (2000). This basic Keynesian idea is as appropriate today as it was then.

When thinking about public expenditure and indebtedness, of course, it is always well to remember that for every borrower there is a lender—a feature as true of public borrowing as it is of private borrowing. While governments bonds are liabilities in the accounts of governments, they are assets on the balance sheets of private-sector lenders. As assets, they increase the wealth of individuals. They are also the vehicles through which monetary authorities conduct open-market operations; they furnish a secure bulwark against financial turmoil in the portfolios of pension funds and mutual funds; they enhance the liquidity of asset markets that is so essential for interbank lending and the smooth functioning of credit channels; and they provide an avenue through which foreign governments (and financial firms) can recirculate the earnings from their overseas activities. In performing these (and other) functions as assets, government bonds may stimulate consumption, investment, and growth, both locally and globally, and they may do this almost as directly as does the initial government expenditure that their issuance allowed.

These macroeconomic realities are not altered by thinking microeconomically, as some have claimed, unless one is prepared to believe in a number of manifestly fictional presuppositions, such as the existence of perfect capital markets, the absence of liquidity constraints, or the lack of feedback effects between financial markets and the real economy. Likewise, one has to pretend that the complex interactions of decisions by a multitude of private-sector agents can be captured as a single "representative" agent of a whole economic system. Just as it seems easier to lament the passing of the day at sunset than it is to contemplate a new day beginning when that same sun rises on the other side of earth, it is all too easy to be paralyzed into inaction by the thought of massive public debt—the more so if macroeconomic realities are not kept firmly in view.

On the domestic monetary policy front, the scope for any further influence on the economic activity seems to be narrowing. With the exception of the Eurozone, where the European Central Bank has been excessively timid, monetary authorities have reduced interest rates to near zero. They have also engaged in quantitative easing to about as large an extent as seems feasible. Thus, monetary authorities have little room for additional maneuvering.

Furthermore, monetary policy changes are notoriously unreliable when economic activity is in sharp decline. The economy is not like a sailing ship where, when the wind goes out of the sails, there may well be a demand for more canvas. When the strength of aggregate demand falls in an economy, the demand for loans typically falls, too. Borrowers, whether investors or consumers, are unlikely to be numerous when inventories and unemployment are rising; and when prospective profits, the volume of trade and confidence are in free fall. In these circumstances, cheap money may do very little to change their minds—it is often not so much that banks are unwilling to lend as that borrowers are unwilling to borrow. Charles Kindleberger made this same point quite nicely in relation to the Great Depression: "the interest rate may be low in historic perspective but high relative to investment opportunities so that it fails to encourage loans" (1973/1986, p. 128). Likewise, cash in hand thanks to quantitative easing may also be of little avail if its principal use is to run down or service preexisting debt.

On the fiscal front, the Bush administration's Emergency Economic Stimulus Act (2008) and the Obama administration's American Recovery and Reinvestment Act (2009) embodied most of the discretionary fiscal measures applied in the United States. The former almost exclusively involved revenue measures; the latter gave greater weight to expenditure measures (although it did contain some corporate tax relief and even more targeted relief to individuals). A further fiscal stimulus comes from the operation of automatic stabilizers. Taken together, these programs constituted a package larger than any other undertaken in the last fifty years—and they approached the size (relative to GDP) of the recovery measures deployed by President Roosevelt in the 1930s. Only during World War II have we witnessed any stimulus on so grand a scale. There is little doubt that a fiscal stimulus on this scale had a positive effect. But the real questions are, Was it enough to close the U.S. output gap and return the economy to high growth? and Was it enough to revive the level of global effective demand and growth?

The answer to the first question is, no. If one looks at OECD forecasts, with all the caveats that must be applied to such predictions, it appears that the United States (and other nations that have embarked on a policy of discretionary fiscal policy) may only just get its head above water in the medium term. Table 4.3 summarizes some of the main OECD predictions; even when rates of growth begin to be positive, it will be some time before investment, consumption, and especially employment recover to their pre-crisis levels. The answer to the second question is, also no—as was bound to be the case without a measure of harmonized fiscal action across the whole of the G20. The disappointing outcomes of successive G20 meetings shows how difficult a objective this might be to achieve.

When the same global economic circumstances are faced by all nations, trade surpluses and deficits exhibit a sort of global redistribution. The volume of world trade may be adversely affected when the fiscal policies of the major players differ. In the case of trade between, say, two large open economies, one following a policy of fiscal expansion and the other a policy of fiscal contraction, the contractionary policies of one may neutralize the expansionary policies of the other. Worse still, the volume of trade may fall and deepen the downturn.

In the context of fiscal stimulus packages, there has been much talk of fiscal sustainability. This is as it should be. There is absolutely nothing wrong with fiscal sustainability; quite the contrary, it is the target to be aimed at. What is wrong with much of the conversation on fiscal sustainability is the idea that it is to be secured by keeping in check the current government spending, deficits, and debt. In times of deep recession, however, what is needed is not less spending activity but more. If the aim is to balance the budget "tomorrow," during a slump we should not seek to balance it "today." In fact, were such a strategy of seeking balance to be tried in the present, the budgetary position would only worsen in the future. Similarly, if we wish to have a stable and sustainable ratio of public debt to GDP tomorrow, we will need to raise that ratio (perhaps quite dramatically) today.

If the Obama administration is to succeed, it must resist those ever lounder siren voices claiming that "their" tax dollars ("today" or "tomorrow") that are being used to finance the recovery program. But "their" tax dollars are not needed "today". It is the dollars of investors and savers looking for the low-risk, above-market rates of return that gilts provide, that are financing the recovery.[6] When the returns on most other investment vehicles remain historically low and/or are of ambiguous or indeterminate riskiness, those dollars are not being drawn away from more productive uses of the funds. Instead, they are, so to speak, being taken out from under the mattress. Nor will those tax dollars be needed "tomorrow." Recession-induced deficits are, in large part, self-correcting.

Table 4.3 OECD economic interim projections: Selected economies

	2004	2005	2006	2007	2008	2009	2010
United States							
Gross domestic product (volume) market prices	3.6	2.9	2.8	2.0	1.1	–4.0	0.0
Gross domestic product (deflator) market prices	2.9	3.3	3.2	2.7	2.2	1.8	0.5
Unemployment rate (% of labor force)	5.5	5.1	4.6	4.6	5.8	9.1	10.3
Government net lending (% of GDP)	–4.4	–3.3	–2.2	–2.9	–5.8	–10.2	–11.9
Consumer price index (% change from previous year)	2.7	3.4	3.2	2.9	3.8	–0.4	0.5
Japan							
Gross domestic product (volume) market prices	2.7	1.9	2.0	2.4	–0.6	–6.6	–0.5
Gross domestic product (deflator) market prices	–1.1	–1.2	–0.9	–0.7	–1.0	2.2	–1.0
Unemployment rate (% of labor force)	4.7	4.4	4.1	3.9	4.0	4.9	5.6
Government net lending (% of GDP)	–6.2	–6.7	–1.6	–2.5	–2.6	–6.8	–8.4
Consumer price index (% change from previous year)	0.0	–0.6	0.2	0.1	1.4	–1.2	–1.3
Germany							
Gross domestic product (volume) market prices	0.7	0.9	3.2	2.6	1.0	–5.3	0.2
Gross domestic product (deflator) market prices	1.0	0.7	0.5	1.9	1.5	1.6	0.5
Unemployment rate (% of labor force)	9.7	10.5	9.7	8.3	7.3	8.9	11.6
Government net lending (% of GDP)	–3.8	–3.3	–1.5	–0.2	–0.1	–4.5	–6.8
Consumer price index (harmonized % change from previous year)	1.8	1.9	1.8	2.3	2.8	0.6	0.5
France							
Gross domestic product (volume) market prices	2.2	1.9	2.4	2.1	0.7	–3.3	–0.1
Gross domestic product (deflator) market prices	1.6	2.0	2.5	2.5	2.2	1.2	0.6
Unemployment rate (% of labor force)	8.8	8.8	8.8	8.0	7.4	9.9	10.9
Government net lending (% of GDP)	–3.6	–3.0	–2.4	–2.7	–3.4	–6.6	–8.3
Consumer price index (harmonized % change from previous year)	2.3	1.9	1.9	1.6	3.2	0.4	0.6
United Kingdom							
Gross domestic product (volume) market prices	2.8	2.1	2.8	3.0	0.7	–3.7	–0.2
Gross domestic product (deflator) market prices	2.5	2.2	2.6	2.9	2.4	2.3	1.6
Unemployment rate (% of labor force)	4.8	4.8	5.4	5.4	5.7	7.7	9.5
Government net lending (% of GDP)	–3.7	–3.3	–2.7	–2.8	–4.4	–9.3	–10.5
Consumer price index (harmonized % change from previous year)	1.3	2.0	2.3	2.3	3.6	2.0	1.7

Source: OECD, 2009b. *Fiscal packages across OECD countries: Overview and country details*. Paris: OECD.
Note: Data show % change from previous year unless otherwise indicated.

Either the projects to which they have been devoted are completed in a few years, or the recovery (even a slow one) so reduces that part of government expenditure attributable to the operation of automatic stabilizers (by far the largest element of growth in the deficit during a recession) falls away. And all of this happens without mention of the powerful effect of fiscal multipliers.

It is not necessary to guess what the effects will be of doing the opposite—of becoming a "government of thrift" and introducing an "age of austerity," as the leader of the UK's Conservative Party has crazily proclaimed to be his strategy—since we have an actual experiment in progress that will show the effects of cutting deficits in times of economic crisis. The guinea pigs are the citizens in Hungary, Ireland, and Iceland (see table 4.4), where the IMF has moved in and insisted on "fiscal responsibility." In what looks to be a replay of songs from the 1970s and 1980s, the IMF has made its assistance conditional upon these economies' bringing their budgets into balance over a four-year horizon. This is breathtakingly ill-advised. It is exactly the opposite of what is called for. The consequences of these conditions for the unfortunate citizens of these countries are not hard to predict: slow growth, high unemployment, and almost unaltered (or worsening) fiscal balances. Table 4.4

Table 4.4 European Commission forecasts, 2007–12: Hungary, Iceland, Ireland

	2007	2008	2009	2010	2011	2012
Hungary						
GDP growth (annual % change)	*1.1*	*0.5*	*−6.7*	*1.1*	*2.8*	*3.2*
Unemployment (annual %)	*7.4*	*7.8*	*10.0*	*11..1*	*11.0*	*10.3*
Budget balance (% of GDP)	*−4.9*	*−3.4*	*−4.4*	*−3.8*	*−4.7*	*−6.2*
Iceland						
GDP growth (annual % change)	*6.0*	*0.3*	*−6.8*	*−3.5*	*0.7*	*2.1*
Unemployment (annual %)	*2.3*	*4.6*	*7.2*	*7.8*	*7.3*	*6.3*
Budget balance (% of GDP)	*5.4*	*−11.5*	*−9.9*	*−6.2*	*−4.2*	*−3.2*
Ireland						
GDP growth (annual % change)	*6.0*	*−3.0*	*−7.6*	*−0.2*	*0.9*	*1.9*
Unemployment (annual %)	*4.6*	*6.3*	*11.9*	*13.7*	*13.5*	*12.7*
Budget balance (% of GDP)	*0.2*	*−7.1*	*−14.4*	*−32.3*	*−10.3*	*−9.1*

Source: European Commission: Directorate-General for Economic and Financial Affairs. *Economic Forecast*. Spring 2009. *European Economy* 3/2009; *European Economic Forecast*, Autumn 2010. *European Economy* 7/2010.

shows the European Commission's forecasts. It does not look at all good in the medium term.

It is hard not to agree with something Evsey Domar said at the end of the Second World War on the subject of public debt:

> the public debt and its burden loom in the eyes of many economists and laymen as the greatest obstacle to all good things on earth. The remedy suggested is always the reduction of the absolute size of the debt or at least the prevention of its further growth. If all the people and organizations who work and study, write articles and make speeches, worry and spend sleepless nights—all because of fear of the debt— could forget about it for a while and spend even half their efforts trying to find ways of achieving a growing national income, their contribution to the benefit and welfare of humanity—and to the solution of the debt problem—would be immeasurable. (1944, p. 823)

If a further illustration is needed to understand the actual effects of attempting fiscal sustainability through large-scale cuts in current expenditures (sometimes coupled with selective tax concessions that supposedly give incentives to business and the wealthy to invest)—a refrain that one hears often enough—the United States in the 1980s springs immediately to mind. During the 1980 presidential election campaign, candidate Ronald Reagan declared that he intended to get government "off our backs" and "out of our pockets." Once elected, he half succeeded. He certainly got government "off their backs," but unluckily he put an unrestrained global market there in its place. This, as a series of financial crises and a worldwide recession have since taught us, turned out to be very much a mixed blessing. However, by the end of Reagan's tenure in the White House, the government was even deeper "into people's pockets" than it had been eight years earlier. Between 1980 and 1988, the federal deficit nearly tripled (from $69 billion to $171 billion), and as a percentage of GDP, it rose by 2%. As figure 4.1 shows, during the 1980s, the federal debt to GDP ratio nearly doubled, from 32% to 56%.[7]

The message is simple enough: dramatically reduce current spending (and even cut certain taxes under the banner of providing "incentives to invest"), and you are likely to *increase* the deficit *and* the public debt, not decrease it. The consequences on unemployment are equally well known: it goes *up* and not down.[8] Do all of this when the economy is in, or only just emerging from, a recession, and these negative economic consequences will be all the more severe. In an uncharacteristic moment

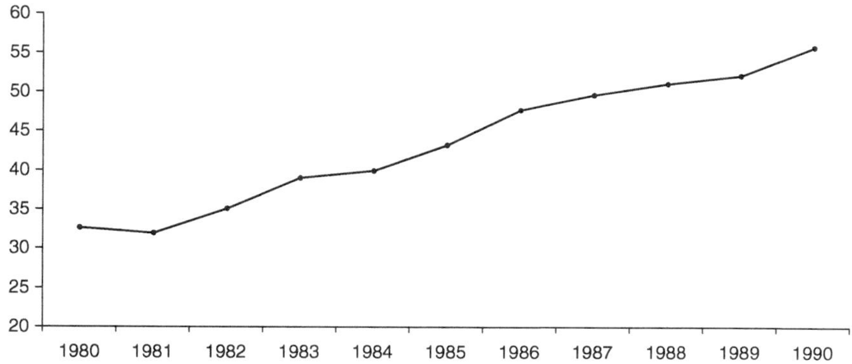

Figure 4.1 U.S. federal debt as a percentage of GDP: 1980–1990
Source: U.S. Treasury: *Historical Debt Outstanding,* available at www.usgovernment spending.com).

of economic perspicuity, the elder George Bush dubbed the Reagan approach "voodoo economics."[9]

The dangers of being overwhelmed by the ideology of austerity are legion. Not only does it undermine recovery but it also diverts attention away from what needs to be done. For example, one sometimes hears ill-considered calls from otherwise plausible austerity ideologues for a return to the "great days" of the 1980s and 1990s when, they tell us, we supposedly learned that markets, rather than governments, solve all of our economic worries. They neglect to mention that the 1980s was the decade of the Reagan-Thatcher recession, and that the 1990s, which were supposed to be the years when that earlier pain would give way to future gain, were instead the years of bubbles, irrational exuberance, and....

Listening to the laments of those who spend sleepless nights worrying over the deficit and the debt, it is almost as if the fact that the international economy was brought to the edge of an abyss by a dangerously out-of-control global financial system (one in need of fundamental reengineering)—and that we were saved the pain of an even deeper recession by countercyclical loan expenditure by governments—has been forgotten. While that financial system stands in need of root and branch reform, all that the opponents of stimulus can come up with (apart from austerity) are ideas like compulsory insolvency-insurance schemes for financial firms, limited checks on proprietary trading activities, constraints on short selling, more muscular regulation, and taxes on bankers' bonuses. It is like trying to earthquake-proof a building after it has fallen down. It is doubtful whether such measures would have prevented the last crisis; they will certainly not prevent the next one.

When it comes to judging the ideology of austerity, we should not forget our history. Faced with a financial crisis in the 1990s, Japanese policymakers were seduced by the ideology of austerity. They did all the things (and more) that the current crop of well-groomed austerity-merchants recommend. The result was a "lost decade" that has lasted twenty years. In 1937, Franklin D. Roosevelt capitulated to the same pressures and the tentative U.S. recovery was stopped in its tracks. National output fell by one-third, and the already high unemployment rate increased to near 20%. Contemplating this history, the words "first time as tragedy, second time as farce" spring to immediately to mind.

When British politicians engaged in the premature reversal of stimulus measures tell us that the price *will* be austerity, yet the president of the European Central Bank tells us that it *will not* threaten output and employment, it is difficult to have confidence that anyone actually knows what he or she is doing (or even why). When the government of Germany embarks upon an austerity program despite having a very low deficit-debt profile, telling us that it will *increase* growth and employment, while the chief economist of the IMF tells us that the same policies elsewhere (in Spain, Greece, Portugal, and Ireland, in particular) will *lower* growth and employment, what possible sense is the ordinary citizen to make of it all?

The lexicon of austerity seems to be designed only to muddy the waters further. The government budget has cyclical and structural components; so far, so good. The *cyclical* component has risen dramatically as a result of stimulus measures. But why we, therefore, need to reduce the *structural* component of spending by curtailing state pensions and other social security entitlements, freezing the pay of public sector workers like teachers, and raising the retirement age is not at all clear. Then there is "fiscal responsibility," "fiscal consolidation," and "fiscal sustainability." Again, all perfectly worthy objectives; but when their achievement is said to mandate *only* fiscal contraction, no matter what the prevailing economic circumstances happen to be, something far from "responsible" seems to be going on. It is rather like insisting that 30 mph is the only "responsible" driving speed, no matter what the prevailing road and weather conditions might be. It is plain bad advice; and sometimes very dangerous, to boot.

Of course, even with appropriate rescue and recovery measures in place, the risks involved in mistaking these solutions for the much needed longer-term measures of financial reform are not small. Those dangers are apparent in some of the stances adopted in certain European economies, especially France and Germany. The financial-reform measures their leaders have called for are certainly needed if long-term financial stability is to be secured. But their resistance to effective stimulus measures involving fiscal expansion—a resistance shown in practice by the very modest loan-expenditure measures that they have already implemented—is likely to retard rather than accelerate their recovery from the slump. Unemployment in France and Germany is already above the OECD average, and it seems likely that unemployment will grow more rapidly, and be more protracted, than in those other OECD economies that have opted for more substantial discretionary fiscal packages.

Reform Measures

Scarcely a start has been made on the longer-term reform of the international financial system. It is in this area where the power of vested interests and ideas, economic and political, are most powerful. It is also in this area where resistance to much needed change is likely to be most stubborn. But it is this area that is most at stake. Without wholesale reform, even if we eventually struggle through the recession, history might repeat itself.

Perhaps the greatest danger, however, is that authorities may somehow convince themselves that they do not need to change what they were doing, that they just need to do it better. In seeking to ensure that financial firms comply with transparency and internal risk-management requirements, as authorities have been doing ever since the deregulation of financial markets in the 1980s—and in replacing a sensible regulatory framework that encouraged a diversity of business models among financial firms with one that encourages the adoption of the same business model across the whole sector—we have watched financial markets lurch between sentiments that see almost no risk anywhere to those that see risk everywhere, at great cost to the stability of the system. When financial firms are all acting on the same information, and when they are all responding in essentially the same way, using the same business model, these swings in market sentiment can be hugely destabilizing—as we have now come to realize.

Such swings in market sentiment have been behind the asset-price bubbles (driven by excessive leverage) that we have seen in the United

States, Japan, the UK, and elsewhere over the last twenty years or so; they have been behind the invention of new financial instruments like those asset-backed securities that have been so troublesome in the present crisis; they have been behind international financial crises like the ones in Asia and Russia in the 1990s; and they were behind the unwillingness of major banks to lend (even overnight) to other major banks that gave us the "credit crunch" of 2008. None of this is irrational from the point of view of individual banks or financial firms. Yet it would be dangerously irrational for authorities to allow these systemic risks to persist into the indefinite future. For years now we have known that the best advice one could give a risk-averse individual investor is to not put all of his or her eggs in one basket. Today, the same advice could well be given to authorities interested in minimizing systemic risk. A diversity, not uniformity, of financial firms in the financial sector, with diverse business models and with different regulatory requirements, is the way to a more stable future.

But let us end where we began, with President Kennedy speaking at Yale in 1962. What he said then might well be said again today:

> There are three great areas of our domestic affairs in which[,] today[,] there is a danger that illusion may prevent effective action. They are, first, the question of the size and the shape of the government's responsibilities; second, the question of public fiscal policy; and third, the matter of confidence, business confidence or public confidence, or simply confidence in America. (1962)

We should not forget, however, that having success in making the kind of economic changes needed today also depends, to a considerable extent, on the predominant political context and the prevailing climate of opinion. Popular, credible, trusted, purposeful, and newly elected politicians are powerful vehicles for implementing change. President Obama's first 100 days showed just how powerful these factors could be in accelerating the rate of change in ideas and policy innovation. But it is not just a matter of doing broadly the "right thing" (if it were as simple as that; the opinion-poll ratings of the former British Prime Minister prior to the election loss would have been sky-high rather than at rock-bottom). We may be witnessing the end of a period in American history when our understanding of what the market actually can do is eclipsed by a dogmatic creed that says it can do everything. To paraphrase Barack Obama's words, used in a different context during the 2008 Democratic

Primary debates, we do not just need to get ourselves out of the financial crisis and recession, we also need to change the mind set that got us there in the first place. Barack Obama still can do it. But he will need to go back onto the offensive; he will need to follow through on further stimulus measures; and he will need to resist the cries of his opponents for the imposition of conservative finance and austerity. None of this will be easy.

Notes

This is a revised version of a lecture delivered by Murray Milgate, Japan, in April 2009.

1. This is not to proclaim the end of ideology or an end to politics. If fundamental change in the techniques of economic management is to be achieved and sustained, then battles of ideas will remain to be fought and won, and effective politics will be every bit as decisive as it has always been.

2. In the last months of 2008, they included Bear Stearns, Merrill Lynch, Lehman Brothers, Bank of America, Wells Fargo, Washington Mutual, Fannie Mae, Freddie Mac, Citibank, Indymac, Silver State, and Wachovia in the United States. In Britain and Europe, they were Dexia, Northern Rock, Bradford and Bingley, Alliance and Leicester, Royal Bank of Scotland, Lloyds TSB, and Halifax Bank of Scotland.

3. One need only look at the movements in U.S. equity prices in the weeks leading up to the announcement of the results of the "stress tests" on the major banks in April 2009, or the action on bond markets to the pricing of Greek debt in the first months of 2010, to see how influential these ramifications might be.

4. Of course, their associated reluctance to deploy any creative fiscal measures whatsoever only amplified in the real economy the effects of their failure to deal with nonperforming loans in the financial sector. So much for the classical dichotomy.

5. In 2008, the outgoing Bush administration implemented all of its fiscal stimulus as tax cuts. In 2009, the incoming Obama administration used only about one-third of its program for tax cuts. Since expenditure measures have greater multiplier effects than tax-cutting measures, this appears to be a positive move.

6. James Tobin, back in 1963, made an acute observation about deficits that has not entirely lost a relevance to us today. In the United States, he said, "when no one else borrows the surpluses of the thrifty, the Treasury ends up doing so. Since the role of debtor and borrower is thought to be particularly unbecoming of the federal government, the nation feels frustrated and guilty. Unhappily, crucial decisions of economic policy too often reflect blind reactions to these feelings. The truisms that borrowing is the counterpart of lending and deficits the counterpart of surpluses are overlooked in popular and Congressional discussions of governments budgets and taxes. Both guilt feelings and policy are based on serious misunderstanding of the origins of federal budget deficits and surpluses" (1963, p. 50).

7. At the same time, between 1980 and 1989, real wages fell by about 1% per year.

8. One might think that the experience in Britain during the Thatcher decade was better in at least one respect—in the UK, the government budget was indeed balanced while following such policies. But once one allows for the massive, one-off, windfall receipts to the government coffers arising from the extensive privatization programs completed by that administration, the same picture of the actual budgetary consequences of spending cuts and tax concessions emerges there, too.

9. At the time, of course, Bush was running against Ronald Reagan for the Republican Party's presidential nomination. When he later joined the Reagan ticket as his vice-presidential running mate, he seems to have become a convert.

5

Useful Bubbles

Economic bubbles do not have a good press. Alan Greenspan's famous label of "irrational exuberance," applied to the "bubble" in dot-com shares in the 1990s, says it all: irrational—who would be in favor of that? And exuberance—clearly the central banker's term for "frenzy."

In economic discourse, the term "bubble" is indeed intended to conjure up an image of a mania, a process in which a price or prices are continuously bid upward in a frenzied spiral, in which greater and greater bids are made in the confident belief that prices will be bid ever higher, that the bubble will last forever. Goods (or more accurately, titles to goods) are bought not for their intrinsic characteristics, nor for the reasonable income they might earn, but for the potential capital gain embodied in the ever-spiraling price. Anyone who fails to get on the ladder will lose out, and may reasonably fear being condemned to future penury. The bubble doesn't simply appear to create instant wealth for some; it actually *does* create instant wealth, redistributing the wealth of society to those with the courage and foresight to invest in the bubble and away from the timid and short-sighted—and "the devil take the hindmost" (Allen and Gale, 1999, 2000).

The classic bubble was the great Dutch tulip mania of 1636–37, when the accelerating rise in the price of particular exotic tulip bulbs in the autumn of 1636 spread to the prices of common bulbs (Posthumus, 1929; Garber, 1989, 1990; Fridson, 1995). In the single month of January 1637, prices of ordinary tulip bulbs increased twenty times over. As the frenzy showed signs of slowing, the Dutch government anticipated the reaction of future governments to their bubbles by reassuring citizens that "there was no reason for the bulbs to fall in price." But in February, prices fell back to a twentieth of their peak value. And then they kept on falling, ruining buyers and dealers until, it is said, tulip bulbs were worth no more than onions.

In more modern times, perhaps one of the most extraordinary bubbles was that in Japanese real estate at the end of the 1980s. Between 1980 and 1989, the price index of residential real estate rose four times over. At the peak, it is said that a few acres of downtown Tokyo were worth more than the entire state of California. Unlike the case of tulips, the Japanese real estate bubble did not end in total collapse. Real estate prices stayed high. But crucially they stopped rising, trapping those who had speculated on ever rising prices, and it precipitated a severe debt crisis in the Japanese banking system and a decade of economic stagnation from which Japan is still struggling to escape. The "bubble economy" ended Japan's four decades of extraordinary postwar growth.

Or consider the dot-com boom. During the years in which the NASDAQ soared to ever-greater heights (let us remember that from 1991 to 2000, the index rose from 500 to over 4500), it was almost a matter of approbation that a new supposedly high-tech company had no prospect of making a profit. The rising index was all that mattered. Yet from March 2000 to March 2001, the index fell from 4500 to 1750.

It is the bursting of the bubble that is most feared. The upward spiral makes some commentators uncomfortable—there are always Jeremiahs who will condemn a get-rich-quick culture. But they are few and far between, and are often roundly condemned. As J. K. Galbraith pointed out in his famous study *The Great Crash, 1929,* "In 1929 [prior to the crash]...pessimism was not openly equated with efforts to destroy the American way of life. Yet it had such connotations" (1954, p. 94).

Contemporary commentators on bubbles typically argue that the good times and the price rises will go on forever. Famously, the distinguished Yale economist Irving Fisher commented in the autumn of 1929 that "stock prices have reached what looks like a permanently high plateau" (quoted in Galbraith, 1954, p. 95). Seventy years later, in 1999, just before the collapse of the dot-com boom, the equally distinguished Princeton economist Alan Blinder (1999) compared the U.S. economy to "Ol' Man River, who just kept rolling along."

They were both wrong. Bubbles do burst. And the bursting of the bubble brings with it substantial financial disruption. Those who have overextended themselves collapse into bankruptcy; financial institutions desperately cut credit to rebuild their balance sheets; the distortions and neglect characteristic of the obsessive mania are now manifest in dislocated production systems, unemployment, and general economic misery.

And it's not just those who have fed the mania who are hurt. As Alfred Marshall wrote:

> The evils of reckless trading are always apt to spread beyond the persons immediately concerned.... When rumours attach to a bank's credit, they make a wild stampede to exchange any of its notes that they may hold; their trust has been ignorant, their distrust is ignorant and fierce. Such a rush often caused a bank to fail that might have paid them gradually. The failure of one caused distrust to rage around others and to bring down banks that were really solid; as a fire spreads from one wooden house to another until even fireproof buildings succumb to the blaze of a great conflagration. (1923, p. 305)

Bubbles are also frowned upon because the collapse of the bubble is often accompanied by the revelation of numerous swindles that have been launched amid the general euphoria (Kindleberger, 1978/1996, chap. 5). The South Sea Bubble of 1720 was, of course, a swindle. But it was accompanied by even more exotic scams, a favorite being the announcement of "An Undertaking of Great Advantage that would be Revealed in Due Course." The perpetrator charged two guineas a share and made off with £2000, keeping his secret intact by failing to attend a meeting with the investors. Recent American financial scandals have shown that the tradition of the boom-time swindle is alive and well.

It is little wonder that, in his classic study *Manias, Panics and Crashes*, Charles Kindleberger (2002, p. 26) declares that "Manias and panics... are associated on occasion with general irrationality and mob psychology," to which may be added "the irrationality of the gullible and the greedy in succumbing to swindlers and defalcators." In the whole of his book, Kindleberger does not have a good word for bubbles.

Useful, Not Rational

But here we shall attempt to row against this powerful tide of condemnation and suggest that bubbles might be useful. It should be made clear right away that we need to define *useful* in a very limited way—that is, as producing some positive consequences. This is not to join those who, in an attempt to bridge the chasm between economic theory based on the core concept of rational economic man and the historical evidence of bubbles and manias, have in recent years developed a theory of "rational" bubbles (Blanchard and Watson, 1982). Indeed, it will be suggested later the idea of a rational bubble is rather limited, depending as it does on the consideration of rational individual actions while neglecting outcomes for the economy as a whole. Even when economy-wide consequences are taken into account in these models, they are typically confined to a medium term of benign equilibrium, devoid of the harsh consequences of panic and crash.

Ignoring modern ideas on rational bubbles will probably disappoint those who are looking forward to a more formal theoretical discourse. The chapter may also disappoint any economic historians who might reasonably expect a less cavalier approach to evidence than what will be offered here. But this attempt is to bring a wide range of ideas to bear on this particular problem—and as far as pure theory and precise history are concerned, there are a lot of people who could do the job far more effectively.

Finally, keep your contemporary economic and political antennas switched on. While many examples will be drawn from the nineteenth and early twentieth centuries, bubbles are very much a characteristic of today's economy (as, indeed, are swindles), and the policy questions their existence poses are, if anything, are more important than ever.

Bubbles and the Beauty Contest

Before addressing the question of whether there are useful bubbles, it is helpful to devote some time to considering the morphology of a bubble—that is, why do bubbles happen and what are their building blocks?

It is clear that bubbles are essentially financial phenomena. They may focus on tulips or real estate or railways. But in all these cases, just as much as manias in currency markets or on the stock exchange, they are driven by *financial* speculation. Indeed, the fact that there might be something real associated with the bubble is irrelevant—the tulips are not for growing and looking at, they are for dealing in. It is the title to the tulips that matters—the escalating prices of the dealers' IOUs, or of the stocks and shares, or of real estate deeds, or of complex financial derivatives that matter. These are readily tradable, and it's the dynamics of their prices that holds the key to their understanding. So, to understand bubbles we must look to the fundamental operations of financial markets.

Keynes, in his *General Theory,* provided the best characterization of how financial markets really work. He described the operation of financial markets as a beauty contest. This was no Miss World Competition, in which there are tearful losers and a single, jubilant winner. Instead, Keynes was referring to a particular sort of newspaper competition that readers above a certain age might even remember.

> [P]rofessional investment may be likened to those newspaper competitions in which the competitors have to pick out the six prettiest faces from a hundred photographs, the prize being awarded to the competitor whose choice most nearly corresponds to the average preferences of the competitors as a whole; so that each competitor has to pick, not those faces which he himself finds prettiest, but those which he thinks likeliest to catch the fancy of the other competitors, all of whom are looking at the problem from the same point of view. It is not a case of choosing those, which, to the best of one's judgement, are really the prettiest, or even those which average opinion genuinely thinks the prettiest. We have reached the third degree where we devote our intelligences to anticipating what average opinion expects the average opinion to be. And there are some, I believe, who practise the fourth, fifth and higher degrees. (1936, p. 156)

In Keynes's contest, beauty is not in the eye of the beholder. Instead, the game is won by those who can accurately assess what others think others think others think is beautiful. In financial markets, it is knowing what others believe to be true about the movement of the market that is key to knowing how markets will indeed move. The market is driven by participants' beliefs about what average opinion believes average opinion believes (see also Allen, Morris and Shin, 2003).

It is worth making a comment at this point about rational bubbles. Given an individual's opinion that average opinion expects a price to rise, then it is entirely rational for an individual to seek out the profit-making opportunities that the bubble offers. Indeed, given the probabilities attached to the price's rising and to the bubble's bursting, it may be readily demonstrated that an individual who invests is acting in accordance with rational expectations. But the outcome for the economy as a whole is nonetheless irrational. It is this irrational outcome of the rational acts that *really* matters. Calling the bubble rational does not get us very far.

Given that a beauty contest is driven by what average opinion believes average opinion believes average opinion to be, how can we be sure that financial markets are stable and liquid?

Liquidity and Stability

The answer to the above question lies in the composition of traders (actual and potential) in the financial markets. If the traders are heterogeneous—that is, they have heterogeneous beliefs about the future, heterogeneous economic and financial goals, heterogeneous information, and so on, then in any one market for a particular financial instrument there will typically be some who wish to sell and some who wish to buy—the market will be liquid.

But suppose market participants are homogeneous, with the same beliefs, the same goals, and the same information. Then, when all want to sell also none want to buy. The market is totally illiquid—the price collapses, *in extremis* to zero, and the asset is worthless. The desperate desire for liquidity also arises when homogeneous beliefs in a future rise in an asset price result in everyone's wanting to buy. The price is bid up and up, and there is lust for more and more buying power to inflate the bubble further. There is a severe lack of liquidity, not because it's not easy to sell the asset—there are plenty of buyers around—but because there is not enough money around to buy the asset at ever more inflated prices.

In these circumstances, there is a great incentive to invent new techniques of buying. In other words, there is a tremendous incentive for financial innovation, overcoming the bounds of current financial practice and any difficulties in feeding the bubble. Indeed, it may well be that it is financial innovation, or changes in financial policy, that provides the liquidity that sets off the bubble in the first place.

Often, the financial innovation enhances the later disaster when the bubble bursts. In 1636, for example, a new phenomenon appeared in Dutch financial markets. Traders of tulip bulbs began meeting in taverns, in groups called "colleges," where trades were regulated by few rules. Since tulip bulbs are not available until June, and must be planted by September, any purchase between September and June has to be a contract for future delivery. Thus, a futures market in bulbs was created. As in today's futures markets, neither party intended delivery on the settlement date, only a payment equal to the difference between the contract and the settlement price. So they traded on the margin, having resources that are only to cover the expected price difference. When prices collapsed, and margins were called, there was no money to meet the cost of settlement. Contemporary waves of financial innovation have fueled more recent bubbles, with similar consequences. As prices begin to fall, a cumulative debt deflation spreads from the overextended commitments of market participants to the economy as a whole.

How can beliefs—even beliefs about what average opinion believes average opinion believes—have such a profound influence on the determination of prices, and of economic activity in general? The answer to this question has two components.

First, the price of the financial asset today is derived from its *expected* future price—so what people expect to happen is fundamental to the dynamics of today's price and hence to the dynamics of the bubble. The trouble is that we have very little evidence about what others expect. There are some futures markets for some commodities, stocks, and currencies, but they are subject to irrational manias just as much as are spot markets. Second, the asset is *relatively* fixed in supply. If, as the price is bid up more, and more of the good the asset represents is forthcoming, then the rise in price is mitigated and the bubble will deflate. The tulip mania could never have been sustained into the summer once it spread to ordinary tulips, and there was the immediate prospect of a flood of new bulbs.

There is a delicate balance here. The growth of a bubble in a company's shares will to some extent be fed by the appearance of new companies that, by their very existence, validate its prospects. The dot-com bubble was undoubtedly enlarged by the spectacular launch of new companies. But in due course the very plethora of investment opportunities will dilute the flow of funds to individual stocks and undermine their potential profitability.

Perhaps to these two basic components there should be added a third—the belief by individuals caught up in a bubble that either the bubble will go on forever or that they have the skill and foresight to get out in time. For example, none other than Sir Isaac Newton sold out his shares in the South Sea Company in April 1720, at a solid profit of 100%. Sadly for our confidence in the rationality of the great scientist, he was subsequently gripped by the prevailing mania, reentered the market at what proved to be the peak, and ended up losing £20,000.

The belief that you will get out in time is reinforced by the incentive structure of modern institutional investing. A dealer who ignores the profitable opportunities of a bubble will be fired. A dealer who buys into the bubble as does everyone else, and then loses his shirt (or, more accurately, his customers' shirts), does not necessarily lose his job. As Keynes put it, "Worldly wisdom teaches that it is better for reputation to fail conventionally than to succeed unconventionally" (1936, p. 158).

Finally, it might be asked if Keynes's characterization of financial markets is correct, how in the world do we ever observe any stability in the financial markets? Why are we not continually fluctuating, to take a popular political phrase, between boom and bust? The answer lies in a number of factors. First, there are a wide range of forces reinforcing the heterogeneity of market traders. Second, policymakers have reacted to past bubbles by regulating financial markets in a manner that diminishes the propensity to replicate those past bubbles ("past" bubbles, because so often the regulator is reacting to yesterday's bubble-creating financial innovation, and will still be caught out by tomorrow's). Third, markets may be stabilized by convention—that is, by public knowledge and beliefs that are strongly and widely held.

This last point is worth elaborating a little. Even markets that are inherently unstable are sometimes stable beyond all reason, resembling the cartoon character that runs off the cliff and remains, for some time, suspended in midair, running vigorously. The stability of the Thai bhat prior to the collapse of the Thai real estate bubble in 1997 is a case in point. The most powerful convention of all is that imposed by governments. When the exchange rates of the future euroland currencies were declared prior to being irrevocably fixed on January 1, 1999, the markets rapidly converged on those rates.

So, to sum up, we should not be surprised to encounter bubbles in markets driven by average opinion's beliefs about average opinion's beliefs. Those markets are predominantly markets for the titles to relative fixed quantities of assets. For the bubble to be sustained, there must be a growing pool of liquidity to feed the mania. Then follows debt deflation, as prices stop rising and begin to fall.

"Useful"

How can anything about a bubble deserve the label "useful"? Of course, even the worst event can have unintended positive consequences. The Second World War, for example, brought about changes in the social structure of Britain that many would regard as beneficial, but that would hardly be an argument for the usefulness of global conflict. For a phenomenon to be deemed useful, the positive consequences must be part of the intrinsic character of the event, not an unintended consequence. Of course, the positive consequences may be heavily qualified; there may be far better ways of achieving the same outcome, but nonetheless positive they are.

Financial Innovation

The overriding pressure from the demand for liquidity provides a powerful incentive for financial innovation. I have already discussed the financial innovations of the tulip mania. It has been argued that these innovations, damaging as they may have appeared during the subsequent debt deflation, paved the way for the development of the Dutch financial sector that was a dominant world force in the eighteenth century and remains a significant force to the present day. Consider, too, the British railway boom of the 1830s. Joint stock companies already existed in the UK, but they were to be the main driver and main financial innovation in the boom, able to provide capital on a scale far greater than ever had been required for, for example, the erection of cotton mills. They established the joint-stock company as the major system of governance for the second half of the nineteenth century and beyond.

Or take the subsequent European railway and real estate boom of 1847–48. When the boom collapsed in March 1848, it threatened to take the Schaaffhausen Bank of Cologne with it. In an attempt to stabilize the financial situation, the Prussian government allowed the bank to be converted into a joint-stock company, contrary to a standing policy of opposition to credit expansion. This precedent paved the way for the substantial expansion of German banks in the 1850s, with important consequences for German growth. Then, there was the great American railroad and steel boom of the 1870s that was funded by the new investment banks and that gave a huge boost to institutionalized finance.

And in modern times, the dot-com boom resulted in the growth of the American venture-capital business from a relatively small, unimportant sector of the financial services industry into a major source of financial support for innovation. Despite being hit hard by the collapse of the NASDAQ in 2000, the venture-capital system, along with the more complex risk-management instruments developed in the boom, has survived to fund the next wave of innovation.

All of these financial changes have a fundamental characteristic: they are designed to mobilize finance in new ways to feed the bubble, and in doing so they typically extend the scope of financial markets, drawing funds from a wider population than ever before.

The bursting of the bubble resulted in many a financial innovation being the object of much opprobrium, often quite rightly, as in the case of brokers' loans on late-1920s boom-time Wall Street. But it is remarkable how many survived the subsequent regulatory examinations of the authorities and were incorporated into more secure financial structures—more secure, that is, until the next time.

There remains a difficult question of cause and effect. Financial liberalization or innovation has been cited by many authors as the initial stimulus for the bubble, rather than the consequence. While every historical instance will be somewhat different, we rather suspect that the truth is that there is a bit of both—financial liberalization provides the initial impetus to prices. Then as the frenzy develops, further financial innovation is necessary to sustain an ever-growing flow of funds. Note, for example, that if investment is to continually grow (even grow steadily), then the stock of debt must not just expand; it must also expand at an accelerating speed. If investment is growing ever faster, then the acceleration in the stock of debt is compounded.

Transforming Technologies

It is not only the financial innovations produced by bubbles that are useful. So are the technologies that are developed as part of the bubble and that stay with us far longer.

For example, in February 1793, the canal mania that had been financed by refugee capital from France collapsed, but the canals remained. In December 1836, the first great railway boom, financed by new joint-stock banks, collapsed, bringing significant ruin to new landlord investors, but the railroads remained. In October 1847 came the collapse of the second great railway boom, this time financed by the new innovation of selling railway securities by installment, thereby spreading the subsequent ruin among a wider population, but the railroad system grew. Then, 1873 saw the collapse of the first great U.S. railway boom, funded by new financial instruments and an inflow of European capital, producing ruin that spread now on an international scale, though Americans realized benefits in railroad development. The stock market boom of the late 1920s had been associated in part with the growth of new industries—the internal combustion engine, electricity, the building of the suburbs. The collapse, transmitted through a fragile international financial system, was a worldwide event, but these inventions helped everyone prosper eventually. And, of course, the 1990s brought the dot-com boom; the full consequences of its collapse are still not yet clear, and the financial results had ramifications around the world. For example, new financial techniques of credit-risk transfer via derivative instruments have meant that European insurance companies were carrying far more of American financial risk than they realized, but new technologies spread worldwide as well. So, when the U.S. banking system was hit by multiple defaults in the past few years, part of the bill was passed on to the Europeans.

All of these events have a similar theme. The bubble was associated with large-scale investment in a new technology—a new technology that would in due course transform the entire economy. When each of these bubbles collapsed many investors were ruined and there was great financial distress. But society was left with canals, railways, automobiles, and roads to drive them on—even a fiber-optic network and the Internet. The financial bubble has burst; investments of real social value have been left behind.

This point should not be exaggerated. As Peter Mathias (1969) has pointed out, many of the canals were built "with different widths and depths, and much inefficient routing." As far as the railways were concerned "this was to be duplicated on an even larger scale." Railway promotion was originally a matter of setting up routes where the need was evident and the engineering practicable. Then it spread to routes where demand was doubtful and the engineering was full of problems. Plans for up to twenty-seven different railway lines from London to Brighton do not suggest that this was a particularly efficient investment process.

In an article in the *Financial Times*, Dan Roberts (2001) described telecommunications investments in the late 1990s as a "trillion dollar scrap heap." He argued that in 2001, only 1% to 2% of the fiber-optic cable buried under Europe and the United States had so far been "lit." When they tried to sell the assets, court-appointed receivers of bankrupted companies were recovering, on average, less than 10% of the original cost of building the networks.

However, despite the manifest inefficiencies of the investment processes during these bubbles, there is a persistent theme that cannot be ignored: significant, transforming technological change is introduced by a bubble. It was a bubble that made the finance available. It was a bubble that apparently directed national resources toward major economic transformations.

The Economics of a Useful Bubble

Economic analyses that associate bubbles with positive economic outcomes are rather rare. In an echo of Nicholas Kaldor's argument (1959/1964) that a steady rate of inflation is good for investment, since it shifts wealth from lenders to borrowers, Jacques Olivier (2000) suggests that bubbles may be "growth enhancing" just so long as the bubble is in the price of equity. Olivier argues that equity bubbles will raise the market value of firms, thus encouraging entrepreneurship, firm creation, investment, and growth. On the other hand, speculation on other types of assets that draws funds away from investment is unambiguously growth impairing.

In a not dissimilar mode, Mathias Binswanger (1999) developed a model of what he calls "sustainable bubbles," in which dynamic efficiency will be enhanced and real investment will be increased "if bubbles are sustained for a long time." This seems to be somewhat contrary to the reality of bubbles. (Binswanger, writing in 1999, apparently expected the U.S. stock market bubble to be sustained indefinitely.)

I take an entirely different position, proposing that the usefulness of bubbles derives from their effect in alleviating social inefficiencies that derive from rational individual actions. In other words, I suggest that, in the absence of bubbles, rational individual actions result in a socially irrational outcome, and that the bubble, by inducing irrational acts in individuals, may (and only, may) shift the economy toward a more socially rational position.

Problems of Scale

The first individual irrationality arises from problems of scale. That is, in a perfect capital market, as portrayed in the economics textbooks, individuals will be willing to invest up to the point where the return on capital falls to such a level as not to cover the cost of their borrowing. In this scenario, a child from a poor background would be willing to borrow the amount necessary to invest in an education at Eton and, I suppose, Oxford.

You can see the flaw right away. First, it is highly unlikely that a financially disadvantaged child will be given the opportunity to borrow, even if he or she wanted to. Second, it is likely that the child will view the scale of borrowing to create far too great a risk that there would be no adequate return. On both these grounds, the child will underborrow and underinvest.

Nor is the tendency to underinvest solely a characteristic of financially ill-informed individuals. In 1993, Metallgesellschaft AG, Germany's fourteenth largest industrial company, was almost ruined by losses in excess of $1 billion suffered in derivatives trading in the oil market by a U.S. subsidiary and by the refusal of the company's lead banker, Deutsche Bank, to finance the trading strategy further. It was argued by some distinguished economists that the fault lay not with Metallgesellschaft's trading strategy but with Deutsche Bank's refusal to fund the financial strategy over the longer period in which it would bear fruit. In other words, the problem was Deutsche Bank's unwillingness to invest on the scale required. But this argument rests too strongly on the proposition that the capital market is "perfect," in the sense that it is possible to borrow virtually unlimited sums today with the prospect of gain a long time in the future. In fact, rational risk aversion is likely to rise with the sheer scale of borrowing, a phenomenon known as the "principle of increasing risk." In the Metallgesellschaft case, it was lack of willingness to allow it to accumulate yet more debt that created severe problems for the firm (Mello and Parsons, 1995).

Similar problems were presented by the development of canals, and in yet more dramatic form by the appearance of a dramatically new transport technology—railways. The scale of the investment required in railways went far beyond what even the rich could rationally commit. If investment had relied on rational calculation, then it would have been enormously difficult for substantial projects to take place, other than investment in small, task-specific industrial lines. Irrationality saved the day. Individuals and firms took on far more debt than they rationally should. Their personal overcommitment ensured that the railways were built.

Public Goods

The second individual irrationality arises from the public goods problem. A "public good" in economists' jargon is not the same as a public good in everyday speech. In everyday parlance, a public good is a good or service produced by the public sector. For an economist, it is quite different: a public good is a good for which there is noncompetitive consumption. An apple is not a public good because consumption is competitive. If you eat it, it is not available for me to eat. But a radio program is a public good; it doesn't matter how much you listen to a particular station because I can listen to that station as much as I like, too. Similarly, an uncongested road is a public good. Your presence on the road doesn't prevent my using itas well—until, that is, it becomes congested.

It is typically irrational for an individual to invest in a public good. We don't subscribe individually for radio programs—they are paid for by advertising revenue, by charitable donation, or by government-imposed levies. (The possibility of encrypting radio or television signals enables the broadcaster to extract consumer surplus.) We only pay for toll roads to escape congestion (or perhaps the cost of a diversion). Suppose that there is a proposal to connect an isolated village to a main road some distance away. If all the inhabitants of the village are asked individually whether they will contribute to the cost of building the link, their rational answer is no since, if the link is built, they will be able to use it anyway. So the link is not built.

Now, the characteristic of many of the bubbles considered above is that the value of the investment in a new technology (perhaps defining a new era; see Sampson, 2003) depends crucially on the creation of a system—a connecting system of canals, or railways, or suburbs and suburban roads, or fiber-optic cables linking computers. It is generally impossible for an individual to invest in exclusive use of the new technology, and it is irrational to participate in a shared investment.

Again, irrationality comes to the rescue. The euphoria of the bubble persuades investors to commit themselves to investment in the overall system far beyond any rational calculation. But more important, it overcomes the isolation of the individual investor. The mania grips everyone and transforms isolated, selfish individuals into what might best be called "quasi-social investors." Society is bonded by greed.

Long-term Thinking

The third individual irrationality arises from the fact that returns may be too long deferred, arising too far into the future. The argument is an obvious extension of those already made. Individuals are reluctant to invest for the long term—they have a time preference that values returns in the short term above returns in the longer term. The problem with so many major investments in new technologies is that the returns seem to be so far in the future that it would be irrational for any individual to commit today. But irrationality comes to the rescue. The mania induces investment in firms that have never made a profit and have no prospect of making a profit in the foreseeable future—but that produce goods and services that result in a net increase in social welfare.

So bubbles are useful. Not only do they encourage financial innovation but also they overcome serious inefficiencies of a competitive market that would otherwise inhibit important economic and social progress. The mania suppresses the fear of the scale of change and of the uncertainty of the future; it overcomes the isolation of the individual investor; and it provides funds on a scale necessary to transform the economic infrastructure of society.

This may not be a very sensible way of getting the job done. The same deficiencies could, for example, be overcome by the state. The state can mobilize funds on a sufficient scale; as might be expected, it is the probably the best vehicle for investing in public goods. And the state does not have the "defective telescopic vision" that creates myopic time preference. In many of the areas of investment that have been characterized by bubbles, it was indeed the state that made many of the investments, often after the collapse of the bubble, and often in the interest of national defense. The U.S. government funded over 40% of nineteenth-century investment in U.S. railroads, and the Defense Department built the original Internet. The responsibility for investment in roads and electricity networks has been taken in many countries by the state.

So bubbles are not efficient, not in any way optimal, nor in any interesting way rational. But they may be useful. The case for useful bubbles was beautifully put by T. S. Ashton in his famous study, *The Industrial Revolution, 1760–1830*:

> The canal mania of 1790–4 undoubtedly led to some waste of national resources in ill-advised projects, but, taken as a whole, the investment in waterways brought, not only substantial dividends to shareholders, but an increase in the real income of the public in general.... The cost of bulky or heavy commodities such as coal, iron, timber, stone, salt, and clay was greatly reduced; agricultural regions which had been remote from the market were brought within the widening circle of exchange; the fear of local famine, of both food and fuel, was removed; and the closer contacts with others which the new means of communication afforded had a civilising influence on the populations of the Potteries and other inland areas. There was a redistribution of activities; old river ports such as Bewdly and Bawtry declined, and new communities grew up at nodal points like Stourport. The competitive position of more distant centres of production was improved, and rents in those nearer to the markets fell, or

failed to rise as they otherwise could have done. The incomes paid to those that dug the new canals, when spent, resulted in a raising of the level of employment generally. The offer of transferable shares, with prospects of high profit, accustomed men to invest their resources outside the restricted field of the Funds and the chartered trading companies, and so played a part in the rise of an impersonal market for capital. Perhaps the most important result, however, of the movement initiated by Bridgewater and Brindley was that it trained up a new race of engineers, equipped to meet the calls which the age of the railways was to make on their skill, endurance, and capacity for disciplined effort. (1948, p. 84)

That all sounds rather useful.

Note

This chapter was written by John Eatwell and appeared originally in *Contributions to Political Economy* (2004).

6

Unemployment on a World Scale

From 1950 to 1970, all the major industrial countries enjoyed employment levels at or near full employment. This was also a time in which world trade grew more rapidly than in any equivalent period before or since, and in which productivity growth (that is, the absorption of technological change) was faster than at any time before or since. Inflation was also low relative to later experience; it was a Golden Age of Western capitalism. Over the same period, there was a sustained improvement in economic performance in almost all of the Third World, maintained in large part by the steady growth of demand emanating from the industrial countries.

A distinct break occurred around 1970, with a sharp increase in trend levels of unemployment. The increase was greatest in the major countries of the European Union, with West Germany experiencing an almost eightfold increase (from a very low base). Only Italy had a relatively low increase, but this was from what was, for the 1960s, a high base. Canada and the United States, both relatively high-unemployment countries in the 1960s, also suffered "only" 50% and 130% increases, respectively, in average levels of unemployment. Japan's experience is exceptional, having very low unemployment in the 1960s and from that low base suffering only a 120% increase (see table 6.1).

The economic disruption visited upon the 1970s by oil price shocks, together with the deflationary measures taken by G7 governments in reaction to the oil price rise, might be thought to have been the source of the deterioration in G7 economic performance. The OECD estimated

Table 6.1 Unemployment in the G7, 1964–73 and 1983–92

	A. 1964–73	B. 1983–92	B/A
West Germany	0.79	6.03	7.63
France	2.23	9.70	4.35
Italy	5.48	10.13	1.85
UK	2.94	9.79	3.33
USA	4.46	6.69	1.50
Canada	4.23	9.64	2.28
Japan	1.22	2.71	2.22

Source: OECD Main Economic Indicators.
Note: Annual standardized unemployment rates as % of the labor force, averaged for each ten-year period.

that 20% of the loss in OECD real income in the mid-1970s was due to the trade effect of the oil price rise. The remaining 80% of the loss was due to the concerted deflation policies that characterized the responses of the Western economies to the price increase.

But the oil price rises of the 1970s are not an adequate explanation of sustained high unemployment. For not only had the Western economies absorbed similar rises in prices of raw materials during the Korean War without a similar slowdown, but also these new high trend levels of unemployment persisted into the 1980s and 1990s, and were not notably affected by the collapse in oil prices and other commodity prices in 1986. It was these high trend levels of unemployment that underpinned the yet higher unemployment figures produced by the "slowdown" in the G7 economies—so that G7 unemployment in the period cannot possibly be considered to have been purely cyclical. It was, instead, a combination of a long-term trend and the cyclical factors associated with recessions in Europe and Japan. Indeed, it may well have been that the recessions were simply another step up in the long-term general level of unemployment. This suggests that unemployment in the G7 could be tackled by standard countercyclical policies. A new approach was required.

The commonality of the unemployment experience throughout the G7, outweighing the particular economic fortunes of individual countries, was especially striking. The particular circumstances of each country did, of course, affect the distribution of unemployment between them. But the common experience suggests that the causes of high unemployment are to be found in factors that affected all G7 countries in a broadly similar manner, rather than in the individual circumstances of each country. To appreciate the range of policies that might have been capable of tackling the G7 increase in unemployment requires identifying the common factors underlying that increase.

Likely candidates for a common source of increased unemployment are: (1) the pace of labor-saving technological change; (2) structural changes in world trading relationships associated with the increasing mobility of capital and the rapid growth of Third World manufactured exports, particularly from China and the Pacific Rim; and (3) changes in the international financial environment and consequential changes in the macroeconomic polities of the G7 countries, which in turn impacted the growth performance of developing countries, notably through a reduced rate of growth of world trade and low commodity prices.

The Pace of Technological Change

It has been a common view since the early nineteenth century that technological change is a threat to jobs. In the 1950s and 1960s, automation was regarded as the key menace. In the 1970s and 1980s, the impact of information technologies was often cited as potentially job destroying.

Whatever technological changes may have done to the *composition* of employment, there is no evidence that the speed of technological change was behind the growth in unemployment throughout the G7. If it were, then there should have been an acceleration of productivity growth in the 1980s and 1990s as new techniques sharply reduced the labor input required per unit output. In fact, the reverse occurred. There was a sharp slowdown in productivity growth, a slowdown that was greatest in Japan and least in the United States and the UK (in both of which productivity growth was relatively low in the earlier period). Indeed, the slowdown in productivity growth was everywhere greater than the slowdown in the overall growth of demand, which means that the slowdown in productivity contributed to the creation (or at least the preservation) of jobs, rather than their distribution (see table 6.2).

In each of the G7 countries, the slowdown in productivity growth was less pronounced in manufacturing than in the economy as a whole. Insofar as the growth of demand for manufactures also slowed, the fact that manufacturing productivity growth was relatively buoyant resulted in substantial job losses in manufacturing, notably in the UK. An exception to the general trend was manufacturing employment in Germany, which toward the end of the 1980s resumed a (slight) rising trend, though this was overwhelmed by a subsequent downturn (see table 6.3).

The loss of jobs in manufacturing was exacerbated by a change in the relationship between the growth of demand and the growth of jobs. In the 1960s, growing demand was associated with increasing jobs. In the 1980s, growing demand was satisfied (even more than satisfied) by productivity growth, and jobs were lost. It is not clear to what extent the failure of manufacturing to create jobs as in the past was due to the slowdown of demand, and to what extent it was the result of a change in the relationship between the rate of growth of demand and the rate of technical progress.

Whatever might have been the case, it seems likely that a higher rate of growth of demand for manufactures, although it would probably bring with it a higher rate of productivity growth too, would at least have stemmed the loss of jobs. And there was certainly a potential for a higher growth of demand for manufactures. Even in the most advanced of the G7 countries there were substantial proportions of the population who did not have access to the number and quality of manufactured

Table 6.2 Overall productivity growth: GDP per person employed

	A. 1961–70	B. 1981–90	B/A
West Germany	4.3	1.9	0.45
France	5.0	2.0	0.40
Italy	6.2	1.9	0.31
UK	3.3	2.0	0.60
USA	1.9	1.1	0.58
Japan	9.1	3.0	0.33

Source: *European Economy*, Annual Economic Reports.

Table 6.3 Manufacturing productivity growth in the G7

	A. 1964–73	B. 1983–92	B/A
West Germany	4.0	2.4	0.60
France	5.3	2.6	0.49
Italy	5.1	2.6	0.51
UK	4.2	3.6	0.95
USA	3.1	2.8	0.90
Canada	4.0	2.6	0.65
Japan	9.6	5.7	0.59

Source: *OECD Main Economic Indicators.*

goods that their fellow citizens regard as necessary to sustain a normal standard of living.

Structural Changes in the World Economy

An issue of growing importance is whether the rise in competition from the newly industrializing countries, particularly those on the Pacific Run, jeopardized job creation in the traded-goods sectors of the G7 countries. The possibility of securing full employment by a higher growth of domestic demand is significantly diminished if the competitive strengths of G7 industry are overcome by the potent combination of low Third World wages and ever more mobile capital.

There was a distinct acceleration in the penetration of developing country manufactures into G7 markets. In 1968, just 1% of G7 domestic demand for manufactures was satisfied by imports from the Third World. By 1980, developing countries' markets share had risen to 2%; by 1988, to 3.1%; by 1993, to 4%. Developing countries manufactures accounted for 10% of G7 manufactured imports.

Competition from the Third World certainly led to a loss of jobs in particular sectors (typically low-skill tradables) either directly, owing to loss of markets, or indirectly, as innovation in response to Third World competition led to the adoption of less labor-intensive techniques, particularly low-skill-intensive techniques (Wood, 1994). But if, despite these sectoral effects, the *overall* balance of trade was unchanged, there would be no net effect on aggregate demand. Where there is any impact on the overall relationship between aggregate demand and employment depends on the structure of demand in the economy, including demand for nontradables, the scale of trade with Third World countries, and the pace and content of technological change in the various sectors of the economy.

In fact, leaving aside the impact of the oil price rises, there tended to be a *surplus* in the balance of trade between G7 and the more dynamic of the Third World countries; indeed, these countries were typically the fastest growing markets in the world. This was particularly true in the 1970s. Thereafter, overall G7 trade moved closer to general balance with this group of countries.

The impact of low-wage competition from the newly industrializing countries is not dissimilar from the competition that the northern European countries experienced from southern Europe in the late 1950s.

That competition, which resulted, for example, in the growth of Italy's share of world manufactured trade from less than 2% to over 6% in twenty years, did not result in unemployment in northern Europe. On the contrary, throughout the period in which competition was most intense, northern Europe suffered from a labor shortage, with about 10 % of the labor force in West Germany and France being immigrants. The structural changes associated with the development of Italy took place in the context of generally high growth rates. The structural adjustments heralded by the rapid growth of manufactured exports from the developing countries appeared threatening because of persistent slow growth in the G7.

If competition from the newly industrializing countries did result in increasing deficits with the G7, then they could be dealt with (to some extent) by the traditional method of changing the exchange rate between surplus and deficit countries. The effectiveness of exchange-rate changes will, of course, be limited if the penetration of G7 markets was due to the technological superiority of the imports. For example, the impact of Korean steel on the U.S. market is typically attributed to technological superiority of the product in an industry in which labor costs are a very low proportion of total costs. Whatever the character of Third World competition might be, the growth and prosperity of the G7 rests on maintaining its technological vitality, both in the quality of research and innovation and in the quality of the labor force.

Changes in the International Financial Environment and Their Impact on Macroeconomic Policies and Employment in the G7

The key to understanding the growth in unemployment throughout the G7 in the period would appear to be the third common element: the slowdown in the trend rate of growth of demand (table 6.4). This slowdown occurred around 1970, and has persisted.

Real GDP growth in developing countries revealed a similar pattern. However, this similarity masked the fact that in the intervening period, developing countries' growth was sustained at a relatively high level. From 1973 to 1982, real growth in developing countries averaged 4.7% per year, compared with 1.9% in the United States, 2.4% in the European community, and 3.9% in Japan. Moreover, aggregate figures for developing countries disguised significant differences in growth in different parts of the world, particularly in growth of GDP per capita. In the

Table 6.4 Growth of real GDP—the "slowdown"

	A. 1964–73	B. 1983–92	B/A
West Germany	4.5	2.9	0.64
France	5.3	2.2	0.42
Italy	5.0	2.4	0.48
UK	3.3	2.3	0.69
USA	4.0	2.9	0.72
Canada	5.6	2.8	0.50
Japan	9.6	4.0	0.42
Developing Countries	5.6[a]	3.7	0.66

Source: *OECD Main Economic Indicators*; UNDO Industry in the 1980s, 1985; UN, 1993. *World economic survey*. New York: United Nations.
[a] 1960–70.

period 1983–92, GDP per capita fell in Latin America (at a rate of –0.1%), in Africa (–0.9%), in West Asia (–3.3%), and in the developing countries of the Mediterranean region (–1.5%); but grew in South and East Asia (+3.8%) and China (+7.9%).

The persistence of slow growth in demand into the 1990s seems to have been predominantly caused by the change in the structure of international finance and the consequent impact on the structure of domestic macroeconomic policies. The slowdown has from time to time been attributed to a number of other factors, including the growing profit squeeze at the end of the 1960s, the exhaustion of easy opportunities for technological catchup with the United States, and, of course, the impact on the growth of demand of the rise in raw material prices, particularly oil prices. But none of these seems to have an explanatory power comparable with that provided by changes in international financial relationships (see Glyn, Hughes, Lipietz, and Singh, 1990).

Two fundamental institutional changes marked a clear break in the international environment: first, the collapse of the Bretton Woods system, with its fixed exchange rates, in the early 1970s, which resulted in the 1970s and 1980s being an era of floating rates; second, the deregulated global markets of the 1980s having replaced the regulated financial markets of the 1960s.

There has been extensive analysis of the inability of the post–Bretton Woods trading and payments system to deal with international trading imbalances other than by deflation and growing unemployment in weaker countries—a deflationary impulse that has proved contagious.

Less attention has been paid to the fact that this deflationary pressure is reinforced by the deregulation of global markets and the huge growth in short-term capital flows.

Financial markets began to be dominated by short-term flows that sought to profit from changes in asset prices—in other words, from speculation. Growth in the scale of such speculation, relative to other transactions, was particularly marked in the foreign exchange markets. It is estimated that in 1971, just before the collapse of the Bretton Woods system, about 90% of all foreign exchange transactions were for financing trade and long-term investment, and only about 10% were speculative. By the 1990s, those percentages were reversed, with well over 90% of all transactions being speculative. Daily speculative flows regularly exceeded the combined foreign exchange reserves of all the G7 governments.

The explosive growth in short-term speculative flows originated from a powerful combination of the carrot of profit and the stick of financial risk. To an important extent, speculation is an inevitable outcome of the abandonment of fixed rates. Under the Bretton Woods system, there was little profit to be had in speculation, since currencies moved only in very tight bands—apart, that is, from the very occasional change in parity. Indeed, the Bretton Woods system provided quite remarkable stability. For example, the core currencies of the European Monetary System, locked together in the 1980s in the Exchange Rate Mechanism (ERM), enjoyed greater stability in relation to one another during the Bretton Woods era than they have been able to achieve since. In the face of that Bretton Woods stability, it was not worthwhile maintaining the large-scale currency dealing facilities with which we are familiar today—even if the contemporary regulatory structures had not placed significant barriers in the path of short-term capital flows.

However, once Bretton Woods had collapsed, and significant fluctuations became commonplace, opportunities for profit proliferated, the regulatory structures that had inhibited flows of capital were challenged as "inefficient" and "against the national interest," and the infrastructure of speculation was constructed. The Bretton Woods system was finally abandoned in 1973. The United States announced the elimination of all capital controls in January 1974.

The incentive to deregulate international capital flows, which was created with the abandonment of fixed rates, was decisively reinforced by the need to hedge against the costs that fluctuating exchange rates imposed on the private sector. Under the Bretton Woods system, foreign exchange risk was borne by the public sector. With that system's collapse, foreign exchange risk was privatized. This privatization of risk imposed substantial strains on the domestic and international banking systems, however. The need to absorb and cover foreign exchange risk demanded the creation of new financial instruments, which in turn required the removal of many of the regulatory barriers that limited the possibilities of laying off risk and a restructuring of financial institutions.

Combined with other, domestic pressures for the removal of financial controls, the collapse of Bretton Woods was a significant factor driving the worldwide deregulation of financial systems. Exchange controls were abolished. Domestic restrictions on cross-market access for financial institutions were scrapped. Quantitative controls on the growth of credit were eliminated, and monetary policy was now conducted predominantly through management of short-term interest rates. A global market in monetary instruments was created.

By the 1990s, the sheer scale of speculative flows could easily overwhelm any government's foreign exchange reserves. The ease of moving money from one currency to another, together with the ease of borrowing for speculative purposes, meant that enormous sums could be shifted across the exchanges—especially for short periods of time. Prior to the September 1992 run on sterling, the British government boasted of a $15 billion support facility it had negotiated in Deutsche marks, to be used to defend the parity of the pound. Yet, when the speculative storm broke, that sum would be matched by the sales of sterling by just one prominent player in the foreign exchange markets.

The overwhelming scale of such potential flows meant that governments, as never before, had to keep a careful eye on the need to maintain market "credibility." Indeed, credibility became the keystone of policy-making in the nineties. A credible government was a government that pursued a policy that is "market friendly"—that is, a policy that is in accordance with what the markets believe to be "sound." Particularly favored were measures designed to meet a "prudent" predetermined monetary target, such as maintaining a given exchange-rate parity or a given growth rate of the money supply. Governments that failed to pursue sound and prudent policies would be forced to pay a premium on the interest costs of financing their programs. Severe loss of credibility would lead to a financial crisis.

The determination of what is credible, and how governments lose credibility, is a product of the way that speculative markets actually work. In his *General Theory,* Keynes likened the operations of a speculative market to a beauty contest. He was not referring to a 1930s equivalent of the Miss World contest. He had in mind a competition that was then popular in the British tabloid Sunday newspapers in which readers were asked to rank pictures of young women in the order that they believed they would be ranked by a "celebrity panel." So in order to win, the player should express not his or her own preferences, but the preferences he or she believed were held by the panel. In the same way, the key to playing the markets is not what the individual investor considers to be the virtues or otherwise of any particular policy, but what he or she believes everyone else in the market will think.

Since the markets are driven by average opinion about what average opinion will be, an enormous premium is placed on any information or signals that might provide a guide to the swings in average opinion and as to how average opinion will react to changing events. These signals have to be simple and clear-cut. Sophisticated interpretations of the economic data would not provide a clear lead. So the money markets and foreign exchange markets become dominated by simple slogans—larger fiscal deficits lead to higher interest rates; an increased money supply results in higher inflation; public expenditure is bad, private expenditure is good—even when those slogans are persistently refuted by events. To these simplistic rules of the game add the need for governments to publish their own financial targets, to show that their policies are couched within firm financial frameworks. The main purpose of insisting on government transparency and a commitment to financial targeting is to aid the average opinion in guessing how the average opinion will expect the government to respond to changing economic circumstances, and how the average opinion will react when the government fails to meet its goals.

The demands of credibility imposed broadly deflationary macroeconomic strategies on the G7. In the 1960s, the managed international financial framework permitted expansionary, full-employment policies that were contagious both domestically, encouraging private investment, and internationally, underwriting the growth of world trade. In the 1980s, the deregulated financial framework encouraged policies that elevated financial stability above employment. This ratcheted up real interest rates, which in turn reduced domestic investment and slowed the growth of world trade.

Financial instability has a severe impact on the ability of companies to invest with confidence, and, indeed, on their ability to survive. The globalization of financial markets has meant that, whereas international disequilibria may in the past have been manifest in exchange-rate movements, they now have an impact on interest rates in domestic money markets. The instability of local interest rates has meant that international financial pressures are felt by small and medium-size firms operating in the home market, and not only by large companies operating internationally.

These new pressures on small firms have had major implications for any drive to create new jobs. Between 1979 and 1991, employment by the Fortune 500 companies in the United States fell from 16.2 million to 12 million. In contrast, the U.S. Bureau of Labor Statistics estimated that, of the net total of 18.5 million jobs that were created in the 1980s, 12 million were created by new, mainly small companies. Small and medium-size firms are the job engines of the G7, and it was these firms that were most severely hit by the financial instability transmitted through the global money markets.

Instability has had a further negative effect on policy. It severely reduced the scope of the fiscal cooperation that G7 countries so desperately need to engineer a concerted attack on unemployment. With exchange rates fluctuating, the distribution of the gains of such a concerted strategy is highly uncertain. But if the payoff is unknown, it is difficult for governments to commit themselves to a cooperative strategy, particularly when that strategy carries the risk of loss of credibility.

Lessons for a Global Full-Employment Strategy

The golden age of full employment was a product of a particular combination of international relationships—a combination that collapsed in the early 1970s. Much of the rise in G7 unemployment through to the 1990s can be attributed to that collapse. If this argument is correct, then the pursuit of a full-employment policy must involve either withdrawing from the international pressures that create unemployment (the "war" or "siege" economy solution) or the creation of an international environment that replicates the expansionary framework of Bretton Woods. Simply to pose the issue indicates the scale of the task. However, there is no intrinsic reason that we should not be able to create a new international regime that would underwrite national full-employment policies.

Going back to Bretton Woods is not a feasible proposition. The Bretton Woods system rested on the economic dominance of the United States. That economic dominance produced a worldwide desire for dollar reserves and the consequent ability to fund international imbalances by flows of U.S. capital. Bretton Woods was not a multilateral system. It was led by the United States, and it was therefore incapable of dealing with the imbalances caused by the relative economic decline of the United States itself.

Neither of the two other dominant economies, Germany and Japan, occupied a position comparable to that of the United States in the immediate postwar period. Leaving aside the temporary impact of reunification, Germany has been running a large and persistent current account surplus for the previous thirty years. But long-term capital flows out of Germany have never been sufficient to fund the counterpart deficits in other countries in the way that U.S. capital flows did in comparable circumstances earlier. As far as Japan is concerned, the yen has not achieved the role in international trade played by the dollar even today, especially in third-party transactions. While Japanese exports amount to 16% of total G7 exports, only 7.5% of G7 exports are involved in yen. By contrast, 42% of G7 exports are invoiced in dollars, even though the United States is the source of only 21% of those exports.

A new international financial framework must be a genuine multilateral arrangement. At the core of that new system should be a renewed commitment to securing the currency stability necessary to underwrite the coordinated international expansion needed to avert worldwide recession. The present largely ceremonial summits of the G7 and the G20 need to be replaced with meetings that actually dealt with substantive issues. A permanent secretariat might even be created with the skills and authority to manage the international payments system.

It is often argued that a new stable currency system is simply not feasible in a world of deregulated finance linked by the modern technology of the money markets. This argument fails to take into account the fact that fluctuating rates are themselves the motivating force behind the very existence of the large-scale speculative infrastructure. Moreover, while the speculators may be able to borrow very large sums for short periods of time, the central banks, as the creators of currencies, can, collectively, provide indefinitely large sums for just as long. New cooperation between the major central banks and the creation of new techniques of domestic monetary control (and sterilization) are vital if stability is to be restored.

It will not, of course, be possible to create a new stable system if there are persistent trade imbalances that are not funded by long-term capital flows. Today, the fundamental imbalance is between the United States and China. European Community trade is broadly balanced—and has been for more than a decade. The losses suffered by Chinese financial investments in the United States suggest that financing a persistent U.S. deficit is going to prove difficult. Sustained growth and expanding trade will, therefore, require action to correct trade imbalances. The alternative is either persistent instability or the stability of permanent recession.

Any international agreement to buttress economic policy coordination with a framework of stable exchange rates must be reinforced by action to monitor and perhaps regulate short-term international capital flows. Attempting to maintain stability in international currency markets under the current deregulated regime is like trying to cross an uneven field carrying a large volume of water in a shallow pan. It would be much easier if the pan contained a number of baffles to prevent all the water from sloshing in unison from side to side. That is, financial "baffles" are needed to slow down the rush of short-term capital from one currency to another.

The technical problems involved in creating such suitable baffles in the international financial markets are typically overstated. The fact that trading today is typically by electronic transfer makes effective monitoring easier than ever before, and with international agreement, it would not be too difficult to link the legal right to trade with the requirement to accept appropriate monitoring. Effective monitoring is the starting point of effective management. Both will be possible only if there is full and consistent cooperation among the major economies, in the pursuit of agreed-upon objectives.

This will require the creation of an entirely new institutional framework, not previously encountered in the history of modern capitalism. The Bretton Woods era was not a period of policy coordination; the system of fixed exchange rates was buttressed by strict capital controls and by active trade policies, against which the dominant economic power, the United States, did not retaliate.[1] Individual countries were able, therefore within bounds to pursue national economic objectives. That these added up to a reasonably coherent set of international growth rates is, to a substantial degree, attributable to the combination of managed trade and a persistent U.S. deficit on combined current and long-term capital accounts that sustained the growth of world demand. The sustained high levels of employment were the outcome of the resultant structure of national policies—interdependent, yes; coordinated, no.

A similar reliance on national policies was the basis of the recovery from the recession of the 1930s. The recovery heralded by the abandonment of the gold standard, and the successive devaluation of currencies against gold, was not due so much to the devaluations (after all, it was not possible for all countries to devalue against each other, and the countries that did not devalue were not big enough relative to the world economy to act as deficit-absorbing engines of world demand). It was instead due to the adoption of national expansionary policies—notably, cheap money policies fortified by capital and trade controls—once the need to maintain the monetary orthodoxy of the gold standard had been abandoned (Temin, 1989; Kitson and Michie, 1994).

The problem of international unemployment is rooted in the developments in the international trading and financial system since 1973. The pressure to liberalize goods markets and, most important, financial markets, has created a deflationary climate that has infected the worldwide economy. Within this deflationary climate not only is it difficult to implement the structural reforms required in the weaker developed countries, but also the development of formerly backward economies such as South Korea, Taiwan, and China is seen as a threat and an excuse for yet another deflation and deregulation.

The theory of international economic policy, the policies that emanate from that theory, and the institutions that implement the policies are all constructed on the model of an optimally self-adjusting market system. The history of the international economy lends no support for this model, however. On the contrary, a sustained revival of international economy and the attainment of higher levels of employment, let alone the attainment of full employment, require replacement of that model with an analysis that recognizes the need for institutions that ensure sustainable growth of world effective demand, so that expansion, rather than deflation, becomes contagious.

Notes

This chapter is a newly revised version of a paper written by John Eatwell, which appeared as the first chapter of his book *Global Unemployment: Loss of Jobs in the 1990s.*

1. For a full account of the trade policies of this era, particularly the "management" of trade by Germany, France, and Japan, and the response of the United States, see Shonfield, 1965.

7

International Financial Liberalization

The impact of the liberalization of international financial markets on the scale of cross-border capital flows has become an increasingly familiar tale. Yet the extraordinary growth in international capital flows makes it a tale worth retelling. This growth in capital flows is the product of the most important systemic transformation of the world economy since the establishment of the new world order at the end of World War II. Its current and potential impact on the organization and operation of developed and developing economies demands detailed evaluation. Indeed, it is the key to the world's economic future.

The Scale of Capital Flows

In 1973, daily foreign exchange trading around the world ranged from between $10 billion to $20 billion per day. But on January 1, 1974, the United States abolished all restrictions on international capital movements, following the same move by Canada, Germany, and Switzerland during 1973. Britain scrapped all controls in 1979, Japan in 1980, France and Italy in 1990, and Spain and Portugal in 1992.

Following the abolition of controls, the volume of international capital flows began to grow exponentially. During the 1970s, foreign exchange trading led the way. By 1980, according to the Bank for International Settlements (BIS, 1993), foreign exchange trading had reached a daily average of $80 billion, and the ratio of foreign exchange trading to world trade was about ten to one. By 1992, daily trading averaged $880 billion, a ratio to world trade of fifty to one. In 1995, daily trading averaged $1,260 billion, a ratio to world trade of nearly seventy to one, and equal to the entire world's official gold and foreign exchange reserves (BIS, 1996). These figures are for an *average* day's trading and would be greatly exceeded on days of high activity, such as in September 1992, when the pound sterling was forced out of the European Exchange Rate Mechanism (ERM) and the French franc was under sustained speculative attack. As is clear from table 7.1, by far the greatest proportion of currency trades were very short run. Given that the vast majority of trades are not for the finance of trade in goods or services or long-term investment, these short-term trades must be based on expectations of gain to be derived from changes in the value of the financial assets. In the broadest sense, they are speculative.[1]

In the 1980s, it was the turn of the international bond markets. From 1983 to 1993, total cross-border (cross-currency) sales and purchases of U.S. Treasury bonds rose from $30 billion to $500 billion. Sales and purchases of bonds and equities between foreigners and U.S. residents rose from 3% of U.S. GDP in 1970 to 9% in 1980, to 135% in 1993. Over the same period, cross-border securities transactions in the UK rose from virtually nothing to more than 1000% of GDP. Woodall (1995) cites an IMF estimate that "total cross-border ownership of tradable securities in 1992 was $2,500 billion."

The growth in trading was accompanied by a growth in the stock of international bank lending, from $265 billion in 1975 to $4,200 billion in 1994. The McKinsey Global Institute estimated that the total stock of all financial assets traded in global (i.e., open) markets rose from $5,000

Table 7.1 Maturity of net global foreign exchange transactions, April 1992 and April 1995 (percentages) x = *number of days maturity*

	Spot*		Forward#	
	$x \leq 2$	$2 < x \leq 7$	$7 < x \leq 365$	$365 \leq x$
1992	47.3	33.9	18.2	0.6
1995	43.5	38.1	17.5	0.8

Sources: BIS, 1993. Survey of Foreign Exchange Activity in April 1992. Basle. BIS, 1996. Central Bank survey of foreign exchange and derivatives market activity, *1995*. Basle.
* Single outright currency exchanges with cash settlements within two business days. Excludes the spot leg of swaps.
\# Swaps, outright forwards traded on exchanges or "customized" and currency options at their notional value. Cross-currency swaps of interest and amortization installments not included.

billion in 1980 to $35,000 billion in 1992—equal to twice the GDP of the OECD countries. By 2000, McKinsey forecasted that the stock of globally traded assets would reach $83,000 billion—about three times the OECD GDP (Woodall, 1995).

It is no accident that the explosive growth of international capital flows coincided with the 1973 collapse of the Bretton Woods system of fixed exchange rates. Apart from comparatively rare realignments, fixed rates offered only the profits of limited arbitrage. The fluctuating rate system that took its place stimulated capital flows with a powerful cocktail of the carrot of speculative profit and the stick of financial risk, laced with the proceeds of extensive arbitrage.

To an important extent, profit-seeking speculation is an inevitable outcome of the abandonment of fixed rates. Under the Bretton Woods system, there was little profit to be had in speculation, since currencies moved only in very tight bands—apart, that is, from the very occasional change in parity. Indeed, the Bretton Woods system provided quite remarkable stability. For example, the core currencies of the European Monetary System, locked together in the 1980s in the ERM, were less stable in relation to one another than they had been during the 1950s and 1960s. In the face of Bretton Woods stability, it was not worthwhile creating the infrastructure of large-scale currency-dealing facilities with which we are familiar today—even if the contemporary regulatory structures had not placed significant barriers in the path of capital flows. Nonetheless, in the 1960s, growing speculative capital flows and the consequent pressure on fixed parities, notably the dollar price of gold, played a large part in the demise of the Bretton Woods system (Triffin, 1960; Black 1987; De Grauwe, 1987). But once Bretton Woods had collapsed and significant fluctuations in exchange rates became commonplace, then opportunities for profit proliferated, regulatory structures that inhibit flows of capital were challenged as "inefficient" and "against the national interest," and the modern infrastructure of speculation was constructed.

The incentive to deregulate international capital flows was powerfully reinforced by the need to hedge against the costs that fluctuating exchange rates imposed on the private sector. Under the Bretton Woods system, foreign exchange risk was borne by the public sector. With that system's collapse, foreign exchange risk was privatized.

This privatization of risk imposed substantial strain on the domestic and international banking systems. The need to absorb and cover foreign-exchange risk demanded the creation of new financial instruments, which in turn required removal of regulatory barriers that limited the possibilities of laying off risk, and a restructuring of financial institutions. Combined with other domestic pressures for the removal of financial controls, the collapse of Bretton Woods was a significant factor in driving the worldwide deregulation of financial systems. Exchange controls were abolished. Domestic restrictions on cross-market access for financial institutions were scrapped. Quantitative controls on the growth of credit were eliminated, and monetary policy was now conducted predominantly through the management of short-term interest rates. A global market in monetary instruments was created.

The "Official" Position on Capital Controls

With the appearance of the new global financial market came an equally fundamental shift in the official assessment of the value of capital controls. Liberalization of international capital movements was not one of the objectives of the 1944 Articles of Agreement that established the International Monetary Fund (IMF). The goal of convertibility was associated with current account transactions alone. Indeed, debate at the Bretton Woods conference revolved around whether Article VI of the Articles of Agreement should not merely permit the imposition of capital controls but also should require the IMF and other countries to assist in the enforcement of any member's controls against capital flight. This had been Keynes's objective from the first draft of his plan for a Clearing Union. In due course, pressure from the U.S. Department, the Federal Reserve Bank of New York, and Wall Street bankers resulted in the adoption of the compromise embodied in Article VI.[2] Under that article, member states are allowed to impose permanent controls and the IMF is required to ensure that its credits are not used to fund capital flight, but neither the Fund nor other countries have any obligation to assist in the enforcement of a country's capital controls.

The IMF's practice today is exactly the opposite of both the letter and the intent of Article VI. Not only is IMF lending now conditional on measures that enhance the attractiveness of borrowers to international investors (including the lifting of capital controls), but also IMF assistance has been provided explicitly to enable countries to withstand capital flight without imposing controls. The IMF reaction to the 1994 Mexican crisis is the most dramatic example of this approach. In order to eliminate the contradiction, the Fund's managing director, Michel

Camdessus, has proposed that Article VI be revised. In its place would be a requirement that the currencies of all member countries be freely convertible for all capital transactions in order "to lock in the freedom of capital movements already achieved and encourage wider liberalization" (Camdessus, 1994).

The World Bank has also become active in the encouragement of capital market liberalization. Its affiliate, the International Finance Corporation, is fostering stock-market development in developing countries and encouraging them to open their capital markets to foreign portfolio investment (Sudweeks, 1989). Encouragement of the growth of stock markets is a fundamental pillar of the World Bank's proposals for pension reform (World Bank, 1994; Singh, 1995).

The alteration in the practice of the Bretton Woods institutions reflects a change in the conventional wisdom. The experience of the Great Depression led Keynes (1933, p. 236) to argue, "above all, let finance be primarily national," a view that was maintained in the Bretton Woods negotiations not only by Keynes but by White, too. Today, however, the belief that a freeing of capital flows is "efficient," that it brings about the convergence of long-term interest rates and optimizes the global allocation of capital, has been accepted by even the most careful commentators.[3] For example, in considering Richard Marston's demonstration (1993) that in Britain, Germany, and the United States, "capital controls imposed during the Bretton Woods period led to large covered interest differentials"; Barry Eichengreen (1993, pp. 626–627) comments, "Post-World War II capital controls were a potential source of allocational inefficiency. *Thus,* there was nothing particularly admirable about financial market performance under Bretton Woods" [emphasis added]. Paul Krugman (1993, p. 540) is more equivocal: "The capital controls of the Bretton Woods era may not have made a good deal of sense—but then the free capital flows of our own time do not make much sense either."

What is lacking on both sides of the argument are clear criteria for the evaluation of the impact of liberalization. Later in this chapter, the impact of international financial liberalization is assessed against a list of explicit claimed benefits. It is found that empirical evidence, with respect to both developed and developing countries, is not supportive of these claims. There follows an analysis that seems to accord more closely with the facts and has an assessment of the impact on public policy. Lastly, the chapter examines the impact of financial liberalization on the private sector of the real economy.

Assessing the Experience of Liberalization

Criteria for Evaluation

The argument that liberalization will enhance economic efficiency derives from some basic propositions in economic theory. Before turning to an examination of the facts, it may be useful to consider that theoretical framework, within which the experience of liberalization is typically presented.

Theoretical Arguments for the Efficiency of Liberalization

Implicit in virtually all arguments in favor of liberalization is the first part of the Fundamental Theorem of Welfare Economics (that competitive markets yield Pareto optimal equilibria) combined with the Efficient Market Hypothesis (that financial markets use information efficiently).

The argument that competitive markets are "efficient," and hence that capital controls are "inefficient," rests on the Fundamental Theorem, even though the concept of Pareto optimality has well-known limitations. A corollary of the same argument proposes that, in the absence of distortions, economies typically operate at or near full capacity, at the "natural rate of unemployment." The Fundamental Theorem presumes a perfectly competitive economy, with no externalities, in which consumer tastes are innate and the economy is always in equilibrium (Graaf, 1957). If these conditions do not hold, then the conclusions of the theorem do not hold. Nor is a partial fulfillment of these conditions necessarily superior to their total absence (Lipsey and Lancaster, 1956; Bohm, 1987). The associated Pareto criterion famously ignores all issues of distribution. An economy in which one individual is fabulously rich while others live in grinding poverty may be Pareto optimal.[4]

The Efficient Market Hypothesis portrays financial markets as efficient gatherers and transmitters of information (Malkiel, 1987). When that information includes knowledge of the "true" behavior of the economy ("the fundamentals"), then financial assets embody the true value of their real counterparts, creating an environment in which rational agents trading in these assets can make Pareto-efficient decisions. With rational expectations, agents do not make decisions about the future that are systematically proven to be wrong. Accordingly, asset prices tend to gravitate toward the means of normal probability distributions of the present values of their net revenue streams. The present value embodies all the (incomplete) information on the fundamental determinants of net revenue streams while the variance represents errors owing to information failures. If the fundamentals remain unchanged, the variance will tend to shrink, but changes in the fundamentals, including unexpected changes in government policies, will increase volatility. Policy intervention will increase efficiency *if and only if* the government has a better understanding of economic efficiency and is better informed than the markets.

While the Fundamental Theorem is about the efficiency of the real economy, the Efficient Market Hypothesis is about the link between financial markets and those true "fundamentals."[5] Combined, they present a picture of economic efficiency as dependent upon free markets for goods, labor, and finance—and a minimalist state. Market liberalization is accordingly beneficial because it involves the removal of market distortions, which are by definition inefficient.

This approach comes dangerously close to assuming what it purports to prove. Even if the Pareto criterion is accepted as an appropriate definition of efficiency, use of the Fundamental Theorem and the Efficient Market Hypothesis presupposes that market conditions correspond, at least approximately, to the conditions necessary for the proof of the theorem. If they do not, then defining particular market controls as "allocationally inefficient" is a leap of faith.

Five Expected Benefits of Financial Liberalization

A far better approach, and one that corresponds more closely to the realities of economic policy, is to evaluate measures in terms of the attainment of specific goals, such as economic growth, or levels of employment, or the distribution of income, or at a more microeconomic level, cost minimization, innovation, and the growth of markets. In fact, the benefits that are claimed to derive from the liberalization of capital markets are typically presented as a combination of theoretical advantages and practical policy goals. These benefits can be summarized as:[6]

1. In a world of free capital movements, savings will be directed to the most productive investments without regard for national boundaries. Hence, capital will flow from capital-rich developed countries to opportunity-rich emerging economies.
2. Increased competition will create a more efficient financial system, offering better opportunities for savers, as well as lower costs for borrowers.
3. New financial instruments such as derivatives (futures, swaps, and options) help firms to manage financial risk more effectively.

4. The long-run result should be higher investment and growth.
5. The markets provide a healthy discipline for governments, which encourages better economic policies and performance.[7]

These five claims are predominantly derived from a combination of the conclusions of the Fundamental Theorem—competitive markets will tend to enforce productive efficiency ("savings are directed to the most productive investments") and allocative efficiency ("better opportunities for savers")—together with the Efficient Market Hypothesis: financial markets operate so as to process information efficiently ("new financial instruments"), and certainly better than governments could ("the markets provide a healthy discipline that encourages better economic policies and performance").

The fundamental difficulty that arises in assessing these claims is, of course, that changes in so many factors other than financial liberalization will have had some impact on the various performance indicators. It is not easy to test the claims for any particular benefit. The proposition that the deregulation of A will lead to higher values of B may appear to be refuted by a fall in B, but it could well be claimed that the fall in B would be even greater if A had not been changed. While statistical tests can never be "conclusive," the only possible response to the problem of counterfactual argument is to assemble as much evidence as possible, identifying as precisely as may be done the role of specific variables and relationships, and, of course, to provide a plausible theory explaining the link between A and B.

Comparing Reality with Expectations

Are Savings Directed Toward More Productive Investments?

If there were truly a single international capital market, then savings would be "directed to the most productive investments without regard for national boundaries." Hence, there would be no correlation between the rate of savings in any one nation-state and the rate of investment in that nation-state. Feldstein and Horioka (1980) assessed the degree of capital market integration by estimating the cross-section equation:

$$(I/Y)_i = a + \beta(S/Y)_i + u_{ie} \tag{1}$$

where I/Y is the ratio of investment to national income and S/Y is the ratio of domestic savings to national income. They found that the estimate of β was close to 1, suggesting a close correlation between investment and national savings, and an absence of international capital market integration. Feldstein and Bacchetta (1991) found a value of β equal to 0.79 for the period 1980–86, still significantly different from zero but lower than the estimate of 0.91 for the 1960s and 0.86 for the 1970s, a trend confirmed in Feldstein (1994). A very large number of subsequent examinations have found the Feldstein-Horioka result (that β is not significantly different from 1) to be remarkably robust (Coakley, Kulasi, and Smith, 1995).

Another way of presenting the same result is to point to the fact that current account imbalances do not, in the medium term, typically amount to large proportions of national income (see table 7.2). Even in the 1980s, when current account imbalances rose sharply above earlier ratios (as is consistent with the lower correlation between investment and national savings), they did not exceed 3% of GDP. This compares with the average UK current account surplus of 4.5% of GDP over the period 1880–1913. Financial liberalization in the modern era may have produced very large *gross* capital flows, but it has not been associated with larger *net* international flows of capital than those experienced under the gold standard before the First World War. One might suspect that the majority of trans-border flows may be responding to different incentives from optimizing the allocation of real investment.[8]

This lack of integration of national capital markets is further indicated by the persistent divergence of real rates of return (Blundell-Wignall and Browne, 1991). Frankel (1992) decomposes the real rate of interest into the covered interest differential, the exchange risk premium, and the expected real depreciation. He finds that there has been substantial convergence of covered differentials (as does Marston, 1993), but currency premia (exchange risk plus expected real depreciation) are

Table 7.2 Current account balance as a proportion of GDP

	1964–1973	1974–1983	1984–1993
Canada	0.85	1.50	2.74
France	0.28	1.06	0.43
Germany	1.11	1.13	2.92
Italy	1.93	1.69	1.08
Japan	1.08	0.78	2.76
United Kingdom	1.33	1.35	1.93
United States	0.40	0.49	2.19

Source: OECD National Accounts, OECD Main Economic Indicators.
Note: Average of absolute values of annual ratios of current account balance to GDP.

high. This suggests that differentials in national real rates of return are sustained, at least in part, by the barrier of currency risk. This hypothesis is strengthened by the findings of Sinn (1992) and Bayoumi and Rose (1993) that there is no correlation between regional savings and investment rates within countries, and Bayoumi's (1990) finding that there was no correlation between national savings and investment in the gold-standard era. It seems that exchange-rate fluctuations inhibit the full integration of capital markets and provide the opportunity for national governments to pursue relatively independent monetary policies.[9] The existence of separate currencies and national jurisdictions appears to create a more powerful tendency to balance the current account than is the case between regions of a single currency area.[10] The peculiar ability of the United States to sustain a persistent current account deficit reinforces this conclusion.

That peculiar ability has ensured that the net transfer of resources has not been from the "capital-rich developed countries" to "opportunity-rich emerging economies," The largest net transfer in the period 1983–1992 has been to the United States, at an average rate of $100 billion per year. Over the same period, the net transfer to all developing countries amounted to an average of $1 billion per year, and almost all of that inflow was concentrated in the final two years of the period (UN, 1993). Indeed, for most of the 1980s, resources were transferred out of the developing world. During the 1980s, the United States became the world's biggest debtor—hardly an example of capital flowing from capital rich to capital poor. And the flow to the United States has not diminished. In 1994, the net transfer to the United States was $112 billion; in 1995, $119 billion (UN, 1996).

There has, however, been a dramatic change in the mid-1990s with respect to flows to developing countries. In 1993, net transfers to developing countries on an expenditure basis (excluding additions to reserves) rose to $45 billion, and in 1994, to $48 billion. Of this latter amount, $20 billion went to Latin America (UN, 1995). These inflows have been the result of capital liberalization, the development of stock markets, and the consequent inflow of portfolio investment, together, in Southeast Asia, with an increase in foreign direct investment. The growth of portfolio investment in Latin America, replacing the bank lending that precipitated the debt crisis, has slackened the credit constraint under which these economies have suffered since the early 1980s. Unfortunately, in Latin America the increase in real investment has been only about one-third of the net capital inflow (Devlin, Ffrench-Davis, and Griffith-Jones,

1995). The beneficial effects of capital inflows have been overshadowed by the impact of stock-market volatility, particularly following the Mexican financial crisis in 1994.

The cautionary comment of Mussa and Goldstein (1993, p. 293) should be borne in mind: "Over the past two decades, the developing countries that relied most on foreign saving—defined as the top one-third of countries ranked by the ratio of all capital flows to GNP—tended to have higher inflation, higher fiscal deficits, lower investment, and lower growth than those that relied less on foreign saving."

As noted above, while *gross* capital flows have been very large, *net* flows have been very small and have tended to flow toward the developed countries, particularly the United States. Furthermore, flows of finance do not necessarily correspond to flows of real investment. The evidence is not consistent with the claims that the integration of international financial markets has created a market where flows of real savings ignore national boundaries, and in which there has been a flow of capital toward the "opportunity rich" developing world. In so far as there has, in the past five years, been a flow of capital toward "emerging markets," it is a flow that has proved to be very volatile, with investors reluctant to purchase other than the most liquid of financial assets. The role of these emerging markets is discussed further below.

Are There Better Opportunities for Savers and Lower Costs for Borrowers?

That liberalization, and the consequent explosion in the size and variety of asset markets, has created a wider range of placement opportunities for savers is undeniable. This is particularly evident in the changing pattern of assets held by institutional investors. In the United States and Japan, the proportion of pension funds' assets invested in foreign securities was negligible in 1980, but by 1993, it had risen to over 7% and over 12%, respectively. Over the same period, the commitment to foreign assets by British pension funds rose from 10% to over 20% of total assets (Edey and Hviding, 1995, table 10). The greater choice and spread implicit in portfolio diversification will, *ceteris paribus*, produce welfare gains to savers (Obstfeld, 1993).

The growth of institutional investors (see table 7.3) has been a major factor behind the growth of the global capital market. So has financial innovation, which, as noted above, is an essential component of the management of risk. Expanding institutional investment and widening innovation have stimulated each other. The competition between

Table 7.3 Financial assets managed by collective institutions as a percentage of household financial assets

	1980	1985	1990*
Canada	20.4	24.9	29.7
France	10.6	23.6	36.3
Germany	22.6	29.0	35.1
Italy		2.9	16.1
Japan	15.6	20.2	26.4
United Kingdom	41.5	53.1	58.6
United States	20.0	26.0	31.2

Source: BIS, 1992. 62nd annual report. Basle.
* For Italy and United Kingdom, 1989. Collective institutions are pension funds and life assurance companies, and collective investment institutions.

institutional investors manifests itself as a persistent requirement to demonstrate superior returns in order to attract more funds. Successive high short-term gains are more effective in this respect than longer term returns. This is so even if over a number of years the overall return on successive short-term investments is no greater, and perhaps even somewhat smaller, than a long-term investment. An institutional investor pursuing a short-term strategy that tops the performance tables in nine years out of ten will tend to attract more funds than the long-term investor who performs extremely well once in ten years. Edwards (1993, p. 50) reports that, in the United States, "the typical stock is now held for an average of a little over two years, compared to over four years ten years ago and seven years in 1960. The average holding period for institutional investors is less than two years, compared to almost five years for individuals." The enormous flow of funds into institutional hands requires a persistent search for new investment opportunities in which the returns are high and there is a ready opportunity of exit. Innovation is geared toward these two goals.

However, there is no evidence whatsoever that the liberalization of financial markets, and the massive expansion of financial assets that has come in its wake, has led to any lowering of costs to borrowers. On the contrary, in all G7 countries, real interest rates have risen sharply in the 1980s, as compared with the Bretton Woods era of capital controls. Other than in the exceptional period of the 1970s, when very high and volatile inflation rates in an era of sharp oil price rises resulted in negative real interest rates in many G7 countries, the period in which capital flows were strictly controlled enjoyed the *lowest* real long-term interest rates of modern times.

Table 7.4 Long-term real interest rates in the G7

	1870s–1890s	1900–1913	1956–1973	1974–1980	1981–1993
Canada		1.6	2.2	0.3	6.7
France	4.2	1.8	1.0	0.4	5.7
Germany	3.4	3.5	3.0	3.0	4.5
Italy			1.1	-5.0	4.2
Japan			0.3	0.5	4.4
United Kingdom	2.9	2.7	1.8	-3.3	4.5
United States	6.1	2.3	1.1	-0.3	5.6
Average	4.1	2.6	1.7	0.0	5.1

Sources: OECD *Historical Statistics*; OECD *National Accounts*; Homer and Sylla, 1991.
Notes: Average refers, for all periods, to the average of France, Germany, United Kingdom, and the United States. Conversion to real terms is by GDP deflator.

The only comparable period is that from 1933 to 1939, when restrictions were also imposed, and the average real interest rate (for France, Germany, the United Kingdom, and the United States) was only 1.7%.

By contrast, real long-term interest rates in the 1980s were the *highest* in modern times. This places a very considerable burden on borrowers, whether they are governments or private agents, and greatly increases the danger of national and international debt burdens rising exponentially as real interest rates exceed rates of GDP growth.[11] High interest rates were also typical of the late nineteenth-century gold standard, an earlier period of free capital movements, despite the fact that exchange rates were very stable (see table 7.4). In neither period of open international financial markets does the prediction of "lower costs for borrowers" correspond to the facts.

These broad observations are reinforced by the findings of Alesina, Grilli, and Milesi-Ferretti (1994) and Grilli and Milesi-Ferretti (1995). In analyses that incorporate a range of institutional variables (such as central bank independence and the political leanings of the government), they find that both in a sample of OECD countries, 1950–89, and in a wider sample of 61 countries, 1966–89, capital controls are associated with lower real interest rates.

Do Derivatives Help Firms to Manage Financial Risk?

The privatization of foreign-exchange risk with the collapse of Bretton Woods has been a major motivation behind the liberalization of international capital markets. It is in the foreign exchange markets and the commodity markets to which they are closely related that derivatives originated, and it is therefore no surprise that increased risk has promoted an enormous expansion in the scale and variety of derivative instruments. The BIS (1996) estimated that the notional principal outstanding in financial derivatives had risen from just over $1,000 billion in 1986 to around $56,500 billion in 1995.[12] A little less than 30% of these are traded instruments, the rest being provided over the counter. Turnover in derivatives markets stood at a daily average of $1,450 billion in 1995, 40% of which comprised exchange traded contracts (BIS, 1996).

The post–Bretton Woods era has been characterized not only by significantly greater fluctuations in exchange rates but also by greater variability in interest rates. Woodall (1995) states that an estimated 85% of America's *Fortune 500* companies make some use of derivatives to insulate themselves from swings in interest rates and currencies. The growth of derivatives markets is part of the process of liberalization. In a world of fixed rates and capital controls, derivatives had a far smaller role than they do today. It is clearly true that liberalization has spawned derivatives. It is equally true that fluctuating rates and liberalization have *created* the demand for derivatives.[13]

The essence of derivatives trading is the hedging of risk. Risk is, of course, transferred from one side of the transaction to the other. The pooling of risk, by the familiar principle of insurance, simply spreads the gains and losses more thinly. Nonetheless, the expansion of derivatives trading has led to some suggestion that risk has actually been increased. In an important sense, this alarm is well founded. While the underlying risk associated with any given asset may not have changed, the sheer complexity of the structure of derivative positions limits the ability of firms to monitor and manage risk effectively. The well-publicized examples of the abuse of derivatives markets in the cases of Orange County and Barings Bank indicate the difficulties that senior executives may have in understanding what is being done in their names. Similar difficulties are faced by the regulators.[14]

A further element of risk may be introduced by the very mathematical models that are used to price derivatives. Those models are typically derived from the physical sciences and are based on the characteristics of the probability distributions of random movements. The fundamental Black-Scholes model, for example, is based on the assumption that price movements follow the same log-normal distribution as the Brownian motion displayed by many physical phenomena. In fact, as far as price movements are concerned, more price changes tend to be concentrated at the extremes than the log-normal distribution would predict.[15] In these circumstances, the mathematical models that drive much of today's programmed trading will tend to price events at the extremes incorrectly.

Even more important is the problem that may undermine even the best-designed derivatives hedge: liquidity. In 1993, Metallgesellschaft AG, Germany's fourteenth largest industrial company, was almost ruined by losses in excess of $1 billion suffered in derivatives trading in the oil market by a United States subsidiary, and by the refusal of the company's lead banker, Deutsche Bank, to finance the trading strategy further. It is now widely accepted that the hedging strategy employed was misconceived, representing not a hedge but a speculation (Mello and Parsons, 1995). However, Christopher Culp and Merton Miller (1995) have defended Metallgesellschaft's trading strategy, arguing that the fault lay with Deutsche Bank's refusal to fund the financial strategy over the longer period in which it would bear fruit. This raises another question: even if it were well designed, is it right to analyze the hedging strategy *as if* Metallgesellschaft faced a perfect capital market and could therefore borrow virtually unlimited sums today with the prospect of gain a long time in the future? Risk aversion is likely to rise with the scale of indebtedness, a phenomenon that Kalecki (1937) referred to as the "principle of increasing risk."[16] In the Metallgesellschaft case, lack of liquidity created severe problems for the firm alone. Aversion to risk is infectious, rises with indebtedness, and can provoke a general rush to cash that destroys even the most sophisticated hedging strategies and so can pose systemic risk. Liquidity ultimately rests on a diversity of perceptions of asset values. Where there is a tendency for perceptions to be shared and transmitted, there is an enhanced possibility of cumulative liquidity crises. In these circumstances, the "management of financial risk" is an illusion.

The proposition that financial liberalization has been accompanied by the benefits of growing numbers of derivatives must, therefore, be heavily qualified. Liberalization and fluctuating exchange rates have created many of the risks that derivatives are designed to hedge.[17] The growth of derivatives markets may increase systemic risk, both because the very complexity of some derivative instruments and hedging strategies creates severe informational problems for both management and regulators and because derivatives trading may increase exposure to liquidity crises.

Has the Result Been Higher Investment and Growth?

This is the most important test of all, for it derives not from criteria generated within particular theoretical models but from practical policy goals. A higher rate of growth, all other things being equal, results in the higher standards of living that are, after all, the fundamental objective of economic activity. Of course, a simple assertion about the benefits of growth must itself be qualified to take into account any implications for the content and distribution of national income, and for environmental degradation. But growth and sustainable human development are highly correlated. Hence, for the purpose of this chapter, the criterion for distinguishing between beneficial and damaging financial regimes is whether growth is higher or lower, and high rates of investment are presumed to be associated with high growth.[18]

Of course, investment and growth are sensitive to a very wide range of factors. However, disappointing results over the last twenty years throw doubt on any hope for the positive impact of financial liberalization.

Table 7.5 (which is adapted from Felix, 1995) presents an examination of changes in the share of investment to GDP as between the Bretton

Table 7.5 Investment to GDP ratio as compared with the 1960–71 average (*Numbers of countries with ratio higher or lower*)

	1972–81	1982–91
All countries (54)		
Decade ratio higher	32	19
Decade ratio lower	22	35
All non-oil exporting countries (45)		
Decade ratio higher	25	15
Decade ratio lower	20	30
OECD countries (20)		
Decade ratio higher	7	4
Decade ratio lower	13	16
Latin America (10)		
Decade ratio higher	7	1
Decade ratio lower	3	9
East and South East Asia (7)		
Decade ratio higher	6	6
Decade ratio lower	1	1

Source: Felix,1995. Financial globalization versus free trade: The case for the Tobin tax. UNCTAD Discussion Paper no. 108. Using data source World Bank, 1994. *Averting the old age crisis: Policies to protect the old and promote growth*. New York: Oxford University Press.
Notes: OECD countries are Australia, Austria, Belgium, Canada, Denmark, Finland, France, Germany, Greece, Ireland, Italy, Japan, Netherlands, New Zealand, Norway, Spain, Sweden, Switzerland, the UK, and the US. Latin American countries are Argentina, Brazil, Chile, Colombia, Dominican Republic, Ecuador, Guatemala, Mexico, Peru, and Venezuela. South and Southeast Asian countries are Hong Kong, Indonesia, S. Korea, Malaysia, Philippines, Singapore, and Thailand.

Woods era of fixed exchange rates and capital controls (1960–71) and the current regime of floating rates and open capital markets. The sample of countries covers all OECD, Asian, and Latin American countries whose 1983 GDP exceeds $10 billion; all Middle Eastern and North African countries with GDPs above $7.5 billion; and all sub-Saharan African countries with GDPs above $5 billion—a total of fifty-four countries.[19] The comparisons in the table are ordinal because of the variable quality of the data (Felix, 1995, p. 6). In each category, the table presents the number of countries for which the average investment/GDP ratio in that particular decade was higher, or lower, than the 1960–71 average. It is clear that the predominant tendency has been for investment to fall as a share of GDP. Moreover, declines have become more pronounced in the period 1982–91 as capital liberalization has become more widespread, with two-thirds of the countries in the sample experiencing declines. Three-quarters of OECD countries had lower investment/GDP ratios in the 1980s than in the 1960s, as did nine out of ten Latin American countries. Investment in Latin America had typically been higher in the 1970s, but was cut sharply by the accumulation of high levels of indebtedness. Only in East and Southeast Asia was there a persistent pattern of higher rates of investment in the later periods. Most of the G7 countries also experienced declining investment/GDP ratios in the 1980s, the two exceptions being Canada and Japan.

Given that investment is highly correlated with domestic savings, a declining ratio of investment to GDP suggests a fall in the overall domestic propensity to save (private plus public). Other things being equal, this will be associated with a lower rate of growth. In developed

Table 7.6 Investment to GDP ratios in the G7, 1964–1973 and 1983–1992

	A. 1964–1973	B. 1983–1992	B/A
Canada	18.3	21.5	1.17
France	24.0	20.6	0.86
Germany	26.0	20.3	0.78
Italy	26.9	21.3	0.79
Japan	29.7	30.2	1.02
United Kingdom	18.8	17.7	0.94
United States	19.2	18.3	0.95

Source: OECD, *National Accounts, various years.*
Note: Gross domestic fixed capital formation as a % of GDP, averaged for each 10-year period.

economies, low levels of investment and slower GDP growth will tend to be accompanied by growing unemployment and declines in *public* saving (often in the form of increasing public deficits), whether due to rising social expenditure or reduced tax revenues. In Japan, where the investment/GDP ratio in the 1980s did not fall,[20] social security spending is particularly low, and high levels of employment have been maintained by the absorption of workers into low-productivity nonfinancial services

Table 7.7 Growth rate of GDP per head as compared with the 1960–1971 average (*Number of countries with the average growth rate for the period higher or lower than 1960–1971*)

	1972–1981	1982–1991
All countries (total 57)		
Growth rate higher	18	10
Growth rate lower	39	47
All non-oil exporting countries (total 48)		
Growth rate higher	11	7
Growth rate lower	37	41
OECD countries (total 20)		
Growth rate higher	1	2
Growth rate lower	19	18
Latin America (total 10)		
Growth rate higher	4	1
Growth rate lower	6	9
East and Southeast Asia (total 7)		
Growth rate higher	5	3
Growth rate lower	2	4

Source: Felix, 1995. Financial globalization versus free trade: The case for the Tobin tax. UNCTAD Discussion Paper no. 108. Using data source World Bank, 1994. . *Averting the old age crisis: Policies to protect the old and promote growth.* New York: Oxford University Press.

Table 7.8 Growth in GDP per head in the major economies

	A. 1961–70	B. 1979–90	B/A
France	5.0	2.0	0.40
Germany	4.3	1.9	0.45
Italy	6.2	1.9	0.31
Japan	9.1	3.0	0.33
United Kingdom	3.3	2.0	0.60
United States	2.3	1.1	0.58

Sources: European Economy, Annual Economic Reports; OECD *National Accounts*, 1979–1991.

(Eatwell, 1995b). In developing countries, a declining share of investment is accompanied by a growing share of output associated with informal employment.

The growth of output per head in the major economies has fallen to between 60% and 30% of the growth rates that prevailed until 1972. The lesser falls have been experienced in those countries in which growth was relatively low in the earlier period. The inferior economic performance of the G7 countries in the 1980s as compared with the 1960s has also been manifest in rising unemployment and declining rates of productivity growth in the manufacturing industry (Eatwell, 1996).

The overall conclusion is disturbing. Far from there being an increase in investment and growth, the decade of the 1980s (characterized by financial liberalization and very large increases in gross financial flows among countries) has also seen a sharp deterioration in economic performance in the G7, the OECD as a whole, and in virtually all developing countries with the exception of some countries in East and Southeast Asia. Of course, the fact that liberalization and deteriorating economic performance have coincided does not prove that one has caused the other. But given that inferior economic performance is a common phenomenon shared by almost all countries, then it is appropriate to look for a common change in circumstances that might have affected them all. The change in the international financial system since 1973 is just such a common change. At any rate, there is no evidence of a link between financial liberalization and higher investment and growth—quite the opposite.[21]

Do Liberal Financial Markets Provide a Healthy Discipline that Encourages Better Economic Policies?

There can be no doubt that liberal financial markets do affect economic policy, sometimes in a quite dramatic manner. Indeed, a common characterization of financial liberalization is that it severely constrains the exercise of discretionary policies by national governments (Bryant, 1987; Keohane and Milner, 1996). But this introduces the question of whether the impact is "healthy" and, indeed, how "healthy" should be defined.

While the first question will be systematically explored in the third section of this chapter, the discussion can be introduced here by a few remarks about how "healthy" should be defined. A minimal definition might be that a healthy economic policy should not contain elements that are in direct contradiction with one another. An excellent example of a policy stance that is internally contradictory was that adopted by the

British government in the summer of 1992. At one and the same time, the government attempted to use monetary policy to maintain a fixed parity between the pound and the Deutsche mark and to weather a severe recession characterized by rising unemployment and falling asset values (particularly house prices). However, the level of interest rates required to maintain the external parity exacerbated domestic economic problems. The policy stance became literally incredible. No one could possibly believe that the government would be prepared to raise interest rates to protect the exchange rate while further depressing domestic asset prices and deepening the recession. It was this contradiction that was exploited by the financial markets in a speculative run that forced the pound out of the Exchange Rate Mechanism (ERM) and precipitated a 20% devaluation against the Deutsche mark.

While the day of the devaluation has been labeled "Black Wednesday," the event has been hailed by many commentators as a return to rational economic policy and the beginning of the recovery from recession.[22] In this sense, the behavior of the markets may be said to be "healthy" in that they exposed a policy stance that was internally contradictory—but that is all. There is nothing in the markets' behavior in this case from which to infer any evaluation of the relative merits of using monetary policy, either to maintain the exchange rate parity or to expand the domestic economy. For at the same time as the contradictions of British policy were exposed, the French government managed to convince the markets that it was willing to sacrifice all other policy objectives to the maintenance of the parity between the franc and the Deutsche mark. Once any hint of a contradiction was eliminated, speculation against the French franc ceased.[23]

So, a clear distinction must be drawn between the healthy exposure of contradictory policies and the healthy alignment of policy with a particular theoretical conception of economic efficiency. The former does not depend on any particular theory of the workings of the economy. The latter attempts to identify a desirable, or even ideal, economic policy and relate financial policy to the attainment of that ideal. A desirable policy can be defined only in terms of some expected relationship between action and outcomes—that is, in terms of a theory of the economy. Neoclassical welfare economics is the dominant theory of economic policy in microeconomics and macroeconomics (although in macroeconomics the prevalence of ad hoc theorizing makes for a more varied policy framework). There is even a tendency to identify the conclusions of neoclassical theory with "the fundamentals." Why the relationship between the financial sphere and the real sphere may be less than healthy will be explored in the next section.

Summing Up

When confronted with the actual experience of liberalization, we see that the representative list of "benefits" is not convincing. None of the five benefits appears to have been substantially realized; and in many cases, the liberalization of international financial markets has been associated with a sharp deterioration in economic performance. Of course, although the accumulation of evidence is disturbing, the coexistence of liberalization and poor economic performance might be only coincidence. Nonetheless, it is worth exploring whether this result can be accounted for by a different analysis of the behavior of financial markets from that which sustains the conventional wisdom.

Explaining the Record of Liberalization

The issue to be considered is the relationship between the operations of the financial markets and a "healthy" economic policy. The analysis in this section will suggest that the behavior of financial markets can impose a deflationary bias on the real economy.

Financial Markets and the Real Economy

Two theories of the real economy appear to play a major role in forming the perceptions of financial market operators. The first deals with unemployment, the second with fiscal deficits.

The Non-Inflation Accelerating Rate of Unemployment

The behavior of the bond markets today suggests a prevailing market view according to which, other than in the most depressed conditions, any indication of higher levels of activity and employment will result in higher interest rates. The fear of impending increases in interest rates, and of consequent capital losses, precipitates a sell-off in the bond market, raising the long-term rate of interest, as expected. Depending upon the national origins of the sell-off, the exchange rate may rise as well. Higher interest rates, whether or not aided and abetted by a higher exchange rate, tend to result in a slowdown in the growth in output and employment, aborting policies designed to increase activity.

The presumed link between activity and accelerating inflation is associated with the concept of a natural rate of unemployment (Friedman, 1968; Phelps, 1968). If, as the natural rate hypothesis suggests, the economy has a persistent tendency to gravitate toward the natural rate, deviating from it only in the short run, then any systematic upswing in activity will precipitate accelerating inflation with upward pressure on interest rates.[24] But is the hypothesis correct? Does it indeed truly represent the "fundamentals" of the real economy? If not, then the actions of the financial markets are not "healthy."

Some doubt is cast on the value of the concept of the natural rate by its propensity to shadow the actual rate of unemployment. In 1970, with actual unemployment at 4.8%, the Economic Report of the President suggested that the natural rate of unemployment in the United States was 3.8%. In 1979, with the actual rate at 5.8%, the estimated natural rate had risen to 5.1%. By 1983, with the actual rate at 9%, the Economic Report of the President estimated the natural rate at 7% (Gordon, 1987). Commenting on a similar peripatetic tendency of the "natural rate" in European economies, Robert Solow (1990, p. 70) argues that:

> European experience can only be taken as evidence against the meaningfulness of a stable and well-defined natural rate.... Attempts to salvage the idea of a well-defined equilibrium unemployment rate require the equilibrium rate itself to have undergone drastic change between the 1970s and the 1980s. To any reasonably sceptical person, it all smacks of the invocation of epicycles to salvage Ptolemaic astronomy, but apparently with rather less success.[25]

Solow points to evidence that the relationship between inflation and unemployment can be altered by macroeconomic policy. Just as the low growth of the past decade has raised the natural rate, so boosting demand, while it may raise inflation in the short run, will in due course lower the natural rate. In other words, active macroeconomic policy could be a way to cure "structural" unemployment. Yet, it is exactly the possibility of a short-term increase in inflation that alarms the bond market and results in the negation of expansionary policies. The bond market behaves as if the economy is at or about the natural rate of unemployment.

The higher levels of unemployment characteristic of the 1980s may be in part attributable to this persistent tendency of the bond market to regard the rate of unemployment as the natural rate. Reactions to changes in the level of activity are typically asymmetric: all increases in activity are likely to precipitate falling bond prices while decreases in activity are evidence of praise-worthy financial discipline.

Markets' Reactions to Fiscal Deficits

The impact of the natural-rate hypothesis on market behavior is reinforced by the markets' attitude toward fiscal deficits. Increases in fiscal deficits are believed to be inflationary and to precipitate increases in interest rates. Consequently, deficits incur the displeasure of the bond market. There is a clear relationship between national budget deficits and the real rate of interest (Orr, Edey, and Kennedy, 1995; BIS, 1995). Once again the market is imposing persistent deflationary pressure.

Other than in exceptional years, the current account balances of the OECD countries taken as a whole fluctuate closely around zero. Accordingly, the sum of fiscal deficits must be equal to the excess of private savings over private investment—that is, roughly

$$S_i(G - T) = S_i(S - I) \quad (2)$$

where G is government expenditure, T is tax revenue, S is private-sector saving, I is private- sector investment, and S_i indicates the summation over all OECD countries.

The decline in investment and in activity that has been characteristic of the 1980s will tend inevitably to be associated with rising fiscal deficits. The problem is, which causes which? Similarly, the steady increase in public-sector debt that has been another characteristic of the 1980s may not so much be a product of profligate government borrowing in liberalized capital markets as be a result of the decline in investment relative to private-sector saving.[26] In both cases, the theoretical issue is whether the causal relationships between the financial balance of the government sector and the financial balance of the private sector can be clearly identified. Which are the independent variables and which the dependent variables?

The theory underpinning the bond markets' response to public-sector deficits is the fiscal counterpart to the natural-rate hypothesis. Just as the operation of the competitive labor market is supposed to ensure that the economy always gravitates toward the natural rate of unemployment, so the operation of a competitive capital market is supposed to ensure the balance between savings and investment at the natural rate. Accordingly, it is argued that government deficits "crowd out" private-sector investment; and indeed, as equation (2) indicates, public deficits must be accompanied by an excess of private savings over private investment. The increase in private savings is, according to the Ricardian Equivalence Theorem, a rational consumer reaction to the increase in government debt (Barro, 1974). However, investigation of the "crowding out" phenomenon has indicated that crowding out is a characteristic of the operations of financial markets, not of the underlying real economy (Blanchard, 1987). This in turn suggests that the behavior of the financial markets is creating a self-fulfilling prophecy: public spending crowds out private investment because the market reaction to public spending is to raise long-term interest rates. The high interest rates demanded by the bond markets tend to produce downward pressures on private-sector investment and upward pressures on the private savings rate, further exacerbating fiscal deficits.

The typical reaction of bond markets to changes in the labor market and in the government's fiscal stance suggests that they behave as if the economy will tend to be in a perfectly competitive equilibrium, ensuring that there is an underlying tendency toward full employment and an efficient allocation of resources. If this is not a true model of the economy—that is, if the economy does not operate in this fashion—then the markets' "discipline" may well be inappropriate and damaging. This will be particularly true if the financial markets operate in a manner that is in some respects self-fulfilling—that is, the market determines the fundamentals—which leads us to a quite different explanation of the relationship between financial markets and the real economy.

How Market Views Are Formed

The interpretation of the impact of financial-market liberalization is, as has been seen above, heavily dependent upon the theory of the real economy and of the interaction between the real economy and financial markets. An examination of how market views are formed suggests an alternative to the orthodox combination of neoclassical welfare economics and the Efficient Market Hypothesis. In this alternative theory, the level of output in the economy is determined by the level of effective demand, and it is assumed that there is no tendency for that demand to gravitate to a level commensurate with full employment growth. Financial markets influence output, and the trend of output, via their impact on effective demand.[27]

In his *General Theory*, Keynes provided quite a different description of financial market behavior, and of the interaction between real and financial markets, from that assumed by the conventional wisdom. Keynes likened the operations of financial markets to a "beauty contest." He was not referring to a 1930s equivalent of the Miss World contest, in which judges declare a winner. He had in mind a competition then popular in the British tabloid Sunday press in which readers were asked to rank pictures of young women in the order that they believed would correspond to the average preferences of the competitors as a whole. So in order to win, the player should not express his or her own preferences, nor even the genuine preferences of average opinion, but instead should anticipate "what average opinion expects average opinion to be" (Keynes, 1936, p. 156). In the same way, the key to success in the financial markets is not what the individual investor considers to be the virtues or otherwise of any particular policy but what he or she believes everyone else in the market will believe everyone else will think.

Since the markets are driven by average opinion about what average opinion will be, an enormous premium is placed on any information or signals that might provide a guide to the swings in average opinion and to how average opinion will react to changing events. These signals must be simple and clear-cut. Sophisticated interpretations of the economic data would not provide a clear lead. Hence, the money markets and foreign exchange markets become dominated by simple slogans—larger fiscal deficits lead to higher interest rates, an increased money supply results in higher inflation, public expenditure is bad, falling unemployment always leads to accelerating inflation, and so on.

However, such slogans could not dominate market behavior if the simple economic propositions embedded within them were consistently shown to be false. Profits could be earned by those who ignore the slogans—those, for example, who buy bonds as unemployment falls or fiscal deficits rise. If such behavior were to be successful, "average opinion" would tend to change. So if the "true model" of the real economy were the neoclassical model, then "average opinion" would tend to oscillate around the predictions of neoclassical theory. The peculiarity of the Keynesian model is that monetary and financial factors are assigned a dominant role in the determination of real economic performance. The "true model" is not independent of the behavior of financial markets. It is, therefore, possible for "average opinion" to become self-fulfilling. If the markets believe that higher fiscal deficits result in higher real rates of interest, then so they will. Of course, "average opinion" is not formed in a vacuum. It has its own history and is heavily influenced by fashionable theories and by the exercise of the financial powers of national governments, particularly the more economically powerful ones. The history of capital-market liberalization might be represented as a swing in the balance of influence from a postwar theory of economic policy that enjoined national governments to limit international capital movements to the present-day theory that encourages free capital movements and the abdication of national regulatory powers.[28]

Keynes's characterization of the operation of financial markets suggests two ways in which financial-market liberalization might result in deterioration in overall economic performance. First, a market that operates as a beauty contest is likely to be highly unstable and prone to occasional severe loss of liquidity, as all opinion tends to shift in the same direction. This will increase the cost of capital and sometimes lead to severe capital shortages—both factors that will tend to discourage investment and reduce levels of activity in the medium term. Second, the operation of the beauty contest in a liberal environment may produce systematic changes in the behavior of both public and private sectors. Although these changes may succeed in reducing instability, they achieve this only at the cost of a medium-term deterioration in overall economic performance. Both effects, which have bearings on policymaking, will be introduced here. In the final section, there is an evaluation of the impact on private-sector performance.

Consequences for Public Policy

An Erratic Discipline

The tendency of financial markets to move erratically is an important qualification of the alleged "healthy" discipline they impose on governments. Woodall (1995) points out that IMF as argues the discipline exercised by capital markets over policy is neither infallible nor is it applied smoothly and consistently and herself suggests that "discipline is often doled out erratically, with waves of excessive optimism being followed by excessive pessimism." There have been three prominent examples of erratic market behavior: (1) the rise and fall of the dollar in the 1980s—the index of the dollar effective exchange rate swung from 105 in 1980, to 145 in 1985, to 100 in 1990;[29] (2) the rise and fall of world bond markets in 1993 and 1994; and (3) the crisis in the Mexican peso at the end of 1994. What is particularly striking about the second and third examples is that they are both clearly linked to financial market liberalization.[30]

As far as the fluctuations in the bond market are concerned, the BIS (1995) attributes the fall of bond prices to:

1. Overshooting in 1993 (i.e., excessively high prices).
2. Speculative excesses fueled by "leverage which allowed participants to take large exposures with relatively little own capital, either by borrowing or using derivatives."
3. "Institutional features and market practices" including hedging strategies. Moreover, "an important force linking yield movements across markets was the generalised retrenchment by non-resident, especially US, investors." (pp. 112–116)

The overall conclusion is that there is significant potential for "medium-term deviations from realistic views about sustainable levels (fundamentals).... Such misalignments have great potential costs in terms of a misallocation of resources. They also heighten the risk of abrupt and disorderly corrections and hence of broader financial instability" (BIS, 1995, p. 116).

It was just such a "disorderly correction" that in 1995 forced the United States and the IMF into the unaccustomed role of lender of last resort to the Mexican money markets and that compelled Mexico to increase its already crippling burden of foreign debt. Mexico had been pursuing the policy stance recommended by the IMF: a stable exchange rate with the dollar to act as a "nominal peg" to the inflation rate, and liberalization of its capital markets (by selling dollar-denominated instruments). As the stable exchange rate encouraged imports, capital flowed in to cover the deficit and acquire a 20% return. The possibility of devaluation, a perfectly rational step in the light of Mexico's steadily deteriorating current account and overly restrictive monetary policy, produced a dramatic rush out of Mexican paper, provoking a classic liquidity crisis and real recession in Mexico (Taylor and Schlefer, 1995). As the BIS (1995) comments, the crisis was precipitated by financial factors despite the fact that external deficits in Mexico have this time coincided with both microeconomic and macroeconomic 'fundamentals' that were healthy by any standards. The Mexican economy, far from staying "healthy," became distinctly "unhealthy," with severe social consequences.

The Mexican example also exposes an ambiguity in the use of the term "fundamentals." In some discussions, this term is used to suggest the "true model" of the economy. In others, it is used more pragmatically to mean simply a position that is sustainable. Of course, if the "true model" is indeed "true," then these two interpretations can amount to the same thing. But if it is not, then the definition of what is sustainable may itself be a function of self-fulfilling behavior of the financial markets.

If financial markets are to promote "healthy" policy, then the model of the economy implicit in market behavior must be a "true" model, for if it is not, the discipline enforced by markets may not be healthy. This does not mean that the outcome implied by market behavior will not indeed be forthcoming—only that that outcome will not necessarily correspond to real economic efficiency. There is nothing efficient about zero inflation and 10% unemployment, for example. If market behavior is not based on a true model, or if the performance of the real economy is not independent of financial market behavior, then erratic and disorderly market movements are not merely "overshooting" or temporary fluctuations around a true mean. They may be the determinants of systematically inefficient behavior.

Governments in Search of Credibility

The liberalization of financial markets has clearly reduced the power of governments to manipulate the economy. In fixed exchange rate systems (such as the ERM), governments face the "impossibility problem": the impossibility of sustaining fixed exchange rates, free capital movements, and an independent monetary policy. With flexible exchange rates, control over short-term rates is recovered, to some degree, but long-term rates are still subject to the whims and judgments of the international bond traders. Moreover, control over short-term rates is recovered only if, as with the U.S. Federal Reserve Bank, the authorities are apparently unconcerned about movements in the exchange rate[31]—a rare luxury, and perhaps a costly one. The markets also place powerful constraints on the exercise of fiscal policy. Orr, Edey, and Kennedy (1995) find that real interest rates are highest in countries with the largest structural budget deficits and current account deficits (other than the United States).

If the financial markets are simply enforcing the logic of real economic efficiency, strengthening the self-adjusting powers of competitive markets, then the "disciplining" of governments would be benign; but if markets are pursuing the rules of a beauty contest and imposing self-fulfilling prejudices on the workings of the real economy, then the outcome may be very damaging. The overwhelming scale of potential capital flows means that governments must today, as never before, attempt to maintain market "credibility." Credibility has become the keystone of policymaking in the nineties (King, 1995). A credible government is a government that pursues a policy that is "market friendly"—that is, a policy that is in accordance with what the markets believe to be "sound" and "efficient." Particularly favored are measures designed to meet a "prudent" predetermined monetary target or imposing nominal anchors on monetary policy, and on balancing the budget (preferably by cutting public expenditures rather than raising taxes). Governments that fail to pursue "sound" and "prudent" policies are forced to pay a premium on the interest costs of financing their programs. Severe loss of credibility will lead to a financial crisis. The determination of what is credible, and how governments lose credibility, is a product of the beauty contest.

The BIS (1995) sums up the situation:

> In the financial landscape which has been emerging over the past two decades, the likelihood of extreme price movements may well be greater and their consequences in all probability further reaching.... At the macro level, the new landscape puts a premium on policies conducive to financial discipline. Strategically, a firm longer-term focus on price stability is the best safeguard, one which can only be achieved with the support of fiscal discipline.

The BIS then warns, "yet such a safeguard is by no means always effective." (p. 85)

The costs of losing credibility can reverberate over many years, and reacquiring credibility can be very costly in real terms. So if governments are risk averse, the demands of credibility will impose broadly deflationary macroeconomic strategies. In the 1960s, the managed international financial framework permitted expansionary, full-employment policies that were contagious both domestically, encouraging private investment, and internationally, underwriting the growth of world trade. In the 1980s, the deregulated financial framework has encouraged policies that elevate financial stability above growth and employment. This has ratcheted up real interest rates, which have in turn reduced domestic investment, reduced the growth of world trade, and slowed the rate of growth of effective demand.

All of this is not surprising in the light of the basic Keynesian proposition that the real economy is not self-adjusting—that is, that markets are just as likely to settle into a low-growth, high-unemployment equilibrium as into any other pattern. Keynes pointed out that the idea of self-adjustment was convincing only because of a common confusion between the efficiency that the markets may impose on the operations of an individual firm and the fact that the markets do not ensure that the economy as a whole is maintaining an efficient level of employment, or in a longer term perspective, an efficient balance between consumption and investment. In Keynes's characterization of the operations of a market economy, it is clear that the behavior of financial markets may well be an important factor driving the economy toward a low-growth, high-unemployment equilibrium. The markets are neither omniscient nor benign. When their influence is combined with the persistent search for government "credibility," defined in terms of "sound money" and "prudent" deflationary policies, then the low-level position is the most likely outcome.

Liberal Financial Markets and the Private Sector

It has been argued so far that liberalized financial markets have imposed deflationary pressures on world levels of growth, productivity, and investment. These pressures on both the public and the private sectors derive primarily from the sheer scale of potential capital flows and from the potential volatility of those flows.

Volatile financial markets generate economic inefficiencies. Even if fluctuations take place around a "true" level, volatility creates financial risk. Even if the facilities exist for hedging that risk, the cost of financial commitment is raised. More generally, volatility may well result in decisions being made on the basis of false information, and that may induce a general reluctance to take any step that will increase exposure to unpredictable fluctuations in exchange rates or interest rates. A simple premise might be: the greater the volatility, the greater the reluctance to undertake any exposure to fluctuating variables. The greatest danger of all in open capital markets is, of course, posed by a general loss of liquidity.

A further question raised by the liberalization of international capital markets is the extent to which instability is transmitted between markets. As has often been noted, one of the most interesting aspects of the stock market crash in October 1987 is that it was a worldwide phenomenon. Prices were marked down in all stock markets around the world, with no particular reference to the "fundamentals" in each particular country. It is now generally accepted that this was a classic example of "contagion," of a beauty contest in which markets were reacting to the news of markets. King and Wadhwani (1988) have shown that the correlation coefficient between hourly changes in London and New York rose after the crash, an observation that is consistent with the idea that the extent of contagion grew after October 19th. When allowance is made for time zone trading and interactions between Tokyo, London and New York are examined in turn, this finding is confirmed. The value of the contagion coefficient measuring the impact of New York on London depends on volatility.

Developed Economies

Analyses of financial instability typically focus on short-term volatility, often monthly or even daily price movements. It is not surprising to find that short-term volatility in money markets has increased since the end of the Bretton Woods system. On average, the monthly volatility of G7 exchange rates has tripled, with far larger increases in volatility being experienced by countries outside the core of the ERM. There has been no tendency for volatility to decrease in the 1980s and early 1990s, but equally, after the sharp increase between the 1960s and early 1980s, there has been no further tendency for volatility to increase, despite the fact that currency trading has increased enormously (see table 7.9). There is a clear link between international speculative flows, the exit of Italy and the United Kingdom from the ERM in 1992, and the greater exchange-rate volatility subsequently experienced by those countries.

As shown in table 7.10, a similar increase in volatility is evident in bond yields, although this, too, has generally eased a little in the 1990s when the amount of international bond trading increased sharply. There has also been some correspondence between short and long rates, with increased volatility of short-term interest rates (Shiller, 1988).

No consistent trend toward increased volatility is observable in equity markets either, even though volatility was a little higher in the 1980s; see table 7.11. Stock market volatility has been shown to be only weakly related to volatility in the real economy, although William Schwert (1989) has argued that there is a link, albeit a weak link, between volatility and recession.

There is only limited evidence of a significant impact of short-term financial volatility on the real economy. Writing in the early 1980s, Andrew Crockett (1984) argued that the large majority of empirical studies on the impact of exchange rate variability on the volume of international trade are unable to establish a systematically significant link between measured exchange rate variability and the volume of international trade. Joseph

Table 7.9 Volatility of effective exchange rates

	1960–69	1980–1985	1986–1989	1990–1994
Canada	0.2	0.9	1.0	1.1
France	1.0	1.1	0.8	0.7
Germany	0.7	1.0	0.8	0.9
Italy	0.3	0.7	0.6	1.9
Japan	0.3	2.4	2.4	2.4
United Kingdom	1.0	2.0	1.8	2.0
United States	0.2	1.8	2.1	1.5

Source: Edey and Hviding, 1995. An assessment of financial reform in OECD countries, OECD Economics Department Working Paper no. 154.
Note: Standard deviation of monthly changes (percentage points).

Table 7.10 Volatility of bond yields

	1960–1969	1980–1985	1986–1989	1990–1994
Canada	0.13	0.58	0.27	0.31
France	0.11	0.42	0.38	0.31
Germany	0.10	0.28	0.20	0.22
Italy	0.11	0.43	0.37	0.46
Japan	0.27	0.37	0.52	0.38
United Kingdom	0.17	0.43	0.43	0.36
United States	0.18	0.58	0.34	0.23

Source: Edey and Hviding, 1995. An assessment of financial reform in OECD countries, OECD Economics Department Working Paper no. 154.
Note: Standard deviation of monthly changes (percentage points).

Table 7.11 Volatility of share price

	1960–1969	1980–1985	1986–1989	1990–1994
Canada	3.5	5.7	5.0	3.5
France	4.6	7.2	7.9	5.3
Germany	4.0	3.0	6.1	4.1
Italy	5.0	6.5	7.8	6.6
Japan	4.3	2.6	4.1	5.8
United Kingdom	3.5	3.4	5.7	3.7
United States	6.9	3.8	3.9	2.8

Source: Edey and Hviding, 1995. An assessment of financial reform in OECD countries, OECD Economics Department Working Paper no. 154.
Note: Standard deviation of monthly changes (percentage points).

Gagnon (1993), in an analytical study, suggested that the impact of volatility on trade is likely to be negative but small. Examining the wider impact on the real economy with data covering forty-nine countries, Baxter and Stockman (1989) found no link between the performance of the real economy and the exchange-rate regime (fixed or floating). However, an empirical study by Linda Goldberg (1993) found that exchange-rate volatility had a clear negative impact on investment in U.S. industry, although the observed negative effects were quantitatively small. Her results are in accord with John Huizinga's findings (1994) that:

> for United States manufacturing industries the move to flexible exchange rates was in fact accompanied by significant and widespread increases in uncertainty about real wages, the real price of materials inputs, the real output price.... Higher uncertainty about real output price was shown to be negatively correlated with the investment rate and productivity growth.... Higher uncertainty about real wages was also...negatively correlated with the investment rate, but positively correlated with productivity growth. Higher uncertainty about the real price of materials inputs was...positively correlated with the investment rate and productivity growth. (p. 211)

Huizinga's study distinguishes between periods of fixed and fluctuating rates, rather than using measures of volatility as such. In doing so, he illuminated an important point. It would appear that short-term volatility in exchange rates is not the relevant measure for the impact of international capital liberalization on the medium-term performance of the real economy. Liberalization was accompanied in the 1970s and 1980s by huge medium-term swings in exchange rates, with no obvious relationship to the needs of the real economy. For example, the appreciation of the pound sterling effective exchange rate by over 20% between 1978 and 1981 was accompanied by a doubling of the UK inflation rate. The consequent increase in the real exchange rate resulted in a rapid deterioration in the balance of trade in manufactured goods and a fall in domestic manufacturing output of 20%—declines from which British manufacturing has not fully recovered. Similarly, the 40% swings in the U.S. effective exchange rate in the 1980s were associated with the growth of the U.S. current account deficit to over $160 billion in 1987 (with a counterpart deterioration in the federal budget deficit).

Giorgia Giovanetti (1991) has shown that the impact on the competitiveness of a given change in a fluctuating rate is significantly less than the same change in a fixed, but adjustable, exchange rate. The rationale for this result is not hard to find. Under a fixed-rate system, an adjustment of the rate results in a new pattern of international prices that can be used, with reasonable confidence, as a framework for long-term decision making. The same absolute change in a fluctuating exchange rate will not be expected to persist in the same way, and therefore will be less of an incentive for long-term change. Of course, exchange-rate movements today are far more affected by changes in asset prices than by the requirements of purchasing-power parity. But insofar as altering exchange rates is a means of adjusting to differences in international competitiveness, then fluctuating rates, by the very nature of the uncertainties that they create, will require larger swings in relative parities than are really appropriate—a further contribution to international instability.

As well as exchange-rate instability, the 1980s have experienced both an increase in the volatility of bond rates and a sharp increase in the real level of the long-term bond rate. There is a clear body of evidence that links the volatility and high rates of return demanded in deregulated capital markets to bond default and corporate failure. Gertler and Hubbard (1988) have argued that the impact of volatility on a firm's net worth will limit its ability to borrow, and that smaller firms can be hard hit by the impact of high interest rates on the cost of loans. Combined with the well-known evidence presented by Fazzari, Hubbard, and Petersen (1988) that retained profits are the key determinant of investment, these results suggest that the impact of high and volatile interest rates on cash flow will lead to a significant deterioration in corporate performance, especially for those companies with high debt-equity ratios.

In a short briefing paper, Keating and Wilmot (1992) present a startling illustration of the impact of the creation and demise of the Bretton Woods system on the default rate on corporate bonds (see their figure 1). The Bretton Woods era is characterized by historically low default rates, while defaults rose sharply as that era ended and climbed steadily through the 1980s. This pattern showing the impact of liberalization on corporate survival is confirmed by a study of U.S. business failures by Michele Naples and Arben Arifaj (1995). Naples and Arifaj verify the fact that the corporate failure rate was peculiarly low in the Bretton Woods era and rose sharply in the 1980s. They also find that the real interest rate and the corporate debt-equity ratio are significant explanatory variables of that failure rate.

What is particularly striking about these observations is that they suggest that deregulation of national and international capital markets has raised the cost of capital and introduced instability into the local financial environment of middle America. The corporate survival rate was sustained in the Bretton Woods era by a combination of macroeconomic steady growth and the microeconomic benefits of low interest rates and financial stability. The globalization of financial markets has meant that, whereas international disequilibria may, in the past, have been manifest in exchange-rate movements, today they have an impact on interest rates in domestic money markets. The instability of local interest rates means that international financial pressures are felt by small and medium-size firms operating in local markets, not only by large companies operating internationally.

Emerging Markets

As was noted above, the growth of equity markets in developing countries has played a positive role in encouraging a flow of capital toward developing countries and in relaxing financial constraints on economic activity, particularly in Latin America (Devlin, Ffrench-Davis, and Griffith-Jones, 1995). The World Bank, through the International Finance Corporation, is actively encouraging the development of equity markets in developing countries and is encouraging them to liberalize their capital markets as the most effective way of attracting international capital. The conventional wisdom is effectively summed up in a report by the World Institute of Development Economics Research (1990), which called for the repeal of Article VI of the IMF Articles of Agreement. It was argued that the need to attract foreign capital in non-debt creating forms *is only one reason, and not the most important reason, why developing countries should wish to foster their emerging equity markets.* Equity markets are a vital part of economic development—they encourage savings, help channel savings into productive investment and encourage entrepreneurs to improve the efficiency of investments. This wider report, therefore placed the role of the foreign investor within the context of the general desirability of the growth of equity markets for domestic resource mobilisation reasons as well as for tapping foreign savings and know-how on market organization and technology.

As Singh (1993) points out, this argument fails to take account of the substantial body of literature that demonstrates that relatively sophisticated equity markets in developed countries are not effective either in ensuring an efficient allocation of savings or in encouraging efficient decision making by entrepreneurs. It also ignores the widely accepted view that "bank-based" systems of corporate finance have superior development records to "stock-market based" systems (Frank and Mayer, 1990; Pollin, 1995). Moreover, Singh reports that there is little or no evidence of an increase in aggregate savings for most developing countries as a result of greater new issues activity on the stock market. In some of the countries (e.g., Mexico, Turkey) aggregate savings actually fell during the 1980s (Singh, 1993.)[32]

However, Singh and Hamid (1993) have shown that even though the development of stock markets does not increase savings, equity finance is nonetheless a very important form of funding for industry.[33] New issues are far more important in the funding of manufacturing companies in developing countries than is the case in developed countries, where new equity finance is a very small component of the corporate flow of funds. Whereas in U.S. industrial companies, retained earnings provide over 90% of the corporate sources of funds (Corbett and Jenkinson, 1994), in South Korea only 13% of funds were internally generated, and across the entire sample, an average of 32% of funds were internally generated. Although there were very wide differences between countries, new equity provided, on average, 40% of funds in the developing economies compared with a negative contribution (owing to takeover activity and "buy backs") of -9% in the United States.

Given the importance of new issues in the financing of corporate growth in developing countries, the very high volatility of those markets casts a cloud over the success of emerging markets in attracting capital flows. The short-term volatility of stock prices is significantly greater than in the G7. Over the period 1985 to1989, the standard deviation of monthly price changes was 37 in Argentina, 21 in Brazil, 8 in South Korea, 15 in Taiwan, and 24 in Turkey (compare the figures for developed countries in table 7.11).

Of even greater importance are the violent medium-term swings to which these markets are prone. Singh (1993) reports that between 1982 and 1985, share prices of the Brazilian stock exchange rose five fold (in U.S. dollar terms), two years later they had fallen to 28% of their 1985 value. In the first nine months of 1987, share prices on the Mexican market rose 6-fold. However in October 1987 prices fell to a tenth of their previous level. In Taiwan, the largest Third World stock market, between 1987 and February 1990 the share price index rose by 330 percent to reach a peak of 12,600, the index then fell to a quarter of its value (3160) by September 1990.

It is difficult to associate such volatility with efficiency or to consider it mere "overshooting."[34] Instability is also likely to discourage international capital flows into emerging markets and provoke the sort of liquidity crisis suffered in Mexico. The BIS (1995) comments that "capital inflows—inflated by volatile short term movements—can reach levels that are not sustainable. In the process, the exchange rate and other financial asset prices can overreact in ways that are inimical to long term goals.... In some countries, recent developments in securities markets have constituted a potential source of systemic risk. (p. xxx) In the light of experience, both the BIS and the IMF recommended that developing countries consider imposing short-term capital controls to discourage excessive capital inflow.

Conclusions

Effects of Liberalized Financial Markets

The broad lines of a potential explanation of the relationship between liberalized international financial markets and the performance of the real economy can now be discerned. Given that financial markets operate as a beauty contest, and the real economy has no automatic tendency to converge to full-employment growth, then the simple rules of the game embodied in the policy positions believed by market participants to be held by other participants will be imposed on the economy. The downside risks involved in flaunting the rules of the game will create a deflationary bias in government policy and in the private sector of the real economy. This is reinforced by the very high costs of debt in a situation in which real interest rates typically exceed growth rates by a substantial margin. High interest rates are themselves the outcome of the attempt to maintain financial stability in a potentially volatile world. So the postwar goal of "a high and stable level of employment" is abandoned and replaced by the goals of the "long-term price stability"—the path to which is defined according to the rules of the game.

The easing of bond yield volatility in the 1990s probably reflects widespread adjustments to financial market constraints, rather than improvements in the functioning of the markets themselves. Policy has been adjusted to accommodate the pressures of volatile markets, and this explains the decline in the instability observed in the nineties. Private-sector decision makers have also adapted to the new low-level situation. With governments no longer committed to the maintenance of full-employment levels of effective demand, the prospective growth of sales is reduced and the attractions of investment curtailed. Falling private-sector investment will tend to precipitate some deterioration in the government's fiscal balance, further exacerbating deflationary pressures.

It is potential volatility that creates the pressures on government policy. As governments increasingly accept the new rules, and as demands for "international surveillance" and "openness" enforce those rules with increasing ferocity, observed volatility may diminish.[35] A relatively slow-growth, high-unemployment, monetarily stable system can endure indefinitely. This is the case even in circumstances of rapid technological change. New technologies might be expected to spark off a Schumpeterian wave of new investment, but with macroeconomic balances maintained in a carefully constructed deflationary stance, the impact of new technologies is felt more on the composition of activity than on the rate of growth. The low overall rate of growth ensures that the average rate of productivity growth remains low (Eatwell, 1995b).

A low rate of growth, with low ratios of investment and saving to GDP, will not lessen the influence of the bond market. Even though the flow of savings may be diminished, the stock of financial assets remains enormous, and it is the turnover of that stock which determines long-term interest rates. As liquidity increases with the creation of ever more sophisticated financial products, the stock market begins to operate like a bond market. Institutional investors increasingly demand that dividend rates be maintained, irrespective of corporate performance, thereby imposing a further deflationary burden on corporate cash flow.

In sum, a liberalized, sophisticated financial system, with a premium placed on the possibility of exit, is a fragile financial system. That fragility is manifest in:

1. Liquidity crises, some of which have substantial reverberations in reduced real output.
2. Risk aversion in the private sector, which produces a bias toward the short term and a corresponding reluctance to invest for the long term.
3. Risk aversion in the public sector, producing a bias toward deflationary policies.
4. Persistent demands for greater "flexibility" to increase the possibilities of exit.

The development of new derivative products to manage the risk that the liberal financial system has itself created has in turn produced new systemic risks. Indeed, the complexity of such instruments leaves them vulnerable to sudden loss of liquidity as opinion swings in one direction or another.

The explanation presented here of the impact of international capital liberalization is consistent with the deterioration of economic performance in the post–Bretton Woods era. It does not, of course, prove causation. It simply comprises a set of hypotheses on the operation of financial markets and the real economy, and the interaction between them, which would suggest that liberal financial markets with very high turnover would tend to impose deflationary pressures on the economy.[36] As regards developing economies, the benefits that the abolition of financial controls have brought to emerging markets must be heavily qualified by the instability that is inherent in the ease of exit demanded by investors. Granted, increased flows of direct, real investment probably require agreement to unrestricted repatriation of profits—but probably not the instant-exit conditions demanded by financial markets.

Lessons Learned

If the foregoing hypotheses do, indeed, capture the essence of the current operation of the international economy, this raises the question of what could be done to improve the relationship between the operation of the international financial system and the overall efficiency of the real economies of the world. It is often argued that nothing can be done to change the present system, since capital flows can overwhelm a large number of measures decided by any one government. This is certainly true. But it is equally true that the foundation stones of the world financial system are the monetary instruments issued by a small number of major governments. The U.S. dollar, the Deutsche mark, the yen, and the pound sterling were on at least one side of the transaction in 80% of currency trades in 1989 and 1992, and 77% of trades in 1995 (BIS, 1996, table F-3). Ultimately, those governments acting together have the potential to control capital flows.[37]

But that potential will be manifest only if governments themselves espouse a different theory of economic policy than the orthodox view that currently dominates economic and political debate. In many cases, the assumed superiority of a liberal market strategy derives not just from conventional theory but also from a belief in the inherent economic incompetence, and even venality, of governments—an unflattering picture that some governments themselves seem to have adopted. Of course, there are a number of examples for which such pessimism is justified. Yet in the longer term, successful economic development has always been associated with active developmental states (Gerschenkron, 1962; Amsden, 1989; Singh, 1994). State intervention has also contributed to short-run efficiency. Within the Bretton Woods system, active macroeconomic management was successful in maintaining high levels of output and employment (Eichengreen, 1993). Examples of bad and incompetent policy are not sufficient justification for handing the future of the economy over to an economic environment of liberalized markets that renders systematic policymaking impossible. Rather, they should encourage the creation of an environment within which good and competent policy can be effective.

As was argued above, restrictions on capital flows have not necessarily been associated with poor economic performance. It is worth remembering that Western reconstruction after World War II, surely one of the great economic policy achievements of modern times, was conducted in an environment of tight capital controls. Even current account convertibility was typically not permitted before 1958, by which time the success of reconstruction was assured. By contrast (though the two cases are not totally comparable), in process of transition by the Central and Eastern European economies, there was a rush to convertibility and to relaxation of capital controls. This liberal environment for trade and finance has not been notably successful in attracting capital to the reconstruction effort (from 1992 to 1994, foreign direct investment for the entire region was only about the same as foreign direct investment in Malaysia) and has produced the bizarre result that the Russian Federation is a significant net capital exporter (EBRD, 1995). All successful examples of the creation of modern industrial economies, from nineteenth-century Germany (Gerschenkron, 1962) to the modern Republic of Korea (Amsden, 1989), have been associated with interventionist policies in both trade and finance. History suggests that a laissez-faire international regime may well hinder, rather than help, the process of transformation in Central and Eastern Europe (Eatwell, Ellman, Karlsson, Nuti, and Shapiro, 1995).

The importance of the theoretical framework that informs economic policy is also clear in the interwar period experience. As Peter Temin (1989) has made clear, the Great Depression of the 1930s was a product of both the loss of international financial control (the UK was unable to sustain the international system as it had done before the First World War, and the United States was unwilling to do so) and the fact that governments were convinced of the necessity of deflationary policies. They had no alternative theory that would lead them to act otherwise. Without a change of "theory" by governments, without a willingness to pursue growth-oriented policies, no formal structure of financial controls would deliver recovery in OECD countries. Without a change of policy to encourage higher growth in the north, the prospects for successful growth strategies in the south were seriously reduced. Developing countries, however, could question this legacy by adopting a pragmatic stance on financial liberalization and by considering whether the benefits of financial liberalization outweigh its costs and help foster the goals of sustainable human development.

It took the experience of the Great Depression and of economic management during World War II to change the stagnationist theory that wrought such damage in the 1930s. In the same way, it is unlikely today that a significant reassertion of control over international financial structures is possible without an equally major change in priorities and analyses by major governments. Such changes have historically been associated with the aftermath of worldwide economic and political disruption.

Notes

This chapter was written by John Eatwell and first appeared as a UNDP Office of Development Studies Discussion Paper (Number 12). Acknowledgment is due to Sara Sawhney for research assistance and to Edward Amadeo, Barry Eichengreen, Ricardo Ffrench-Davis, Tony Porter, Ajit Singh, Paul Streeten, and Charles Wyplosz for a number of incisive criticisms.

1. "Speculative" trades may be made in hope of capital gain, or to hedge against potential capital loss, or to seek gains by arbitrage.

2. Keynes had the support of the UK Treasury and the Bank of England. Initially, Harry Dexter White and the U.S. Treasury supported Keynes's position, but the American position was watered down under pressure from Wall Street (Helleiner, 1994).

3. Less careful writers simply assume what should be proved. For example, Blundell-Wignall and Browne (1991) begin an examination of the macroeconomic consequences of financial liberalization with the statement, "it is a premise of this study that financial liberalization is an important step toward better-functioning market economies."

4. If no one can be made better off without someone else being made worse off, then an economy is said to have reached a state of Pareto optimality. Moreover, the so-called Third Theorem of Welfare Economics demonstrates that there is no logically infallible way to aggregate the preferences of individuals and so to solve the problem of distribution. Allan Feldman (1987, p. 894) sums

up the state of welfare economics as, "We feel we know, as Adam Smith knew, which policies would increase the wealth of nations. But because of all our theoretical goblins, we can no longer prove it."

5. In circumstances in which decisions affect the path of the economy through time, the assumption of competitive markets that underpins the Fundamental Theorem must be supplemented by the rational expectations hypothesis. Even so, there is no presumption that the competitive economy is stable. Not only might there be multiple equilibria (Obstfeld, 1986) but also there exists no general proof of the global stability of competitive equilibrium (Fisher, 1983). Taken by itself, the Efficient Market Hypothesis embodies no presumption that the real economy is in a competitive equilibrium. It is a hypothesis about the use of information by financial markets; however, that information may be generated.

6. These claims were spelled out in a survey of global financial markets and their policy implications (Woodall, 1995). They are the "conventional wisdom" on the subject. For example, Bayoumi and MacDonald (1995, p. 552) also assert that "open capital markets can provide the same services across countries that they provide within a single economy, allowing more efficient use of funds for investment and improving the allocation of consumption over time. These gains, which are similar to those accruing to individuals from capital markets within a country, were the logic behind the general move toward international financial liberalization since the late 1970s."

7. Woodall (1995, p. 6) argues that "a government's loss of powers is reason to cheer, not fear: all that is being lost is the power to pursue damaging policies and practice economic deception by letting inflation rip."

8. An alternative approach to the Feldstein-Horioka result has been to investigate whether capital is sufficiently mobile to permit consumers to insulate themselves against national shocks, smoothing consumption and ensuring that consumption paths in individual countries are highly correlated with aggregate consumption across all countries. Although conclusions are less clear cut, there is little evidence of perfect capital mobility (Bayoumi and MacDonald, 1995).

9. The separation of British and German monetary policy following Britain's exit from the ERM in September 1992 is an example of currency risk in a fluctuating exchange rate system "insulating" interest-rate differentials.

10. A deficit in the current account, whether of a country or region, must be matched by a net inflow of capital. The net inflow will be composed of direct investment and borrowing. Insofar as borrowing predominates, the deficit region will tend to accumulate indebtedness, limiting the possibility of future deficits. Within nation-states, the accumulation of debt in deficit regions tends to be mitigated by transfer payments (Commission of the European Communities, 1977).

11. The ratio of debt to GDP will grow exponentially if the real rate of interest is greater than the real rate of growth. On the implications of this relationship for the U.S. external debt, see Godley (1995).

12. This figure is an underestimate, since it excludes UK data on foreign exchange forwards and swaps, as well as transactions between nonreporting entities. Including these trades would add around $7,000 billion to the total (see BIS, 1996).

13. The same may be said of nonforeign exchange derivatives. Under the headline "Volatility Is Making Hedges Grow," Suzanne McGee (1995, 12th June,

C1) reported in the *Wall Street Journal* that "price uncertainty and market volatility are driving producers and consumers of energy products and metals to hedge their exposure in greater numbers than ever before. The result: Wall Street dealers are gleefully anticipating surging sales of commodity derivatives to these companies."

14. The collapse of Barings provides an excellent example of the challenges faced by the regulatory authorities. Prior to the collapse, Mr. Eddie George, the governor of the Bank of England, wrote in *The Observer* of July 24, 1994, that: "We now have an expert team monitoring derivatives who are getting even better every time they go in to see a firm. What they are reporting back from the most active players in the market is very reassuring. These people know what they are doing whether it's at director level or the chaps on the desk." In a similar vein, Mr. Brian Quinn, the Bank of England director in charge of banking supervision, wrote in the *Bank of England Quarterly Bulletin* in August 1994 that "I believe both the market participants and the regulatory authorities have come a considerable way in identifying the capital needed for derivatives and all other instruments carrying market risk." Yet the Report of the Board of Banking Supervision's inquiry into the Barings collapse concluded: "We believe the Bank should explore ways of increasing its understanding of the non-banking businesses (particularly financial services businesses) undertaken by those banking groups for which it is responsible" (para. 14.35). And "The Bank should ensure that it understands the key elements of the management and control structures of those banking groups where it is responsible for consolidated supervision" (para. 14.37).

15. Why this might happen is discussed in the third section below.

16. On this point, Mello and Parsons (1995, p. 116) argue: "We think Culp and Miller play down the funding risk too much and lean far too much on the idea that Metallgesellschaft's creditors and shareholders should have readily coughed up extra cash. Culp and Miller have argued in the abstract that Metallgesellschaft *could not* have really faced a liquidity constraint, except as Deutsche Bank and others foolishly chose not to continue financing the oil business....Speaking of Deutsche Bank as if it had unlimited pockets is simply not facing up to the real-world constraints that had already been evidenced."

17. Derivatives such as commodity futures were originally developed to hedge environmental risks, such as harvest failures, rather than risks inherent in the operation of markets themselves.

18. The relationship between investment and growth is, of course, not simple. High rates of investment may be wasteful and may lead to a long-term slowdown in growth rates. But in this chapter, the accumulation of capacity is presumed to enhance the output and growth potential of the economy.

19. Ethiopia, Syria, and Tanzania meet these criteria but are excluded from table 7.5 because of lack of data. They are included in table 7.7.

20. In the past three years, there has been a sharp fall in Japanese investment, virtually no growth in GDP, a sharp increase in unemployment, and a growing public-sector deficit.

21. The chapter by Alesina, Grilli and Milesi-Ferretti (1994) and the paper by; Grilli and Milesi-Ferretti (1995), referred to above, consider the relationships among a variety of institutional variables, including capital controls and economic performance. They find a positive, though weak, relationship between capital controls and growth of income per head. The relationship is strongest in

the Alesina et al. chapter, which studies twenty OECD countries over the period 1950 to 1989.

22. There is some disagreement about exactly what the beneficial impact of Black Wednesday consisted of. The most obvious point is that the devaluation of a previously overvalued exchange rate improved the trade performance of the economy and provided a stimulus to effective demand via increased net exports. But the increase in exports in 1993–94 was predominantly due to the growth of overseas markets, rather than any increase in competitive market share, and the share of imports in national expenditure actually increased (Eatwell, 1995a). Of far greater importance than the exchange-rate effect was the relaxation of monetary policy that became possible once the uncertainty associated with the new floating rate regime permitted some decoupling of British and German interest rates (Eatwell, 1994a).

23. There was no speculation against the currencies of Austria, Belgium, or the Netherlands—countries for which the commitment to the maintenance of the parity with the Deutsche mark was "credible" (Crockett, 1993).

24. There are, of course, other theories of inflation that would produce the same outcome. Those models that claim to identify a Non-Inflation Accelerating Rate of Unemployment (or NAIRU), determined by structural factors and the acceleration related to the level of effective demand, lead to conclusions similar to that derived from the natural-rate hypothesis, even though the presumed behavioral mechanisms are different. There is, for example, no tendency for the economy to gravitate toward the NAIRU; and inflation is determined by the level of effective demand, not the rate of growth of the money supply (Rowthorn, 1977; Parkin, 1987).

25. In like manner, Tobin (1980, p. 41) argues that "It is hard to resist or refute the suspicion that the operational NAIRU gravitates toward the average rate of unemployment actually experienced."

26. It is notable that the fiscal surpluses enjoyed by the British government in the late 1980s were associated with a sharp fall in the private-sector savings ratio. It could be argued that it was not government prudence that produced the surplus but a lack of prudence by the private sector.

27. Today, Keynesian theory is typically interpreted in terms of "rigidities" that inhibit the ability of markets to ensure a gravitation toward full-employment equilibrium. In other words, an underemployment equilibrium is a special case of the full-employment model, distinguished only by the imperfections (market failures) that prevent the attainment of Walrasian equilibrium. An alternative interpretation is that Keynes's vision is of an underemployment equilibrium determined by a level of effective demand that displays no tendency, even in the best of all possible worlds, to gravitate toward full employment. This is not a special case of the neoclassical model, but an alternative to it. These issues are surveyed and analyzed in Eatwell and Milgate (1983).

28. The emphasis on "theory" in this sentence is perhaps excessive. The abandonment of the Bretton Woods system was not necessarily the preferred choice of most governments, but resulted from international financial developments that they were increasingly incapable of controlling.

29. A similar story might be told of the pound, which swung wildly from over $2.40 in 1980, to near $1.00 in 1986, to $2.00 in 1990—hardly a reflection of "fundamentals."

30. Another good example of the damage that imprudent financial flows can do is the large-scale bank lending to developing countries in the late 1970s, particularly to Latin America, which precipitated the debt crisis from which real output has barely recovered.

31. Exchange-rate uncertainty drives a wedge between national interest rates, but the decoupling depends on the maintenance of uncertainty.

32. A study by Cho and Khatkhate (1989) of financial liberalization in five Asian countries (Indonesia, Malaysia, Philippines, South Korea, and Sri Lanka), cited by Singh (1993, p. 247), concluded: "financial reform, whether comprehensive and sweeping or measured and gradual, does not seem to have made any significant difference to the saving and investment activities in liberalized economies. It was believed until recently that removal of repressive polices would boost saving. The survey in this paper of the consequences of reforms does not reveal any systematic trend or pattern in regard to saving (and also investment), though it clearly demonstrates that reform has greatly contributed to the financialization of savings." Devlin, Ffrench-Davis and Griffith-Jones (1995, p. 250), commenting on the Latin American experience, 1991–93, observe that "Mexico—although experiencing a particularly large influx of private capital—has not seen... a recovery of growth in the period," and for Latin America as a whole, "national savings were crowded-out by external savings."

33. Singh and Hamid (1992) examine a sample of 50 of the largest manufacturing companies over the period 1980 to 1988 in each of nine countries: India, Jordan, Malaysia, Mexico, Pakistan, South Korea, Thailand, Turkey, and Zimbabwe.

34. Singh (1993) cites the description in *The Economist* (September 9, 1989) of the Taiwan stock market as "a rigid casino with a phenomenal turnover." In 1989, the average total value of shares traded on the Taipei stock market was nearly $3 billion, $1 billion more than in London and just half the value of a day's trading in New York.

35. Schwert's finding (1989) that stock market volatility in the United States was high during the 1930s runs contrary to this image of a long-run stable depression. However, Bayoumi and Eichengreen (1994, p. 820) find that "under fixed rates, monetary policy had to be adjusted to stabilize the exchange rate, flattening the demand curve and thereby increasing the output response and reducing the price response to aggregate supply shock. Following the shift to floating, monetary policy was freed, steepening the demand curve and increasing price volatility relative to output volatility."

36. These were, of course, the hypotheses that provided the theoretical underpinning of Keynes's position at the Bretton Woods conference.

37. This potential is acknowledged even by proponents of financial liberalization. For example, in rejecting the "Myth of the Powerless State," Pam Woodall (1995) argues that the "myth" was propped up by politicians unwilling to take public responsibility for their liberalizing decisions. "The world has changed, the global economy has indeed arrived: nonetheless, the emasculated state is a myth.... The barriers that politicians have lowered can be raised again.... In finance, technology makes the changes harder to reverse, but by no means impossible... given the will, governments can do it."

Part Two

Analytical

8

The Imperfectionists

The key issues in any consideration of the operation of the market mechanism can be revealed by the answers given to two questions. The first question is whether the determination of relative prices in a market economy involves determination of the size and composition of output and, in particular, whether the level of output is such that labor is fully employed (in the sense that, at the going wage, all workers willing to offer labor would be able to find employment). The second question is whether variations in relative prices are associated with variations in output, such that the economy tends toward a level of output compatible with the full employment of labor. Each of these questions can be supplemented with a further question: if not, why not?

The significance of these questions can be illustrated in terms of the most elementary piece of orthodox neoclassical analysis. This analysis involves the argument that the price of a commodity is determined by the relationship between demand and supply. According to this account, equilibrium, determined at the intersection of a function relating price to quantity demanded and another function relating price to quantity supplied, is defined as "market clearing." When this view of price determination is extended to the economic system as a whole, the equilibrium position of the economy is characterized by a set of market-clearing prices, with associated quantities (levels of commodity output and levels of factor utilization) such that the markets for all commodities and all factors of production clear. In particular, the labor market clears at the equilibrium level of the wage (relative to the associated set of equilibrium prices).

In terms of this familiar approach to the analysis of price formation, the answer to the first question is obvious. Equilibrium prices and equilibrium quantities are determined simultaneously. If there exists an equilibrium set of prices, then there exists an equilibrium set of outputs—equilibrium in the sense of market clearing, including the full employment of labor, as defined above. Furthermore, this theory of the simultaneous determination of prices and quantities is typically presented in such a way—by juxtaposing demand and supply functions—that the idea that prices adjust automatically so as to clear markets, thus pushing the economic system toward a full-employment level of output, seems to follow as a self-evident corollary of the theory. (It does not, in fact, follow as readily as might appear at first sight, since the stability of an equilibrium is less easily demonstrated than its existence; but we will leave these difficulties to one side for the moment.[1])

Here, then, we have the orthodox neoclassical account of the operation of the market mechanism in a nutshell: the equilibrium set of outputs (and levels of factor utilization) is determined simultaneously with the equilibrium set of prices (of commodities and factors of production); variations in relative prices, sparked by an imbalance between demand and supply, will be associated with variations in quantities in a direction that ensures that both prices and quantities tend toward their equilibrium levels. Neoclassical analysis, therefore, answers in the affirmative the first two questions posed above.

An analysis of unemployment may then be derived directly from these relationships between prices and quantities. Any inhibition to the tendency of prices and quantities to find their equilibrium (market-clearing) levels will leave the economic system in disequilibrium with, perhaps, either an excess demand for labor or an excess supply of labor (that is, unemployment). An enormous variety of analyses of unemployment are constructed in this way.

The general tenor of the neoclassical analysis of the causes of unemployment is that, while the economy would be self-regulating in the best of all possible worlds (i.e., the implicit tendency toward the full employment of labor would be realized), the market is *inhibited* from fulfilling this task by the presence of certain frictions or rigidities. In the literature on the problem of unemployment, examples of such inhibitions are legion. They include sticky prices (particularly sticky or even rigidly fixed wages and/or sticky interest rates); institutional barriers to the efficacy of the price mechanism, such as monopoly pricing (by firms or individual groups of workers); inefficiencies introduced into the working of the real economy by the operations of the monetary system; and the failure of individual agents to respond appropriately to price signals because of disbelief in those signals, the disbelief being derived from uncertainty about the current or future state of the market, or from incorrect expectations concerning future movements in relative prices, or from false conjectures about the actual state of the market.

Examples of frictions and rigidities can be multiplied at will—any factor that causes the market to work *imperfectly* will do. It will be convenient, therefore, to group all the authors of the myriad arguments of this kind under the general heading of "imperfectionists."[2]

From what has already been said, the usefulness of such a classification should be obvious. For, although this kind of argument comes in many varieties, each is no more than a particular species of the genus. Underlying the arguments is a fundamental similarity: if the particular aspect (or aspects) of the economic system that gives rise to the breakdown of the market mechanism were to be absent, then the system would tend toward the full employment of labor (and other factors of production). In all cases, the analysis of unemployment is viewed as no more than an aspect of the neoclassical theory of value and distribution. According to this approach, whether a relatively optimistic or pessimistic stance is taken with respect to the efficacy of the market mechanism in promoting full employment, the analysis of output and employment is part and parcel of the theory of relative price determination. This is so even in the case of those imperfectionists who feel that the essential workings of the theory are distorted gravely in the real world.

In marked contrast to the analyses outlined above are those theories of employment that propose no particular functional relationship between prices and quantities. The central proposition of neoclassical analysis—that the theory of value and distribution is also the theory of output—is rejected, together with the connected notion that appropriate variations in relative prices will promote variations in quantities, so moving the economic system in the direction of a full-employment equilibrium.

Unfortunately, this rejection of the neoclassical theory of value and distribution—of the entire apparatus of demand-and-supply analysis—has not always been backed by rigorous analytical arguments; this is so much so that it has sometimes been confused with an imperfectionist position. A striking example of this is the rejection by a number of writers of the neoclassical theory of value, and their advocacy of the idea that relative prices, far from being determined by demand and supply, are determined by a markup over normal prime cost where this markup is insensitive to variations in the conditions of demand (see, for example, Kalecki 1939; Nield 1963; Godley and Nordhaus 1972). Quite apart from the obvious shortcomings of "markup" analysis as a theory of price formation—it is in essence a proposition about the stability of the ratio between prices and costs rather than a theory about the determination of either of those magnitudes, or even of the size of the ratio—this attempt to separate the study of relative price determination from the analysis of output may readily be confused with an imperfectionist argument based on sticky prices arising from the presence of monopolistic or oligopolistic influences in commodity markets.[3] Moreover, the bald assertion that prices and quantities do not bear the well-defined functional relationship to one another that is postulated in neoclassical theory does not provide a satisfactory analytical basis upon which to build a critique of the neoclassical position.

Yet the requisite critique does exist, and a prominent theme of this book is that this critique is to be found in the outcome of the debate over the neoclassical theory of value and distribution and its treatment of capital as a factor of production on a par, so to speak, with land and labor. While this debate is seen by many as a rather esoteric controversy in the more abstract realm of economic theory, its implications are more far-reaching than has hitherto been appreciated. The central conclusion of the debate may be summed up, in broad terms, as follows: when applied to the analysis of a capitalistic economy (that is, an economic system whereby some of the means of production are reproducible), the neoclassical theory is logically incapable of determining the long-run equilibrium of the economy and the associated general rate of profit whenever capital consists of more than one reproducible commodity. Since, in equilibrium, relative prices may be expressed as functions of the general rate of profit, the neoclassical proposition that equilibrium prices are determined by demand and supply (or, more generally, by the competitive resolution of individual utility maximization subject to constraint) is also deprived of its logical foundation.

The relevance of this critique of the neoclassical theory of value and distribution to the problem of the missing critique of the neoclassical theory of output and employment should be apparent from what has already been said. Because the neoclassical analysis of the determination of prices and the determination of quantities is one and the same theory (that of the mutual interaction of demand and supply), the critique of the neoclassical theory of value is simultaneously a critique of the neoclassical theory of output and employment. Therefore, the first of the two questions that were posed at the outset of this chapter must, on the grounds of the requirement of logical consistency alone, be answered in the negative. The second question, from which neoclassical theory derives the idea that under the operation of the market mechanism there is a long-run tendency toward a determinate full-employment equilibrium, is rendered superfluous.

But this is not all. If the general (or long-run) case of the neoclassical model has bee shown to be logically deficient, then all imperfectionist arguments—which are derived by examining the implications of the introduction of particular (or short-run) modifications into the general case—are incapable of providing a satisfactory analysis of the problem of unemployment. This is not to say that many of the features of the economic system cited by the imperfectionists will have no role to play in a theory of employment based on quite different foundations from those adopted by the neoclassicals. After all, much of the credibility of imperfectionist arguments derives from their pragmatic objections to the direct applicability of the assumptions of the more abstract versions of demand-and-supply theory. But pragmatism is not enough. The implications of more realistic hypotheses must be explored in the context of the general theoretical framework within which they are applied. Since the account of a self-regulating market mechanism that operates according to the theory of demand and supply is unacceptable on the grounds that it is logically inconsistent, any analysis of unemployment that in turn derives its rationale from that very model is also unsatisfactory. The mechanisms of demand-and-supply theory are just not there.[4]

The question that immediately arises is this: if the neoclassical theory must be rejected, then what approach to the study of these questions are we to adopt? On this question, the gap may be filled with a return to the study of value and distribution developed by the old classical economists and rehabilitated by Piero Sraffa (1960). According to this theory, the size and composition of output is taken as a datum in the determination of relative prices—hence no functional relationship between prices and quantities is involved (Eatwell, 1977). From the perspective of the classical characterization of the workings of a market economy, the analysis of value and distribution is conducted separately from the analysis of output. Of course, in adopting this theoretical stance, neither the old classical economists nor their modern counterparts would deny that all aspects of the market system (prices, distribution, and output) act and react upon one another. Their argument is, rather, that the analysis of the determination of relative prices is conducted assuming the size and composition of output to be given (that is, without taking into account, at this stage, the implications of changes in output). Likewise, the analysis of output is conducted assuming prices and distribution are given. Once the explanation of the determination of these variables has been accomplished satisfactorily, their interactions may then be examined in a more complex narrative; but this additional investigation leaves the process of determination of the relevant variables unaltered. These *separable* explanations of the forces that determine relative prices, distribution, and output, and the *subsequent* consideration of the interactions between them, are the hallmark of the classical approach to economic history. It should not be confused with the necessary simultaneous determination of these magnitudes that neoclassical theory entails.

Thus, we arrive at the basic conclusions concerning the relationship between theories of output and theories of value to which the attempt to answer our two initial questions has led. Alternative analyses of unemployment can be distinguished on the basis of whether the study of the factors determining output (and employment) is separable from the study of value and distribution, or whether the analysis of output and employment is treated as an aspect of the theory of value and distribution. The discredited neoclassical theory and its imperfectionist variants fall into the latter category; the classical theory of value falls into the former.

Moreover, since the study of markets along classical lines leaves open the question concerning the determination of the normal levels of output and employment, the development of the classical alternative leads directly to the requirement of providing a satisfactory theory of output that is not essentially connected with the analysis of value. The interesting new idea that emerges from the general line of inquiry being pursued in this book is that Keynes's theory of effective demand provides just such an analysis of output and employment.

The proposition that the level of activity is determined by the level of expenditure, and that the volume of savings is maintained (in the long run) in equality with the amount of investment by variations in the aggregate level of output, does not rely for its general validity on any theory concerning the joint determination of equilibrium relative prices and quantities such as that provided by the neoclassicals. Indeed, precisely the reverse is true: the theory of effective demand when applied to the long-period analysis of output and employment is compatible with such joint determination of prices and quantities. Keynes's use of the propensity to consume as the links between investment, output, and saving replaces the neoclassical mechanism of adjustment that is supposed to operate via variations in relative prices (and, in particular, the rate of interest). The theory of effective demand thus establishes a normal level of output that is not necessarily that which ensures the full employment of labor. The neoclassical presumption that there will always be forces at work (however weak the imperfectionists may asset their influence to be) tending to push output toward the full-employment level has no place in Keynes's economics.

This, of course, refers only to Keynes's original contribution in the *General Theory* of a theory of output and employment based on the principle of effective demand. Unfortunately, however, Keynes detracted from the strength of his own argument by reintroducing elements of the neoclassical theory of value and distribution in his discussions of the determinants of the volume of investment. By proposing a functional link between distribution (the rate of interest) and the amount of investment in the form of the marginal efficiency of capital schedule, the possibility reemerged that appropriate variations in the rate of interest will initiate changes in the level of investment that would tend to push the economic system toward full employment. To obviate this possibility, Keynes was led to defer to the liquidity-preference theory of the rate of interest, and so to the role of uncertainty and expectations, which ensures a stickiness in the rate of interest—an essentially imperfectionist argument.[5] This is exactly the kind of argument that, for almost fifty years, mainstream writers, ignoring the radical implications that Keynes himself felt would follow from the application of the principle of effective demand to the determination of the normal levels of output and employment, have asserted to be the only appropriate interpretation of Keynes. Thus, paradoxically, we have witnessed the spectacle of a supposedly "Keynesian alternative" that rests on just the sort of imperfectionist arguments that are everywhere apparent in the writings of Marshall and Pigou, Keynes's arch theoretical adversaries.

The presence of both radical and orthodox elements in the *General Theory* calls for two observations. The first concerns the problem of the interpretation of that book. A careful examination of Keynes's central arguments in the constructive parts of the *General Theory* reveals that an interpretation that emphasizes the radical, as opposed to the orthodox, strands of thought therein is more consistent with the substance of Keynes's positive arguments, as well as being more in line with Keynes's own views on the significance of his contribution. Moreover, on Keynes's own authority, the orthodox elements are not essential to his main thesis. The second observation relates to the theoretical consistency of those orthodox elements themselves. For, it turns out that the critique of the neoclassical theory of value and distribution is also a critique of the idea that there exists an inverse relationship between the amount of investment and the rate of interest (that is, Keynes's marginal efficiency of capital schedule). When taken together, these two facts imply that the marginal-efficiency-of-capital theory of investment must be dropped, and that only the principle of effective demand can be retained. But in the reconstruction of a more consistent approach to the study of value, distribution, and output, this is a positive step, for it is the principle of effective demand that provides the basis for an analysis of output that does not involve the simultaneous determination of prices and quantities and that is, at the same time, perfectly compatible with the classical theory of value and distribution.

This straightforward perspective may be obscured by a number of issues that must be dealt with before we can proceed: the relationship between the long run and the short run in the analysis of output and employment, the change in the notion of equilibrium in modern neoclassical theory, the treatment of uncertainty and expectations, and the relationship between macroeconomics and microeconomics.

Long Run and Short Run

In orthodox neoclassical circles, Keynes's economics is typically characterized as consisting essentially of a short-run theory of output. Although the definition of the "short run" is sometimes left unstated, there can be little doubt that it is thought to be analogous to Marshall's famous distinction between the short-run and long-run equilibrium of the firm. Such interpretations of Keynes's economics as a short-run theory usually cite in support of their case Keynes's own usage of the term in the *General Theory*. Yet a careful examination of the context within which Keynes adopts this concept reveals that he is using it in an altogether different sense from Marshall.

For Marshall, the short run and the long run both refer to the same given set of circumstances. The short run is that state of the economy in which the system has not yet fully adjusted itself to an equilibrium between demand and supply that is consistent with the given set of circumstances (firms, for example, may not yet have adjusted the level and composition of their production to the composition and level of demand). The long run, on the other hand, is that state of the economy where full adjustment has taken place. Borrowing the terminology of Adam Smith, Marshall regarded these long-period normal positions as centers of gravitation of the system—that is, positions toward which the economy would tend to be pushed under the influence of the more systematic and persistent forces that characterize its operation.

The significance of this distinction between long-run and short-run analysis when it is applied within the context of neoclassical demand and supply theory is readily apparent. For, although the conclusions of the long-run version of this theory imply the full employment of labor (and other factors of production), in any short-run situation in which complete adjustment has not occurred, there will be no guarantee that the long-run conclusions apply. In particular, there may well be unemployment in the short run. Of course, there is still the presumption that there will be a tendency for such short-run unemployment to be eliminated as the operation of the price mechanism sets in motion forces that drive the economic system toward its long-run, full-employment position. Thus, since short-run analysis is derived directly from long-run analysis, it can have no meaning independent of that long-run analysis. The conclusions of short-run neoclassical theory temporarily modify, but do not overturn, the validity of the conclusions of the long-run theory; they stand in relation to long-run conclusions in the same way as the particular case stands in relation to the general case. Whatever theory is offered for the determination of long-run variables, it is not left behind by moving to a consideration of short-run deviations. When one seeks to discover the theoretical foundations of any short-run analysis, one must look to its basis in the associated long-run theory.

From this essentially simple perspective, it becomes apparent that many imperfectionist analyses of unemployment are no more than examples of short-run neoclassical theory where, for example, full adjustment is inhibited by relatively sticky prices. The label of "Keynesian" is, then, often misleadingly applied to such arguments by drawing on one or other of the more memorable of Keynes's pre-*General Theory* statements, such as "in the long run we are all dead." The problem is that while such an argument was undoubtedly at the bottom of the discussion in Keynes's early writings, in particular the *Tract on Monetary Reform* and the *Treatise on Money*,[6] the idea that such an analysis underlies the central propositions of the *General Theory* is seriously to be questioned.

In the *General Theory*, Keynes's short-run analysis is quite different in content from anything that is to be found in Marshall. For, while this Keynesian short run refers to a set of circumstances where "we take as given the existing skill and quantity of available labour, the existing quality and quantity of available equipment, and the existing technique" (Keynes, 1936, p. 245), it is invoked not in order to establish the possibility that complete adjustments to a long-run full employment equilibrium of the neoclassical kind will not occur but, rather, in order to abstract from those more slowly working secular changes due to accumulation, technological progress, and population growth or decline. This procedure, by allowing Keynes to focus on the persistent and systematic forces that act to determine the levels of output and employment, is more directly analogous to that traditionally adopted for the construction of a long-period theory—the important difference being that the determining circumstances offered by Keynes (that is, the theory of employment and output based on the principle of effective demand) are not those of demand and supply that form the basis of the conventional neoclassical wisdom.

The Change in the Concept of Equilibrium

The debate over the issues covered by the chapters in this book has been made rather more difficult than it might have been by the change in the concept of equilibrium used by neoclassical economists. This change, the origins of which may be traced to the interwar period (Milgate 1979), has been shown by Garegnani (1976) to be a reaction to the logical deficiencies of the neoclassical analysis of value and distribution—deficiencies that were fully exposed in the capital theory debate.

The change in the concept of equilibrium has involved abandonment of the notion of equilibrium of the economy as the center of gravitation toward which the competitive decisions of profit-maximizing entrepreneurs would tend to push the system—a center of gravitation consequently characterized by a *uniform* rate of profit on the cost of production of the capital used in each particular line. Modern neoclassical economists have replaced this traditional notion of equilibrium by a concept of equilibrium as a position in which all markets clear, including markets for an *arbitrary* stock of capital goods, where there is no presumption that the rate of profit on the reproduction cost of capital goods will be uniform. Since this type of equilibrium is typically presented as a temporal sequence of instantaneously cleared markets, it may be called an intertemporal equilibrium. There are a number of versions of such intertemporal equilibria, ranging from Hicks's temporary equilibrium to the Arrow-Debreu full intertemporal equilibrium. However, all versions suffer from the same fundamental deficiencies. Since they are positions of the economy in which the rate of profit is not uniform, they are positions from which profit-maximizing entrepreneurs would tend to move away. Hence, they cannot be characterized as centers of gravitation—as positions to which the economy would tend to move.

Nonetheless, this unsatisfactory concept of equilibrium has been adopted as the new object for neoclassical demand-and-supply theory. Incapable of providing a logically coherent explanation of the determination of *long-run* equilibrium, the same theoretical apparatus is now applied to the new conception of equilibrium. And imperfectionist arguments are likewise transmuted to the new environment. Since the essence of the imperfectionist position is the inability of the economy to achieve market-clearing equilibrium, the same analysis applies whether the (logically unsuccessful) attempt is made to characterize the long-period position as market clearing, or whether the analysis is applied to the new intertemporal definition of equilibrium. Indeed, the fact is typically ignored that the equilibrium from which the imperfectionist position deviates (and in terms of which it is defined) is not the long-period position of the economy; formal results on intertemporal models are interpreted as if they applied to a model in which the equilibrium was a competitive center of gravitation.

The development of imperfectionist arguments within the intertemporal general equilibrium setting is, therefore, doubly disingenuous. Disequilibrium arguments are developed in terms of a concept of equilibrium that is itself a "disequilibrium" in the sense that it is a point from which profit-maximizing entrepreneurs would tend to move away. And these arguments are then applied to concrete analyses of wages, unemployment, fiscal and monetary policy, and so on (presupposing (incorrectly) that the equilibria they define *do* capture the dominant forces of the economy and hence *do* define a center of gravitation. Yet there is little point in discussing policy issues if it cannot reasonably be supposed that general tendencies in the economy are captured by the notion of equilibrium that serves as the benchmark for that analysis. Intertemporal equilibrium manifestly fails to meet this requirement.

There are general analytical reasons for rejecting the concept of equilibrium used in modern general equilibrium theory (see Garegnani,

1976). When attempts are made, via imperfectionist arguments, to derive results that might be used to interpret the actual behavior of the economy, the sterility of the underlying concept of equilibrium is starkly revealed.

It is important to stress that our arguments should not be mistaken for the advocacy of what has been referred to above as long-period analysis to the exclusion of everything else. The true point is rather different—it is that if one wishes to conduct an adequate disequilibrium analysis, one must first be satisfied that the equilibrium analysis from which the disequilibrium is *necessarily* derived is acceptable in terms of two connected and minimal conditions: that the equilibrium *theory* satisfies the requirement of logical consistency and that the *notion* of equilibrium (which expresses the object that the theory is to explain) captures the persistent and systematic forces that work through competition toward equalization of the rate of profit on the supply price of capital. Early neoclassical theory, which chose as its object the long-period positions of the system, clearly met the second condition, but it failed, as the capital theory debates of the 1960s manifestly showed, to meet the requirements of logical consistency. Modern neoclassical economics, based on the notion of intertemporal equilibrium, fails to meet the second condition. Imperfectionist arguments (or disequilibrium analysis) derived from either of these two versions of neoclassical economics must, therefore, be rejected, even if for somewhat different reasons.

Uncertainty and Expectations

Much confusion has been introduced into the debate on theories of unemployment by the variety of roles given to uncertainty and expectations. Uncertainty concerning future events is a fact of life, and expectations concerning the likely path of the economy undoubtedly affect economic decisions. But it is not immediately obvious what role these essentially unobservable factors should play in the formulation of economic analysis.

Economic analysis attempts to identify the fundamental causal relationships underlying the working of a market economy. The multiplier, for example, traces the impact of investment on the aggregate level of output. The effects of mistakes made by individuals because of their past uncertainties concerning future events will be revealed by the objective circumstances of today. For example, past uncertainty over the future demand for a given product may have led to its being underproduced, and this will clearly be evident by either a market price above the product's long-run normal price, or by run-down stocks, or a lengthening of order books, or any combination of these. The influence of uncertainty is just one of those multitude of influences that cause the day-to-day circumstances of the economy to deviate from the long-run normal position. Uncertainty and expectations may, thus, be confined to the category of temporary or nonsystematic effects, as distinct from the persistent and systematic forces that act to determine the long-run position.

If, on the other hand, an attempt is made to locate uncertainty and expectations within the class of the persistent, systematic forces characterizing the workings of the economy, then the analysis becomes bereft of any definite result—the behavior of the economy being as arbitrary as the hypothesis made about the formation of expectations.

A very interesting example of the arbitrary character of assumptions on the formation of expectations is provided by models of so-called rational expectations. The essential proposition of the rational expectations hypothesis is that individuals rationally use the economic information available to them, so that the expected value of their prediction of the future magnitudes of economic variables is equal to the prediction that would be made by the relevant and correct economic theory. Hence, the expected value of forecasting error is zero. The position of the economy may be affected only by random events or imperfect information—expectations do not matter. In this way, the rational expectations hypothesis removes the role of expectations as far as determination of the long-run position of the economy is concerned; this is left to be characterized in terms of dominant behavioral relations that are specified independently of uncertainty. In this latter sense, in exposing the true nature of the theory used, rational expectations models are a considerable advance over the imperfectionist models that attempt to analyze unemployment in terms of the arbitrary imperfections introduced into the operation of the price mechanism by erroneous expectations (or, in some cases, by an all-pervasive uncertainty that renders the price mechanism completely impotent).[7]

What is wrong with the rational expectations hypothesis is not that the role of expectations as an element in the general analysis of economic behavior is reduced—that is a forward step. Rather, what is wrong is that, first, the model adopted by the rational expectations theorists is the neoclassical theory of value and output; and second, that the role of expectations is purged from the system by making manifestly improbably assumptions on the economic behavior of individuals, rather than by the recognition that such factors have no role to play in an economic analysis that is to have any definite content.

The treatment of expectations as secondary would seem to sit ill with the obvious point that uncertainty is a fact of economic life and that many economic decisions necessarily involve some estimation of future events. However, the point is that economic theory should be confined to those phenomena that may be analyzed in terms of the concrete behavioral relations of a market economy, and should eschew those phenomena about which nothing definite can be said. Uncertainty may be a fact of life, but the market economy operates systematically in an uncertain world, and it is those systematic operations that are the proper subject matter of economics. Neoclassical analysis has accustomed economists to placing unreasonable faith in subjective propositions. But when subjective factors are projected from the present into the future, what was unreasonable becomes ridiculous.

The confusion introduced by appeals to the role of uncertainty and expectations is particularly clear in the analysis of investment. Investment decisions must be affected in some way by estimations of the future, but there is no reason to suppose that these estimations follow any systematic pattern. Indeed, there is no reason to suppose that investment can be analyzed in terms of a simple parametric model. In neoclassical theory, investment is reduced to an element within the theory of value and distribution, the function relating investment to the rate of interest being confronted with a function relating saving to the rate of interest in order to determine the equilibrium volume of saving and investment. As the capital theory debates have shown, this view of investment is logically untenable. How, then, is investment to be analyzed?

Investment is accumulation, and the process of accumulation in market economies is a process that varies in character from one historical period to another—indeed, from one specific economy to another. Some generalizations can be made; for example, the rate of investment will probably be positively affected by the rate of growth of demand, by the rate of technological change, even by growth in population. But attempts to construct a general model would seem to be misconceived. There is no general behavioral mechanism determining investment that is analogous to the mechanism linking investment and output, or that linking the level of real wages and the rate of profit.

Macroeconomics and Microeconomics

Up to this point, we have deliberately refrained from commenting on a now customary issue in Keynesian economics: the relationship between macroeconomics and microeconomics. The explanation for this omission is that it would not have been possible to set this distinction in its appropriate analytical context without first having traced the basis of the neoclassical theory of output (and employment) to its foundation in the neoclassical explanation of the determination of relative prices. For this distinction between macroeconomics and microeconomics was introduced into neoclassical economics largely in an attempt to accommodate the seemingly incompatible conclusions drawn, on the one hand, by Keynes in the *General Theory* concerning the levels of output and employment and, on the other, by the orthodox theorists of value and distribution.

Initially, the distinction between macroeconomics and microeconomics became associated in neoclassical literature with the idea that the differences in the conclusions arrived at by Keynes (macroeconomics) and those arrived at by the theory of value and distribution (microeconomics) were somehow to be accounted for by the doctrine that what is true for the individual producer or consumer (microeconomics) need not be true for these individuals treated in the aggregate (macroeconomics). This doctrine spawned a more serious and voluminous literature on the "problem of aggregation" and led eventually to a whole program of research devoted to unearthing the microfoundations of "Keynesian macroeconomics."

It should be clear, however, that this approach to the discussion and development of Keynes's contribution to economic theory is no more than the familiar imperfectionist theme in another guise: the question is merely one of reconciling the possibility of prolonged unemployment with the key implication of the neoclassical theory of value and distribution that there will always be forces at work in a market economy tending to push the system toward a configuration of relative prices compatible with the full employment of factors of production (including labor). Indeed, when the literature on the formal problem of aggregation seemed to be leading only toward successively more perplexing mathematical conundrums—thus leaving "Keynesian macroeconomics" with apparently no foundation in the neoclassical theory of value and distribution—the problem began explicitly to be tackled in the imperfectionist framework by investigating what modifications could be introduced into the theory of value and distribution (microeconomics) so as to produce "Keynesian" conclusions.

As we have seen, such attempts to accommodate Keynes in an imperfectionist framework, like the neoclassical theory upon which it is based, have been applied indifferently to the analysis of long-period normal equilibrium and to the analysis of intertemporal equilibrium. Similarly, a microeconomic foundation for "Keynesian macroeconomics" has been sought within both of these systems. In both cases, the argument has been returned to the point from which it began: the necessity of modifying the orthodox view of price formation to deal with an analysis of unemployment. But, given the logical inconsistency of the long-period version of the neoclassical theory of value and distribution, together with the fact that the alternative neoclassical approach, couched in terms of the notion of intertemporal equilibrium, does not provide a satisfactory object of analysis, the attempt to derive macroeconomic conclusions from a microfoundation taken from either of these neoclassical approaches to the theory of value, distribution, and output is unacceptable.

In the final analysis, it would seem better to avoid the use of the terms "macroeconomics" and "microeconomics," if only because their use obscures the substantive analytical point at issue in the debate over the connection between them—that is, the relationship between a theory of output and a theory of value and distribution.

Concluding Remarks

By now, it should be clear that one of the main aims of this book is to smoke out the imperfectionist interpretations of Keynes's theory of output and employment and to reveal them in a clearer analytical perspective. At best, these interpretations are no more than an uneasy and misleading compromise between concerned pragmatism and an unwieldy and unsatisfactory theory of value and distribution based on demand and supply. At worst, they represent mystifying apologetics for this discredited economic theory itself.[8]

On the positive side, we try to provide in this volume the essential ingredients of a framework for demonstrating the manner in which the classical theory of value may be regarded as being congruent with Keynes's principle of effective demand. The potential for a reconstruction of economic theory along these lines is not difficult to grasp—some of the new perspectives it entails have been outlined in this chapter. Of course, many difficult analytical problems remain to be settled, not the least of which are those to be found in the important areas of the theory of money and the theory of capitalist accumulation. Yet it is not too much to hope that, starting from the more appropriate analysis of value, distribution, and output that emerges here, a measure of perseverance and consistency of purpose will yield fruitful results in these crucial fields of study.

The implications of this new approach can be summed up in the answers it provides to the two questions posed at the beginning of this chapter. First, the determination of relative prices in a market economy does *not* involve the simultaneous determination of the size and composition of output. Prices and quantities are determined by separable, though interacting, forces. The level of output associated with long-run normal prices is not necessarily the full-employment level. Second, variations in relative prices are determined by forces that have no immediate relation to the forces determining the level of output. The economic system will certainly tend toward its center of gravitation, but that center is not necessarily a full-employment position.

The simple reason full employment disappears from the picture is that relative prices just are not determined in accordance with the principles of the neoclassical theory of demand and supply. Instead, the level of employment is determined by the level of effective demand—a magnitude that is not susceptible to systematic variation in the face of changes in relative prices, the wage rate, or the rate of profit. When the discussion of economic policy is conducted within the framework provided by these simple propositions, it will acquire a more logically consistent and empirically relevant content.

It is not without interest to recall, in conclusion, some remarks of Keynes that seem not only to capture the general flavor of the arguments just presented but also to suggest the particular analytical task that lies ahead:

> On the one side are those who believe that the existing economic system is, in the long run, a self-adjusting system, though with creaks and groans and jerks, and interrupted by time lags, outside interference and mistakes.... On the other side of the gulf are those who reject the idea that the existing economic system is, in any significant sense, self-adjusting.... The strength of the self-adjusting school depends on its having behind it almost the whole body of organised economic thinking and doctrine of

> the last hundred years. This is a formidable power. It is the produce of acute minds and has persuaded and convinced the great majority of the intelligent and disinterested persons who have studied it. It has vast prestige and a more far-reaching influence than is obvious. For it lies behind the education and the habitual modes of though, not only of economists, but of bankers and business men and civil servants and politicians of all parties.... Thus, if the heretics on the other side of the gulf are to demolish the forces of nineteenth-century orthodoxy... they must attack them in their citadel. No successful attach has yet been made.... They have made no impression on the citadel. Indeed, many of them themselves accept the orthodox premises; and it is only because their flair is stronger than their logic that they do not accept its conclusions. (Keynes, 1973, 13: 486–89)

Notes

This is a newly revised version of a paper written by John Eatwell and Murray Milgate and published as the first chapter of their *Keynes's Economics and the Theory of Value and Distribution.*

1. The fact that neoclassical theory lacks adequate stability properties highlights a major weakness of the demand-and-supply approach. Even in the best of all possible worlds, in which all of the most abstract assumptions on preferences and technology required by this theory are satisfied, it is not possible to prove, without resort to additional assumptions devoid of acceptable economic content (like weak gross substitutability between all commodities), that demand and supply functions yield stable equilibria—let alone to show that these equilibria may sensibly be regarded as centers of gravitation that underlie the necessarily complex day-to-day behavior that the economic system will exhibit. In fact, the difficulties associated with the proof of stability raise serious doubts about the usefulness of the whole demand-and-supply approach to the question of existence of equilibrium. If one is to have any faith in the notion that the mutual interaction of demand and supply captures the persistent and systematic forces at work in a market economy, then it would not be too much to expect that these systematic forces would be strong enough in themselves to reestablish equilibrium in the fact of a one-off disturbance from equilibrium and in absence of any market imperfections. Since this is the very question that neoclassical stability analysis addresses and fails to answer adequately, one is naturally led to doubt the appropriateness of isolating the forces of demand and supply as the supposedly dominant factors at work. An equilibrium that cannot be shown to be the point toward which the economy would, *ceteris paribus,* tend cannot be said to capture the systematic forces determining either the equilibrium of the system or its direction of movement.

2. It should be noted that by referring to this kind of analysis as "imperfectionist" we do not intend to imply that the envisaged failure of the market mechanism to operate in the way depicted by the underlying demand-and-supply theory necessarily derives from imperfections of competition.

3. Thus Malinvaud (1977) cites the results of Godley and Nordhaus (1972) in support of his orthodox imperfectionist position.

4. The spectacle of professional economists' crossing swords in the daily newspapers over whether governments should be advised to adopt those economic policy measures that are suggested by the general neoclassical model, or whether they should be more sensible and adopt those policies suggested by a more "realistic" modification of that model while conceding that, at a general theoretical level at least, they are all on the same side of the fence, is rivaled only by the remarkable propensity of orthodox economic theorists to ignore, or interpret as confirmation of the presence of frictions or rigidities, the steadily accumulating literature of applied economics that has failed to find evidence that any of the neoclassical mechanisms are actually present in the real market economies.

The theory that states the equilibrium position is determined by supply and demand should be carefully distinguished from the proposition that competition (sometimes called the law of supply and demand) tends to establish normal prices, the magnitude of which is determined by forces captured in a different theory altogether (see Eatwell, 1982).

5. An alternative imperfectionist argument, which has less textual basis in the *General Theory*, invokes the idea of a relatively inelastic investment demand function so that even if the rate of interest were "free" to vary, the volume of investment would be "unresponsive" to such variations.

6. Indeed, it is from the former of these two works, dating from 1923, that Keynes's more celebrated estimates of the length of the short run are drawn—not from the *General Theory* at all.

7. Unfortunately, some credibility was given to these imperfectionist exercises by Keynes's appeal to the role of uncertainty (notably in Keynes, 1937a); an appeal motivated by the unfortunate consequences attendant upon his reintroduction of the price mechanism into the analysis of output, in the form of the marginal efficiency of capital schedule. This has lead many anti-neoclassical writers erroneously to locate the essential novelty of the *General Theory* in the role attributed to expectations, rather than in the new theory of saving and investment, thus blurring the distinction between a separable analysis of output and an analysis of output that is merely based on imperfectionist arguments.

8. As an example of the latter, "But of course it is absolutely correct to maintain that every feature of an actual economy which Keynes regarded as important is missing in Debreu.... But it is also true that Debreu and other have made a significant contribution to the understanding of Keynesian economics just by describing so precisely what would have to be the case if there were to be no Keynesian problems" (Hahn, 1973a, p. 34).

9

Effective Demand and Disguised Unemployment

The two issues that dominated the employment experience of the major industrial countries between the 1970s and the 1990s were the common rise in unemployment they all experienced; and the diversity in the scale and content of that rise between the economies of Western Europe, on the one hand, and those of Japan and North America (particularly the United States), on the other. A satisfactory explanation of this outstanding feature of the macroeconomic performance of the industrial economies must explain both.[1]

Conventional approaches sought to explain the differential employment outcomes of Europe and North America primarily in terms of imperfections in the operation of labor markets. The clear implication of such explanations was that if the labor-market imperfections had been absent, or less pronounced, then the economy would have converged to full employment.[2] But these old-fashioned explanations now seem unconvincing. While a wide variety of factors affected the macroeconomic landscape—including the age structure of the population, government employment schemes, labor hoarding, and employment in the black economy—the most important determinant of the common experience of growing unemployment was the slowdown in the growth of aggregate demand that occurred throughout the major industrialized economies in the 1980s. Furthermore, it seems that the differential experience of the major industrial countries in this period was attributable to the interaction between changes in the growth of effective demand and national labor-market structures, rather than imperfections per se.

In short, it is to the role of the growth of effective demand that one must turn to understand what went on.

The analysis that follows adopts a simple Keynesian perspective to do just that. The level of effective demand is taken as an independent variable (at least in what will be identified as the advanced sector of the economy), and accordingly, unemployment is not attributable to the presence of imperfections but, rather, to the fact that the level of effective demand (or, over time, the rate of growth of effective demand) is too low.[3]

While the behavior of effective demand is the key to the common growth in unemployment in the major industrialized economies, the characteristics of national labor markets were important in the analysis of their differential experiences. For, as will be shown, it was the impact of labor-market policies that determined whether there was any employment *in excess of that which might be expected from the growth in effective demand*. The factors influencing this "additional" employment will be the main focus of this chapter. It will be argued that this additional employment is likely to be greater wherever unemployment benefits are either low or of short duration, or where low-productivity employment is subsidized or protected. The scale of additional employment is determined by the supply of labor. The activities undertaken by the additionally employed will be characterized by significantly lower productivity than is typical of the advanced sector of the economy. This additional employment is, in fact, *disguised unemployment*, in the precise sense that a higher level of effective demand would result in workers' being reallocated to jobs with much higher productivity per person employed. This chapter will both analyze the origins and structure of disguised unemployment and provide an illustrative estimate of the magnitude of disguised unemployment from 1979 to 1990.

Disguised Unemployment: Analysis

The approach adopted in this chapter is based on ideas first developed by Joan Robinson (1937). She argued that the level of employment in the economy was determined as the sum of the employment determined by effective demand (taken as an independent variable) and the level of disguised unemployment. She defined disguised unemployment in the following manner:

> In a society in which there is no regular system of unemployment benefit, and in which poor relief is either non-existent or "less

> eligible" than almost any alternative short of suicide, a man who is thrown out of work must scratch up a living somehow or other by means of his own efforts. And under any system in which complete idleness is not a statutory condition for drawing the dole, a man who cannot find a regular job will naturally employ his time as usefully as he may. Thus, except under peculiar conditions, a decline in effective demand which reduces the amount of employment offered in the general run of industries will not lead to "unemployment" in the sense of complete idleness, but will rather drive workers into a number of occupations—selling match-boxes in the Strand, cutting brushwood in the jungles, digging potatoes on allotments—which are still open to them. A decline in one sort of employment leads to an increase in another sort, and at first sight it may appear that, in such a case, a decline in effective demand does not cause unemployment at all. But the matter must be more closely examined. In all those occupations which the dismissed workers take up, their productivity is less than in the occupations that they have left. For if it were not so they would have engaged in them already. The wage received by a man who remains in employment in a particular industry measures the marginal physical productivity of a similar man who has been dismissed from it, and if the latter could find an occupation yielding him a better return, he would not have waited for dismissal to take it up. Thus a decline in demand for the product of the general run of industries leads to a diversion of labour from occupations in which productivity is higher to others where it is lower. The cause of this diversion, a decline in effective demand, is exactly the same as the cause of unemployment in ordinary sense, and it is natural to describe the adoption of inferior occupations by dismissed workers as *disguised unemployment.* (1937, pp. 83–4)

She went on to argue that the disguised unemployed would typically have a marginal propensity to consume equal to one. Hence, any diversion of demand from "the general run of industries" to the products of the disguised unemployed would be offset by the extra demand that their expenditures add to the system. Accordingly, the potential scale of disguised unemployment is independent of the level of effective demand for the products of the general run of industries.

In effect, Joan Robinson portrayed a dual economy. In one sector, the advanced sector (A), the level of employment is determined by effective demand; in the other, the backward sector (B), the level of employment is determined by the supply of labor to that sector. The distinction between the sectors might be reinforced by deploying the arguments embodied in theories of segmented labor markets. But this would obscure the core point—namely, that the *potential* productivity of labor in the two sectors is exactly the same; it is effective demand that is lacking. Those who are working in sector B are measured as employed in the employment statistics. But given the insufficient level of effective demand, they are disguised unemployed. If only effective demand were higher, sector B jobs would disappear, and with them the disguised unemployment:

> we may say that unemployment is present when an increase in the output of capital goods (not offset by an increase in thriftiness) would lead to an increase in the output of consumption goods. Let us apply this criterion to disguised unemployment. If a revival of investment were to occur, dismissed workers would be called back from the hedgerows and the street-curbs into their normal occupations. The wages they now receive represent a command over consumption goods which they prefer to the product of their former hand-to-mouth efforts. The output of consumption goods, as evaluated by consumers, has therefore increased. Hence, according to our definitions, unemployment existed before the revival of investment took place, even though every individual worker was busy all day long. There has been no increase in employment reckoned by heads, but there has been an increase in employment reckoned in terms of output, because efficient methods of production have been substituted for inefficient methods. (Robinson, 1937, pp. 85–86)

Joan Robinson had recognized the possibility of jobless growth.

This analysis has been simplified by the assumption of a homogeneous labor force. In circumstances in which effective demand is increasing, this assumption is likely to be more viable in the medium term than in the short term. In the short term, an expansion of effective demand may run up against a barrier of relatively unskilled sector B workers, whose prior exclusion from sector A has eroded their potential productivity in sector A employment. In the medium term, the desire to meet growing demand will induce companies to invest in the expansion of sector A workforce. The most dramatic example of the medium-term flexibility of the labor force was the increased employment of women in Britain during World War II. In response to the very high demand for labor, the total employed population increased by 2.9 million (14.5%) between 1939 and 1943. Eighty percent of that increase consisted of women who had not been previously employed or who had been housewives (Parker, 1957, p. 482). Yet levels of productivity comparable to, or even exceeding, the levels achieved by the earlier, predominantly male labor force were rapidly achieved.

This example suggests that the definition of disguised unemployment should be extended to cover inactivity—that is, to include the participation rate, where the participation rate is a function of the level and rate of growth of effective demand. The persistence of high levels of male unemployment in Britain from the 1970s resulted in a large number of men withdrawing from the labor force altogether.[4] The high level of male unemployment and nonemployment was also a major stimulus to an increased supply of female labor in an attempt to balance family budgets. The demand for part-time labor, in turn, increased the supply of part-time workers. Surveys of "discouraged workers" and of "involuntary part-time workers" are designed to capture something of this variety of disguised unemployment. The components of the analysis of unemployment in this period were, therefore:

1. The factors affecting the level of aggregate demand, and in turn defining the common experience.
2. The factors affecting the level of disguised unemployment, and hence defining the differential experience.

Disguised Unemployment: Evidence

Identification of disguised unemployment requires an examination of both the levels and the rates of change in output and employment between and within sectors of the economy. This raises a number of significant statistical difficulties. It is, for example, extremely difficult to identify disguised unemployment within an industry, yet this makes an important contribution to disguised unemployment. The widespread growth of self-employment may be an indication of growing sector B employment within relatively dynamic industries. But sorting out type A and type B employment within an industry would require detailed micro and survey analysis that goes beyond the scope of this chapter.

A further major difficulty here is the traditional problem of measuring the growth of output and productivity in service industries. No difficulty is presented in comparing the value of output per head between, say, manufacturing and services, as is appropriate in defining sectors A and B. But any dynamic analysis of the impact of productivity growth on employment presents the problem of measuring "real" output. In many services, this can be done only by measuring the incomes of those working in the industry, an approach that necessarily weakens any conclusions about rates of productivity growth (but not, of course, the increase in peculiarly low-paid jobs). In this chapter, employment and output in public-sector services are excluded from the analysis, even though public-sector employment may be an important "sponge" in some circumstances.

This section uses data on sectoral outputs provided in the OECD National Accounts for four sectors—agriculture, manufacturing, construction, and services—and one subsector, services excluding finance, insurance, real estate, and business services (or "services excluding finance," for short). Employment is defined as all persons active in the sector, not just employees, in order to include the self-employed and all forms of casual work in the identification of B sectors. The analysis is conducted over the (roughly) peak-to-peak trade cycle of 1979 to 1990.

Identification of disguised unemployment requires, first, an examination of benefit levels and their likely impact on sector B employment; second, the identification of employment in sector B; and third, an estimate of "true" unemployment—that is, measured unemployment plus disguised unemployment.

The Reservation Wage

Wage flexibility, or the freedom for real wages to adjust to equate the demand for labor to the supply of labor, was a central concept in the OECD *Jobs Study* of the period in question. It argued that "[b]oth theory and empirical evidence suggest that lower labour costs stimulate employment in the private sector, and all measures which reduce wage pressures at a given level of unemployment ultimately show up in better labour market performance" (OECD, 1994a, p. 51).

However, nowhere in the *Jobs Study* was there an explicit consideration of the theoretical "evidence" cited. Indeed, one of the peculiarities of the *Jobs Study* was a lack of theoretical specification. For example, despite its overt concern with the problem of aggregate unemployment, virtually all of the analysis was conducted at the level of partial equilibrium. There was no consideration of the fact that, as was argued above, even within the neoclassical model that was the underlying motivation of the argument, wage flexibility was not a sufficient condition for the attainment of full employment. If an increase in employment is to be sustained, then increased investment must absorb the increased savings that the higher level of activity will produce. If, for any reason, investment fails to increase, then the higher level of employment cannot be maintained, even though wages are perfectly flexible. Despite the key role of investment in the determination of the level of employment, there was in the *Jobs Study* no sustained analysis of the determination of the level of investment, nor of the relationship between investment and employment.[5]

By contrast, in this chapter it is presumed in Keynesian fashion that, given technological conditions, the level of effective demand determines the level of employment in sector A. In sector B, employment is determined by the supply of labor to sector B activities. This supply of labor to sector B, and hence sector B employment, is determined by the reservation wage. A major influence on the level of the reservation wage is the level of benefits available to the unemployed (Table 9.1).

For example, if there is no benefit, then the only unemployed will be those who can live off the earnings of someone else. Other than in this case, anyone without a job in sector A must find some way of getting by.

The provision of benefits will provide a choice between getting by and unemployment.[6] Since the reservation wage is related only to sector B employment, there is no reason to expect any relationship between benefit levels and aggregate employment. In fact, there is, if anything, a negative relationship between benefit levels and unemployment: countries with higher benefit-replacement rates tended to have lower unemployment (OECD, 1994c, pp. 172–78).

Leaving the case of Italy aside for the moment, the data suggest a sharp differential between mainland European levels and coverage of benefits, and the levels and coverage of benefits in Japan and the United States, with the UK lying between mainland Europe and the United States. On this basis, it might have been expected that in the United States and in Japan, the reservation wage would be low, and therefore in those countries there would have been a tendency for declines in sector A employment to lead to increases in sector B employment, not increases in overt unemployment. In mainland Europe, higher benefit levels would be associated with higher unemployment. An OCED analysis (1994c) of trend changes (that is, changes between trade cycles) in benefit entitlements and changes in unemployment yields results consistent with the hypothesized positive relationship. The elasticity of the unemployment rate with respect to the mean benefit level is estimated as being equal to one. The elasticity above the mean is greater than one.

Table 9.1 Benefit replacement rates and benefit coverage, 1991

	Average replacement rate	Beneficiaries/unemployed
Canada	28	129
France	37	98
Germany	28	89
Japan	8	36
Italy	3	*na**
UK	18	71
USA	11	34

Source: OECD, 1994c. *The OECD jobs study: Evidence and explanations. Part II: The adjustment potential of the labour market.* Paris: OECD.
* No comparable statistic is available for Italy. However an EC survey of benefit recipients suggested that the Italian figure would be low.
Note: The average replacement rate measures the average benefit entitlement before tax as a percentage of previous earnings before tax. The beneficiaries/unemployed ratio expresses the ratio of the number of unemployment beneficiaries to the total number unemployed as measured by the ILO Labour Force Survey.

The Italian case is an oddity, with very low benefit rates being associated with relatively high levels of unemployment. Clearly, alternative means of subsistence must have existed in Italy, which enabled the unemployed to survive. It has been widely suggested that this consisted of a larger black economy—that is, higher sector B employment that was not officially recorded than was typical of other countries. It should be remembered that the proportionate increase in unemployment in Italy was the lowest of the Western European economies (from a high base).

The OCED *Jobs Study* (1994c, p. 175) found that the trend slowdown in the growth of aggregate demand was overlaid by cycles in demand, in which changes in the level of unemployment were smaller when the benefit levels have been lower. It is through the cycle that the expansion and contraction of sector B employment might be expected to dampen the impact of changes in effective demand.

A further indication of the impact of forces determining the reservation wage and the supply of labor to sector B is a change in the dispersion of wages. In Canada, the UK, and the United States, wages paid to the lowest decile diverged from the median wage. In the United States, the median wage itself fell, precipitating a fall in real wages of more than 1% per year between 1980 and 1989.

In France, Germany, and Italy, the growth in real wages for the lowest decile was greater than the increase in the median real wage. In Germany, this meant an increase in real wages for the lowest paid of

Table 9.2 Trends in lowest decile wages relative to the median, 1973–1991

	First year	Final year	M_f/M_1
Canada (1973–90)	0.52	0.44	109
France (1973–91)	0.62	0.66	119
Germany (1980–90)	0.67	0.71	127
Italy (1979–87)	0.67	0.75	104
Japan (1979–90)	0.63	0.61	118
UK (1973–91)	0.68	0.59	134
USA (1975–89)	0.41	0.38	96

Source: OECD, 1993.
Notes: The terms "First year" and "Final year" refer to the data for the first and final years shown after the specification of the country. The third column is the real median income in the final year relative to the real median income in the first year. The figure in the third column for Japan is the relative level of real compensation per employee in the business sector in 1990 relative to 1979.

over 2.5% per year between 1983 and 1990. In Japan, the relative position of the lowest paid was virtually unchanged. In the UK, a rapid increase in median real wages was accompanied by a sharp increase in inequality, while in Canada and the United States, an already unequal distribution of income has become even more unequal. The widening of the distribution of earned incomes in North America suggests a lowering of lower decile wages that may have been associated with the growth of sector B unemployment, particularly in the face of low U.S. benefit levels. Something of the same phenomenon seems to have been emerging in the UK, as income inequality increases sharply. The Japanese case was very different. Low benefit levels would suggest a low reservation wage. But the relatively egalitarian distribution of earned incomes suggests that B sector employment may nonetheless be relatively well remunerated. The evidence suggests that levels of sector B employment are likely to be high in Canada, the United States, Italy, and Japan.

Sector B

"Disguised unemployment" is defined as employment in very low productivity sectors. The benchmark was the performance of the German economy. With high benefits and broad coverage, it might be expected that disguised unemployment would have been low in Germany—or, to put it another way, that the dispersion of the levels of value productivity per head would be less in Germany than in other industrial economies. This was indeed the case. Other than in agriculture, the value of output per head was almost invariably at least 80% of the value of output per head in manufacturing. So, as a rule of thumb, for each country, "very low" is defined as being at a level of output per head of less than 80% of output per head in national manufacturing industry.

Tables 9.3 and 9.4 illustrate the rationale for separating non-financial services from the rest of the services sector. The high value of output per head in the financial sector seriously biases the overall output figures in services.

Particularly striking were the very low levels of productivity in agriculture generally, and in Japanese and (in 1990) Italian agriculture, in particular. Very low levels of output per head were also found in Canadian, Japanese, and U.S. nonfinancial services. Equally striking was the high level of output per head in services within the European Union (including Italy), with only British nonfinancial services sliding into Sector B at the end of the period as wage differentials in Britain widened. More generally, there was a fall in relative productivity in nonfinancial services in all industrial economies as unemployment increased.

However, an important distinction must be drawn between what happened in low-productivity agriculture and what happened in low-productivity nonfinancial services. While aggregate unemployment increased, in agriculture, absolute employment fell and in nonfinancial services, both absolute employment and the share of employment rose (and in the UK, rose sharply). Given that disguised unemployment is conceived as a sponge that absorbs workers who lose sector A jobs and are unable to acquire satisfactory benefits, it may be unreasonable to

Table 9.3 Value of output per head relative to manufacturing, 1979

	Agriculture	Manufacturing	Construction	Services	Services (X)
Canada*	78	100	125	73	52
France	52	100	75	110	86
Germany	43	100	83	113	89
Italy	42	100	89	120	91
Japan	26	100	77	89	68
UK	83	100	99	114	84
USA	86	100	81	97	76

Sources: OECD, 1979–91; Annual Abstract of Statistics, 1993;Survey of Current Business, Nov. 1993.

* Canada 1980.

Notes: Private-sector employment as a proportion of total employment. Services (X) = private services excluding the financial sector.

Table 9.4 Value of output her head relative to manufacturing, 1990

	Agriculture	Manufacturing	Construction	Services	Services (X)
Canada	57	100	105	67	46
France	53	100	65	110	83
Germany	45	100	80	120	95
Italy	32	100	81	111	84
Japan	22	100	87	84	63
UK	80	100	101	97	68
USA	70	100	69	90	69

Sources: OECD, 1979–91; Survey of Current Business, Nov. 1993.
Notes: Private-sector employment as a proportion of total employment. Services(X) = private services excluding the financial sector.

classify employment in sectors with falling employment as disguised unemployment. Of course, it could be argued that without the disguised, low-productivity effect, employment in agriculture would have fallen even more rapidly than it did. Without a clear-cut means of differentiating between these two cases, disguised unemployment will be estimated, first including all sectors in which productivity was less than 80% of productivity in manufacturing and then excluding those sectors in which employment was falling.

Tables 9.5, 9.6, 9.7, and 9.8 provide detailed information on the pattern of the value of output per head for each year 1979–90 for Germany, Japan, the UK, and the United States. The German experience is totally different from that in the other three countries. In Germany there was no tendency whatsoever for sectoral value productivity to diverge (apart from a brief episode in German construction, 1984–89). Yet such a divergence occurred in each of the other three countries, though the changes were most pronounced in the UK and the United States, and least pronounced in Japan. In Japan the value of output per head in nonfinancial services, already low, tended to decline further relative to manufacturing in the late 1980s. Japan also had the highest proportion of its labor force working in nonfinancial services (45%), other than in Canada (53%). In the UK and the United States, there were sharp declines in relative productivity in nonfinancial services over the whole period. Both countries also experienced sharp increases in the proportion of the labor force working in nonfinancial services. In the United States, the proportion of such employment increased from 39% in 1979 to 43% in 1990. In the UK, the increase was even sharper, from 31% in 1979 to 38% in 1990.

Disguised Unemployment and "True" Unemployment

The analysis of the preceding section provides the raw material for the calculation of disguised unemployment and for the determination of "true" rates of unemployment—that is, the rates of unemployment

Table 9.5 Value of output her head relative to manufacturing: Germany, 1979–1990

	Agriculture	Manufacturing	Construction	Services	Services (X)
1979	43	100	83	113	89
1980	42	100	89	118	93
1981	43	100	87	120	93
1982	48	100	84	121	92
1983	42	100	81	120	91
1984	43	100	78	120	90
1985	39	100	74	117	88
1986	40	100	75	113	86
1987	37	100	77	116	90
1988	41	100	77	116	90
1989	46	100	79	116	90
1990	45	100	80	117	93

Source: OECD, 1979–91.
Note: Services(X) = private services excluding the financial sector.

Table 9.6 Value of output her head relative to manufacturing: Japan, 1979–1990

	Agriculture	Manufacturing	Construction	Services	Services (X)
1979	26	100	77	89	68
1980	23	100	76	90	69
1981	23	100	80	89	69
1982	23	100	77	87	68
1983	24	100	71	87	68
1984	24	100	71	87	66
1985	24	100	72	88	67
1986	24	100	75	88	71
1987	23	100	81	86	65
1988	22	100	82	86	64
1989	22	100	85	86	64
1990	22	100	87	84	63

Source: OECD, 1979–91.
Note: Services(X) = private services excluding the financial sector.

Table 9.7 Value of output her head relative to manufacturing: UK, 1979–1990

	Agriculture	Manufacturing	Construction	Services	Services (X)
1979	83	100	100	116	84
1980	87	100	100	113	83
1981	88	100	98	107	79
1982	87	100	94	101	74
1983	76	100	95	99	71
1984	86	100	92	95	69
1985	71	100	88	91	67
1986	74	100	89	96	71
1987	74	100	91	93	68
1988	70	100	96	92	69
1989	73	100	93	88	63
1990	86	100	91	90	64

Source: OECD, *National Accounts*, 1979–91.
Note: Services(X) = private services excluding the financial sector.

Table 9.8 Value of output her head relative to manufacturing: USA, 1979–1990

	Agriculture	Manufacturing	Construction	Services	Services (X)
1979	86	100	81	97	76
1980	71	100	82	99	77
1981	80	100	76	97	75
1982	70	100	76	96	74
1983	54	100	73	95	73
1984	68	100	73	94	73
1985	68	100	74	95	73
1986	63	100	76	95	73
1987	62	100	74	92	70
1988	59	100	72	91	70
1989	67	100	71	91	69
1990	70	100	69	90	69

Source: OECD, *National Accounts*, 1979–91;*Survey of Current Business*, Nov. 1993.
Note: Services(X) = private services excluding the financial sector.

measured as the sum of published unemployment rates and disguised unemployment. Having classified sectors as belonging to category B, the next task is to measure disguised unemployment. Disguised unemployment is defined as a number of jobs that would need to be lost if a sector is to attain a level of value productivity per head equal to 80% of the level of productivity in manufacturing—that is, the typical relationship in Germany. As noted above, this calculation is conducted both including and excluding those sectors in which employment is falling. The estimates of disguised unemployment are set out in table 9.9.

The highest levels of disguised unemployment were, as expected, in Canadian services, in Italian and Japanese agriculture, and in American, Japanese, and British nonfinancial services. The high level of disguised unemployment in UK nonfinancial services in 1990 emerged despite the well-known high rate of productivity growth in retail services. This may have been the result of the rapid growth of low-productivity self-employment in the service sector in those years. The scale of disguised unemployment in Japan was extraordinary, and totally transforms the traditional employment picture of the economy.

In table 9.10, the figures for disguised unemployment are added to published unemployment figures to give what may be called the "true" unemployment rates. One significant result is that the supposed superiority of the North American labor market immediately disappears. Instead, the "true" unemployment rate in North America greatly exceeds the rate of unemployment in Germany and is comparable to that in France and the UK. The Japanese "true" unemployment rate is the second highest in the G7. If the identification of disguised unemployment is correct, these high rates of "true" unemployment are the consequence of the slowdown in the rate of growth of effective demand.[7]

By far the greatest proportion of disguised unemployment was to be found in Japan and in Canada. In the UK and the United States, disguised

Table 9.9 Disguised unemployment in the G7 countries, 1979 and 1990 (thousands)

	Agriculture		Manufacturing		Construction		Services		Services (X)	
	1979	1990	1979	1990	1970	1990	1979	1990	1979	1990
Canada*	*15*	*154*	–	–	–	–	554	1,285	1,860	2,769
France	*678*	*447*	–	–	*117*	*330*	–	–	–	–
Germany	*652*	*224*	–		–	–	–	–	–	–
Italy	*1,446*	*1,342*	–	–	–	–	–	–	–	–
Japan	*5,384*	*4,391*	–	–	218	–	–	–	3,442	6,216
USA	–	*376*	–	–	–	868	–	–	1,422	7,007

* Canada 1980 and 1990.
Notes: Disguised unemployment in *italic type* occurs in sectors in which employment is falling. Disguised unemployment in roman type occurs in sector in which employment is rising.

Table 9.10 "True" unemployment rates

	1979			1990		
	Published	"True"'	(B–A)/B	Published	"True"	(B–A)/B
including sectors with falling employment						
Canada*	7.4	24.0	0.69	7.5	29.0	0.74
France	6.0	9.5	0.37	8.9	11.9	0.26
Germany	2.9	5.1	0.43	4.9	5.5	0.11
Italy	7.8	14.5	0.46	11.1	16.5	0.33
Japan	2.1	18.3	0.88	2.1	18.7	0.89
UK	4.5	4.5	0.00	5.9	11.6	0.49
USA	5.8	7.1	0.19	5.5	12.1	0.55
excluding sectors with falling employment						
Canada*	7.4	24.0	0.69	7.5	27.9	0.73
France	6.0	6.0	0.00	8.9	8.9	0.00
Germany	2.9	2.9	0.00	4.9	4.9	0.00
Italy	7.8	7.8	0.00	11.1	11.1	0.00
Japan	2.1	8.7	0.76	2.1	11.8	0.82
UK	4.5	4.5	0.00	5.9	11.6	0.49
USA	5.8	7.1	0.19	5.5	10.3	0.47

Sources: OECD, 1979–91, 1993, and own calculations.
* Canada 1980 and 1990. (B-A)/B= ("true"–published)/"true".

unemployment in 1990 was nearly half "true" unemployment—that is, "true" unemployment was double the published rate. In mainland Europe, disguised unemployment was around a third of "true" unemployment, and vanishes altogether if those sectors with falling employment are excluded from consideration. Moreover, whereas disguised unemployment was increasing as a proportion of "true" unemployment in Canada, Japan, the UK, and the United States, in mainland Europe it was falling as a proportion of "true" unemployment.

Disguised Unemployment or "Flexibility"

The OECD *Jobs Study* attributed the low measured rate of unemployment in North America to the flexibility of labor markets, particularly in the United States, as measured by low rates of worker protection. The OECD policy conclusion was that steps should be taken to increase labor-market flexibility in Europe by weakening worker protection, lowering minimum-wage levels, reducing unemployment benefits, and so on.

The analysis presented in this chapter suggests a quite different interpretation of the data. It attributes the low measured rate of unemployment in North America and in Japan to the presence of very high levels of disguised unemployment. Disguised unemployment was growing in Britain as benefits were cut and inequality increased. The disguised unemployment that existed in mainland Europe was predominantly due to the subsidization of inefficient employment in European agriculture.

In effect, there were three strategies being pursued in reaction to growing unemployment: the mainland European "benefits strategy," the U.S. and (increasingly) UK "impoverishment strategy," and the Japanese "protection strategy." It may well be argued, of course, that disguised unemployment at low wages is superior to unemployment on relatively high benefits, and reasonably well-paid employment in protected sectors is, in social terms, best of all.

But whatever the circumstances in individual countries, the policy conclusion is the same. The rate of growth of effective demand was everywhere too low relative to the growth of sector A productivity, and steps should have been taken to remove the constraints on the expansion of demand by an appropriate mix of fiscal and monetary policies. If measures to expand demand had been implemented, the expansion might have proved contagious.[8] Constraints may have been imposed by the fear of inflation, or by international financial considerations, or both. But if most B sector employment persisted for a long time, the most important constraint would become the difficulty of transferring labor from sector B to sector A. This is akin to the familiar problem of returning the long-term unemployed to the labor force, but it is typically overlooked, given that sector B labor is disguised unemployment.

Increased flexibility, in the sense of the removal of workers' protection, did little to increase employment in sector A. Indeed, the figures for "true" unemployment suggest that the highly regulated German labor market was the most efficient. However, elimination of unemployment benefits would reduce the level of measured unemployment to very low levels, if not eradicate it altogether. This would be because the unemployed would be forced into disguised unemployment.

An increase in disguised unemployment was clearly a waste of resources, since labor was working at a level of productivity below its true potential. Moreover, high levels of disguised unemployment when associated with very low wages probably discouraged productivity-boosting innovation in other sectors, thereby slowing down the overall rate of productivity growth. The experience of Japan, where disguised unemployment was associated with a relatively egalitarian structure of wages, and where productivity growth was relatively high even in sector B industries, is instructive in this respect.

The analysis suggests that the rise in unemployment between the 1970s and the 1990s was not due to rigidities or imperfections in the labor market, but to those factors, international and domestic, that inhibited an increase in the rate of growth of effective demand. There was substantial surplus labor either openly unemployed or hidden in disguised unemployment.

Notes

This is a newly revised version of a paper written by John Eatwell that appeared originally as the third chapter of Jonathan Michie and John Grieve Smith's *Employment and Economic Performance*.

1. The high rates of labor force growth in North America and Japan was matched by high rates of job creation. In North America, there was an 80% increase in the number of jobs since 1960. In Japan, the number of jobs increased by 40%. In the Western European economies, employment increased by only 10%. Of course, comparing rates of job creation does not mean very much. It would have been impossible for the European Union to create as many jobs as North America, simply because the European rate of population growth was so much lower. The fundamental question is not why European job creation was low in absolute terms, but why job creation in Europe did not keep pace with its (slower) rate of population growth.

2. It should be noted that this argument typically embodied a serious theoretical error—namely, in presuming that a well-behaved labor market was sufficient to ensure full employment. Suppose, for example, that the volume of investment is totally inelastic with respect to the interest rate, and that the propensity to save is positive; then, even a perfectly well-behaved labor market will not ensure full employment.

3. Nor is the level of effective demand itself regarded as a function of relative prices. The role of market imperfections (typically rigid wages or prices, but including the impact of "uncertainty" or "false conjectures") in models of unemployment is examined in some detail elsewhere in this volume. The objective of this chapter is to present a positive interpretation of the unemployment experience of the 1970s to the 1990s. Hence, critical analysis of alternative explanations is kept to a minimum.

4. Jonathan Wadsworth (1994) has shown that the inactivity rate among males aged 16–64 rose from 3% in 1975 to 12% in 1993. The sum of unemployed men and inactive men gives a total of nearly 4 million men, one in four, out of work. Moreover, Wadsworth shows that the inactivity rate falls when there are sharp upturns in the employment rate.

5. In a cross-section study, Robert Rowthorn (1995) found a strong positive relationship between investment and employment in manufacturing, and a positive relationship between investment and employment in the service sector. He interpreted the role of investment as that of loosening capacity constraints, and hence lowering the level of unemployment at which inflationary pressures

will emerge. This interpretation could be extended to encompass the dual role of investment: creating capacity and creating demand.

6. Some sector B employment may be permitted as a supplement to benefit.

7. The expression "true" rate of unemployment refers here only to the addition of disguised unemployment to the published rate of unemployment. It does not involve any adjustments to allow for other concerns that have been expressed about the published rate.

8. It is often argued that a coordinated expansion of demand is required. The problem is that while it is widely agreed that a coordinated expansion of demand is desirable, it never happens. There are a number of good reasons for this, which are surveyed in Eatwell (1994a). It is important to note that the Bretton Woods system did not work by means of macroeconomics coordination. Instead, it worked because of a framework of circumstances that permitted governments to pursue national macroeconomic policies without too much fear of international financial disruption.

10

Theories of Value, Output, and Employment

Theories of value and theories of the general level of output (as opposed to theories of the output of particular commodities) are often treated separately, too little regard being paid to the congruence of the particular theories advanced. The objective of this chapter is to examine alternative theories of the determination of the general level of output in the light of the theories of value with which they are associated. The ultimate purpose of the exercise is to suggest a critique of attempts to reinterpret Keynesian analysis within the framework of orthodox neoclassical general equilibrium theory (microeconomics) and to contribute to the constructive task of relating Keynes's principle of effective demand to the framework of an older tradition of economic analysis dating back to the classical economists and Marx.

The first section of this chapter is devoted to a discussion of the long-period method in theories of value and theories of output. The second and third sections deal with theories of output set within the framework of classical and Marxian analyses—first the classical version of Say's Law, then Marx's rejection of Say's Law and his discussion of the possibility of crises. The fourth section presents the neoclassical version of Say's Law, exemplified by Irving Fisher's theory of investment. The fifth section turns to Keynes's theory of output as presented in the *General Theory* and subsequent articles, and the sixth section presents the interpretation of the *General Theory* generally known as the Neoclassical Synthesis. The seventh section is devoted to a critique of general-equilibrium analyses of rationing and unemployment. Finally, in the eighth and ninth sections, it is demonstrated that a more satisfactory critique of neoclassical theories of output than that advanced by Keynes himself may be found in the critique of the neoclassical theory of value and distribution based on the analysis of Piero Sraffa's *Production of Commodities by Means of Commodities*; and that the framework of the classical analysis of value and distribution provides a congenial setting for the Keynesian theory of output. Moreover, the characteristics of a capitalist economy, identified by Marx as creating the possibility of crises, are just those characteristics that define the institutional setting for the principle of effective demand.

This is clearly a rather extensive program, and some of the topics will necessarily be treated in a somewhat sketchy fashion. The purpose of this perhaps excessively rapid Grand Tour is to provide an overview of the issues involved and, hence, to establish the central theme in a disparate literature. The reader would do well to keep in mind that the relationship between saving and investment is the crucial link between a theory of output and a theory of value. Much of our discussion will accordingly focus on the manner in which the saving–investment relationship is formulated in the variety of theoretical structures examined.

The Object of Analysis

In relating theories of output to theories of value, we must specify the object of the joint analysis with particular care to ensure consistency in the characterization of the economic circumstances to which the theories refer (see Milgate, 1982). A primary issue in the development of theoretical knowledge in the social sciences (or, indeed, in any science) is the problem of abstraction and the definition of abstract categories. This problem has two dimensions: first, the *object* on which the inquiry is to be focused must be defined in terms that will permit statements of general validity; second, the *theory* that is to explain the magnitude or state of the object must itself be constructed at a particular level of abstraction. Although these two dimensions are not unrelated, they are essentially sequential. If they were to be simultaneous (as they are in intertemporal general equilibrium models), the object might be defined to fit the theory, and the theory would in consequence reveal little other than its own structure.

In defining the object of the analysis and identifying the forces that determine it, the assumption is made, implicitly, that the forces of which the theory is constituted are the more dominant, systematic, and persistent. Transitory and arbitrary phenomena are abstracted from intentionally, as are those forces related to specific circumstances as opposed to general use. The dominant forces are expressed in algebraic form, as functions and constants, and constitute the *data* of the theory. The model may then (if it has been specified correctly) be solved to determine the magnitude of the object. It is known that, except by a fluke, the magnitude determined as a solution will not be exactly that observed in reality. It cannot be, since a variety of transitory forces, known and unknown, have been excluded. Nonetheless, since the theory is constructed on the basis of dominant and persistent forces, the magnitude determined by the analysis is the *center of gravity* of the actual magnitude of the object. Whether this center of gravity is a temporal constant or takes different values through time does not affect the essence of the method.

The development of abstract categories—in particular, the sequential formulation of object and theory—may be traced in the evolution of economic thought (see Milgate, 1982, ch. 2). The seventeenth and eighteenth centuries saw the progressive development of the social division of labor and the emergence of wage labor as the dominant system for the social organization of production. At this time, the idea emerged that prices—the parameters of markets, and hence the entire economic system—might be subject to the influence of systematic laws. On the basis of this insight, Adam Smith constructed the abstraction of an economy organized entirely through competitive markets, and he isolated the problem of price formation as a necessary element in the search for an understanding of the laws determining the operations of the economy. To distinguish the dominant from the transitory, Smith characterized the competitive market as establishing natural or average rates of wages, profits, and rents. When the price of a commodity is just that which provides for the payment of the land, labor, and "stock" used in its production at their natural rates, then the commodity sells at its *natural price* (Smith, 1776, Book 1, ch. 7).

While natural prices were held to be the outcome of the persistent forces in the economy, *market prices,* the prices which actually rule at any one time, are influenced by a variety of transitory or specific phenomena, elements which may be excluded from the analysis of the more permanent forces in the economy. The natural price is characterized not only as a single price for each commodity, but also by a uniform rate of profit on the value of capital invested in each particular line. Indeed, as Ricardo argued, it is the active role played in the organization of production by the capitalists seeking the maximum return on the finance they have invested in means of production that is the basis of the tendency toward natural prices (Ricardo, 1951a, p.91). Marx elaborated on this point by emphasizing that the tendency toward the equalization of the general rate of profit and the exchange of commodities at their prices of production (as he called natural prices) "requires a definite level of capitalist development" (Marx, 1967, p. 177). So, the associated categories of natural price and of the general rate of profit were an integral part of the characterization of the capitalist economy.

The fundamental change in economic theory that occurred in the final quarter of the nineteenth century did not, with respect to prices, lead to any significant change in the definition of the object. The new neoclassical theory was an alternative to the classical theory. As an alternative, it necessarily offered a new and different explanation of the same object. This continuity in the object that accompanied the great discontinuity in the theory is particularly evident in Marshall, who devoted considerable attention to the specification of short-period normal prices and long-period normal prices, the concepts he substituted for the market prices and natural prices of Smith and Ricardo (Marshall, 1961, Book 5, chs. 3,5).

Two important aspects of the specification of this familiar framework for the analysis of capitalist economies should, perhaps, be clarified. First, the notion of the tendency toward a uniform general rate of profit on the supply price of capital goods derives from the twofold character of capital in a market system: money capital and commodity capital. In a system in which production and distribution are organized by means of a generalized process of exchange, money assumes the form of the general equivalent of value, and ownership of money or access to finance endows the ability to own and control the production and distribution processes. Hence, the accumulation of monetary wealth becomes, by the nature of the competitive system, the ultimate objective of each individual capitalist, leading him to attempt to maximize the return on the value of the means of production in which he invests his money. But the production of surplus (profits) in the economy as a whole is not a financial phenomenon; it takes place in the process of production. The realization of a financial return and the organization of the process of production are two dimensions of the same phenomenon—two phases in the circuit of capital, which find their conceptual unity in the general rate of profit.

Second, the determination of natural prices and the general rate of profit are associated with the socially necessary or dominant technique of production. At any one time, a given commodity may be produced by means of a variety of techniques: (1) some "fossils" embodying out-of-date methods, which are not being reproduced since, at existing prices, they would yield a rate of return on their supply price lower than the general rate of profit, but that nonetheless do yield positive quasi-rents; and (2) some superior techniques that are used only by a limited number of producers and yield super profits. The various theories of value and distribution are not concerned with these, but with "the conditions of production normal for a given society" (Marx, 1976, p. 129), the normality being defined by dominance throughout the competitive market.

These considerations amount to the proposition that satisfactory analysis of value and distribution in a capitalist economy should endeavor to explain and determine the normal or long-period position of the system—where by "long period" is meant not that which occurs in a long period of time but, rather, that which is determined by the dominant forces of the system within a period in which those forces are constant or changing but slowly. Hence, if we are to present a coherent analysis of the relationships between prices, distribution, and the general level of output, then the *object*—the determination of which is to be explained by the theory of output—must be the natural, or normal, level of output, itself the center of gravity of the transitory forces that affect output at any given time. Thus, a long-period analysis of the formation of natural prices must be accompanied by a long-period analysis of output.

This proposition would seem to contradict the popular interpretation of Keynes's theory of effective demand as presented in his *General Theory*. Joan Robinson has argued, for example, that Keynes "started from a Marshallian short period. Here we are today with whatever stock of capital equipment, training of labour and business organisation that the past has produced" (Robinson, 1978, p. 5). Similarly, Malinvaud (1977) identified Keynesian analysis with short-run equilibrium.

While there can be no doubt that Keynes developed his theory within what he saw as a short-period setting, it will be argued that it is the long-period implications of his analysis, as a theory of employment, that represents the significant contribution. Indeed, even on its own terms, Keynes's analysis does not warrant the appellation "short period." For example, the fixed composition of the capital stock that defines Marshall's short period plays no role in Keynes's theory of employment; unemployment is, according to Keynes, not due to the shortage of a particular capital good but to a lack of effective demand. Moreover, his assumption that "we take as given the existing skill and quantity of available labour, the existing quality and quantity of available equipment, the existing technique, the degree of competition, the tastes and habits of the consumer, the disutility of different intensities of labour and of the activities of supervision and organisation as well as the social structure including the forces...which determine the distribution of the national income" (Keynes, 1936, p. 245), although it might appear to be intended as a definition of a short period in the Marshallian sense, is really designed to rule out the effect of *accumulation,* for Keynes continued: "this does not mean that we assume these factors to be constant; but merely that, in this place and context, we are not considering or taking into account the effects and consequences of changes in them" (p. 245).

Hence, Keynes rules out changes in the dominant and persistent forces acting *in a given situation*—changes that Marshall argued would lead to "Secular movements of normal price, caused by the gradual growth of knowledge, of population and of capital, and the changing conditions of demand and supply from one generation to another" (Marshall, 1961, p. 379).

Finally, if Keynes had argued in the *General Theory* merely that the economy might be in a disequilibrium in the short period, then he would have added nothing to the prevailing theory (or, indeed, to his own argument in the *Treatise on Money*). Since a short-period position is, by definition, a disequilibrium, the only novelty of his theory might be the particular form the disequilibrium is presumed to take (as we shall see, this is just the approach adopted by proponents of rationing theory; see Strøm and Werin, 1978). There would remain the question of what would, in such circumstances, be the level of output toward which the system would tend to gravitate? Would it, for example, be the full-employment level?

Keynes was not concerned with short-period disequilibria. He claimed that the nature of the components of his theory was

> adequate to explain the outstanding features of our actual experience; namely, that we oscillate, avoiding the gravest extremes of fluctuation in employment and in prices in both directions, round an intermediate position appreciably below full employment and appreciably above the minimum employment a decline below which would endanger life"...[and that] we must not conclude that the mean position thus determined by "natural" tendencies, namely by those tendencies which are likely to persist, failing measures expressly designed to correct them, is,

> therefore, established by laws of necessity. The unimpeded rule of the above conditions is a fact of observation concerning the world as it is or has been, and not a necessary principle which cannot be changed. (1936, p. 254)

The persistent forces establish the long-period level of output: it is these forces and that level that Keynes's theory is designed to explain. In an appraisal of alternative theories of output, and their relationship to theories of value, we should, therefore, bear in mind that (a) the theories of output should be theories that determine the normal level of output in terms of the dominant and persistent forces comprising the theory; and in consequence that (b) in relating a theory of output to a theory of value we will be concerned with the effect that prices and the distribution of income may have on the determination of the normal level of output and the tendency toward it. Following Garegnani (1978–79), we will look to the saving–investment relationship as the key to the elucidation of (a) and (b); and therefore, an important role will be played by theories of the rate of profit, both because this rate is related (in radically different ways in different theories) to the saving–investment relationship and because it provides a link between monetary phenomena and the determination of real output.

Separabilty Between the Theory of Value and the Theory of Output

As we are now well aware (Sraffa in Ricardo, 1951–73, I; Garegnani, 1960; Sraffa, 1960), the classical theory of value takes as its data the size and composition of output, the conditions of reproduction of commodities, and the real wage. These data are sufficient for the determination of relative prices and the general rate of profit. Since output is a datum, there is no place in the theory of value for functional relationships between quantities and prices—or among saving, investment, and the rate of profit. Changes in output will, in general, lead to changes in prices and the rate of profit, but nothing can be said, a priori, about the form of such changes, which reflect variations in the conditions of production. So, the theory of value and the theory of output are formally separable from one another. In Ricardo's case, this separability is expressed in the combination of a comprehensive and consistent theory of value with a theory of output—Say's Law of markets, which is no theory at all.

The law of markets proposed by Say in his *Traité d'Economie Politique* (1803) was constructed from two elements: the first, anti-mercantilist, locating the problem in terms of exchanges of commodities, with money being merely a medium of exchange; the second, physiocratic, portraying the interacting forces of demand and supply within the circular flow of commodities in the process of reproduction. Thus, to purchase a commodity in the circular flow of production, one must produce a commodity—the supply of one commodity *is* the demand for another. Suppose, for example, that a hat maker wishes to buy shoes; he must produce a hat, take it to the marketplace, and attempt to exchange the hat for shoes. If the shoes are available, there will be a balance of supply and demand. If, however, the hat is produced but shoes are not, then there will be a glut of hats and a shortage of shoes. There will be an excess of a particular commodity, but there will not be an excess of all commodities—that, Say argued, is impossible. Ricardo agreed:

> M. Say has, however, most satisfactorily shrewn, that there is no amount of capital which may not be employed in a country, because demand is only limited by production. No man produces, but with a view to consume or sell, and he never sells, but with an intention to purchase some other commodity, which may be immediately useful to him, or which may contribute to future production. By producing them, he necessarily becomes either the consumer of his own goods, or the purchaser and consumer of the goods of some other person. It is not to be supposed that he should, for any length of time, be ill-informed of the commodities which he can most advantageously produce, to attain the object which he has in view, namely, the possession of other goods; and, therefore, it is not possible that he will continually produce a commodity for which there is no demand. (Ricardo, 1951, I: 290)

Two elements of this argument should be noted. First, it refers only to the employment of capital, not to the employment of labor. As in all classical analyses, it is presumed that there will, in general, be unemployed labor. The level of employment is determined by the current level of accumulation and the social productivity of labor. If there is any tendency toward full employment, this must derive either from accumulation having outstripped the growth of the available labor force or by means of some form of the Malthusian population principle. Such forces are quite unrelated to the law, which ensures that capacity is fully utilized. Second, since, in this formulation, supply is demand, then saving—the production of commodities other than for consumption—is investment. This proposition is not based on the ex post identity of saving and investment, but on the characterization of the motivation of production. "It therefore seems possible to conclude that in Ricardo 'Say's Law' was not the result of an analysis of the investment-saving process, but rather the result of the *lack* of any such analysis" (Garegnani, 1978–79, p. 340).

Since full utilization of capacity is assured by the proposition that decisions to save are decisions to invest, and this proposition was accepted not only by James Mill and Ricardo but also by Malthus. Mathus's argument for the possibility of a general glut is, at first sight, rather puzzling. Malthus's confusion is a reflection of his confusion concerning the theory of value and distribution. He identified the general glut with a fall in the rate of profit brought about by an excess supply of capital: "how is it possible to suppose that the increased quantity of commodities, obtained by the increased number of productive labourers, should find purchasers, without such a fall of price as would probably sink their value below the costs of production or, at least, very greatly diminish both the power and the will to save" (Malthus, in Ricardo, 1951, IV: 303).

As Garegnani has shown, this is an extension of Adam Smith's argument that accumulation of capital will lead to a decline in the rate of profit—an argument that Ricardo had already refuted by demonstrating that the rate of profit will fall with accumulation only because wages rise owing to the increased difficulty of producing wage goods. As long as Malthus assumed that saving is spending, there could be no logical foundation for his argument, for there would be no shortfall in the demand for capital; and to Ricardo, the argument that the normal rate of profit might fall with given conditions of reproduction and a given real wage was completely incomprehensible.

The separability of the classical theory of value from the theory of output adopted by Ricardo leaves the way open for a critique of the tautological status of Say's Law and its replacement by a satisfactory theory of output, while the classical analysis of value and distribution is retained. The foundations for the first task were laid by Marx.

Marx on Say's Law and the Possibility of Crisis

Attacks on Say's Law are scattered throughout Marx's works, the most detailed being his critique of Ricardo's theory of accumulation in part two of *Theories of Surplus Value*. There, he argues that Say's Law is false because it is based on a false conception of capitalist production—a conception that likens capitalist production to the barter of use values:

> The conception that over production is not possible, or at least that no general glut of the market is possible is based on the proposition that products are exchanged against products.... It must never be forgotten that in capitalist production what matters is not the immediate use-value, but the exchange value and, in particular, the expansion of surplus value. This is the driving force of capitalist production, and it is a pretty conception that—in order to reason away the contradiction of capitalist production—abstracts from its very basis and depicts it as a production aimed at the direct satisfaction of the producers. (Marx, 1968, pp. 493, 495)

Once it is recognized that capitalist production is organized and directed by the necessity of producing commodities—that is, exchange values—and of transforming those values into the general form of value, or money, the barter analysis is revealed as a profoundly deceptive portrayal of harmonious capitalist accumulation:

> *money* is an essential aspect of the commodity and... in the process of metamorphosis it is independent of the original form of the commodity. Crises are thus reasoned out of existence here by forgetting or denying the first elements of capitalist production: the existence of the product as a commodity, the duplication of commodity in commodity and money, the consequent separation which takes place in the exchange of commodities and finally the relation of money or commodities to wage labour. (Marx, 1968, p. 502)

Marx constructs his analysis of output in two stages: first, he seeks to establish the *possibility* of crises—those conditions that imply "the framework for a crisis exists" (Marx, 1968, p. 509); second, he presents arguments establishing the *actuality* of crises (see Kenway, 1980). The possibility of crises is derived from just those characteristics of capitalistic production that Ricardo has ignored: the commodity and money. The circuits of capital from money to commodity to money, and so on, are the necessary form of the production and expansion of surplus value, but the realization of that surplus is not unproblematic, for the circuit may be broken: "the difficulty of converting the commodity into money, of selling it, only arises from the fact that the commodity must be turned into money, but the money need not be immediately turned into commodity, and therefore *sale* and *purchase* can be separated" (Marx, 1968, p. 509).

Thus, Marx's notion of the separation of sale and purchase refers to the separation in a monetary economy between a decision to initiate production and the ability to sell the commodities produced. The possibility of crisis is inherent in this aspect of capitalist production.

Marx's discussion of the actuality of crises is less innovative. He falls back on just those conditions of disproportionality and disruption that Ricardo had conceded may occur—the difference being that, given the phenomena that establish the possibility of crises, these conditions lead to crisis, which "is nothing but the forcible assertion of the unity of phases of the production process which have become independent of each other" (Marx, 1968, p. 509). This discussion of the actuality of crises is essentially a short-period analysis, related not to the dominant and persistent forces of the system but to transitory elements. Marx argued forcefully that the positions of Smith and Malthus, whereby an overproduction of capital might lead to a permanent diminution of the rate of profit, were wrong both because of their erroneous theories and because they attempted to present long-run analyses of crises: "When Adam Smith explains the fall in the rate of profit from an overabundance of capital, an accumulation of capital, he is speaking of a *permanent* effect and this is wrong. As against this, the transitory over-abundance of capital, over-production and crises are something different. Permanent crises do not exist" (Marx, 1968, p. 497n).

The character of Marx's discussion is also evident in the contrast between the analysis of the circuits of money capital, in which "it is . . . taken for granted . . . that commodities are sold at their values" (Marx, 1967, p. 24), and the discussion of crises in which "the market prices of commodities . . . fall far below their cost prices" (Marx, 1968, p. 494). But a short-period theory must always be related to some center of gravitation defined by the persistent forces of the system. Transitory disruptions are characteristic of all analyses (including Ricardo's), and though Marx may attempt to argue that such disruptions may be repetitive and severe, it is far from obvious that they can bear the weight that he clearly wishes to place on them unless they are related to a theory of output that contains the possibility of a level of output *permanently* lower than that implied by past levels of accumulation. If a theory of value, based on the conditions of reproduction of a given output, is to encapsulate the dominant and normal forces in a capitalist economy, then that output must also be the outcome of dominant forces. A satisfactory theory of crises must be linked with a theory of output that locates crises as something other than transitory phenomena. Marx failed to provide such a theory because he, like Ricardo, identified saving and investment, proposing no theory of the relationship between them and relying on time lags to create transitory disruption: "If the interval in time between the two complementary phases of the complete metamorphosis of a commodity become too great, if the split between the sale and purchase become too pronounced, the intimate connexion between them, their oneness, assets itself by producing—a crisis" (Marx, 1974, I:15; see also 1968, p. 495).

So, while providing important insights into the possibility of crises, Marx's analysis of the actuality of crises is severely limited by his lack of any theory of the general level of output.

The Neoclassical Theory of Value and the Theory of Output

The construction of the neoclassical theory of value involved the provision of a logical foundation for the idea that prices are determined by supply and demand. This required that a method be found for expressing the forces of supply and demand in homogeneous units as functions of prices (Mill, 1945). The requisite homogeneity was constructed by Jevons, Menger, and Walras in terms of individual utility maximization, balancing marginal utility and marginal disutility at the margin of constrained choice. The essential structure of the model involves the relationship between utility maximization and the constraint provided by a fixed endowment of commodities and/or factors, the process of maximization being based on the possibility of substitution (either direct or indirect) between the fixed elements. Taking as data utility functions, technology, endowments, and the distribution of the endowments, demand and offer functions (or the equivalent sets) may be constructed and counterposed to determine the set of prices and quantities consistent with competitive market clearing. The necessity of simultaneous determination of equilibrium prices and quantities means that the theory of value and the theory of output are the same theory. In marked contrast to classical analysis, the neoclassical theories are completely inseparable. (The peculiar case of the nonsubstitution theorem, in which separability apparently exists, derives from the very basis of neoclassical theory, the possibility of substitution between factors having been assumed away; see Eatwell, 1977).

What we will characterize as the neoclassical version of Say's Law is quite different from the classical version. It consists of two propositions: First, that there exists a set of market-clearing prices for all commodities and all factors. By definition, these prices equalize the supply and demand for all commodities including factors of production—except when commodities are in excess supply at a zero price. It is usually presumed that there is sufficient substitutability in the system to ensure that the price of labor is not zero. Second, that competitive forces will cause prices to tend to their market-clearing levels. Thus, the equilibrium set of prices will contain a wage that clears the labor market and a rate of interest that equalizes the demand for investible funds to the supply of savings.

The present examination of the neoclassical theory of output will consider the version of the theory proposed by Irving Fisher, but the argument that follows is quite general (see also Garegnani 1960, 1978–79). Fisher's analysis is especially useful for our purposes, both because he presents a particularly clear analysis of the relationship between utility-maximizing consumer choice and saving and investment in the determination of the general level of output, and because it provides a particularly apposite basis of comparison with Keynes's analysis, for Keynes identified part of his theory with that of Fisher: "Professor Fisher uses his 'rate of return over cost' in the same sense and for precisely the same purpose as I employ 'the marginal efficiency of capital'" (Keynes, 1936, p. 141).

Fisher conducts his argument in various stages (which he calls "approximations"). The first approximation is an analysis of the exchange of immutable consumption streams; the second approximation includes the possibility of altering consumption streams by productive activity. Within each stage, the argument proceeds from an examination of an individual's saving and spending decisions to the determination of the rate of interest by the market equilibrium of the economy as a whole. For the individual, "the rate of interest is cause, and his lending and borrowing is effect. For society as a whole, however, the order of cause and effect is reversed" (Fisher, 1930, p. 119).

Intertemporal production possibilities are introduced in Fisher's second approximation, in the form of alternative streams of income:

> the owner of any item of capital wealth or capital property, including, of course and especially, his own person, is not restricted to

> a sole use to which he may put it, but has open to his choice several possible or alternative uses, each of which will produce a separate optional income stream. He has, therefore, two kinds of choice: first, the choosing of one from any optional income streams, and secondly, as under the first approximation, the choosing of the most desirable time shape of his income stream by exchanging present income against future. (1930, p. 125)

Saving for the economy as a whole may now be defined as taking part of the flow of production and adding it to the preexisting stock. Production techniques are distinguished by the amount of capital required with a given quantity of land and labor to produce a unit of output.

With the introduction of techniques of production, Fisher needed to postulate a relationship between the stock of capital and the rate of return to investment of capital. He assumed that there are diminishing returns to increased investments of capital, other factors of production being fixed. The set of available techniques defines the transformation frontier:

$$c_2 = f(c_1, x) \tag{1}$$

where c_1, c_2 are consumption per head at time *1* and at time *2*, and x is the initial endowment of capital per head at time *1*. The rate of return on increased saving at time *1*—say, from $x - c^*_1$ *to* $x - (c^*_1 + h)$—is defined as the ratio of gain *minus* sacrifice *over* sacrifice:

$$r = -\,[f(x - c^*_1 + h) - f(x - c^*_1) + (x - c^*_1 + h) - (x - c^*_1)]/ \\ (x - c^*_1 + h) - (x - c^*_1)\dots\dots \tag{2}$$

The limit of (2) as $h \to 0$ is $-(f' - 1)$, or the marginal rate of return over costs.

The relation between the amount of saving and the marginal rate of return gives the demand for saving as a function of the rate of interest. The assumption of diminishing returns to the substitution between capital and labor means that the greater the amount saved, the lower is the marginal rate of return or, alternatively, the lower the rate of interest, the greater is the demand for saving. By the assumptions made concerning individual preferences the supply of saving is lower as the rate of interest is lower. The market rate of interest is that point at which the supply of, and demand for, saving are equal. This rate of interest is equal to the marginal rate of return over the cost of the marginal increase in the stock of capital. Equilibrium in the market for saving and investment will be accompanied by equilibrium in the markets for land and labor.

Hence, in the neoclassical analysis, there exists an analysis of the relationship between saving and investment: the desire to save and the desire to invest are brought into equality by the functioning of the price mechanism. The essential assumption for this to take place is that there be the possibility of substitution between capital and labor, from which is derived the elastic demand schedule for investment as a function of the rate of interest—or, to be more accurate, the combination of the rate of interest and the wage rate that clears the savings–investment market and the labor market.[1]

The existence of a market-clearing set of prices does not, of course, mean that such prices will actually be established. Analyses of short-period disruptions, or of trade cycles and similar disequilibria, by neoclassical economists have, therefore, assumed the form of particular imperfections that limit the competitive tendency toward market-clearing equilibria. Such imperfections might be sticky wages and prices, disruptive monetary and financial phenomena, uncertainty or lack of information leading to miscalculation by economic agents, or simply imperfect competition. All of these are, however, defined by their relation to the market-clearing, full-employment level of output implicit within the neoclassical theory of value.

Keynes's Theory of Output

The argument of Keynes's *General Theory* is constructed in two essentially distinct parts. In the first section of the book, chapters 1 to 10, Keynes advances the proposition that the equality between desired saving and the volume of investment is maintained by variations in the level of aggregate output and employment. Then, in chapters 11 to 18, he attempts to argue that there is no tendency for the level of investment to adjust to a level commensurate with full-employment saving. This involves both the formulation of his own theory of investment and a critique of the neoclassical theory (see Milgate, 1982). The structure of the book thus mirrors the intellectual development that led to the formulation of the basic propositions of the *General Theory*:

> the initial novelty [of the General Theory] lies in my maintaining that it is not the rate of interest, but the level of incomes which ensures equality between saving and investment. The arguments which lead up to this initial conclusion are independent of my subsequent theory of the rate of interest, and in fact

> I reached it before I had reached the latter theory. But the result of it was to leave the rate of interest in the air. If the rate of interest is not determined by saving and investment in the same way in which price is determined by supply and demand, how is it determined? One naturally began by supposing that the rate of interest must be determined in some sense by productivity—that it was, perhaps, simply the monetary equivalent of the marginal efficiency of capital, the latter being independently fixed by physical and technical considerations in conjunction with the expected demand. It was only when this line of approach led repeatedly to what seemed to be circular reasoning, that I hit on what I now think to be the true explanation. The resulting theory, whether right or wrong, is exceedingly simple—namely, that the rate of interest on a loan of given quality and maturity has to be established at the level which, in the opinion of those who have the opportunity of choice, i.e., of wealth holders—equalises the attractions of holding idle cash and of holding the loan. It would be true to say that this by itself does not carry us very far. But it gives us firm and intelligible ground from which to proceed. (Keynes, 1937, p. 250)

The initial novelty is based on the proposition that, while saving is independent on the level of income (output), the volume of investment that entrepreneurs may undertake at any one time is independent of the current level of income. This independence derives from the existence of the monetary system—that is, of money, credit, and finance. The prospective investor can acquire purchasing power, or command over real resources, from the financial sector in excess of the current flow of savings:

> If investment is proceeding at a steady rate, the finance (or commitments to finance) required can be supplied from a revolving fund of a more or less constant amount, one entrepreneur having his finance replenished for the purpose of a projected investment as another exhausts his on paying for his completed investment. But if decisions to invest are (e.g.) increasing, the extra finance involved will constitute an additional demand for money.... But "finance" has nothing to do with saving. At the "financial" stage of the proceedings no net saving has taken place on anyone's part, just as there has been no net investment. "Finance" and "commitments to finance" are mere credit and debit book entries, which allow entrepreneurs to go ahead with

> assurance...if the banking system chooses to make the finance available and the investment projected by the new issues actually takes place, the appropriate level of incomes will be generated out of which there will necessarily remain over an amount of saving exactly sufficient to take care of the new investment. (Keynes, 1937, pp. 247–48)

It is in this crucial sense that Keynes's theory is a *monetary* theory of employment. The independence with which the monetary system endows the investment decision, combined with the propensity to consume and hence the multiplier, establishes a theory of the determination of the general level of output and , in consequence, of employment.

But this particular role of money was not a novel idea. In his analysis of money, Wicksell (1935) had pointed out that the banks may provide capitalists with command over resources in excess of the current level of output. The essential difference is that Wicksell was assuming that the real forces established a natural rate of interest and the natural rate of wages at which capital and labor were fully employed (on Wicksell's monetary theory and its relationship to Keynesian theory, see Garegnani, 1978–79). Keynes, however, was advancing a different theory of the relationship between saving and investment, though the task remained of establishing that there were no forces present in the economy that would push the level of investment toward the full-employment rate.

This similarity between Keynes and Wicksell should alert us to the fact that Keynes's analysis of output does *not* constitute a critique of the neoclassical theory of output, but simply poses an alternative. A suitably "neoclassical" theory of investment could, as we shall see, transform his analysis into something remarkably similar to the neoclassical formulation.

Keynes's analysis of the determinants of investment consisted of two elements. First, he argued that the relationship between the volume of investment and the prospective yield on that investment could be represented by the elastic schedule of the marginal efficiency of capital. Second, to determine the volume of investment, this schedule was related to the rate of interest that, Keynes argued, was determined not by the relationship between the demand for investible funds and the supply of saving but by the demand for the stock of monetary assets. This is derived from the demand for money for transactions purposes, and what is more important with respect to the determination of the rate of interest in any given circumstances, from the speculative demand to hold money as a means of holding wealth, a necessary condition for which is uncertainty as to the future rate of interest (Keynes, 1936, p. 168).

This latter proposition was to play a central role in the subsequent development of Keynes's argument. For his formulation of the determinants of investment immediately raises the question: why does not the rate of interest adjust to that level which ensures a full-employment rate of investment? Keynes's answer rests squarely on the monetary character of the rate of interest, rather than on any inelasticity of the marginal efficiency schedule: "Thus in the absence of money and in the absence—we must, of course, also suppose—of any other commodity with the assumed characteristics of money, the rates of interest would only reach equilibrium when there is full employment" (Keynes, 1936, p. 235).

So, Keynes appears to be resting his case for a less-than-full-employment equilibrium, not on the proposition that a full-employment rate of interest does not exist but on the proposition that monetary phenomena will inhibit (or prohibit) the tendency of the rate of interest to attain the full-employment rate.

The emphasis on the theory of interest is reinforced by Keynes's consideration in chapter 19 of the *General Theory* of the effect of flexibility of money wages on the level of employment. Given the structure of his model, wage flexibility can only alter the general level of activity if the propensity to consume, or the marginal efficiency of capital, or the rate of interest is affected. Examining these relations in turn, Keynes argued that the employment effect of a fall in money wages on the propensity to consume and the marginal efficiency of capital would be either neutral or tend to reduce the level of employment. The only manner, therefore, in which a fall in wages could lead to an increase in employment would be through its effects on the real value of the stock of monetary assets and, hence, on the rate of interest—effects that may be likened to effects of open-market operations designed to increase the quantity of money: "Just as a moderate increase in the quantity of money may exert an inadequate influence over the long-term rate of interest, whilst an immoderate increase may offset its other advantages by its disturbing effect on confidence; so a moderate reduction in money-wages may prove inadequate, whilst an immoderate reduction might shatter confidence even if it were practicable" (Keynes, 1936, pp. 266–67).

Keynes also attempted to lend support to his own theory by criticizing the neoclassical theory of output (Keynes, 1936, ch.14). This critique was based on the propositions that (a) the neoclassical theory of the determination of the rate of interest and of the level of output was false because saving and investment are necessarily equal at any level of employment, and thus there could not be separate schedules of saving and investment the interaction of which would determine the rate of interest; and (b) that the rate of interest was not determined by the relationship of saving to investment but by the demand for the stock of monetary assets.

The first criticism is related to Keynes's assertion that neoclassical economists assumed that the economy operates at full employment, and like that assertion, it does not hold water. The full-employment level of output is not assumed by neoclassical economists; it is proved to be the equilibrium out of the economy. Similarly, while it is obvious that in an accounting sense, saving and investment are identical, this does not mean that the casual relationship between saving and investment may not be characterized by two elastic schedules. If it is supposed that such schedules exist and that wages and the rate of interest are flexible, then Keynes can argue that the system will not tend toward a full-employment level of activity only by supposing that investment does not react in such a manner as to validate a desire to increase saving. Suppose, for example, that the level of output is below the full-employment level. Wages fall, and individual capitalists decide to hire more labor. The consequent increase in output can be sold only if a fall in the rate of interest leads to increased investment that "absorbs" the consequent increase in saving. By such a process, the system tends toward full employment, with saving always equal to investment (in the accounting sense).

Keynes's second criticism, which relies on the juxtaposition of his theory of the rate of interest and the neoclassical theory, is, as Garegnani has shown, seriously undermined by the fact that fluctuations in liquidity preference are based on fluctuations of the expected rate of interest around the conventional or normal rate—but no theory is presented for the determination of that conventional rate. It might be argued, for example, that in the long run, the normal rate would be determined by the real rate of return on capital, itself determined by the long-run relationship of the supply and demand for capital.

So, not only does an important element of Keynes's theory of output rest on the monetary analysis of the determination of the rate of interest, but his critique of neoclassical theory does, too. But the analysis of interest was just that part of his theory that Keynes was to argue is independent of the initial novelty of his position and that does not carry us far. The reason for the seemingly peculiar elevation of the analysis of the rate of interest to the center of the stage has been identified as the weakness of his critique of neoclassical theory once the very tentative critical remarks made in draft concerning the logical status of the neoclassical theory of capital had been removed following criticism by Harrod (Milgate, 1977) and from the necessity of providing an inhibition to the movement of the rate of interest toward the full-employment level once the existence of an elastic demand schedule for investment, the marginal efficiency of capital schedule, had been assumed (Garegnani, 1976).

Keynes was ultimately forced into defending his theory on the rather weak grounds that the effects of uncertainty linked with monetary phenomena would inhibit the tendency of investment to the full-employment level:

> Thus, after giving full weight to the importance of the influence of short-period changes in the state of long-term expectation as distinct from changes in the rate of interest, we are still entitled to return to the latter as exercising, at any rate, in normal circumstances, a great though not a decisive, influence on the rate of investment. Only experience, however, can show how far management of the rate of interest is capable of continuously stimulating the appropriate volume of investment. For my own part I am now somewhat sceptical of the success of a merely monetary policy directed toward influencing the rate of interest. (1936, p. 164)

But skepticism is not enough. The possibility of the establishment of a full-employment rate of interest was inherent in Keynes's model: "It is therefore, on the effect of a falling wage—and price—level on the demand for money that those who believe in the self-regulating quality of the economic system must rest the weight of their argument; though I am not aware that they have done so" (1936, p. 266). He would not have long to wait.

The Neoclassical Synthesis and Beyond

The characterization of Keynes's argument as "Mr Keynes's special theory," and the subsequent integration of apparently Keynesian propositions into the corpus of neoclassical analysis, was launched by Hicks in 1937. This and the development of what has come to be known as the Neoclassical Synthesis has been ably surveyed by Garegnani (1978–79), and there is no need for us to do anything other than summarize the main points of the argument.

The development of the Neoclassical Synthesis was based on the limitation of the effects that uncertainty and instability might be expected to have in the longer run, as opposed to their effects on short-run fluctuations of the economy around the long-run position. In the long run, it might be argued, for example, that the demand for money would not be dominated by uncertainties concerning the deviation of interest rates from the conventional rate, but would instead be derived from the relative convenience and risk involved in holding wealth in money form:

> The theory of risk-avoiding behaviour has been shown to provide a basis for liquidity preference and for an inverse relationship between the demand for cash and the rate of interest. This theory does not depend on the inelasticity of expectations of future interest rates, but can proceed from the assumption that the expected value of capital gain or loss from holding interest-bearing assets is always zero. In this respect, it is a logically more satisfactory foundation for liquidity preference than the Keynesian theory. (Tobin, 1958, p. 84)

Tobin prefaced his reconstruction of liquidity theory with the proposition that what "needs to be explained is not only the existence of a demand for cash when its yield is less than the yield on alternative assets but an inverse relationship between the aggregate demand for cash and the size of this differential in yields" (1958, p. 65).

Having thereby constructed a stable demand function for money, one may readily conclude that, other than in the case in which the demand for money is highly elastic with respect to the rate of interest (Keynes's special theory), a fall in money wages or an increase in the quantity of money will lead to a fall in the rate of interest and a tendency of investment to the full-employment level: "it is the fact that money wages are too high relative to the quantity of money that explains why it is unprofitable to expand employment to the 'full-employment' level" (Modigliani, 1944, p. 255). Employment may be expanded either by a decrease in money wages or by an increase in the quantity of money, if money wages are constant.

The Keynesian analysis of unemployment is, thus, confined to the short-period influence of rigidities and of uncertainty and similar psychological effects. The permanent forces in the economy would establish a full-employment equilibrium if it were not for short-period imperfections that cause deviations, of lesser or greater size and length, from the full-employment level of output.

The Neoclassical Synthesis involves an attempt to derive essentially neoclassical conclusions from a bowdlerized version of Keynesian ideas, focusing in particular on the relationships between the stock of money, measured in wage units, the rate of interest, and the level of investment. An apparently different direction has been taken with the development of theories of "rationing," in which an attempt is made to derive quasi-Keynesian conclusions from restricted versions of neoclassical general equilibrium models—including models of pure exchange and of non-capitalistic production.

Theories of rationing are descended from Clower's (1965) idea of the dual-decision hypothesis relating notional and effective excess demands, and similar developments by Leijonhufvud (1968, 1971). The rationed equilibrium does not necessarily satisfy Walras's Law, and thus in equilibrium some markets, such as the market for labor, may display negative excess demands, while all other excess demands are equal to zero.

The concept of a ration derives from the idea that the quantity traded in a particular market at a given price is determined by the short side of the market. For example, if the Walrasian notional supply and demand functions for labor are indicated by $S_L(w)$ and $D_L(w)$, respectively, where $w = w/p$ is the real wage and at $w = w^*$, $D_L(w^*) < S_L(w^*)$, then jobs are rationed, since workers can only supply an amount of labor equal to $D_L(w^*)$. Similarly, entrepreneurs' opportunities to sell goods may be rationed if the demand for goods is less than the quantity they would be willing to sell at the going price; or buyers may be rationed in the quantity of a good they are able to purchase if the quantity available is less than the notional demand at the going price.

Clower (1965) uses this concept to explain unemployment in a model in which there exists but one good and labor. Suppose that the real wage is at such a level that the notional demand for labor is less than the notional supply; then, the demand for the good will be a function of the real wage and the quantity of labor demanded, which is equal to the effective supply of labor. The money wage and the price level may be such that supply is equal to effective demand in the market for the good. So, if D_i, S_i are notional demands for i, and S, D are effective demands for i, then the situation just described may be characterized as:

$$D_L(w^*) = S^e_L(w^*) < S_L(w^*) \tag{3}$$

$$D^e_G(w^*, D_L) = S_G(w^*) \tag{4}$$

As far as the entrepreneur is concerned, the market for the good is in equilibrium and there is no incentive to increase output and, hence, demand more labor; and equally, there is no pressure to change the good price. But labor is unemployed. The situation has been characterized by both Clower and Leijuonhufvud as peculiar to a monetary economy:

> If the unemployed demanded "payment" in the form of the products of the individual firms, producers would perceive this as demand for a larger volume of output than is being produced. As long as the unemployed did not demand more in exchange than their marginal physical product, competitive producers would have no reason to turn such barter-bargains down. But, just as workers find that their labour is not a source of direct purchasing power over output, producers find that their output is not a means of payment for the purchase of labour inputs. In offering their services to firms that do not produce a balanced basket of consumer goods, workers ask for *money wages*. From the standpoint of prospective employers, therefore, the offer of labour services is not directly connected with a demand for additional output. Not perceiving that more output is called for, individual firms will, consequently, turn such offers down (a) even if no more than labour's marginal value product (evaluated at going prices) is being asked for, and (b) even if no more than the money wage rate that the system would have in equilibrium is being asked for. (Leijonhufvud, 1971, p. 25)

As Hahn has pointed out (1977, p. 31), this is a very limited definition of a monetary economy, and under the conditions postulated, the absence of money would lead to greater market failure than its presence.

But the transmission of information is not really the issue. Suppose, for example, that in a capitalist economy in which all profits are saved, unemployed workers guarantee to employers that they will spend all the wages they might earn on the goods they produce. The information is conveyed, but clearly no capitalist would offer employment, for there would be no possibility of profit—the total increase in expenditure would be equal to the increased wage bill. If employment is to increase, there must be an increase in investment. Here, Leijonhufvud's analysis is quite traditional. He argues that the fall in the rate of interest required to stimulate the investment that will absorb increased saving (he must mean increased potential saving) will be inhibited by liquidity preference (1971, p. 38). Thus, the amount of effective saving will be rationed by the short side of the saving–investment market. The substance of rationing theory comes down to an inhibition on the adjustment of the rate of interest to the market-clearing rate.

A new version of rationing theory that combines the Clower-Leijonhufvud emphasis on relative prices with earlier ideas on the relationship between the average level of wages and prices, the quantity of money, and the overall level of spending has been developed by Malinvaud (1977). In the discussion that follows, we will utilize a simplified version of Malinvaud's model developed by Kahn (1980).

Malinvaud assumed that investment expenditure (and, hence, employment in the investment sector) is autonomously fixed. Variations in the level of output of and employment can then be due only to variations in the output of consumption goods. Saving behavior is determined by a relatively complex analysis in terms of individual utility maximization in the light of dividends, the wage rate, employment, the price of consumption goods, and the size of money stocks. To simplify the story, we assume that all profits are saved and that the pattern of saving out of wages and the expenditure of money stocks (by the employed and the unemployed) are such that the sum of the two is constant at S_w. This assumption is clearly unrealistic if the average levels of wages and prices are very low relative to the size of money stocks, a question to which we shall return later. If investment-sector profits are also fixed at P_1, then total profits in the consumption sector, P_c, are determined from the condition that investment equals savings:

$$I = S_w + P_1 + P_c \tag{5}$$

So, for any given money-wage level, the price of the consumption good must be such as to yield a profit on the total output of consumer goods equal to P_c. This relationship is shown by the curve *DD* in figure 10.1, in which a unit of the consumption good is defined as the average amount produced by one unit of labor employed. The curve is a rectangular hyperbola around the *y*-axis and the level of the money-wage rate.

On the supply side, Malinvaud assumes that an arbitrary capital stock embodying many vintages will be used in ascending order of cost per unit output, so that increased output may only be produced at an increased marginal cost. The resultant well-behaved supply function is indicated by the curve *SS* in figure 10.1. Finally, Malinvaud argues that the essential characteristic of macroeconomic analysis of modern society is that it should be short run; and hence, on the basis of empirical evidence of administered pricing and the determination of wages in a highly institutional environment, "the theory under consideration

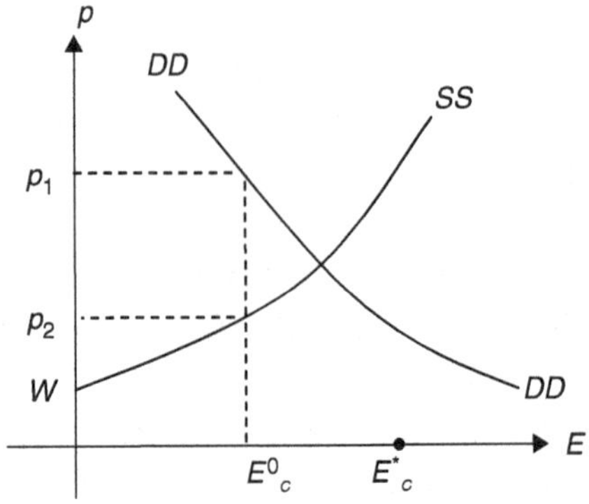

Figure 10.1 Employment in the consumption goods sector

here is justified in assuming full price rigidity, i.e., in working with models in which prices and wage rates are exogenous" (Malinvaud, 1977, pp. 11–12).

The model may now be used to classify types of unemployment with respect to a given configuration of wage rate and consumption-good price. Suppose, for example, that with reference to figure 10.1, in which E_c^* indicates the level of consumption-sector employment that corresponds to full employment in the economy as a whole, and W is the (sticky) money-wage rate, that the price of the consumption good is fixed at p_1. Then, the amount of employment is determined by demand; producers are rationed as to the quantity of consumption goods they can sell; and jobs are rationed to the less than full-employment demand for labor. In these circumstances, a fall in the price (an increase in the real wage) would lead to increased employment. This situation Malinvaud describes as Keynesian unemployment. Now, suppose that the price is set at p_2. Employment is determined by the supply condition; consumers are rationed as to the amount they can buy; and jobs are also rationed. A rise in p (a fall in the real wage) would result in increased employment. This situation Malinvaud refers to as classical unemployment. Finally, if the level of consumption sector employment that would result in full employment in the economy were E_c^o, then any fixed price level between p_1 and p_2 would result in repressed inflation.

The relationship among these three characterizations of the economy is illustrated in figure 10.2. For any given money wage, we may find a price that corresponds to full-employment demand, that corresponds to full employment on the supply side, or that defines the boundary between Keynesian and classical unemployment. Varying the level of

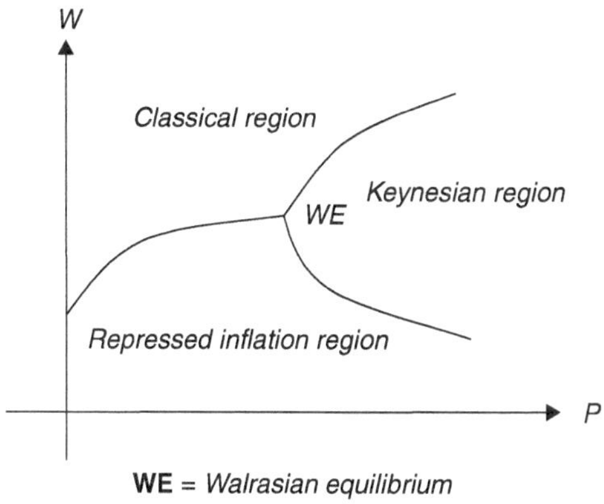

Figure 10.2

money wages and the price level will trace out loci of such wage-price relations, the shape of the curves being considerably influenced by the change in the real value of the stock of monetary assets. There will be a particular real wage and price level, *WE*, which will correspond to full employment—this point Malinvaud refers to as "Walrasian equilibrium."

Malinvaud asserts that if the data of his model were "constant through time... then the long run equilibrium resulting from price theory will be the Walrasian equilibrium," but that "since prices and wages are sticky, we cannot expect the growth path to coincide permanently with the changing Walrasian equilibrium in our short-term model" (Malinvaud, 1977, p. 93). Institutional factors that introduce rigidities into the price system are, therefore, to blame for the economy's not being at a full-employment equilibrium.

Two major criticisms have been made of the Malinvaud model. First, Kahn (1980) has argued that the form of the cost curve on which the analysis depends is incompatible with the assumption of administered prices:

> Fixed or "sticky" prices are found in manufacturing and distribution, where products are not homogeneous and labour costs area constant or decreasing up to the limits of capacity. The result, which has been well confirmed by various empirical studies and is widely known as Okun's Law, is that productivity in industry increases with short run increases in output, while prices are sticky. Flexible prices are found in those markets for a limited range of primary products where products

> are homogeneous, demand to the individual producer is almost perfectly elastic, and costs rise with output due to fixed natural resources. Malinvaud mixes the two. (Kahn, 1980, p. 224)

Second, Hahn (1977) has argued that the rationing model as formulated by Malinvaud (and, indeed, by Clower and Leijonhufvud) amounts merely to the proposition that prices and wages are insufficiently flexible for the determination of full-employment output, without any argument being made as to the origin of such flexibility (Hahn, 1977, pp. 32–33). He argues that inflexibility in the face of, say, persistent unemployment, may be explained in terms of "conjectural equilibria":

> Let us stick for the moment to the labour market and think of money wages as being quoted by the sellers of labour. One now needs to supplement the description of the household by a demand curve conjectured by it.... The household must have some beliefs as to how its ration of labour would respond to a change in the wage it quotes. If there is an equilibrium it is what I call a conjectural equilibrium. That is, it is a state such that actions of agents are compatible and such that, given the conjectures no price can be advantageously changed by any agent.... If an equilibrium is a state where rational actions are compatible and if amongst possible actions one includes changing of price, then there exist non-Walrasian unemployment equilibria. The wage is neither fixed nor arbitrary nor flexible. It is what it is because no agent finds it advantageous to change it. (Hahn, 1977, p. 34)

Hahn has also used the concept of conjectural equilibrium to argue that Malinvaud's identification of a given set of prices with Walrasian full-employment equilibrium is too limited, for rationed conjectural equilibria with unemployment may be associated with the Walrasian prices (Hahn, 1978).

Hahn's argument is illustrated in figure 10.3. The economy consists of two individuals (or two groups of individuals), a and b, with endowments e_a and e_b of commodities x and y. The competitive equilibrium supported by the prices shown involves a selling $(e_a\ s_a)$ of x and buying $(s_a\ t_a)$ of y; b sells $(e_b\ s_b)$ of y and buys $(s_b\ t_b)$ of x. Suppose, now, that a is rationed (by conjecture) to the sale of $(e_a\ c_a)$ of x; then there exists a ration for b—namely, the conjecture that b can only sell $(e_b\ c_b)$ of y—such that the rationed (conjectural) equilibrium is sustained by the Walrasian equilibrium prices.

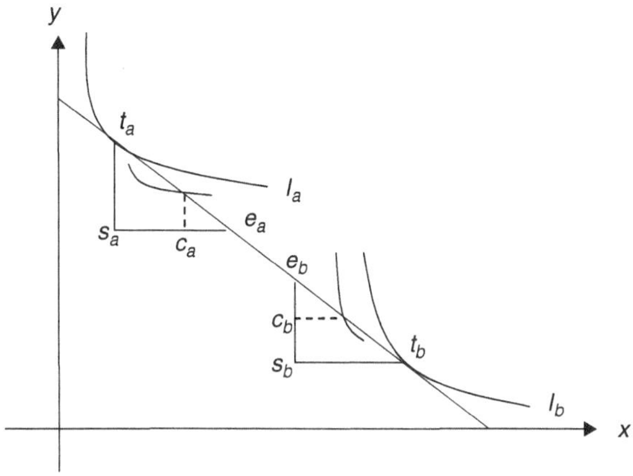

Figure 10.3

But Hahn's criticism does not take us very far (apart from showing how arbitrary is the fixed-price approach). In any disequilibrium, position agents act on false information and these actions may, in the short run, exacerbate and perpetuate the disequilibrium. But the crucial question is whether forces endogenous to the system will push it toward a full-employment position. Hahn admits that it seems likely that, in competitive economies, rationed conjectural equilibria will be unstable and that Walrasian equilibrium will be the only rational conjectural equilibrium possible (Hahn, 1978, p. 3). So, his conjectural analysis reduces to an evocation of monopolistic elements as an explanation for sticky prices or "perceived rations."

However, both Kahn and Hahn seem to miss the main failing of rationing models in general, and Malinvaud's model in particular, which is that such models do not address the fundamental issue in the interpretation of Keynesian analysis—the relationship between saving and investment. In Malinvaud's model, for example, all the weight of adjustment in employment is placed on varying output in the consumption sector, the investment sector being fixed. The label "Walrasian," which he attaches to a full-employment position attained primarily through operation of the real balance effect, is quite spurious, for no Walrasian analysis of saving and investment is present other than the off-hand remark that it "would be still more interesting to introduce into our prototype model a market for bonds with a flexible interest rate and to recognize that 'autonomous' demands depends on the rate of interest" (Malinvaud, 1977, p. 114).

Insofar as rationing models are constructed on Walrasian lines, they amount merely to particular examples of the wide variety of imperfectionist models where particular imperfections are imposed to inhibit the gravitation of prices toward equilibrium. These might even be pure-exchange models. They certainly have nothing essential to do with the central issue of Keynes's *General Theory*—namely, the establishment of an underemployment equilibrium by the normal working of the saving–investment relationship through the multiplier. The rationing models, hence, appear to be a remarkable example of intellectual atavism and spurious sophistication. Under the guise of complex general equilibrium analyses, they contrive to produce pre-Keynesian propositions by means of un-Keynesian devices—and triumphantly label the result "Keynesian."

Keynes's Critique of the Neoclassicals

The variety of attempts to generate neoclassical results in a Keynesian framework, and Keynesian results in a neoclassical framework, together point to important failings in the *General Theory*: the inadequacy of Keynes's critique of the neoclassical theory of output and the important ambiguities introduced by Keynes's marginalist treatment of the labor market and by his portrayal of the marginal efficiency of capital as an elastic demand schedule for investment. Garegnani (1978–79) has argued that these failings may be remedied by application of the results of the debate on the neoclassical theory of capital derived from Sraffa's *Production of Commodities*. We may illustrate this point by reference to the implications of the debate for Fisher's analysis of investment and the rate of interest that, as we saw above, Keynes identified with his own analysis.

But first we will examine Keynes's definition of the marginal efficiency of capital:

> If there is an increased investment in any given type of capital during any period of time, the marginal efficiency of that type of capital will diminish as the investment in it is increased, partly because the prospective yield will fall as the supply of that type of capital is increased, and partly because, as a rule, pressure on the facilities for producing that type of capital will cause its supply price to increase; the second of these factors being usually the

> more important in producing equilibrium in the short run, but the longer the period in view the more does the first factor take its place. Thus for each type of capital we can build up a schedule, showing by how much investment in it will have to increase within the period, in order that its marginal efficiency should fall to any given figure. We can then aggregate these schedules for all the types of capital, so as to provide a schedule relating the rate of aggregate investment to the corresponding marginal efficiency of capital in general which that rate of investment will establish. We shall call this the investment demand-schedule; or, alternatively, the schedule of the marginal efficiency of capital. (Keynes, 1936, p. 136)

Keynes's argument is more complicated than may at first appear, involving as it does assumptions on both the supply and demand conditions for individual capital goods in both the short and long run and, finally, at both individual and aggregate levels—the ultimate objective being the derivation of the relationship between the rate of aggregate investment and the corresponding marginal efficiency of capital in general, or, to put it another way, the general rate of return.

Taking first the short-period aspect of the argument, Keynes's assumption that increased investment in a given type of capital good will lead to higher cost of production—rising supply price—is quite unfounded. Any short-period situation, and particularly a short period in which capacity is widely underutilized, will be characterized by excess stocks of materials and machines in some (maybe all) sectors, with (perhaps) shortages in a few sectors, too. In such a situation, no definite hypothesis may be made as to the likely effect of increased output on cost, though in conditions of widespread excess capacity it seems reasonable to suppose that costs will tend to fall as fixed costs are averaged over higher output. Pressure on the facilities for producing a given capital good will tend to become significant only as full employment is approached, and even then the consequences for the cost of production of an increase in supply of any one capital good cannot be predicted with confidence.

The short-run influence of the demands for capital goods on prospective yield to be derived from further investment is likewise unpredictable, and as to the aggregate effect of all this, nothing can be said at all. Indeed, there is no short-run marginal efficiency of capital in general to say anything about. The relationship that Keynes sought must be a long-run relationship, in the sense that it is sufficiently unambiguous and persistent to allow definite conclusions to be drawn concerning the influence of a given volume of investment on the rate of return.

In the longer run, Keynes himself suggested that increased output will not result in any increase in cost. Any diminution in return must, therefore, derive from the fall in prospective yield as more capital-goods producers compete to sell their services. What, then, is the relationship between the volume of investment and the rate of return in the longer run—that is, in a situation in which the cost-minimizing combination of factors is chosen? At the partial level Keynes first considers, the answer seems clear: if all other prices in the economy are taken as given, then, *ceteris paribus,* it may be argued that there is an inverse relationship between the rate of return and the quantity of capital invested in the production of a given output. But Keynes's argument is on very shaky ground when he attempts to define the relationship for the economy as a whole by simple aggregation of these partial effects, for he can no longer use the *ceteris paribus* condition to keep at bay some fundamental problems.

These fundamental difficulties in Keynes's characterization of the marginal efficiency of capital may be clarified by returning to Fisher's analysis of the incremental rate of return on investment that Keynes tells us is "identical with my definition" (Keynes, 1936, p. 140). Fisher's analysis is based on the substitution of capital for labor in a full-employment equilibrium, and throughout his discussion of the theory of saving, investment, and interest, he imposes a major limitation on his argument; he assumes that all prices, wages, and rents are fixed, and do no vary with variations in the rate of interest (Fisher, 1930, p. 131n). This fixed-price assumption allows Fisher to express all magnitudes in terms of money and to move between discussion of individual behavior and that of the economy as a whole without considering the interrelationship between the rate of interest and prices.

An attempt to generalize Fisher's analysis to a many-commodity model, and hence to relate the determination of prices to the determination of the rate of interest, has been made by Solow (1963, 1967). Solow's model, and the debate it provoked, has been analyzed elsewhere (see Eatwell, 1976); for our present purposes, we need only summarize the main conclusions of that debate.

It is assumed by Solow that the economy is in a stationary state, producing a consumption good—corn—by means of many reproducible inputs and labor. To enable the definition of limits, we may further assume that the technical possibilities of the economy are characterized by a wage-profit frontier that is an envelope to an infinity of wage-profit curves, such that techniques are arrayed continuously along the frontier. Furthermore, consumption and value of capital per head associated with the variations in technique may be described by differentiable functions.

Since the techniques used in the production of corn require inputs of commodities other than corn, the wage-profit line for each technique may assume any negatively sloped curvature. But consumption-good output per capita, c, (net output per head) and the value of produced inputs per capita, k, are continuous differentiable functions of the rate of interest (rate of profit), r, even though the technique in use varies continuously with r:

$$c = z(r)$$
$$k = (\textit{net output} - \textit{wages}) \,/\, \textit{rate of profit} = [z(r) - g(r)] \;/r$$

where $g(r) = w$ is the equation of the wage-profit frontier.

The rate of return over cost of a transition between the technique in use at r and the adjacent technique at $(r + h)$ is the ratio of the value of the difference in the perpetual-consumption streams to the value of the difference in the capital stocks (that is, the sacrifice required to effect the transition):

$$[z(r + h) - z(r)] \;/\; \{[z(r + h) - g(r + h]/ \;(r + h)\} - \{[z(r) - g(r)]/r\} \qquad (6)$$

In the limit, as the number of techniques grows denser, $h \to 0$, and expression *(6)* becomes:

$$z'(r)[\; r^2/ \;\{r[z'(r) - g'(r)] - z(r) + g(r)\} \neq r \qquad (7)$$

The marginal rate of return over cost is not equal to the rate of profit. The equality would hold if and only if:

$$z(r) = g(r) - rg'(r) \qquad (8)$$

This would be the case of an economy having the properties of Samuelson's (1962) surrogate production function, and would indicate that, for all intents and purposes, the economy under consideration was set in a one-commodity world. The inequality does not depend on the presence of reswitching or even perversity. So long as the economy contains more than one produced input, the rate of profit is not equal to the rate of return over cost. More generally, no demand schedule for investment as a function of the rate of interest may be constructed (Garegnani 1978–79).

The lack of any logical foundation for the construction of an elastic demand schedule for investment as a function of the rate of interest is simultaneously a critique of the neoclassical theory of output and a critique of Keynes's concept of the marginal efficiency of capital—which was itself derived from the neoclassical schedule. This follows from the fact that the neoclassical theory of output is synonymous with the neoclassical theory of value, and so an effective critique of the latter necessarily constitutes an effective critique of the former. There is no logically consistent foundation to the idea that variation in relative prices, or in the rate of interest, or in money wages, will cause the system to tend to a full-employment level of output. Keynes's utilization of the notion of a demand schedule for investment may, perhaps, be explained by the pioneering nature of the *General Theory*, in which the main propositions of a new theory of output are combined with vestiges of the old theory; by the need to present an apparently complete theory; and by the pragmatic ambiguity with which many neoclassical propositions were presented in the then dominant Marshallian formulation. Garegnani has argued that:

> the origin of the contrasted meanings attributed to Keynes's theory is to be sought in the doubtful compatibility, from the standpoint of an analysis of long-period tendencies, between the concept of the marginal efficiency of capital and the argument that the level of output plays the leading role in equilibrating planned saving and planned investment. Once the former idea is accepted, it is difficult not to confine the importance of the latter argument to the explanation of the trade cycle and other short-period phenomena. On the other hand, the different conclusions to which Keynes was pointing can be sustained in so far as investment is assumed to be insensitive to the rate of interest, even in the long period. But this assumption is in sharp conflict with the presuppositions of the traditional theory of distribution and cannot find a firm foundation until the critique of that theory has undermined those presuppositions. (1978–79, p. 61)

In other words, once the corrosive influence of the presence of a marginal efficiency of capital schedule is removed, not only is the Neoclassical Synthesis seen to be without logical foundation (as is any other version of pseudo-Keynesian theory, such as that of Leijonhufvud or Malinvaud, which assumes a monotonic inverse relationship between the rate of interest and the volume of investment), but also Keynes's positive contribution, the principle of effective demand, is thrown into more dramatic relief.

The issue is still somewhat clouded, however, by the development of a version of neoclassical theory that, its proponents claim, is immune from the criticism of the traditional neoclassical theory of the rate of profit (or interest). The Arrow-Debreu model of intertemporal equilibrium, in which the equilibrium of the economy is defined as a sequence of temporal market-clearing equilibria, is the culmination of a shift in the domain of economic theory dating from the interwar period. This shift, which began in response to perceived difficulties in the neoclassical theory of capital (Milgate, 1979), was accelerated by the potential challenge of Keynesian theory to neoclassical orthodoxy, and found its most influential expression in the concept of temporary equilibrium in Hicks's *Value and Capital*, involving a change in the fundamental concept of equilibrium that characterizes the object of economic analysis (Garegnani, 1976). The concept of intertemporal equilibrium does not display a general rate of profit on the supply price of capital goods. But if the intertemporal equilibrium is constrained in such a way that the price of all producible means of production must be equal to their cost of production (a much weaker condition, it should be noted, than the imposition of a stationary price vector), the standard neoclassical analysis is, in general, inconsistent unless the endowment of capital goods is expressed as a quantity of value—the old circularity returns. Since the notion of a tendency toward a general rate of profit is an essential part of the abstract characterization of a capitalist economy, the new method of intertemporal equilibrium follows the early versions of Say's Law in assuming away the fundamental aspects of the economic system that it purports to explain—capitalism is assumed away to fit the requirements of the neoclassical theory of value and output.

Yet it is just such Walrasian models that are the typical benchmark for the application of rationing and similar imperfections (including the empirically empty concept of subjective conjecture), and hence, for the argument that Keynesian analysis may be interpreted as an analysis of short-period disequilibrium. The apparent pragmatism implied by the definition of monopoly, lack of information, uncertainty, rigidities, or monetary distortions as short-period phenomena is a triple deception: first, because these concepts are typically incorporated into models from which the very nature of capitalist production is absent; second, because the short period is only a coherent notion when related to the position toward which the persistent forces of the economy will continuously gravitate; and third, because it is by no means clear that any of these phenomena inhibit the long-run forces of capitalist competition (Clifton, 1977).

If, then, we are to take both methodology and analysis seriously, a primary task is to identify those persistent forces that determine the normal, or long-period, position of prices and outputs in a capitalist economy. Once logically consistent and congruent theories of the operation of such forces have been established, then it will be possible to proceed to the analysis of the transitory and specific phenomena that may influence the day-to-day working of the system. We have seen in this section that neoclassical analysis has nothing to offer to this program.

Marx and Keynes

In the search for a satisfactory synthesis of value and output theories, we are thus confronted by a logically consistent theory of value and distribution that is open with respect to the determination of output; and a logically consistent theory of output that has not been integrated satisfactorily with a theory of value and distribution. The task of this final section is to inquire into the possible congruence of the surplus approach to value and distribution and Keynes's principle of effective demand.

Before proceeding to more formal elements of this task, we will, however, consider the relationship between Marx's possibility of crises and the Keynesian theory of output. It was shown in the third section of this chapter that Marx argues that the possibility of crises arises from the essential characteristics of a capitalist economy and in particular from the metamorphoses involved in the circuit of capital from money form, to commodity form, to money form, and so on; and the separation that the ability to hold value in money form permits between the decision to produce and the ability to sell.

But there is more to Marx's conception of the possibility of crises than the fact that a capitalist economy is, of necessity, a monetary economy. Production in a capitalist system is the production of commodities (that is, of exchange values) and the object of investment is the expansion of the production of exchange values, not the production of use values. Thus, as Keynes put it, investment is undertaken for future profit—not for future consumption (Keynes, 1936, pp. 210–12; see also Keynes, 1971, ch. 2). But since Marx advanced no theory of the relationship between saving and investment, his case for the actuality of a general failure to realize the value of output was based on the time lags induced by disproportionalities and the anarchy of capitalist production (Marx, 1968, p. 529).

In this context, anarchy does not mean incoherence, but that what is rational for the individual may be irrational for the system as a whole. In a capitalist economy, the individual capitalist may decide to hold his wealth in terms of money rather than commit himself to future production. This may be a rational act in the light of a pessimistic view of future returns. But with Keynes's principle of effective demand, it may be seen that the outcome will not be irrational merely in the sense of a breakdown, but will lead to a permanently lower level of output from which there is no inherent tendency for the system to move. Permanent crises *do* exist in the sense of permanently lower output, though they do not necessarily exist as a permanently lower rate of profit.

The Keynesian perception of the working of a capitalist system is not inconsistent with the more comprehensive Marxian characterization. Indeed, if Keynes's principle of effective demand is appended as a theory of the actuality of crises, Marx's conception of crises is expanded from a notion of transitory time lags and breakdowns into a theory of output, an essential precondition of which is the existence of a monetary commodity economy.

The formal structure of a model combining a surplus theory of value and distribution with the Keynesian theory of output may best be approached through a consideration of Kalecki's version of the theory of output. Kalecki's version of the principle of effective demand is constructed from two relationships: a rather simplistic theory of distribution based on the idea that the markup contained in individual commodity prices is determined by the degree of monopoly, and a theory of aggregate profits determined by the volume of autonomous investment and the propensity to save out of profits (the propensity to save out of wages being set equal to zero). If the markup is such that the share of profit is equal to π, then from the multiplier condition that:

$$s_p P = I \tag{9}$$

where s_p is the saving propensity out of profits, P total net profits, and I is net investment, we may derive the result that the level of net income, Y, is

$$Y = I \cdot 1/s_p \cdot 1/\pi \tag{10}$$

The problem with Kalecki's model is the inadequacy of his theory of distribution (which, as may be seen in Kalecki, 1971, he constantly revised).

The markup is determined at the level of the individual firm. But the markup of one firm is the cost of another, and unless the ramifications of the interdependence of price formation are taken into account, the ratio π is simply a definition with no theoretical determination. However, this limitation may be overcome, for the markup in any one sector is the outcome of the peculiar circumstances of that sector, and the general rate of profit—the latter being the typically preponderant persistent element in price formation. In his theory, Kalecki does treat the theory of value and distribution and the theory of output separately; and it will come as no surprise that the separability condition we have already seen to be characteristic of the classical theory of value allows us to remedy the deficiencies of Kalecki's approach.

Taking the classical data and assuming, for the moment, constant returns to scale, we can solve for the rate of profit and prices from the equations:

$$p'A(1+r)+p'\ ba'_0=p' \tag{11}$$

where A is the matrix of unit input coefficients, a_0 the vector of labor input coefficients, and b the vector of wage-goods per hour of work. Kalecki's equation (9) may now be re-written:

$$rp'Ax = p'\ n_I(i/s_p) \tag{12}$$

where n_I is the vector of net investments. The value of net investment, $p'\ n_{I'}$ determines, via the multiplier, the combinations of levels of gross outputs x appropriate to the rate of profit and prices determined by equation (11). The level of employment is $a_0'\ x$ and of net output $[I - A]\ x$. Complications and ramifications, including the abandonment of constant returns to scale, may now be added at will.

Formal manipulation apart, the crucial characteristic that permits the combination of the principle of effective demand with the classical theory of distribution in such a simple way is that the latter is *not* based on the principle of supply and demand, but on the proposition that the prices of commodities are determined by their conditions of reproduction and the distribution of the surplus as a uniform rate of profit on the value of capital invested. There is, therefore, no tendency for variation in distribution and prices to be an active factor pushing the system toward the full-employment level of output. This is not to say that there will be no relationship between the rate of profit and the level of investment, but this must be located in the more general context of the process of accumulation.

This brings us to the question of the determinants of investment, an issue that is apparently left open with the dissolution of Keynes's investment theory. An understanding of the determinants of investment can only be attained by locating the problem within the context of a general theory of capitalist accumulation adapted to the specific circumstances of any given time and place. The fundamental characteristic of capitalist accumulation is the competitive struggle for markets. The competitive process is shaped by the evolution and utilization of technology, the cumulative decline of the weak relative to the strong, the policies of nation-states, the penetration of noncapitalist markets, the structure and competition, relations between capital and labor, and pricing policy. All these factors, plus the institutional setting—financial, political, and social—in which they operate, affect the growth of demand and the pattern, scale, and rapidity of accumulation in a complex recursive process. The reduction of a theory of investment to two parameters—expectations and the rate of interest—is as empirically vacuous as it is theoretically empty. It could only be taken seriously in a supply-and-demand model.

How, then, do we interpret the role of uncertainty in the theory of effective demand and more generally in the analysis of accumulation? At the level of the individual capitalist, the uncertainties of the competitive process will have a significant influence on investment plans. But, as Keynes pointed out, this does not mean that the long-period position of the economy "depends of waves of irrational psychology. On the contrary, the state of long-term expectation is often steady" (Keynes, 1936, p. 162). Moreover, in a draft of the *General Theory*, Keynes had argued that having "made clear the part played by expectation in the economic nexus and the reaction of realised results on future expectation, it will be safe for us in what follows to discard reference to expectation. It is important to make the logical point clear and to define the terminology precisely.... But when once this has been done, considerations of practical convenience may legitimately take charge, in the light of the fact that in practice the process of revision of expectation is a gradual and continuous one, carried on mainly in the light of realised results; so that expected and realised results run into and overlap one another in their influence" (Keynes, 1973, p. 397). In a lecture following the publication of the *General Theory*, he commented: "I now feel that if I were writing the book again I should begin by setting forth my theory on the assumption that short-period expectations were always fulfilled" (Keynes, 1973, XIII, p. 181).

Keynes is arguing that the effect of expectations and uncertainties is manifest in the form of the real and persistent forces in the system; but the fact of uncertainty is not the fundamental issue in the interpretation of the systematic behavior of the economy. The issue is what a correct understanding is of the principle of effective demand—the operation of which is independent on the fact of uncertainty. The prevalence of the idea that uncertainty plays a central determining role in Keynes's contribution (rather than simply defining the environment in which the forces of the theory operate) has been attributed to the incorporation by Keynes of ideas on uncertainty into the corpus of the discussion of the *General Theory* (see also Keynes 1937a) in order to keep at bay the tendency to full employment implicit in the elastic marginal efficiency of capital schedule (Garegnani, 1978–79, 1976; Milgate, 1977, 1982). But once that schedule is abandoned, uncertainty can be treated as, on the one hand, an element in the short-period fluctuations of output around its long-period position and, on the other hand, as an element, together with convention, of the general environment in which the systematic processes of capitalist production and accumulation must operate.

In the construction of a theory of normal output, we will come across a difficulty not encountered in the theory of normal price formation. In the latter theory, we argued that prices were determined by the dominant technique; in the former case, however, some output is produced using fossils or superior techniques. The problem has two aspects. First, flexibility in the level of output derives both from the excess capacity carried by capitalist firms as a component part of their competitive strategy and from the fact that if there is a rapid upswing in demand, fossils will be more fully utilized. Nonetheless, the normal level of output in a stationary or slow-changing system would be related to the technical and distributional characteristics of the dominant technique. But, second, there is no reason to suppose that the pace of accumulation is slow, and hence in general, equation (12) must be modified to take account of the actual pattern of accumulation. This will present greater difficulties when the pace and pattern of accumulation is changing than when the pace of change is fairly steady.

This is not to suggest that we should look to the growth models of recent years, with their emphasis on proportionately growing economies, for any significant insight into the actual process of accumulation. Rather, we should ally Keynesian insights to the general theories of the nature of capitalist accumulation that are to be found in Smith and Marx. These theories include recognition that the commodity composition of output (other than the broad divisions between investment goods and wage goods) is of little general relevance in the accumulation of capital.

Although changes in commodity composition, both quantitative and qualitative, may be an important element in competition, the ultimate purpose is the production and accumulation of value in general.

These issues should alert us to the amount of work that needs to be done in order to fully utilize the tools provided by classic Marxian and Keynesian theory. The task involves both ridding the particular theories of inconsistences and obfuscations and elucidating the implications they present for the interpretation of each other. At the core of the resultant analytical schema will stand the surplus theory of value and distribution supplemented by the Keynesian insight into the theory of output.

Notes

This is a revised version of a paper by John Eatwell that appeared as the sixth chapter in Eatwell and Milgate's *Keynes's Economics and the Theory of Value and Distribution* (1983).

1. It is worth noting at this point that neither the classical economists nor Marx saw any role for the rate of profit, or indeed the rate of interest on money, as an equilibrating mechanism in the market for saving and investment. The rate of interest on money was regarded as a derivative concept "merely a portion of the profit, i.e., of the surplus value, which the functioning capitalist, industrialist or merchant has to pay to the owner and lender of money-capital whenever he uses loaned capital instead of his own" (Marx, 1967, p. 370). Hence, the rate of interest was not susceptible to significant variation other than that owing to variation in the social productivity of labor and/or the real wage.

11

Money, Capital, and Forced Saving

According to the conventional wisdom of the quantity theory of money, the ultimate effect of an exogenous change in monetary conditions falls exclusively on the general level of prices. Consideration of the possible effects of such changes on the so-called real variables of the system—the relative prices of commodities, the distribution of income between wages and profits, and the levels of output and employment—is restricted to intermediate situations where full adjustment to altered monetary conditions has not yet taken place. These situations have been the traditional haunt of critics of the more extreme advocates of the quantity theory who tend to play down any real consequences of monetary disturbances. This has been the case since the celebrated Bullionist Controversy and the Currency School–Banking School debates of the nineteenth century, down to debates over the Phillips curve and over the rational expectations hypothesis. However, they have also provided a fertile field for rapid theoretical advances in our understanding of the operation of the monetary system and its role in economic activity.

The interwar years provide a particularly interesting episode in this regard, for they saw not only significant developments in the analysis of these transitional situations but also the emergence of arguments like those of the *General Theory,* whose aim was to break away from the quantity theory framework and to reestablish monetary theory on a new footing. Indeed, there is an important sense in which these latter arguments developed directly out of debates about the transmission mechanism of monetary change within the quantity theory itself. One such debate was that which centered on the implications of monetary changes on the structure and amount of investment and, in turn, on the distinction between voluntary and forced saving. The participants in this debate numbered almost all of the best theorists of the day, and included not only Dennis Robertson, Erik Lindahl, and John Maynard Keynes, but also Piero Sraffa and Friedrich Hayek. The purpose here is to examine the theoretical arguments that lie beneath the analysis of money, capital, and forced saving, and to consider the character and content of the critique that Sraffa launched on Hayek's version of it in the celebrated exchange that took place between the two in 1932 in the pages of the *Economic Journal*. However, I am not so much concerned with the status of this debate in the history of economic thought as I am with those aspects of it that might be relevant to contemporary theory.[1]

Monetary Disturbances and the Level of Investment

Monetary conditions, understood in their broadest sense, include not only the conditions of supply of cash, credit, and other financial instruments but also the terms on which they are made available, the institutional structure of the existing system of banking and finance, its conventional practices and regulatory agencies, and the whole of the legal relations governing the financial system and contractual arrangements denominated in money terms. In modern market economies, monetary conditions seem to bear in one way or another on almost all of the economic relations established between individuals, institutions, and nations. A monetary disturbance, then, takes on the character of a complicated event. Though it may arise initially from an alteration in a limited number of factors—perhaps even just one—it is likely to ramify in a multitude of ways throughout the system. Examples range from the archetypical exogenous change in the available quantity of money (monetary base) to alterations in the policies and practices of private financial institutions or the market and regulatory activities of the central bank.

Of course, to render monetary theory tractable, it is customary to simplify the characteristics of the case considered while attempting to ensure that no essential information is lost. No doubt one of the strongest attractions of the old-fashioned quantity theory is that it reduces such an apparently complicated process to the consideration of a single source of exogenous change and a single, ultimate consequence. In the analysis of the relations between money, capital, and forced saving, the basic question was one that had occupied monetary theorists at least since the time of Wicksell, and it was addressed in a model whose monetary landscape is minimal.

Begin with a closed-market economy where production, relative prices, the wage rate, and the rate of interest are determined "as if" there were no monetary system at all. Taking as given the preferences of individual agents, the initial endowments of the system, and the available techniques of production, we can assume these have the usual properties so as to guarantee the existence of a unique equilibrium. The operation of the market mechanism will produce an outcome such that, at some natural rate of interest, i^*, planned savings just match the desired volume of investment, or $g[I(i^*) - S(i^*)] = 0$. The equilibrium configuration of relative prices, distribution, and the offers and demands for outputs and inputs are determined entirely without recourse to monetary factors. In the language of the day, the twin forces of "productivity" and "thrift" determine the rate of interest. In situations such as these, the volume of output and the aggregate income are established at the normal capacity, full-employment level. This fixes the equilibrium volume of transactions.

If these transactions are imagined to be put into effect with the aid of a medium of exchange—call it money—then, provided its available quantity is known, the familiar quantity equation (in either the Fisher or cash-balance version) will act to determine the general level of prices. Money is neutral, and the celebrated classical dichotomy between monetary and real variables is rigidly in place.[2] This sparse monetary environment can be slightly enlivened by introducing a set of institutions whose function is to deliver the funds accumulated by savers to those desirous of putting them to work in the production of commodities. Such institutions depend for their income on the differentials that exist at any time between their borrowing and lending rates. Notice that there is really nothing that could explain why they should come into existence, nor is there any way of explaining why they should survive. Call this the banking system.

Now, consider a situation in which the rate of interest established by the banking system for the terms of its lending in the market is different from the rate that would ensure compatibility between the plans of individual depositors (savers) and the plans of individual borrowers (investors)—that is, the rate at which the amount of saving forthcoming is equal to the desired amount of investment (assuming tastes and technology remain unchanged). Strictly speaking, such a divergence is not essentially connected with the existence of the banking system we have just introduced. In fact, no feature of a particularly monetary kind is required to explain it. The same situation would prevail if all lending were actually conducted in terms of commodities (deer, beaver, corn, and the like) and the price of one or more of them departed for quite accidental reasons from its cost of production.

Nevertheless, let us for the moment pursue the conventional argument and, with the necessary qualifications in mind, retain its terminology. We call the situation where the configuration of market interest rates now differs from the equilibrium configuration a monetary disequilibrium. Following Wicksell, we call the average market rate of interest the loan or money rate,[3] and the rate that balances planned saving and planned investment, the real or natural rate. In such a situation, what are the consequences of adopting banking practices that continue to allow all the demand for investible funds to be met at the prevailing money rate of interest, independently of the supply of savings forthcoming at that rate?[4] It is to this question that Hayek addressed himself in his *Prices and Production*, the book that Sraffa reviewed in the March issue of the *Economic Journal* in 1932.

Before examining the analysis that leads up to an answer to this question, it needs to be stressed that the key to the initial movement in the volume of investment under such conditions depends on two hypotheses: first, that any relaxation in the terms on which investible funds are made available is expected to be permanent;[5] and second, that at a permanently lower interest rate, producers will wish to augment their stock of capital equipment.

Assume that at time t_0, market rate of interest, i_A, falls below the equilibrium rate i^*. For simplicity, further assume that prior to t_0, the system had been in equilibrium—that is, a cost-minimizing choice of technique had been made such that at i^*, before the disturbance, producers had adjusted their actual capital stock to its desired physical composition and proportion to labor, denoted K^*. Now, at the new lower rate of interest, i_A, producers will only seek to obtain loans if they anticipate that rate to persist and that the new cost-minimizing choice of technique mandates an adjustment to a new desired stock of capital with a different physical composition and a higher proportion to labor, denoted K^{**}. The argument is illustrated in figure 11.1.

Notice that there is no reason to expect any particular path to be taken toward the new position after the initial disturbance. Notice also that, if the change in the rate of interest turns out not to be permanent,

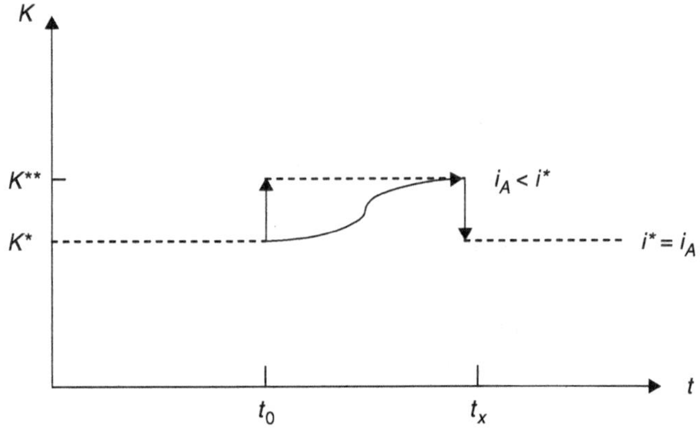

Figure 11.1

say at t_x (a case that will be examined in more detail later), then the system will return to its original position—though not, perhaps, without considerable dislocation and the passage of time. A few of the many possible paths that the system might follow between t_0 and t_x are indicated in figure 11.1. Similar paths could be constructed to depict the actual transition back to the original position after t_x.

From the viewpoint of the real effects of a monetary disturbance, the fact that, in this case, such a disturbance acts initially to increase investment is the most interesting feature of the argument. This is all the more so, since the disturbance entails an expansion of the available quantity of circulating medium.[6] However, the premise behind this plausible enough conclusion is not the plausible enough hypothesis that net investment is synonymous with capital accumulation. Instead, the basic premise is that alterations in the physical composition of the capital stock, favoring methods of production that exhibit higher capital intensity, will be induced by a permanent lowering of the rate of interest. In the kind of analysis we have so far been considering, it is this proposition that ensures the demand for investible funds will rise and fall with the loosening and tightening of the terms upon which they are made available.

Voluntary Saving, Forced Saving, and Over-investment

The transmission of the effects of a monetary disturbance of the type we have just discussed, which Wicksell himself described as a cumulative process of inflation that would give way only when the banking system found its currency reserves depleted (that is, base money, or gold under the gold standard of Wicksell's day), is also the central problem in the debate over forced saving. The argument starts at roughly the same place as Wicksell's cumulative process, but then takes off in a direction entirely its own.[7] As we have seen, the story opens when the banking system grants credits to borrowers whose aim is to use the funds in the production of commodities. Since I am primarily concerned with Hayek's own statement of the matter in *Prices and Production*, let us recall his own starting point: "In a money economy, the actual or money rate of interest...may differ from the equilibrium or natural rate, because the demand for and the supply of capital do not meet in their natural form but in the form of money, the quantity of which available for capital purposes may be arbitrarily changed by the banks" (1931, p. 23).

In the "natural" course of events, so the argument goes, if the demanders and suppliers of capital meet to exchange capital in its "natural form," the excess demand for investible funds consequent upon the lower money interest rate would immediately have a tendency to drive up that rate of interest until the system returned to the original equilibrium at i^*. This will occur as long as the function $g[I(i) - S(i)]$ is continuous and decreasing, and as long as the data remain the same. Savers will not part with their capital "in its natural form" at that rate, or at least will not part with as much of it as investors desire; investors will have to bid up the interest rate in order to induce them to do so.

However, in a money economy, the banking system might simply meet all demands for investible funds at the lower rate i_A. Investment would then actually exceed voluntary saving, and at least in the first instance, there need be no pressure for interest rates to rise. Since these additional amounts of investible funds will be competing for resources that were already fully utilized (the original position was one of equilibrium), a process of rising *nominal* incomes will be set in motion. Whether there are also changes in *real* income during the process depends on the elasticity of output is either significant or negligible. The ensuing inflation would generate forced saving and would close *artificially* the gap between voluntary saving and investment. But this will only be temporary. Either the banking system will run up against reserve requirements, and so be forced to alter the terms upon which advances are being made (interest rate rises), or agents (customarily savers, but this restriction is not essential to the case) will eventually correctly perceive that there has been no alteration in the underlying real conditions (given by preferences, technology, and endowments) and will readjust their actions accordingly (in this way, bringing back into motion an adjustment of the prevailing rate of interest). The case of forced saving is illustrated in figure 11.2.

According to the forced-saving argument, then, the presence of financial intermediaries with some degree of freedom of action in the market allows trading to take place at false prices. Instead of borrowers' finding themselves on the short side of the market at i_A, their demands are met and there is no demand-side pressure on interest rates.

Hayek's own analysis of this process differs from the above only inasmuch as by introducing a distinction between intermediate and final products (which he usually calls producer goods and consumer goods, respectively), he is able to conceive of saving as an alteration in the composition of demand from final to intermediate products. This has the advantage of making clearer the relationship between the terms upon which loans are made available and the structure of production (or the length of the period of production, in Hayek's terminology) of which we spoke in the previous section. This embellishment, however, slightly complicates the story as regards the collapse to the original equilibrium composition of demand and its associated structure of production. According to Hayek:

> [T]his [saving] is not voluntary, and is not made by those who will reap the benefits of the new investments. It is made by consumers in general who, because of the increased competition from the entrepreneurs who have received the additional money, are forced to forgo part of what they used to consume. It comes about not because they want to consume less, but because they get less goods for their money income. There can be no doubt that, if their money

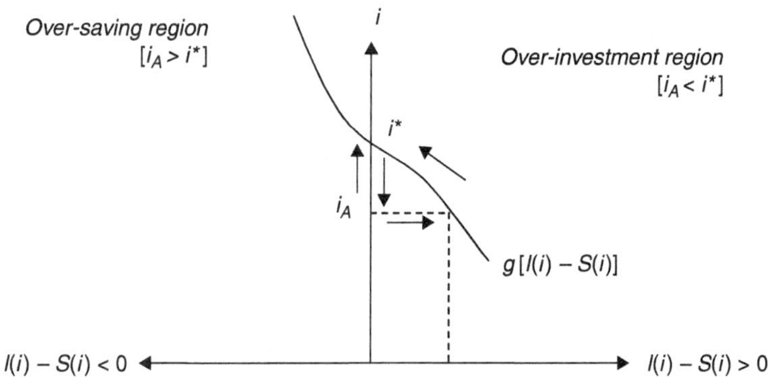

Figure 11.2

receipts should rise again, they would immediately attempt to expand consumption to the usual proportion. (1931, p. 57)

Hayek's argument here about the composition of demand entails, as well, a return to the original (less capitalistic) structure of production—a feature that allows him to emphasize that the return to equilibrium takes the form of an economic crisis of over-investment (see, for example, 1931, p. 58). From a practical point of view, this argument has the effect of redoubling a warning on the perils of inflation.

The case of voluntary saving runs parallel to the above, up to the point of the collapse. Saving again takes the form of a change in the composition of demand between intermediate and final products (and so in the structure of production). However, it is initiated by the voluntary decisions of individuals, rather than by the actions of the banking system. In other words, a change has occurred in the preferences of agents as to the disbursement of their income. In this situation, the existing rate of interest i^* (assuming, as before, the system to have been in equilibrium before the change) is now one at which the new supply of saving will exceed the demand for it—that is, $f[I(i^*) - S(i^*)] < 0$. Investors will find themselves faced with an excess supply, and the rate of interest will fall in consequence, until $f[I(i) - S(i)] = 0$. Denote the rate at which this occurs i^{**}. The case of voluntary saving is illustrated in figure 11.3.

The transition to this new equilibrium is effected entirely through price variations; nothing is said of the deflationary effects that will be associated with the transition, by virtue of the fact that producers of final products are now making losses and will curtail their demand for factors of production. That is, false trading, the possibility for which is set up in consequence of the fact that the point from which the system has to move away (the old equilibrium) is now a disequilibrium, is precluded.[8] In this case, unlike the case of forced saving, the change in the composition of demand, the structure of production (more capitalistic), and the rate of interest are permanent.

It thus becomes apparent that a central difference between the cases of voluntary and of forced saving lies in the fact that, in the former, there is a change in the data of the system whereas in the latter there is not. In the case of voluntary saving, there is a general increase in thriftiness (in figure 11.3, $g[.]$ becomes $f[.]$). In the case of forced saving, thriftiness conditions remain the same. But there is also another difference between the two cases. The analysis of voluntary saving is an exercise in comparative statics. There is no attempt to examine just how the adjustment between

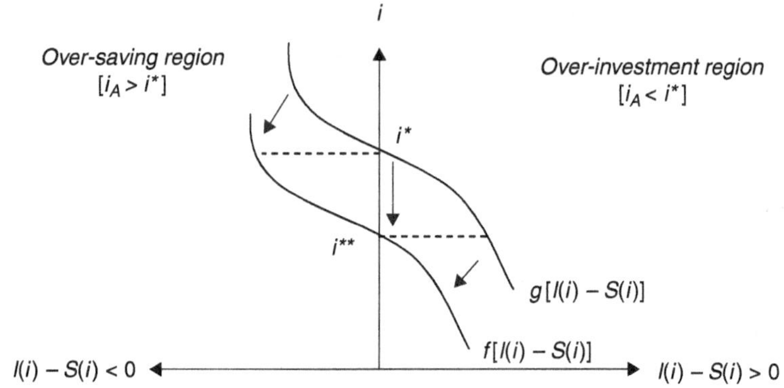

Figure 11.3

these two equilibria might actually be put into effect. The analysis of the case of forced saving, on the other hand, is an exercise in the study of adjustment processes.

It would be remiss not to add, though it is not properly a subject into which I wish to delve, that every outcome attributable to monetary conditions (whether purely monetary or real in character) is, in this line of argument, an unmitigated disaster as compared with the results that would be achieved in the absence of their influence. The maxim of policy, in fact, becomes to neutralize monetary conditions and leave everything else to the market mechanism.[9]

Criticisms of the Concept of Forced Saving

Among the most striking features of the above argument is its monetary landscape. The only relevant feature of money is that it acts as a medium of exchange, and the only relevant feature of monetary institutions is that they channel quantities of circulating medium from one group of agents to another. In fact, the whole argument could be repeated without money and without monetary institutions, in this sense. Of course, even if one were to grant this possibility, it could be maintained that the merit of the argument is that the results would still be true for such a monetary environment, though not only true for that case. Unfortunately, if a more satisfactory account is given of the effects of changes in monetary conditions (even of the attenuated kind allowed in the above argument), then none of the principal conclusions of that case will hold. None of the previously rehearsed results are due to our being in a money economy—and in a money economy, none of the results will follow. Both of these charges were leveled by Piero Sraffa against Hayek's version of the doctrine of forced saving. The essential ingredients of that critique seem to be as follows: In order to repeat the argument without recourse to monetary conditions, recall that the disequilibrium examined in the earlier sections (there, attributed exclusively to the actions of the banking system) would actually arise whenever there was a divergence of the price and the cost of production of one or more commodities in the system. Following Sraffa, assume that the deviation occurs for just one commodity—call it wheat. The consequences of this are set out by Sraffa as follows:

> In equilibrium the spot and forward price coincide...and all the...commodity rates are equal to one another....But if, for any reason, the supply and the demand for a commodity are not in equilibrium (i.e., its market price exceeds or falls short of its cost of production), its spot and forward prices will diverge, and the...rate of interest on that commodity diverges from the rates on other commodities. (1932a, p. 50)

In such a situation, owing to the opening of arbitrage opportunities (i.e., the wheat rate now differs from other commodity rates of interest), borrowing and lending in wheat will take place in response to the difference set up between the spot and the forward prices of wheat.[10] As Sraffa remarks, none of this need be explained by the action of a banking system, but it could be due simply, say, to the fact that "farmers (or, for that matter, the weather) 'arbitrarily changed' the quantity of wheat produced." (Sraffa, 1932a, p. 50) Notice also, that all of this takes place under conditions of direct commodity exchange (barter), without requiring a circulating medium.

Of course, these effects are transitory in character, since the arbitrage opportunities opened in the short run will close when the market price of wheat is adjusted once again to its original cost of production (recall that, as before, it is assumed that there has been no permanent change in the underlying conditions of consumption and production of commodities). The whole process will terminate only when the original equilibrium has been reestablished. It is in this light that one should understand Sraffa's idea that "an essential confusion" arises in Hayek's analysis of forced saving (Sraffa, 1932a, p. 49)—it attributes to the existence of money the possibility of a divergence between market interest rates and the equilibrium configuration, and to the arbitrary action of the banking system, the extension of credit at those market rates when, in fact, monetary conditions need not be involved at all.

This now raises the question as to whether these results, which are not essentially connected with monetary systems, could still be expected to occur in a "money economy" of the kind admitted so far. According to Sraffa, the answer is that they cannot and that, rather, the results of forced saving are likely to be permanent. The argument hinges on the effects of inflation (in fact, of monetary changes in general) on the distribution of income.

The process of rising nominal incomes outlined in the forced saving case is, it will be recalled, one in which all additional money balances are advanced to borrowers who use them to expand the production of intermediate goods—that is, it is associated with a redistribution of income from consumers to producers. Now, in order that the false composition of demand (and structure of production) induced by this process should be reversed, it is necessary that the share of income going to consumers should eventually rise again in proportion to the additional quantity of money. That is, their freedom of action has to be restored, as Hayek puts it. It is on this condition that all of the subsequent readjustments of relative prices envisaged by Hayek, for example, are premised.[11] However, this will only come about if the additional money held by producers is able to find its way back into the pockets of consumers, which, in turn, requires that it "is not absorbed in cash holdings in any additional stages of production" (Hayek, 1932b, p. 242, n. 2).

The essence of Sraffa's criticism of this aspect of the argument is that, on the assumptions of the case, this just cannot happen so that the redistribution of income consequent upon any expansion of the available quantity of money through credits to producers will be permanent.[12] The argument can be summarized as follows: Consider the original situation (under the equilibrium composition of demand) from either the expenditure or the income side (the subscripts p and c designating the producer or intermediate goods sector and the consumer or final goods sector, respectively):

$$e = e_p + e_c; \quad y = y_p + y_c$$

After the issue of an additional quantity of money, δm, which is received by investors and spent exclusively on intermediate products, the new situation becomes:

$$e_1 = e + \delta e = (e_p + \delta e_p) + e_c$$
$$y_1 = y + \delta y = (y_p + \delta y_p) + y_c$$

where $\delta e = \delta e_p = \delta y = \delta y_p = \delta m$. Notice that $y_c/y_1 < y_c/y$ represents the decline in the relative share of consumers in nominal income (on the assumption, maintained throughout, that the velocity of circulation remains unchanged). In neither case are there assumed to be any leakages from the system—that is, on the assumption that saving is equivalent to increased expenditure on intermediate products, we have:

$$s = y - y_c = e_p$$
$$s_1 = (y + \delta y) - y_c = (e_p + \delta e_p)$$
$$s_1 - s = \delta y = \delta m$$

The equilibrium composition of demand (e_p/e_c) can be restored only if there occurs a rise (equal to δm) in the receipts of consumers and that they, in turn, adjust their expenditure on final products accordingly. This could occur only if the volume of transactions required to sustain the new structure of production (embodying a greater quantity of intermediate products) remained unchanged. But since the shift to more capitalistic processes of production entails an increased volume of transactions, this is impossible. In fact, the whole of the additional quantity of money will be absorbed "in cash holdings in additional stages of production." The argument is illustrated in figure 11.4.

The initial fall in the rate of interest is accompanied by an expansion of credits to producers (that is, the available quantity of money increases by $\delta m = M_1 - M_0$). This prompts an increase in the production of intermediate products, represented by the increase in investment from I_0 to I_1 (and an increase in expenditure on them, $\delta e_p = \delta e$). On Hayek's argument, there occurs a shift to a "more capitalistic" structure of production (from K_0 to K_1). Now, this new structure of production, yielding a greater money value of intermediate products (with more stages of production), requires an additional quantity of money of precisely δm to facilitate their transaction. It is perhaps worth quoting Sraffa on this point:

> [It is assumed that] capital will be accumulated in proportion to the quantity of money issued in the form of loans to producers; that the number of stages of production will increase in proportion to the quantity of capital; that the quantity of payments will increase in proportion to the number of stages: as a result, the quantity of payments to be made increases in proportion to the quantity of money, and the whole of the additional money is absorbed in cash holdings for performing such payments. (1932b, p. 250)

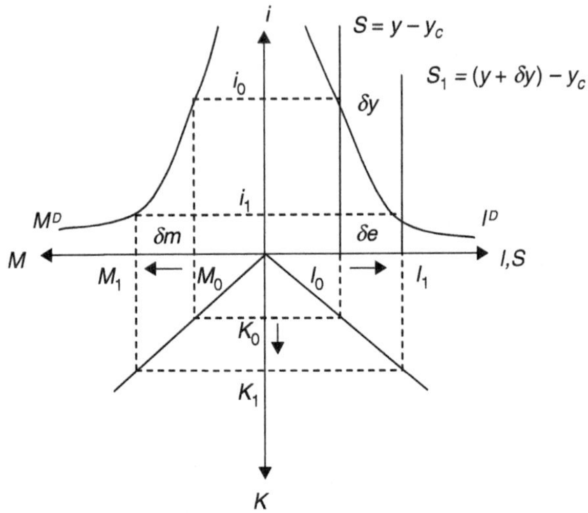

Figure 11.4

There are two other kinds of criticism of the doctrine of forced saving to which I now wish to turn. One of these is due to Keynes and is to be found in the *General Theory*, the other is due to Schumpeter and is to be found in his *Theory of Economic Development*. Let us begin with Schumpeter.

In the case of Schumpeter, forced saving is sidestepped, thanks to an argument that investment (however it might be financed) changes (and enhances) technological possibilities. The Schumpeterian process commences from the same point as the forced saving argument: financial institutions make loans to entrepreneurs at prevailing interest rates, even when these are below the equilibrium rate. As Schumpeter puts it, the possibility of windfall profits arises whenever there is a discrepancy between prevailing and equilibrium interest-rate regimes. In this eventuality, investors approach financial institutions for advances. However, unlike the forced-saving argument, the funds advanced in this way are used to finance changes in production functions (technology), and not simply increases in the volume of investment in available technologies. It is precisely this endogenous change in technology that allows Schumpeter to avoid having to conclude that the system needs to collapse back to the old equilibrium.

In the *General Theory*, on the other hand, the notion of forced saving is eliminated, courtesy of the operation of the principle of effective demand, whereby additional investment generates higher levels of aggregate income (and so, more voluntary savings, under the assumption that the propensity to consume is less than one). It is this effective-demand mechanism that allows Keynes to conclude that the new position is one of equilibrium between voluntary saving and investment, and so to deny the idea of having to return to the original position. His argument against the forced saving idea is worth quoting:

> [T]he notion that the creation of credit by the banking system allows investment to take place to which "no genuine saving" corresponds can only be the result of isolating one of the consequences of increased bank-credit to the exclusion of the others. If the grant of bank credit to an entrepreneur allows him to make an addition to current investment... incomes will necessarily be increased... [and] except in conditions of full employment, there will be an increase of real income as well as money-income. The public will exercise a free choice... to increase their savings. Moreover, the savings which result from this decision are just as genuine as any other savings. (Keynes, 1936, pp. 82–83)

Notice that unlike the Schumpeterian case, this argument does not require that new investment generate changes in productivity conditions. The matter can be put another way. For Schumpeter, investment generates changes in the given production possibilities of the forced-saving case—so *moving* the equilibrium (though that equilibrium is determined along exactly the same lines as in the forced-saving case). For Keynes, on the other hand, it generates increases in aggregate income—so *determining* a new equilibrium (in a manner that differs from the forced-saving case). It is essential to observe that if private investment did not embody the Schumpeterian property, then his argument would reduce to that of the forced-saving school.

However, some interesting relationships exist between the arguments of Sraffa and Keynes. It is quite apparent that Sraffa is concerned with the effects of monetary conditions on the distribution of income, the argument being that when investment is brought about as a result of a reduction in consumption (that is, a redistribution of income from consumers to producers, due, in this case, to inflation), the results of that investment are likely to be permanent.[13] This, it might be noted, is roughly analogous to the redistribution of income between wages and profits that is associated with a wages policy that keeps the rate of growth of money wages below the rate of inflation.[14] The essential difference, of course, is that, in the case of a wages policy, there is no guarantee that the windfall profits that accrue to capitalists will necessarily be invested. (In the discussion over forced saving, this was simply assumed to be the case.) Even in a closed economy, there may be leakages from these windfall profits—savings will not find their way into productive investment, for example, if the prospects for effective demand are especially bleak. In an open economy, barring measures designed expressly to prevent them (like exchange controls), the leakages from domestic "savings" are likely to be significant.[15] Readers of Keynes's *How to Pay for the War* (1940) will recognize the family resemblance between some of these arguments and those that lie behind his ill-fated scheme for compulsory saving.

Returning to the *General Theory*, we find that it is clear Keynes is concerned there exclusively with the effects of monetary conditions on the level of income, the argument being that when investment is going on, the level of real income rises, saving is generated at a rate sufficient to match investment, and the results of the investment process, once it comes to an end, are likely to be permanent. Yet there is, of course, no reason to suppose that an increase of investment must always be effected through a fall in consumption; this would be the case only in conditions of full employment. Nevertheless, whether investment generates saving or is the result of reduced consumption, there will be a permanent change in distribution in another sense—namely, that which comes about in both cases owing to a permanently lower rate of interest and, therefore, a higher rate of real wages. Thus, whether a change in monetary conditions (and now it is the altered monetary practices of the financial system, rather than any alteration in the available quantity of money, that are the relevant change) leads to an expansion of output, or to an increase in the general level of prices, or to some combination of the two, there will be a consequential movement to a new equilibrium distribution (in the second sense) and so to a permanent change in both the structure of production and relative prices.

These two channels of monetary influence on real variables—one that operates via distribution and the structure of production and the other that operates (under conditions of deficient demand) via distribution and the level of production (and employment)— seem to be of more than passing relevance to practical affairs. With the application of a measure of consistency of purpose, as Keynes put it, and with a judicious combination of open-market operations and discount policy, the monetary authorities have available to them channels for altering the money rate of interest and, hence, real production—and these changes will persist. It might be added, although the argument has proceeded on the assumption of a closed economy, that an engineered decrease in domestic interest rates under a system of flexible exchange rates will, via its effect on the demand for assets denominated in domestic currency, exert a downward pressure on the exchange rate, thus tending to improve the net export position of the economy in question. Whether or not these benefits will accrue in full, however, depends on the effects of the monetary policy on the general-level prices and upon any structural biases that may characterize the propensities to import and export. But then, monetary policy is not the only policy instrument that governments have at their disposal for achieving economic objectives.

Viewed from the perspective of the money supply, any activities of the monetary authorities designed to exploit these possibilities will inevitably be expansionary; but the disastrous consequences of such expansions, which were a feature of the old forced-saving argument, are largely, if not entirely, imaginary. It is but a simple step from a realization of this fact to the conclusion that, with monetary targets in place, any action of the kind discussed here would compromise those targets. Indeed, campaigns to restrict central banks to the role of overseers of monetary targeting of one form or another (often involving quite serious proposals for depriving them of their lender-of-last-resort function by legislation) are not only closely related to the argument that lies beneath the forced-saving doctrine but also seem to cut off any real possibility for the conduct of effective monetary policy.

Notes

This chapter was written by Murray Milgate and appeared originally in the *Cambridge Journal of Economics*.

1. We shall, thus, not be concerned with the fact that the idea of forced saving is of more distant origin—dating back officially to Bentham and Thornton (though quite similar notions can be found in Hume and in the debate over the so-called real bills doctrine); neither is there space here to dwell on the discussion of the subject by Malthus and Ricardo consequent upon Malthus's review of Ricardo's *High Price of Bullion* (1810). Nor am I especially interested in the fact that we seem owe the term to Ludwig von Mises. Furthermore, another quite important aspect of the Sraffa-Hayek exchange (relating to Hayek's use of the notion of intertemporal equilibrium and Sraffa's response to it) will not be considered here. On this last point, see Milgate (1979).

2. The reference here is to long-period equilibrium; nothing is said about the applicability of these propositions outside equilibrium. In particular, the super-neutrality of money is not involved.

3. In actual financial markets, the structure of interest rates will reflect differences in the kinds of financial instruments available and the kinds of transactions undertaken. The most obvious factor affecting interest-rate differentials is,

of course, the duration of the loan. In the case where the risk premium can be expressed as a simple function of the duration of the loan, little of substance is lost in adopting Wicksell's idea that that an average of market rates of interest is an appropriate vehicle for analysis. However, when the financial instruments available are themselves heterogeneous, or when adverse selection and moral hazard act in financial markets, then it is no longer so simple a matter to reduce the complex of existing market interest rates to a single magnitude appropriate for short-period analysis. Indeed, in general this will be impossible.

4. This case is analogous to that of a cheap-money policy under the additional assumptions that the monetary authorities have at their disposal means for keeping the complex of market interest rates within some desired range and that credit so advanced is actually invested in domestic production. The first possibility is much more problematic in an open economy than in the closed ones with which this chapter is concerned. The second is problematic in both cases.

5. Expectation formation does not, therefore, conform to the rational expectations hypothesis.

6. The similarity of this argument to that of the short-run Phillips Curve is to be noted.

7. Wicksell, it will be remembered, linking up with the earlier arguments of members of the banking school like Tooke and Fullarton, recognized that as soon as "credit" was introduced into the system in this fashion, the velocity of circulation of "money" became variable and not constant, as the quantity theory required.

8. It might be observed that, unless the rate of interest immediately (or very quickly) falls to its new and lower equilibrium level, such a campaign of saving will prove to be to a large extent abortive (see Sraffa, 1932a, p. 52). To put the matter another way, if the adjustment process from i^* to i^{**} in figure 11.3 is not considered (and it is not by Hayek), one is apt to overlook the possibility of the effects of the oversaving that will exist at i^* (given new thriftiness conditions).

9. This opinion is exemplified at the beginning of Hayek's reply to Sraffa's critique in 1932: "I have been assuming that the body of existing pure economic theory demonstrates that, so long as we neglect monetary factors, there is an inherent tendency towards an equilibrium...; what I tried to do in *Prices and Production*...was to show that monetary factors may bring about a kind of disequilibrium" (1932b, p. 238).

10. For simplicity, it will be assumed that all loans are of the same duration, though nothing that is about to be said actually depends on this simplifying assumption for its validity.

11. See also Hayek, 1931, pp. 85–91; 1932b, p. 242.

12. There are two kinds of redistribution going on simultaneously here that must be kept firmly distinguished. The first is the rise in the real wage concomitant upon the fall in the rate of interest; the second is the alteration in the shares of total income going to wages and profits.

13. It seems hardly necessary to add that Sraffa discusses this case for no other reason than that it is the one Hayek uses.

14. Only roughly, because under a wage policy, unlike the case of a credit expansion, this takes place together with a rise in the rate of profit and a *reduction* in the real wage rate.

15. In the present context, a recognition of this theoretical possibility should stand as a warning against drawing the tempting conclusion that a cheap money policy is, on its own, sufficient to increase investment.

Part Three

Critical

12

Unemployment and the Market Mechanism

> There are…, I should admit, forces which one might fairly well call "automatic" which operate under any normal monetary system in the direction of restoring a long-period equilibrium between saving and investment. The point upon which I cast doubt—though the contrary is generally believed—is whether these "automatic forces" will…tend to bring about not only an equilibrium between saving and investment but also an optimum level of production.
>
> —John Maynard Keynes, 1973, vol. 13, p. 395

Analysis of the level of unemployment in a market economy requires some characterization of the relationship between unemployment and the operation of the market mechanism. The aim of this chapter is to classify the various positions regarding the problem of unemployment, according to the role that differing schools of economic thought ascribe to the market mechanism. It will be possible in this way to reveal the structure of ideas that underlie the differing positions.

Two main groups of writers dominate this discussion. On the one hand, there are those authors who argue that, in the long run, the forces of demand and supply tend to push the economic system toward a full-employment level of activity (or towards a natural rate of unemployment). These authors we shall refer to as the "market-mechanism group." On the other hand, there are those who, while accepting the characterization of a market mechanism that operates under the influence of the forces of demand and supply, maintain that this mechanism is inhibited (or perhaps even totally obstructed) by the presence of a variety of market imperfections, both social and institutional, such as sticky wages and prices, sticky interest rates, and the disruptive impact of uncertainty and disappointed expectations. This latter group, which we refer to as the "imperfectionists," encompasses a whole variety of writers who often have little in common other than the fact that their support for employment policies based on the direct manipulation of the level of effective demand derives from the characterization of unemployment as arising from an obstructed market mechanism.

The major theme here is that the position of the imperfectionists is, in the final analysis, untenable. For, not only is the determining role of imperfections more difficult to sustain the longer the time period considered; but also that the argument that the operation of the market mechanism is inhibited by— say, the role of trade unions or the influence of uncertainty—involves a priori acceptance of the underlying theoretical model of the operation of that mechanism which is provided by the market mechanism group. It all becomes a matter of degree.

It is important to realize that the issue at stake here is not simply one of theoretical interpretation or empirical verification. It is a matter of the utmost practical importance. That is, the formulation and justification of economic policy is rendered arbitrary by the imperfectionist position. The ultimate superiority of a policy of fiscal expansion vis-à-vis a policy of social legislation to, say, unstick the wage is not self-evident. Indeed, if a powerful mechanism of market adjustment *is* present in the economy, then it seems almost perverse not to attempt to harness these (ultimately) beneficial forces. Of course, many of these issues are partially obscured by the distinction between long-run and short-run situations. However, just as short-run movements in the economy are regulated by the more persistent forces governing its long-run tendencies, so short-run policy measures to remedy the consequences of disequilibrium are conditional upon long-run policy prescriptions. If this were the case, the theoretical position of the orthodox market-mechanism school (whether in monetarist, rational expectations, or supply-side guise) would be perfectly secure—for its imperfectionist critics share its characterization of the operation of the market mechanism, albeit with some lack of conviction.

In marked contrast to both of these positions, there is the view presented in the *General Theory* that is particularly clearly stated in the epigraph at the beginning of this chapter (see also Keynes, 1973, 7:254).

Here, the novel idea is not that the market mechanism is obstructed or inhibited—there are, as Keynes said, "automatic [forces] which operate...in the direction of restoring long-period equilibrium"—but, rather, that the way in which this mechanism functions is not such as to establish full employment by clearing the labor market. That is, the market mechanism will not even "tend to bring about...an optimum level of production." However, we shall not dwell on the implications that might follow from this more radical idea (which is fully discussed in Milgate, 1982). Instead, our aim here is to elucidate the theoretical underpinnings of the members of the orthodox market-mechanism group, and thence to analyze their debates with various imperfectionists, examining the extent to which the imperfectionist position in any sense reflects Keynes's contribution.

In the first section, we examine the various interpretations that may be placed on the notion of a self-adjusting market, particularly with respect to Keynes's own view of the market mechanism and the imperfectionist view. In the second section, one of the most prominent and influential of imperfectionist arguments (that unemployment may be attributed to rigid or sticky money wages) is exposed to Keynes's own arguments on the movement of money wages. Finally, in the third section, we examine the debate over the natural rate/rational expectations hypothesis—a debate in which the theoretical poverty of the imperfectionist position has been starkly revealed.

Self-adjustment and the Market Mechanism

The notion that the study of the economic system presupposes an autonomous, law-governed market mechanism is as old as economics itself. From Adam Smith to the present day, economists have been trying to reveal the forces that regulate the operation of the market mechanism and, consequently, to provide an account of the results that those forces tend to produce in the economic system. Indeed, it can be said with some confidence that all of the most important doctrinal disputes in the history of the discipline have been conducted not over whether there are systematic and persistent forces at work in the economy but, rather, what these forces may be. The decline of the classical surplus theory of value and distribution, and its replacement with the neoclassical theory of demand and supply, is, of course, the most prominent example of a change in the characterization of the market mechanism. But the really interesting question in the context of the analysis of unemployment concerns the interpretation of Keynes's challenge to the orthodox position on the market mechanism.

It is well known that Keynes not infrequently couched general statements of his opposition to the orthodox conception of the market mechanism and the notion of self-adjustment in terms that were, at best, somewhat ambiguous. Very early on in the *General Theory*, for example, one reads that the traditional doctrine is "equivalent to the proposition that there is no *obstacle* to full employment" (Keynes, 1973, 7:26, italics added; but see also 14:26). Just one year before the publication of the *General Theory*, Keynes told a radio audience that he disputed the idea that "the economic system is, in any significant sense, self-adjusting" (Keynes, 1973, 13:487). It is obviously crucial to understand correctly the meaning of such statements. Broadly speaking, two views have prevailed. The first of these holds that the statements should be taken to imply that there are no automatic, self-adjusting forces at work in the economy at all: "A theory of unemployment is necessarily, inescapably, a theory of disorder" (Shackle, 1967, p. 133). The second holds that, while there are underlying forces promoting self-adjustment *toward full employment*, the operation of these forces is disturbed by the presence of certain frictions or rigidities. Neither view seems satisfactory.

The first reading can be eliminated readily enough. The strange supposition that Keynes's analysis of unemployment embodies the idea that there are *no* systematic forces at work in the economic system (that is, that the notion of the very existence of a systematic market mechanism, however defined, was itself rejected by Keynes) is contradicted again and again throughout the *General Theory*. One can only wonder at what nonsense, according to this reading, Keynes must have been thinking when he wrote of "the economic machine" (Keynes, 1973, 7:50) and of unemployment being the outcome of "natural tendencies" (7:254), or when, having drawn attention to the innumerable cross-currents at work in the economic system at any given moment, he held that the components of effective demand were "useful and convenient to isolate" because "if we examine any actual problem along the lines of [that] schematism, we shall find it more manageable; and our practical intuition...will be offered a less intractable material upon which to work" (7:249). Indeed, the passage quoted at the beginning of this chapter, though coming from the drafts of the *General Theory*, makes it perfectly clear that Keynes was never in any doubt about the presence of automatic forces in a market economy.[1]

If, therefore, we must conclude that Keynes did not reject the notion of the market mechanism and the related idea of self-adjustment in its most general setting, then there would seem to be a prima facie case for the second interpretation of the remarks cited above namely, that since under the normal operation of the market mechanism self-adjustment promotes the *full* employment of labor, the essence of Keynes's position was to focus attention on the consequences of interferences or obstacles to this process. This is, of course, the view that has dominated the literature, and it is the basis of all imperfectionist analyses of unemployment. However, this reading of Keynes on the notion of self-adjustment, though more widely accepted, is no more firmly grounded than the first.

Let us consider, to begin with, the point in the *General Theory* at which Keynes states that orthodox theory presupposes that there is no obstacle to full employment; at first sight, this appears to provide some textual evidence upon which to base an imperfectionist reading. Now, if this is to be taken as an accurate reading of Keynes, then one would expect to find immediately following it a catalogue of such obstacles—frictions and rigidities that, on this reading, would disturb the underlying tendency toward full employment. Unfortunately, in the very next sentence, one finds Keynes drawing an entirely different implication from his statement than would be required to substantiate an imperfectionist reading. Instead of deferring to obstacles, Keynes states forthrightly: "this is not the true law" (Keynes, 1973, vol. 7, p. 26).[2] This can be read in only one way: that the orthodox doctrine that there is any underlying tendency toward full employment is not a true statement of the general tendencies inherent in the operation of the market mechanism. Indeed, this conclusion is highlighted a few pages further on, when Keynes observes that "it may well be that the classical theory represents the way in which we should like our Economy to behave... but to assume that it actually does so is to assume our difficulties away" (7:34; see also 7:16).

In those passages where Keynes mentions explicitly the notion of self-adjustment, the textual evidence to support an imperfectionist reading is no more convincing. The customary circumstances in which Keynes raises this issue concern the self-adjustment of wages and the self-adjustment of the rate of interest. Since the former case (wage flexibility) will be examined in detail in the next section, we concentrate here on the latter case—self-adjustment of the rate of interest.[3]

It is essential at the outset to define precisely the proposition to which Keynes objected. On this matter, the *General Theory* is perfectly clear: "the weight of my criticism," Keynes writes, "is directed... against the notion that the rate of interest and the volume of investment are self-adjusting *at the optimum level*" (1973, 7:339, italics added). A little later, he observes: "for several millenniums, enlightened opinion held for certain and obvious a doctrine which the classical school has repudiated as childish, but which deserves rehabilitation and honour. I mean the doctrine that the rate of interest is not self-adjusting *at a level best suited to the social advantage*" (7:351, italics added).

There is ample evidence here to suggest that, when Keynes rejected the idea that economy is self-adjusting, he was rejecting a much more specific doctrine than the general idea that the normal operation of the market mechanism tends to produce definite outcomes. It is evident that Keynes was attacking the idea that there is a tendency for self-adjustment *toward full employment* (as the italicized sections of the passages quoted above confirm).[4] In short, we must distinguish carefully, as Keynes sometimes failed to do, between two quite distinct propositions that, in the present context, we keep strictly separate: (a) that the economy is a self-adjusting mechanism in the general sense—that is, it produces definite outcomes; and (b) that the process of self-adjustment is explained by having recourse to the orthodox demand-and-supply theory of the market mechanism that attempts to specify *which* outcomes will be forthcoming. Keynes's quarrel was with the second of these propositions, not the first. Indeed, the second proposition is just another way of stating the orthodox doctrine that, in the long run, there is a tendency for the market mechanism to produce full employment.

Returning to Keynes's remark that he rejected the idea that the "economic system is, in any significant sense, self-adjusting," the key to its correct interpretation lies in that qualifying clause, "in any significant sense." The "significant sense" refers to full employment. What is being rejected here is not the general notion of self-adjustment but the orthodox theory of employment.[5] The imperfectionists might wish to argue that Keynes should not have made such a claim (as Schumpeter, 1954, p. 624; and Leijonhufvud, 1971, p. 22, n. 1, have done), but the fact that he did so bears out our argument that the market mechanism and self-adjustment were basic to Keynes's alternative theory of unemployment.

Keynes's adherence to the general notion of self-adjustment is, perhaps, nowhere more evident than in his discussion of the process through which planned saving and planned investment are brought into equilibrium.[6] For here, although the theory of effective demand indicates that this self-adjusting process (that is, the operation of the market mechanism as it affects employment) does not tend to produce those desirable outcomes that it was asserted to produce, according to the orthodox demand-and-supply characterization of the market mechanism, it is not to frictions and rigidities (or obstacles to the normal operation of the market mechanism) that Keynes appeals for his results.

Given these facts, the development of an imperfectionist interpretation of the *General Theory* was doubly fortuitous from the point of view of orthodox neoclassical analysis. In the first place, it provided the grounds for a rapid absorption of Keynesian economics into what could be held up to be a more practical and relevant version of the older orthodoxy.[7] Second, and probably most important, it eliminated the necessity of scrapping the entire corpus of neoclassical theory—a course that would have been required had the central message of the *General Theory* (that the normal operation of the market mechanism will ensure neither the maintenance of nor a tendency toward the full employment of labor) been taken seriously. Of course, this does not mean that the famous Neoclassical Synthesis was entirely without textual foundation. By skillfully focusing on the crucial weaknesses of the *General Theory*, most notably the marginal efficiency of capital theory of investment and Keynes's unsatisfactory attempts to criticize the internal logic of the classical theory of interest by means of liquidity-preference theory, it was possible to present Keynes's results as special cases, albeit empirically relevant ones, of a more general theory.[8] The same danger exists today.

Despite the apparent rigor and striking popularity of imperfectionist approaches to Keynesian economics in the immediate postwar years, their ultimate reliance on arbitrary inhibitions has proved to be a central flaw. Once their prestige as the accredited theoretical foundation for economic policy formulation began to falter with the manifest failure of the policies they suggested in the late 1960s and early 1970s, authors who advocated a more explicit long-run equilibrium approach to the study of macroeconomic phenomena came to the forefront. This apparent turnaround in the climate of economic opinion, which left Keynesian economists confused and searching for ever more complicated explanations, is not at all surprising. For, in truth, there had been no turnaround at all. The only thing that had happened was that the underlying orthodox theoretical foundations of the imperfectionist position had been reasserted; this reestablished the dominance of analytical coherence over arbitrary realism. Once the imperfectionist position, whose only attraction was the fact that it somehow seemed to be talking about well-defined and easily observable economic phenomena, ceased to reflect the behavior of the economic system, the underlying orthodox analysis of the relationship between employment and the operation of the market mechanism was bound to resurface—if only by virtue of its greater theoretical consistency (see, for example, Friedman, 1974, for a cogent claim to this effect).

Let us consider in detail the failings of the imperfectionist argument, both as an interpretation of the *General Theory*[9] and as a critique of an alternative to the orthodox theory of employment itself. In order to make the discussion manageable, we will focus on two examples of imperfectionist analysis: the hypothesis that sticky wages are the two causes of unemployment, and the hypothesis that incorrect expectations are the culprits.

Wages and the Market Mechanism

The familiar *IS-LM* model, as well as many other interpretations of the *General Theory*, is built around the idea that, with a fixed money supply, inflexible money wages prevent the attainment of full-employment equilibrium. For a closed economy, the system can be summed up in three equations:

$$Y = i\,(r) + G \tag{1}$$

$$M/P = l\,(r) + k\,(Y) \tag{2}$$

$$Y = f\,(P) \tag{3}$$

Equation (1) is the *IS* curve, income (Y) being determined by investment, itself a function of the rate of interest (r), and autonomous expenditures (G).[10] Equation (2) is the *LM* curve, M being the nominal value of the money stock, and P the price level. The demand for the real money stock (M/P) is the sum of the demands for money arising from speculative motive ($l(r)$), and from transactions and precautionary motives combined in $k(Y)$. Equation (3) is the aggregate supply curve. This is derived from the condition of labor market equilibrium and an aggregate production function determining the relationship between employment and output.

Labor market equilibrium is defined by:

$$S\,(P, N) = W = P \cdot D(N) \tag{4}$$

where W is the money wage rate, S the labor supply function, D the labor demand function, and N the amount of labor. If we define:

$$S\,(P, N) = P \cdot L(N) \tag{5}$$

(that is, the price level enters the labor supply function as a multiplicative factor, and money wages are fully flexible in response to price changes), then the labor market clears at an equilibrium real wage:

$$D(N) = W/P = L(N) \tag{6}$$

If, on the other hand, the money wage (W) is fixed ($\delta S/\delta P = 0$) or sticky ($D(N) > \delta S/\delta P > 0$), then labor market equilibrium does not necessarily imply full employment. The latter depends on the demand conditions expressed in equations (1) and (2).

Combining the labor market equilibrium condition (equation 4) with an aggregate production function,

$$Y = g\,(N, K) \tag{7}$$

(where K is the quantity of capital), permits the derivation of the aggregate supply function (equation 3). As long as the money wage is sticky, this will have a positive ($\delta f/\delta P > 0$); the elasticity of the function being dependent not only on the characteristics of the aggregate production function but also on just how sticky the money wage might be. For example, if the money wage is perfectly flexible, then (3) can be replaced by $Y = Y_F$, where Y_F is the full-employment level of output associated with the market-clearing real wage.

Leaving aside the manifest analytical weaknesses of this straightforward modification of orthodox demand-and-supply theory (not the least of which is its use of the discredited marginal productivity theory of distribution in the description of the labor market), we see a question arise that immediately relates to the extent to which this model faithfully represents Keynes's explicit discussion in the *General Theory* of the relationship between money wages and the level of employment. This question is rendered all the more interesting given the fact that Keynes's orthodox predecessors had not failed to notice that money-wage rigidity would act as an obstacle to the tendency they believed the market mechanism possessed to promote full employment (see, for example, Marshall, 1920a, pp. 709–10; Pigou, 1933, pp. 252–56).

There are two closely related aspects of this question that call for attention. The first concerns Keynes's views on the role of any hypothesis about money-wage rigidity in his own explanation of unemployment, and the second concern the role that such a hypothesis would play in what he termed "classical" theory. The rationale for the attribution of an assumption of money-wage rigidity to Keynes (see, for example, Hicks, 1937; Modigliani, 1944; Haberler, 1958, p. 242; Barker, 1980) derives from two rather different sources. On the one hand, the trend toward interpreting the *General Theory* along wholly orthodox lines imposed the theoretical necessity of watering down, at least as far as short-run analysis was concerned, the central conclusion of neoclassical economics: that the operation of the price system might tend to establish, *relatively swiftly*, the full employment of factors of production.[11] On the other hand, some of Keynes's remarks on the subject of money wages in the *General Theory*, when taken out of context and coupled with the erroneous conviction that Keynes's analysis of employment must have been a modification of orthodox neoclassical theory designed to bring it into closer conformity with reality, have been used to bolster this reading.

Unfortunately (at least from the point of view of the proponents of this reading), Keynes is perfectly clear in the *General Theory* that his analysis of unemployment *does not* depend on any assumption of wage rigidity. Although when Keynes conducts his reader through a summary of the essentials of his own theory (in chapter 3), he does assume that money wages "are constant per unit of labour employed," he immediately adds a crucial warning: "this simplification...is introduced solely to facilitate the exposition...the argument is *precisely the same* whether or not money wages...are liable to change" (Keynes, 1973, 7:27, italics added). Indeed, chapter 19 of the *General Theory* is concerned exclusively with the case of money-wage flexibility—and Keynes *does not* reach the conclusion there that this flexibility tends to establish the full employment of labor (see, for example, 7:260–61, 262, 265, 278), as he would have done had it been the case that his analysis was an imperfectionist one based on the hypothesis of money-wage rigidity.[12]

What is more, Keynes's celebrated remark to the effect that "we must have some factor, the vale of which in terms of money is, if not fixed, at least sticky" (7:304, original italics omitted), which follows hard on the heels of a statement that workers are "disposed to resist a reduction in their money-rewards" (7:303), is no more supportive of the money-wage rigidity interpretation than is the analysis discussed in the previous paragraph. For the requirement of stickiness to which Keynes alludes here is adduced not to provide an explanation of unemployment but to ensure stability in the general level of prices—it is required, writes Keynes, to give us "stability of values in a monetary system" (7:304). The argument leading up to this conclusion is sketched by Keynes in chapter 21 of the *General Theory*. It warrants careful consideration.

Starting from the proposition (7:294; see also 7:302) that the general level of prices depends essentially on two *independent* variables—the volume of output (i.e., employment) and costs (under appropriate assumptions, the wage unit)[13]—Keynes enunciates what he somewhat jestingly calls a "Quantity Theory of Money": "So long as there is unemployment, employment will change in the same proportion as the quantity of money; and when there is full employment, *prices* will change in the same proportion as the quantity of money" (7:296, italics in original).

There are, however, a number of important qualifications to this statement,[14] one of which is relevant here for it leads up to Keynes's remark on the connection between price stability and the behavior of money wages. This concerns the possibility that money wages may tend to rise with increases in the quantity of effective demand (the change in which, for simplicity, we shall assume is proportionate with a change in the quantity of money) *below* full employment (7:295, 301–2).

The latter possibility implies that there may exist positions of less than full employment where increases in effective demand (that is, the quantity of money under our assumption) give rise to an increase in money wages, and hence the price level, as well as to an increase in output. Keynes then draws a distinction between these situations—he calls them "positions of semi-inflation" (7:301)—and situations of full employment, where every increase in effective demand is translated into an effect on prices, he calls this "absolute inflation" (7:301). Thus, "[W]hen a further increase in the quantity of effective demand produces no further increase in output and entirely spends itself on an increase in the cost-unit fully proportionate to the increase in effective demand, we have reached a position which might be appropriately designated as one of true inflation" (7: 303).

It is around this critical level that there exists the asymmetry between inflation and deflation of which Keynes often spoke,[15] and in relation to which his remark about stickiness was made. For, if money wages were to rise and fall with every expansion or contraction of effective demand, the price level would be violently unstable. In particular, every contraction of effective demand would so disturb the price level (and note that the process is a cumulative downward spiral in this case) that there would be no point of price stability "until either the rate of interest was incapable of falling further or wages were zero" (7:304). The predisposition of workers not to accept reductions in money wages, the stickiness to which Keynes refers, thus explains the asymmetric behavior, in terms of price versus output responses, above and below this critical level (7:291, 304) in reaction to changes in the quantity of money (which are to be associated with proportional changes in effective demand): "the long-run stability or instability of prices will depend on the strength...of the wage-unit (or, more precisely, the cost-unit)" (7:309). The stickiness is *not* used to explain the level of unemployment, but rather is an explanation (however limited) of the relative stability of the value of money in an economy in which output is not normally at the full-employment level.

We should not leave this subject without also noting that Keynes was alert to the proposition we have already stated in this section of the chapter—namely, that far from being an alternative to the neoclassical theory of employment, the money-wage rigidity hypothesis is part and parcel of that very theory. "Classical theory," wrote Keynes, "rest[s] the supposedly self-adjusting character of the economic system on an assumed fluidity of money wages; and, when there is rigidity... lay[s] on this rigidity the blame for maladjustment" (7:257; see also 7:7–8, 16). This theory of unemployment is, according to Keynes, the orthodox one (see also Keynes, 1973, 14:26, 43; 29:97, for further confirmation of this point). Unsuspecting generations of students have been asked to accept that the very author who claimed to have made such a radical break with the "classical" school and its "habitual modes of thought" actually fell back on what he knew to be the orthodox explanation of unemployment.[16] This error is all the more clearly exposed now that we can appreciate that Keynes's analysis of unemployment does not depend upon any such imperfectionist arguments.

Thus, we arrive at the central conclusion of this section. It was not Keynes's view that his explanation of employment (based on the operation of the principle of effective demand) required a hypothesis of money-wage rigidity. Indeed, far from being "Keynesian," such an explanation was, according to Keynes himself, completely "classical."

Expectations and the Market Mechanism

The analysis of the coexistence of inflation and unemployment posed a serious problem for the standard *IS-LM* analysis. In a situation in which money wages, the price level, and the quantity of money are all increasing, differential variations in the respective rates of increase of these variables will be sufficient to precipitate changes in the real wage and the real value of the quantity of money required for the establishment of a full-employment equilibrium in the labor market (a fact noted by Keynes himself; 1973, 7:9, 15). Thus, the popular inhibition to the operation of the market mechanism—sticky wages—upon which much imperfectionist analysis of unemployment was grounded, is no longer operative. However, instead of alerting the proponents of such models to the inherent weakness in the imperfectionist position—a weakness derived from sharing the same view of the market mechanism as the orthodox demand-and-supply school—the imperfectionists have side-stepped the problem. Not unexpectedly, new inhibitions to the operation of the market mechanism have been "discovered": real wage resistance (Hicks, 1974, ch.3) interest rate inflexibility (Leijonhufvud, 1971, p. 38), and markup pricing behaviour (Tobin, 1980, p. 35).

The opening created by such ad hoc theorizing was exploited to great effect by Friedman (1968) and Phelps (1967, 1968). These authors were able to point out (given that so-called Keynesians and monetarists accepted the same characterization of the market mechanism) that the flexibility present in an inflationary environment could not only restore the power of the market mechanism to generate full employment but also that the uncertainty engendered by that same inflationary experience was sufficient to explain a trade-off between inflation and unemployment in the form of a *short-run* Phillips Curve. Of course, the *long-run* Phillips Curve is vertical at the point where involuntary unemployment is zero—that is, either at full employment or at the natural rate of unemployment (its modern analogue).

The argument is straightforward. Given that relative prices and quantities are determined by the mutual interaction of the forces of demand and supply, then if the general level of future prices is perfectly anticipated, the economy will settle down in a steady-state equilibrium with no involuntary unemployment. Unexpected deviations of actual prices from their expected levels will, however, disrupt equilibrium in, according to Friedman, a predictable way. If nominal prices were higher than expected, unemployment would be lower than the natural rate. If nominal prices were lower than expected, unemployment would be higher than the natural rate. Both effects are, of course, temporary. They give the classic Phillips Curve form to the *short-run* relation between unemployment and the rate of change of the general level of prices. It is important to note that the part of the argument that holds that, in the *long run*, the Phillips Curve is vertical has been overwhelmingly successful. For example, Modigliani was forced to concede that "a specific implication of that model, namely that the long-run Phillips curve is vertical, or, in substance, that in the long-run money is neutral... by now does not meet serious objection from non-monetarists, at least as a first approximation" (1976, p. 119). This measure of agreement is not surprising. It confirms the fact that the imperfectionist and orthodox analyses of unemployment are, ultimately, the same.

All scope for a thoroughgoing theoretical critique of the orthodox pre-Keynesian position having thus vanished, the only path left for the imperfectionist critics was to dispute the central policy conclusion Friedman drew from his analysis—viz., an efficient government policy to promote stable prices was all that was required to ensure that the market mechanism would move the economy to a position corresponding to the natural rate of unemployment (see, for example, Friedman, 1968 and 1980). This path, to the credit of their practical intuition rather than their logical consistency, most imperfectionists were swift to follow. Modigliani, for example, felt the policy conclusion to be of little practical relevance because it was based on too optimistic a view of the empirical evidence (1976, p.119).

The adequacy of the defenses erected against Friedman's initial challenge to the imperfectionist position will be returned to later. It is first necessary to consider some more recent arguments that add a further dimension to the orthodox attack on the imperfectionist position. The arguments in question revolve around the hypothesis that the formulation of expectations is "rational." The significance of this challenge is not difficult to grasp: it attempts to remove uncertainty and expectations from the catalogue of imperfections upon which the neoclassical analysis of unemployment is based.

The issues at stake in this debate may be revealed by applying a simple extension of the model set out in the previous section so as to include anticipations. In this case, the level of output must be expressed as a deviation from that level associated with the natural rate of unemployment—a deviation that will be minimized when expectations are perfectly fulfilled. Any residual deviation from this position arises solely from random shocks. The following model is adapted from the analyses developed by Sargent (1973) and Sargent and Wallace (1976):

$$y_t - \tilde{y}_t = a(p_t - p^e_t) + \varepsilon_1 \tag{7}$$
$$y_t = b_o[r_t - (p^e_t - p_{t-1})] + b_1 gt + \varepsilon_2 \tag{8}$$
$$m_t - p_t = c_o y_t + c_1 r_t + \varepsilon_3 \tag{9}$$

where y, p, and m are the natural logarithms of real national income, the general level of prices, and the (exogenously given) money supply, respectively. The nominal interest rate (not a logarithm) is denoted by r; g is a vector of exogenous demand variables (say, government expenditures). The parameters a, b_o, and c_1 are assumed to be scalars, while

b_1 is a vector conformable to g. The variables ε_1, ε_2, and ε_3 are mutually uncorrelated, normally distributed random variables. The variable p^e_t is the public's expectation of p_t at t–1; $\tilde{y}$ is the level of output associated with the natural rate of unemployment.

Equation (7) is the aggregate supply schedule in the form associated with the natural rate hypothesis. Equation (8) is the *IS* curve, relating income to the expected real interest rate and to exogenous expenditures. Equation (9) is the *LM* curve, or portfolio balance condition, relating the real value of the stock of money to the transactions and portfolio demands for real money balances. Other than the random variables, the model contains four unknowns, y_t, p_t, r_t, and p^e_t. To complete the system, some hypothesis must be advanced on the formation of expectations.

For example, the model might be closed with the supposition that price expectations are formed by the simple adaptive or extrapolative scheme:

$$p^e_t = \lambda p_{t-1} \tag{10}$$

It may then be shown (see appendix for derivation) that:

$$y_t - \tilde{y}_t = a\,[(m_t - \lambda m_{t-1}) + d_1(g_t - \lambda g_{t-1}) + d_2(y_t - \lambda y_{t-1}) + d_3\,\{(\lambda - 1)\,(p_{t-1} - \lambda p_{t-2})\,\}] + \mu \tag{11}$$

Where d_1, d_2, and d_3 are simply redefined parameters, and μ is a combination of error terms.

It is evident from equation (11) that, despite the aggregate supply function being based on the natural rate hypothesis, an important role for a discretionary monetary and fiscal policy remains. By selecting appropriate values for m and g, the authorities can attempt to minimize the fluctuation of actual output around its full-employment level (or, more strictly, its natural rate of unemployment). Active policies are on the agenda because of the manner in which expectations have been supposed to be formed (equation 10). The adaptive expectations hypothesis implies that past mistakes are only slowly corrected, and it is the need to overcome the unfortunate consequences of this stickiness in the process of correction that provides the rationale for government intervention—a very familiar theme indeed in imperfectionist arguments.

But what is the rationale for the adaptive rule on the formation of expectations (equation 10) that has led to this conclusion? If individuals blindly followed this rule, then they would soon discover that they were systematically wrong (wrong, in the sense of making systematic expectational errors). This conflicts with the underlying proposition that individuals attempt to make rational utility-maximizing and profit-maximizing decisions, albeit (typically) with only a limited amount of information available to them. Of course, predictions can possibly be improved only if the economic variables under consideration are subject to determination by systematic forces—that is, if the market mechanism operates according to systematic and persistent laws. As we have seen, the imperfectionists agree that this is the case by deferring to the forces of demand and supply.

The hypothesis of rational expectations, unlike that of adaptive expectations which provides the basis for an imperfectionist position, takes these (shared) underlying propositions seriously. The rational expectations school identifies the forces at work in the market mechanism with those outlined in Walrasian general equilibrium theory—that is, the forces of demand and supply. Notice how a *theory* has simply been taken to *be* objective reality. As Muth (1961), in the case of predictions by firms, argued, "The hypothesis can be re-phrased a little more precisely as follows: that expectations of firms (or, more generally, the subjective probability distribution of outcomes) tend to be distributed, for the same information set, about the prediction of the theory (or the 'objective' probability distribution of outcomes)" (p.316).

The consequence of making this supposition about expectation formation is that for any given prediction of, say, the price level,

$$p^e_t = E\,(p_t \mid \varphi_{t-1}) \tag{12}$$

where E is the expected value operator and φ_{t-1} is the set of information concerning p^e_t at t-1, the expected value of the difference between prediction and event is zero. That is,

$$E(p_t - p^e_t \mid \varphi_{t-1}) = 0 \tag{13}$$

When this hypothesis is introduced into the discussion of unemployment, money, and inflation (see, for example, Walters, 1971; Lucas, 1972a, b; Sargent, 1973), the consequences are dramatic. They can be seen if, following the procedure adopted by Pesaran (1982), we replace equation (10) with equation (12) and complete the model by assuming that expectations are formed rationally (in the sense of equation 13). Then, remembering that the random variables have a zero mean, taking expectations of equations (7), (8), and (9), gives:

$$y^e_t = \tilde{y}_t \tag{7a}$$

$$y^e_t = b_o[r^e_t - (p^e_t - p_{t-1})] + b_1 g^e_t \tag{8a}$$

$$m^e_t - p^e_t = c_o y^e_t + c_1 r^e_t \tag{9a}$$

where $y^e_t = E\,(y_t \mid \varphi_{t-1})$, $r^e_t = E\,(r_t \mid \varphi_{t-1})$ *and so on.*

By subtracting these equations from (7), (8), and (9), respectively, the *unanticipated* change in endogenous variables may be found. For example, subtracting equation (7a) from (7) gives $y_t - y^e_t = a(p_t - p^e_t) + \varepsilon_1$, and so on. Now, since $\tilde{y}_t = y^e_t$ (equation 7a) and $E(p_t - p^e_t | \varphi_{t-1}) = 0$, the deviation of actual income from its natural level may be shown (see chapter appendix) to be:

$$y_t - \tilde{y}_t = z_1(m_t - m^e_t) + z_2(g_t - g^e_t) + \eta \tag{14}$$

where z_i's are combinations of parameters and η is a combination of error terms.

The extent of the influence of monetary and fiscal policy on the level of activity is revealed in equation (14) to be dependent on the deviation of the actual policy from the policy that was expected to rule. If government policies follow an unpredictable course, then they can continue to influence the levels of output and employment. But if the government pursues *any* consistent monetary and fiscal policy, all effects on activity disappear (since individuals can predict policies in the same way as they can predict other economic variables).

Suppose, for example, that current monetary and fiscal policy is based on last year's money supply, fiscal stance, and level of output, plus a normally distributed random element. That is, suppose:

$$m_t - f_m(m_{t-1}, g_{t-1}, y_{t-1}) + \varepsilon_m \tag{15}$$

and

$$g_t = f_g(m_{t-1}, g_{t-1}, y_{t-1}) + \varepsilon_{g.} \tag{16}$$

Since individuals and firms can form rational expectations of government policies,

$$m^e_t = E(m_t | \varphi$$
$$g^e_t = E(g_t | \varphi_{t-1}) = f_{g.} \tag{18}$$

Substituting equations (17) and (18) into equation (14) gives:

$$y_t - \tilde{y}_t = z_1\varepsilon_m + z_2\varepsilon_g + \eta \tag{19}$$

That is, the deviation of actual output from its full-employment level (natural rate) is simply a sum of random events. Only random elements in government policy can have any impact—and precisely what effect that is cannot be known in advance. There is no role for systematic monetary and fiscal policies. The imperfectionist position that relied on the influence of uncertainty and expectations to provide a rationale for interventionist policies has disappeared.

The striking reaffirmation of the laissez-faire position that the above argument entails should have come as no surprise to the imperfectionists. It arises simply from following through in a clear and consistent manner the logic of the presupposition of imperfectionist analysis: that the market mechanism is ultimately governed by the laws of demand and supply. However, the rational expectations hypothesis has been widely criticized in imperfectionist circles. Such criticisms fall into two broad groups: criticisms of the conclusions drawn with respect to monetary policy by the rational expectations variant of the orthodox market-mechanism school; and criticisms of the hypothesis that expectations are formed rationally. Each may be taken in turn.

The rational expectations position has been associated with propositions concerning the neutrality of money—in the sense that the real equilibrium of the system is independent of monetary policy, which serves only to determine nominal magnitudes (Lucas, 1972a). However, as was pointed out by Samuelson (1958), different monetary policies, even if fully anticipated, will have consequences for real variables, primarily through portfolio balance and substitution effects. Buiter (1980) advances these considerations as a critique of the rational expectations school, but it is a critique of limited significance. Samuelson's argument amounts to saying nothing more than that different monetary policies will result in the economy being at different *full-employment* equilibria. Since there is no criterion for choosing between one full-employment equilibrium and another, the fact that strict monetary neutrality does not hold is of very little importance. Indeed, it is no more significant than noticing that multiple equilibria are entirely possible anyway.

The second set of objections to the rational expectations model involves primarily a resurrection of familiar imperfectionist themes: "prices are determined in non-competitive markets by a mark-up process (Modigliani, 1977, p. 120; Tobin, 1980, p. 35; Buiter, 1980, p. 41); "the adjustment of wages and relative prices to their equilibrium levels is sluggish" (Tobin, 1980, pp. 25–27; Buiter, 1980, p. 41); "neither labour markets nor individuals are sufficiently homogeneous to permit the simple derivation of rational expectations results" (Modigliani, 1977, p. 121; Tobin, 1980, p. 26); "empirical evidence suggests that the economy is not typically in a natural rate equilibrium" (Modigliani, 1977, pp. 119, 121; Buiter, 1980, p. 41).

Once again, the pragmatic appeal of these observations should not be permitted to disguise the fact that they in no way constitute an alternative explanation of the underlying relationship between the operation of the market mechanism and the determination of the level of employment. Rather, they are additional considerations to be incorporated into the old orthodox theory to give it a more plausible empirical content. Indeed, if it really is the case that prices and quantities are not determined in accordance with the generally accepted principles of demand and supply, then it is that very theory of the operation of the market mechanism that should be abandoned. However, the unquestioning acceptance of this conception of the market mechanism as applicable to long-run (or equilibrium) analysis, and the discussion of all relevant considerations in terms of deviations from that long-run analysis not only involve the acceptance of the orthodox model of the market mechanism but also consign the analysis of unemployment to an underworld of ad hoc hypotheses. The end of the doctrine of laissez-faire, of which Keynes himself spoke so optimistically over fifty years ago, will not occur until economists realize that the market mechanism is not explained by demand-and-supply theory. And this will not be easy; this homely but inadequate theory has so dominated the discipline that whole generations of economists, industrialists, bankers, politicians, and journalists have grown up believing it to be not just a theory about the real world but the real world itself. Unfortunately, however, no such ultimate truth was discovered when the familiar demand-and-supply curves were first drawn on the back of an envelope.

Conclusion

The orthodox neoclassical theory of value, distribution, and output characterizes the market mechanism as *tending* always to ensure the full utilization of factors of production, including labor. Therefore, the orthodox neoclassical theory of unemployment is based on the imposition of arbitrary imperfections onto the general equilibrium theory of demand and supply. Our argument suggests that this analysis of the relationship between unemployment and the market mechanism is unsatisfactory on four main counts: (1) the attempt to relegate empirical *regularities* into the secondary class of imperfections (of frictions and rigidities) completely ignores the fact that such regularities should be part and parcel of the characterization of the *normal* operation of the market mechanism (not of its abnormal operation as the imperfectionist position requires); (2) there exists a perfectly satisfactory explanation of the relationship between unemployment and the market mechanism, in the form of

Keynes's principle of effective demand, which does not invoke arbitrary imperfections to explain unemployment; (3) the appeal to unknowable imperfections—uncertainty, disappointed expectations, conjectures, and the like—serves to deprive economic analysis of all definite content, thus reducing the discussion of economic policy to the status of guesswork and negating the single most important achievement of economic theory during the past two hundred years—namely, that the market mechanism is governing by systematic, objective forces; and (4) there are fundamental analytical shortcomings to neoclassical theory even when applied to the analysis of equilibrium that suggest that the imperfectionist superstructure is in any case erected on crumbling foundations.

The two examples from the multitude of imperfectionist arguments on which we have focused—the hypothesis that money wages are inflexible and the debate over the natural rate of unemployment/rational expectations position—illustrate clearly the foundations that are common to both the orthodox market-mechanism school and the imperfectionists. The abandonment of these common foundations sweeps away both the theory of employment of the market-mechanism school and the theories of unemployment conjured up by the imperfectionists. This does not mean that some of the empirical regularities utilized by the imperfectionists are now to be ignored. Rather, their importance should be assessed in the context of the more satisfactory theory of employment that is to be found in the characterization of the market mechanism provided by Keynes's theory of effective demand and the surplus approach to the analysis of value and distribution.

Notes

This is an enlarged and newly revised version of a paper by Murray Milgate and John Eatwell that appeared originally as the fifteenth chapter of their *Keynes's Economics and the Theory of Value and Distribution* (1983).

1. The fact that Keynes was dealing with "statements of tendency." as such a stance implies, is clearly revealed in a passage from one of the earliest drafts of the material that was later to become the General Theory: "the orthodox equilibrium theory of economics has assumed... that there are natural forces tending to bring the volume of... output... back to the optimum level whenever temporary forces have led it to depart from this level. But... the equilibrium level towards which output tends to return after temporary disturbances is not necessarily the optimum level" (Keynes, 1973, 13:406). Indeed, the market mechanism and the isolation of determining circumstances are those "formal principles of thought" without which, Keynes noted, "we shall be lost in the wood" (1973, 7:297).

2. It is worth remembering, in this context, that whenever Keynes outlined the basis of the orthodox view that there was a tendency toward full employment

(the law to which this passage refers), he invariably included as part of that statement the possibility of temporary deviations and interferences (see, for example, Keynes, 1973, 7:6, 8, 9, 16, 257, 279; 13:486–87; 14:363–64; 29:97, 102). In this light, it is all the more difficult to understand how imperfectionist interpretations have gained such credibility as accurate readings of the text.

3. On this issue, we are concerned exclusively with Keynes's view on self-adjustment. We will not refer here to the weaknesses of Keynes's theory, which derive from the presence of a traditional, interest-elastic investment demand function—which, once admitted, reintroduces the requirement of a sticky interest rate.

4. See also Keynes, 1973, 14:26; 29:97. This conclusion is further supported by Keynes's frequent substitution of the term "self-righting" for that of "self-adjusting" (see, for example, Keynes, 1973, 14:118).

5. Thus, toward the end of the *General Theory*, Keynes states that his objection is against "the theoretical foundations" of the orthodox school (1973, 7:339).

6. See, for example, Keynes, 1973, 14:211; 29:262–63.

7. Indeed, Hicks made just such a claim in 1937 when he incorrectly attributed to Keynes's analysis of unemployment the postulate of money-wage rigidity. In that article, Hicks argued that "this is the kind of change . . . we ought to be making all the time in response to changing facts" (1937, p. 147). It is difficult to know exactly what facts have changed, since institutional wage determination had evolved in Britain from at least the second half of the nineteenth century; an attempt to rescue a demand-and-supply explanation of wages on the grounds that one-upon-a-time this was so, is rather dubious.

8. Thereby implicitly, and somewhat disingenuously, accusing Keynes of exaggeration in the choice of title for his book (cf. Pigou, 1936, who makes the charge explicit).

9. Clearly, the *General Theory* itself should not be regarded as definitive in all respects. Yet the imperfectionists have used it to give respectability to their arguments, and it seems worthwhile to check the accuracy of their claims against the original.

10. Government deficit spending would be included here.

11. Indeed, a number of imperfectionists, alerted by Leijonhufvud's warning that attributing a money-wage rigidity hypothesis to Keynes was more than a little questionable (see, for example, Leijonhufvud, 1971) have searched out other rigidities. Leijonhufvud himself seems to have chosen the rate of interest (1971, p. 38).

12. This point is elaborated in Milgate (1982, ch.7).

13. This will be the case when, taking technique and equipment as given, all elements of cost change in the same proportion as the wage-unit (see Keynes, 1973, 7:295).

14. The most significant here is that the level of effective demand changes in proportion to the quantity of money. This assumption will be retained through the rest of our discussion of this point (Keynes, 1973, 7:298–99, for a discussion of the effects of relaxing it).

15. Where expansions in the quantity of money above this critical level affect money wages, and hence prices, whereas contractions below it reduce output and employment and need not necessarily alter the price level.

16. One cannot help but imagine that Keynes was contemplating his earlier self, so to speak, when he remarked in the *General Theory* that: "a classical

economist may sympathise with labour in refusing to accept a cut in its money wage, and he will admit that it may not be wise to make it in conditions which are temporary; but scientific integrity forces him to declare that this refusal is, nevertheless, at the bottom of the trouble" (1973, 7:16).

Chapter Appendix

Combining equations (8) and (9) gives:

$$p_t = m_t + d_1 y_t + d_2 y_t + d_3 (p^e_t - p_{t-1}) + c_1/b_o \, \varepsilon_2 - \varepsilon_3 \tag{A1}$$

where $d_1 = c_1 b_1/b_0$; $d_2 = -(b_0 c_0 + c_1)/b_0$ and $d_3 = -c_1$. Using equation (10) and substituting equation (A1) into equation (7) results in equation (11) with $\mu = \varepsilon_1 - (a\lambda c_1 \varepsilon_2)/b_0 + a(\lambda - 1)\varepsilon_{3.}$

Equation (14) is derived by subtracting equation (7a) from equation (7), equation (8a) from equation (8), and equation (9a) from equation (9); and then solving the resultant equations for $y_t - \tilde{y}_t$ (remember that the rational expectation of y_t is $\tilde{y}_t$). Terms have been collected as follows:

$$z_1 = ab_0 / [b_0 + a(b_0 c_0 + c_1)]$$
$$z_2 = ac_1 b_1 / [b_0 + a(b_0 c_0 + c_1)]$$
$$\eta = (b_0 \varepsilon_1 + ac_1 \varepsilon_2 - ab_0 \varepsilon_3) / b_0 + a(b_0 c_0 + c_1)$$

13

The Analytical Foundations of Monetarism

The nature of the relationship between the general price level and the quantity of money (variously defined) has been a matter of dispute throughout the history of economics. Failure to resolve the debate suggests a failure to define in a precise manner, or ever to agree upon, the issues at stake. This failure is evident in the debates surrounding the modern revival of monetarism. Writers who claim that the issues are fundamentally theoretical are opposed by those who argue that it is empirical assumptions that divide the protagonists; and analyses of short-run dynamics—always a fruitful environment for the ad hoc—are counterposed to studies of long-run equilibrium. This chapter will attempt to elucidate some of the issues by examining the theoretical foundations of monetarism. Paradoxically, these foundations do not lie in the realm of monetary theory but, rather, in theories of the determination of real output.

Beginning from the equation of exchange, or monetary identity, $MV \equiv PY$, it is evident that even if the velocity of circulation may be assumed to be relatively stable, determined in the longer run by institutional phenomena, a direct behavioral link between M and P alone requires that Y be independently determined. Thus, the classical version of Say's Law, in which the level of output is determined by the level of accumulation and the social productivity of labor, given that saving and investment are *assumed* equal, was the basis of classical monetarism (on the classical theory of output; see Green, 1982). Similarly, the neoclassical version of Say's Law, in which the level of output is determined in the establishment of a market-clearing set of equilibrium prices, is the basis of modern monetarism: "The price level is then the joint outcome of the monetary forces determining nominal income and the real forces determining real income...I shall regard long-run equilibrium as determined by the earlier quantity theory model plus the Walrasian equations of general equilibrium" (Friedman, 1974a, pp. 27, 48).

The proposition "that changes in the quantity of money as such *in the long run* have a negligible effect on real income" (Friedman, 1974a, p. 27) is not in itself sufficient to sustain a typically monetarist position, for the causation may as well run from price to money as from money to price—indeed, this was the crux of much classical debate[1]—but it is a necessary condition for subsequent development of monetarist propositions. Thus, examination of the characteristics of the theory of real output espoused in monetarist writings is a prerequisite for consideration of the theoretical status of monetarist propositions.

An important corollary to any such examination must be consideration of the characteristics of the equilibrium level of real output as a position to which the economy tends to gravitate and, hence, with respect to which fluctuations in economic variables, both monetary and real, are defined. Thus, not only does Friedman argue that the quantity theory will hold in long-run equilibrium, but he also constructs his analysis of the short-run dynamics of nominal income in terms of the deviations of particular parameters from their permanent or long-run values (see, for example, Friedman, 1974a, pp. 48–61). The short run is dependent upon and derived from the long-run position. The long-run equilibrium is, thus, the key to the entire system, and Friedman defends ably the long-run conception against the charge that "a long run constructed to track the ultimate consequences of anything is a never-never land" (Tobin and Buiter, 1976, p. 273):

> The long-run equilibrium in which, as I put it, 'all anticipations are realised' and that is determined by 'the earlier quantity theory plus the Walrasian equations of general equilibrium' is not a state that is assumed to exist in practice. It is a logical construct that defines the norm or trend from which the actual world is always deviating but to which it is tending to return or about which it tends to fluctuate. The hypothesis that the logical construct does specify the norm or trend in this sense is entirely compatible with the existence of uncertainty, just as the hypothesis that $s = 1/2\, gt^2$ specifies the law of falling bodies is entirely compatible with the existence of air. (Friedman, 1974b, p. 150)

Friedman nowhere spells out what he means by long-run equilibrium, but it is evident from his writings that he is referring to the Marshallian conception (Marshall, 1920, 5:iii, v). Nor does he attempt to justify this characterization of the norm or trend of the economy as a persistent center of gravitation, being apparently content to rest on the arguments built up throughout the development of economic theory, from Smith's conception of natural price to Marshall's long-run normal equilibrium. But in the past forty years, the notion of equilibrium used in economic analysis has undergone a fundamental, though little noticed, change (see Milgate, 1979), and confusion over the specification of equilibrium may, at least in part, contribute to the confusion of monetary debate.

The theoretical foundations of monetarism consist of both a theory of real output and a clearly specified conception of equilibrium. It will be argued below that much confusion has been created by the fact that many of the protagonists in the monetary debates, while sharing the same theory of real output, have adopted different conceptions of equilibrium, and that mutual criticism based on various aspects of the same theory has been erroneously interpreted as being derived from different theoretical bases. In light of these fundamentals, some other disputed issues, such as the proposition that the real equilibrium of the economy is homogeneous of degree zero in money stock and prices, become of secondary importance.[2]

Theory

Arguing that many of those involved in the current debate share the same theory does not mean that they characterize the economy in terms of the same model.[3] What they share is the broad view that prices and quantities in a market economy are determined by the balance of the forces of supply and demand, expressed more or less formally as the market resolution of individual utility maximization subject to the constraints of endowment and technology. Let us label this broad view "neoclassical." Particular neoclassical models may take either aggregative or disaggregative forms, may comprise different specifications of the endowment or of arguments of the utility functions, or may include a wide range of auxiliary constraints (Samuelson, 1947, pp. 30–39) such as sticky prices, probabilistic adjustment or search speeds, uncertainty, misinformation, and so on.

Such differing formulations of the same base theory seem to have been responsible for some of the noncommunication in monetary debates. An example is the comparison of, on the one hand, a variety of model in which normal output is given by real forces and, on the other hand, models in which output is determined by a "Keynesian" *IS-LM* mechanism. Yet these models are essentially the same. Modigliani (1944) has shown that by defining the liquidity preference schedule as a demand curve for money, and the marginal efficiency of capital schedule as the demand function for investment, the Keynesian system may, in the absence of sticky wages, be split into real and monetary parts. The real equations determine the equilibrium output, real wage, and interest rate, and the monetary equation determines the level of nominal wages and prices—resurrecting the Wicksellian image of an equilibrium determined by the interaction of real forces mediated through monetary flows. Since the real forces determine a market-clearing equilibrium, factors of production will be fully employed (or free goods). This conclusion may be modified in those models in which information is transmitted by search as well as prices, and the natural rate of unemployment may not be zero (Phelps, 1970). So, the independence of the determinants of real output from monetary phenomena depends on the absence of stickiness of prices—a plausible assumption in a long-run context.[4] But it is only this stickiness that differentiates monetarist and *IS-LM* models.

A somewhat different confusion has been introduced into the debate by Hahn (1980), who refers to the Friedmanite class of models in which price—determined market clearing occurs, and a class of models of the Clower (1956) or conjectural equilibrium variety (Hahn, 1978), as different theories:

> [T]he proposition that monetary policy that is systematic cannot affect the natural values of real variables is essentially related to the Walrasian model.... But the Walrasian model does not capture any of the market failures macroeconomists have been concerned with for forty-five years. The argument must thus be about appropriate models of the whole economy, and that strikes me as largely a theoretical problem. (1980, p. 6)

Hahn does not propose a new theory in the sense that the apparatus characterizing the behavior of a market economy in terms of maximization subject to constraint is to be abandoned. Instead, a number of imperfections are incorporated into the Walrasian framework, and the same type of equilibrium is then sought. This equilibrium may not be market clearing in the sense that, for a variety of reasons, agents offer or demand quantities other than those that would correspond to equilibrium in a system in which the imperfections were not present. An economy in such an imperfect equilibrium might respond to a variety of fiscal or monetary policy measures in quite a different manner than would an economy without auxiliary constraints.

From the catalogue of imperfect equilibria, Hahn proposes a conjectural equilibrium as an alternative to Walrasian equilibrium, and argues that:

> [The] monetarist view depends on is a unique Walrasian equilibrium and denial of the possibility of rational expectations conjectural non-Walrasian equilibria. It seems tome I have now made the case for the view that quite fundamental theoretical matters are at stake. If further study should show that the notion of rational non-Walrasian equilibrium is not viable, then there would be a great strengthening of the view that systematic monetary policy is ineffective. If, on the other hand, it survives the detailed study it is now rather widely receiving, rather more old-fashioned Keynesian views will survive without violating the axiom of rationality and greed. (Hahn, 1980, p. 10)

But to refer to these models as differing in theoretical fundamentals is profoundly misleading. The theoretical apparatus is essentially unchanged. What is changed is the method by which price signals communicate adequate information concerning demands and offers, and, indeed, how they are interpreted. Hence, the equilibrium will depend on the degree to which one level of communication/interpretation predominates rather than another—that is, the empirical specification of the model.

So, the underlying model of real output adopted by both Friedman and most of his critics is based on the orthodox neoclassical theory of value, output, and employment and variants thereof. Differing conclusions are reached by incorporating a variety of essentially arbitrary imperfections and assumptions about speeds of adjustment. But consideration of the relative importance of different versions takes the argument "out of the realm of those questions that can be considered by *a priori* considerations of internal consistency and logical validity, and into the realm of those questions that can be decided only by empirical considerations of the actual magnitudes of the relevant economic parameters" (Patinkin, 1974, pp. 130–31).

Equilibrium

> I suspect that our difference is a by product of my Marshallian approach to theory... versus Tobin's Walrasian approach.
>
> —Milton Friedman

The context in which Friedman expressed this suspicion was in arguing that a fundamental issue in the evaluation of monetarist propositions is whether a failure to satisfy *perfectly* the theoretical conditions is of any practical importance. His identification of his own position as Marshallian refers to the general method of long-period equilibrium, in which the determinants of long-period positions are the dominant and persistent forces of the economy, and specific imperfections or chance events are the causes of short-run fluctuations around the long-run position.

The origins of this method are to be found in Smith's *Wealth of Nations*. Smith was faced with the dual task of characterizing a market economy at such a level of abstraction that statements of general validity might be made about its behavior and of building a theory to provide the material for such statements. The former task required the identification of the objective force in a market economy that endows its operations with systematic character—the force of competition. Competition creates the tendency toward a uniform wage for each category of labor, a uniform rent for each quality of land, and a uniform rate of profit on the value of capital invested in each particular line as capitalists adjust the composition of the capital stock in search of maximum profits. If these uniformities were established, then commodities would sell at their natural prices. Since in reality the full effects of competition are disrupted by chance events or specific (as opposed to general) circumstances, commodities will sell at their market prices, which competition will always push toward natural prices. Market prices are concrete phenomena and not susceptible to theoretical generalization.

Theoretical generalization involves the abstraction from the complexity of reality of those forces that are believed to be dominant, and the combination of these forces into a formal model. It is obvious that, except by a fluke, the solution of the model will not determine the actual magnitudes of the variables under consideration since, by definition, so many concrete forces have been excluded by abstraction. But the implicit assumption is that these forces are not dominant, and hence the determined magnitudes will be centers of gravitation to fluctuations of the actual magnitudes.

Thus, Smith's conception of natural price linked the empirical characteristics of a competitive market to the necessity of theoretical abstraction. Smith's concepts of natural and market price were refined by Ricardo and Marx, and then adopted by the early neoclassics. Natural prices were redefined as long-run equilibrium prices. A significant modification made at this time was that, between the abstract long period and the concrete market price, a further abstract notion was introduced—that of short-period equilibrium. However, this new notion was generally confined to partial equilibrium analyses where its dubious status as a center of gravitation was of relatively little significance and where it might be assumed, *ceteris paribus*, that the rest of the economy is in long-run equilibrium. Thus, the short run was defined as a specific deviation from the long run—that is, it had no independent existence other than as a deviation from the long-run normal position.

It is to the long-run normal equilibrium that Friedman consistently refers in expositions of his theory. In this context, it is quite reasonable for him to regard imperfections as being essentially short-run phenomena that will be overcome by the long-run force of competition, and the effects of which will be confined to fluctuations around the long-run position. Hence, although perfect conditions are never fully attained "as a practical matter sufficiently correct results will be obtained by treating them *as if* they were perfectly satisfied...I continue to believe that the fundamental differences between us are empirical, not theoretical; that what we really differ on are precisely what effects are and are not 'minor,' not on whether an effect is precisely zero' (Friedman, 1976, pp. 310, 312).

However, Friedman has failed to notice that the differences between himself and his Walrasian critics possess a further dimension, for the Walrasians are basing their critique on a quite different conception of equilibrium.[5] Under the pressure of Keynes's theoretical critique of the foundations of orthodox theory, and of some partially perceived difficulties in the theory of capital, the notion of long-run equilibrium and the associated normal prices and general rate of profit were abandoned, and were replaced by an equilibrium characterized as a temporal sequence of general short-period equilibria, displaying, consequentially, no general rate of profit. Originated by Hayek and Lindahl (see Milgate, 1979) the new notion of equilibrium was introduced into the English-language literature by Hicks (1939). The simplest form of this intertemporal equilibrium is that incorporating perfect foresight and complete futures markets presented by Debreu.

No longer confined to partial equilibrium analysis under the protective umbrella of the *ceteris paribus* assumption, the new short period, defined purely in terms of market clearing without reference to any long period, purportedly defines the temporal path the economy will actually adopt. The basic characteristic of a short-period equilibrium is that it contains all the information (auxiliary constraints) that define it as a short period *within* the determination of the equilibrium. Since the intertemporal equilibrium is, in this sense, all-enveloping, the idea of imperfections causing fluctuations around a short-period equilibrium does not make any sense—the equilibrium is fully defined, warts and all.

Thus, the new neoclassical economics of intertemporal equilibrium does not contain the vocabulary of the old, which specified centers of gravitation and fluctuations around them. A short-lived equilibrium is something from which the economy moves away, not toward. So Tobin and Buiter refer to a long-period position as a "never-never land," and Hahn wishes to incorporate all in imperfections of his conjectural analysis into the specification of the equilibrium, rather than having them determine short-period fluctuations around the long-period normal position. In these circumstances, Friedman's old-fashioned notions of approximation and not-quite-perfect models make no sense. Models and equilibria are completely specified.

Evaluation

We have, therefore, established two distinct though interrelated sources of confusion in contemporary monetary debates: (1) the belief of particular writers that they are advancing different theories that are fundamentally the same, which has led not only to failure to communicate but also has severely diminished the effectiveness of critiques of the monetarist position; and (2) that writers have used different conceptions of equilibrium, which in turn has led to quite different interpretations of the role of imperfections in short-run and long-run analyses.

As has already been noted, Friedman argues that the theory of real output underlying his monetary theory is that, in the long run, output and employment will be at their natural level—that is, at "the level that would be ground out by the Walrasian system of general equilibrium equations, provided there is embedded in them the actual characteristics of labour and commodity markets, including market imperfections" (Friedman, 1968, p. 8). An immediate neo-Walrasian reaction to this argument would be to point out that it is well known that no proof of the existence of equilibrium in an economy with imperfect markets is available (Hahn and Neild, 1980; Roberts and Sonnenschein, 1977). But this would miss the point.

To avoid confusion and to provide the strongest ground for Friedman's propositions, let us suppose the economy to be perfectly competitive, with fully flexible wages and prices manipulated by a Walrasian auctioneer. Friedman could then argue that the long-run Walrasian equilibrium with associated outputs, prices, and general rate of profit would be established by the real forces of individual utility maximization subject to the constraints of endowment and technology. Given this real equilibrium, then, he could with confidence set about building models of the short-run dynamics of nominal income and of the relationship between the quantity of money, the value nominal income, and the long-run price level. But he would be wrong.

For, as a result of the work on the theory of capital done in the last two decades, we now know that it is not logically possible to solve a neoclassical system for the determination of long-run equilibrium (Robinson, 1953; Garegnani, 1960; Sraffa, 1960; Symposium, 1966; Garegnani, 1970). Put more generally, outside a one-commodity world, there exists no logical foundation for the proposition that long-period quantities, prices, and rate of profit are determined by the forces of supply and demand. This logical failure applies to all versions of neoclassical theory—Austrian, Marshallian, Walrasian, and Wicksellian (Garegnani, 1960, pt. 2).

Since this point is less familiar in the context of Walrasian systems, it may prove useful to express it in modern terms. We begin with the specification of a private enterprise economy by Debreu (1959, p. 79) in terms of preferences, endowments, and technology—the endowments of capital goods being each specified in terms of their own physical units. Since the work of Wald (1936), it has been known that the system can be solved only for economically meaningful values of quantities and prices if it is expressed in terms of inequalities. In particular, the price of any producible commodity will, in equilibrium, be *less than* equal to its cost of production. If the price of a capital good is, in equilibrium, less than its cost of production, the rate of return over cost on that good will be less than the general rate of return ruling in that time period on the capital goods for which the equality holds. There is no general rate of profit, and changes in the composition of the capital stock would lead to higher profits—a typical short-period situation.

Expressed in terms of inequalities, the system solves. Now, impose the condition that in each elementary time period there be a uniform general rate of profit (not necessarily the same rate in different periods)—that is, that the demand prices of all capital goods be equal to their costs of production. This amounts to adding a new set of constraints to an already determinate system. The model will be overdetermined and will not solve.

This general failure of neoclassical long-period models may be expressed in a variety of ways. In the early stages of the capital theory debate, attention was focused on the successful demonstration that no logical foundation can be provided for the existence of an elastic, well-behaved demand schedule for capital as a function of the general rate of interest. Since such a schedule provided the logical foundation for the marginal efficiency of capital schedule, the critique removes all logical status from the *IS-LM* models. Similarly, it is not possible to construct a consistent analysis of the labor market in terms of supply and demand—that is, it cannot be shown that real wages and a long-run natural rate of employment (and unemployment) are determined by supply and demand. In orthodox neoclassical analysis, the demand curve for labor is derived from the possibility of substitution of labor with other factors of production, including capital. The inadequacies of the neoclassical theory of capital are thus replicated in the inadequacies of the neoclassical theory of the labor market. It may be concluded that there is no logically consistent neoclassical model of long-period employment, real output, relative prices, and the general rate of profit.

The logical failure of neoclassical long-run analysis provided a major impulse for the abandonment of the notion of long-run equilibrium and its replacement by intertemporal equilibrium. The proof of the existence of intertemporal equilibrium is, on its own terms, logically sound. This raises the question of whether Friedman's analysis may be based on intertemporal equilibrium rather than long-period equilibrium. Unfortunately, it cannot. A central aspect of Friedman's analysis is that the real output determined independently of monetary forces should be the center of gravitation to any fluctuation of the economy brought about by unanticipated changes in the quantity of money. The intertemporal equilibrium is not satisfactory on this count. First, as Hahn and Nield (1980) point out, with respect to the stability of the mathematical functions defining the equilibrium, "absolutely no satisfactory theoretical answer is available" (see also Arrow and Hahn, 1971, ch. 12). Second, and more important, quite apart from the characterization of the mathematical functions, the intertemporal equilibrium is not a center of gravitation toward which the economy would tend and around which it would fluctuate. Any chance fluctuation away from a given sequence of short-period equilibria will establish a new sequence; it will not set up pressures pushing the system back to the old sequence. The old long-period notion derived coherence from the fact that it defined a center of gravitation in terms of the general outcome of capitalistic competition. The new intertemporal equilibrium lacks coherence because while, on the one hand, it purports to define the equilibrium of a competitive economy, on the other hand, it is a point from which any chance deviation will be reinforced, not counteracted, by competitive forces. Thus, despite its logical rigor, the Arrow-Debreu general equilibrium model cannot serve as a basis for Friedman's monetary analysis or, for that matter, of any analysis of a competitive market economy (for a full discussion of this point, see Eatwell, 1982).

Conclusion

We have concentrated on Friedman's monetary analysis not only because he was the most prominent proponent of monetarist ideas but also because he clearly regarded his work as a serious foundation for the analysis of economic policy and, hence, the issue of the concept of equilibrium as a center of gravitation was important to him. It would be quite possible to erect formally consistent monetarist models on the basis of the Arrow-Debreu determination of real output, but such models could not be advanced as the basis for analysis of the short- and long-run dynamics of market economies. It should perhaps be emphasized that the issue is not simply one of formal mathematical stability. It is true that even in an economy with a single capital good and many other nonreproducible factors, in which long-run (uniform rate of profit) and Arrow-Debreu equilibria are identical, no general proof of stability is available (as Tobin and Buiter, 1976, show), and that this severely weakens all neoclassical analysis. But my point is more general. Given the objective and omnipresent force of competition, the long-run position characterizes the center of gravitation established by that force. The same competitive forces ensure that the intertemporal equilibrium cannot be a center of gravitation.

Friedman was left, therefore, with two unpalatable options: either to adopt the Arrow-Debreu framework and eschew any pretense of policy relevance; or to locate his analyses overtly in single-produced means-of-production worlds, such as that of Solow (1970), from which they cannot escape and within which it is extremely difficult to provide any rationale for the existence of money and of monetary policy.

A final comment should perhaps be made on the supposed wealth of empirical evidence that, it is sometimes said, supports monetarist hypotheses. Those who wish to appeal to such evidence should take suitable warning from the production-function fiasco. Despite the fact that the theoretical foundations of the aggregate production function were known to be extremely weak (the one-commodity world once again), literally thousands of studies have produced the empirical evidence that such functions fitted the characteristics of a variety of economies. It took Fisher's (1969, 1971) demonstration that the studies were based on a statistical artifact to call a halt to the production of nonsense. Shaikh (1975) later demonstrated that the statistical specification the good fit was an *algebraic* necessity.

Economists should learn to take their theory seriously before attempting to sustain logically inconsistent theories with empirical evidence. As Friedman himself argued in his Nobel Prize Lecture (quoting Pierre du Pont), "Bad logicians have committed more involuntary crimes than bad men have done intentionally" (Friedman, 1977, p. 471).

Notes

This chapter was written by John Eatwell and appeared originally as the eleventh chapter of Eatwell and Milgate's book *Keynes's Economics and the Theory of Value and Distribution* (1983).

1. Kaldor's argument (1970) that the money supply is endogenous, not exogenous, is a revival of the classical controversy.

2. The role of the homogeneity postulate in the debates is most ambiguous. While Friedman appears generally to ignore the problem, he relies heavily on the Pigou effect to refute Keynesian propositions on the long-run level of employment. Hahn (1971) and Tobin (1974) both cite the failure of the homogeneity postulate as important theoretical evidence against Friedman, and yet attempt to contest his analysis on other grounds. The ambiguity seems to derive from a feeling that the effects of nonhomogeneity do not significantly alter the results of the standard neoclassical model in which homogeneity is presumed and equilibrium prices and outputs are determined by real forces.

3. Kaldor (1970) and Cripps (1977) are exceptions to this generalization. It should, however, be noted that neither Kaldor nor Cripps presents a critique of the theory of real output used by Friedman. Instead, they either contrast Friedman's monetary theory with their own or attempt to refute his propositions on institutional and empirical grounds.

4. Tobin and Buiter (1976) present a model in which the flexible-price, full-employment equilibrium position of the economy is altered by a change in the state's fiscal policy financed without any change in the money supply. By so

doing, they demonstrate that the equilibrium is not independent of the structure of spending decisions by one of the economic agents. They do not demonstrate that the real equilibrium is dependent on the supply of money given the spending preferences of all agents, including the state.

5. As will be evident from what follows, the term "Walrasian" refers to modern (post-1939) general equilibrium theorists, not to Walras himself, whose concept of equilibrium was the traditional long-period position characterized by a uniform "rate of net income."

14

Controversies in the Theory of Employment

The high and persistent levels of unemployment being experienced in most Western economies have moved the controversy over the analysis of employment to center stage There would probably be general agreement that much of macroeconomic theory has been found wanting when it comes to adequately explaining this outstanding feature of our recent experience. Nor does macroeconomics seem to be any more successful in suggesting tolerably satisfactory and workable remedies for the problem. Not only is there today a plethora of competing theories and models, but even the framework within which these theories are developed and the criteria by which they are to be compared and criticized are not agreed upon. Furthermore, this collapse of theoretical consensus has its counterpart in the arena of policy debate—alternative theories of the desirable role of government policy abound. Indeed, the theory of employment appears once more to have become the kind of open question that it was between the wars, and contemporary macroeconomic controversies have returned to many of the questions which dominated the 1930s debates in monetary theory and the theory of employment (before the term macroeconomics had been invented). It might not be out of place, therefore, to reconsider the issues that were then in the fore and to attempt to identify the origins of our present confusion.[1]

Such an exercise is not only of historical interest. It can also shed light on the manifest contemporary failure of the propositions of Keynes's *General Theory* to maintain the theoretical hegemony that they had at one time apparently established and on the analytical issues at stake today.

The usefulness of the exercise in this contemporary arena is enhanced not only by the cyclical tendencies clearly evident in the evolution of economic thought but also by the fact that theoretical issues themselves are often more starkly, if somewhat more crudely, expressed when they are first raised than when they are revived after fifty years of controversy and refinement, with the corners rounded off and deeply etched analytical differences smoothed over or even erased.

Modern controversies in the theory of employment, as well as the parallel controversies of old, are intimately bound up with the relationship between any theory of employment, on the one hand, and the theory of value and distribution with which it is associated, on the other. Put in this rather old-fashioned way, the proposition may at first sound somewhat unfamiliar. But nowadays the idea is a very common one—it is the precisely the relationship that is at issue in the search for the microeconomic foundations of macroeconomics, and it has contained the essence of the problem all along. It appeared in the 1930s in the form of alternative theories of interest, focusing, of course, on the role of the rate of interest in bringing (or failing to bring) planned saving into equality with desired investment. Although those controversies centered almost exclusively on the question of the degree to which interest-rate flexibility might be counted on to secure full employment, this was but part of what would today be called the general equilibrium characteristics of the economy.

In that vision of the economy, equilibrium outputs and levels of factor utilization are determined simultaneously with the equilibrium prices of commodities and factors of production through a process of reallocation and transformation of endowments in conformity with the maximizing behavior of price-taking agents. Under appropriate assumptions about preferences and available techniques of production, an agent's planned supply of the factors of production can be expressed as a function $s_j(p, \mu_j)$ and planned demand as a function $d_h(p, \mu_h)$, where for any given nonnegative vector of relative prices (p), planned supply will be technologically feasible and profit maximizing and planned demand will be feasible (in the sense that it is within the agent's budget set $x: px \leq p\mu_i$) and utility maximizing. It is, then, possible to show that there will exist a set of nonnegative prices and an input-output vector such that utility is maximized for all consumers, profit is maximized for all producers, and all markets are clear. Market clearing here entails not only the idea that the unhindered operation of the price mechanism will produce outcomes whereby the supply of produced commodities will adjust to the demand for them, but also where the supply of labor forthcoming will be adjusted to the demand for its services. It follows that questions concerning the possibility of a failure of markets to clear, when posed in a general equilibrium system, may also be viewed in the context of interferences to the operation of the price mechanism.

Given the similarities between these methods of constructing explanations of unemployment, it is not surprising to find that such theories typically locate the problem in the short run—it is in the short run that frictions, rigidities, and uncertainties are admitted to be relevant, even in arguments that envisage price flexibility and market clearing in the long run. The idea is that the long-run position is determined by certain systematic and persistent forces at work in the economy, and it is enforced by competitive pressures that tend to establish a uniform price for each commodity, a uniform wage for each quality of labor, and a uniform rate of return on the value of capital invested in different lines of production. This essentially Marshallian conception of the long run, and of the associated short-run fluctuations around the long-run position, provide the framework within which the controversies in the theory of employment of the 1920s and 1930s took place. Many writers explicitly developed their theories of unemployment (or, what amounted then to the same thing, their theories of the trade cycle) on Marshallian short-run grounds; the work of Hawtrey, Lavington, Robertson, and Pigou fits very well into this category. Others, while less explicit on the subject, followed an essentially similar procedure; one may think here, for example, of the work of the Swedish disequilibrium theorists.

While a number of interrelated elements characterize this approach, four seem to be of paramount importance. First, the explanation of unemployment is based on rigidities or imperfections in the operation of the price mechanism. Second, the analysis is expressed in terms of either short-period equilibrium or of disequilibrium. Third, the rigidities are exogenously imposed upon an otherwise perfectly functioning market mechanism—either from pragmatic observation of the working of actual institutions (say, trade unions that resist wage reductions) or from modeling the imperfect, and hence disruptive, behavior of particular agents (say, monetary authorities). Fourth, the long-run equilibrium for the economy is characterized both by long-run normal prices and by the dual long-run normal outputs and levels of factor utilization.[2]

Obviously enough, given these features of the traditional landscape, debate may be joined at either of two quite different points: at the particular specification of any short-run imperfection (there can be an almost indefinitely large number of these), or (and this is a more fundamental issue) whether to accept or reject the characterization of the determinants of the long-run equilibrium. This latter, more radical task seems to have been that upon which Keynes embarked in the *General Theory*—although his own arguments were not always entirely consistent and sometimes failed to carry the weight he wished to assign to them. Our failure (or inability) to follow Keynes's lead has left contemporary debate with essentially the same set of choices for the analysis of unemployment that existed in 1936.

An insistence on the centrality to contemporary debate of a distinction between short-run and long-run analyses of unemployment may appear somewhat puzzling to the modern reader. After all, this famous distinction has been all but eradicated from the discourse of rigorous economic theorizing, surviving, perhaps, only in partial equilibrium studies of the theory of the firm. Its place has been taken by the concepts of intertemporal equilibrium and temporary equilibrium, and models of implicit contracts, asymmetric information, and the like. With these innovations, the traditional conception of long-run equilibrium as the center of gravitation of short-run disequilibrium was abandoned and with it the idea of capital markets as continually promoting a tendency toward evening-out returns to investments in different lines of activity, as the cornerstone of the whole theoretical edifice has been abandoned. These developments of the concept certainly complicate the relationship between the old controversies and the new, but they do not diminish their relevance.

The Old Controversies

There is a significant sense in which the publication of Keynes's *Treatise on Money* in 1930 marked the culmination of a broad theoretical effort that had been gathering momentum since the end of the First World War, which had begun to call into question the view that the economic system was capable, if left to its own devices, of securing (relatively quickly) desirable outcomes like full employment and price stability. Prior to the war, important building blocks for such an analysis had been laid down by Wicksell, but much of the refinement seems to have had to await the impetus to study provided by the conditions of economic dislocation that followed in its wake. The whole of the theoretical part of Keynes's *Treatise* was devoted to a discussion of the causes and characteristics of "disequilibrium" and to the advocacy of specific measures of monetary policy in the absence of which, so Keynes argued, it was futile to expect any rapid or uninterrupted return to stability and prosperity. Keynes himself had been working in this direction throughout the 1920s, along broadly parallel lines to those taken by Hawtrey, Lavington, and Robertson.

The starting point for Keynes's argument in 1930 was the celebrated fundamental equations, which expressed the formulas for determining the price level of consumption goods (p) and the price level of output as a whole (π):

$$p = e/y + [(\hat{\imath} - s)/z]$$
$$\pi = e/y + [(i - s)/y]$$

where nominal income (e) is the sum of factor incomes (that is, $\Sigma_i a_i n_i$; *for i factors,* $1 \ldots . n$, factor rentals a_i, and levels of employment n_i), and the volume of saving (s) is the sum of the differences between individual incomes (h individuals, $1 \ldots . m$) and individual current consumption ($\Sigma_h [e_h - c_h]$). For any individual, the choice as to the disposition of income between consumption and saving is assumed to be dependent on the prevailing rate of interest (r). The value of current investment (i) is equal to savings plus (minus) any windfall profits (losses) that might arise if actual income (e_a) differs from e as defined above. Since nominal income is defined in terms of money costs of production, that part of it that is earned in the production of investment goods ($\hat{\imath}$) is equivalent to their money costs of production. For any individual investor, the volume of investment depends on the prevailing rate of interest (r). Aggregate output (y) is made up of the flow of output of consumption goods (z) and the net flow of output of investment goods (k).[3]

According to Keynes in 1930, equilibrium occurs when planned saving and desired investment exactly balance—that is, when $i(r) = s(r)$. The rate of interest at which this balance is achieved is Wicksell's natural rate. In the absence of exogenous changes, the general level of prices is stable and factors of production are fully employed. Notice that if, in this situation, m is the available quantity of money and v its income-velocity of circulation, then $e = mv$, and Keynes's fundamental equations reduce to the familiar quantity theory equation:[4]

$$\pi = p = e/y = mv/y$$
$$mv = py$$

The above provides us with enough of the original theoretical apparatus to isolate the essential ingredients of the old controversy in the theory of employment—or, more accurately, the essential ingredients of it as they stood prior to its next major installment, the *General Theory*.

The argument runs along familiar lines, and may be illustrated using figure 14.1. At *A*, the system is in equilibrium with market and natural interest rates equal ($r_M = r_N$); planned saving exactly corresponds to desired investment and factors of production are fully employed. A disequilibrium between saving and investment will arise when, say, $r_M > r_N$; this has the effect of retarding investment (by increasing the cost of production of new investment goods) and stimulating saving. At a point such as C in figure 14.1, there will be an excess supply of saving (*CB*) that can be expected to persist until variations in the rate of interest and relative prices are set in motion—an adjustment process that in this instance converges to the original equilibrium at *A*. This adjustment process was the center point of theoretical debate. Keynes argued that it was slow in its operation and that in the absence of specific monetary policy measures, disequilibrium could be expected to persist for considerable periods of time. Indeed, as early as 1924, Keynes had been looking to monetary policy "for the ultimate cure of unemployment" (Keynes, 1973, 19:223).

More orthodox writers, like Hayek, argued that disequilibrium would be self-correcting (though at the expense of temporary dislocation), but that no policy measures should be undertaken in the interim (other than tight control of the available quantity of money). Others even went so far as to claim that the adjustment process might alter the equilibrium itself (say, by moving *SI* to something like SI_1)—though the question of just how logically consistent such an argument might be did not surface at the time.

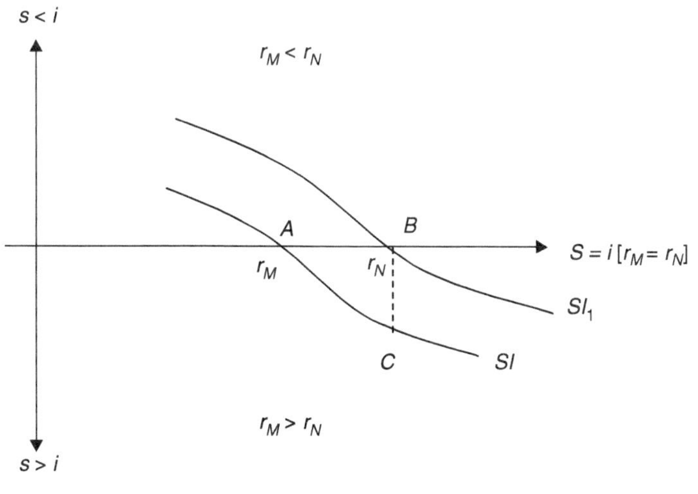

Figure 14.1

Of course, by tending to focus almost exclusively on movements in the general level of prices (consequent upon divergences between planned saving and desired investment), rather than on changes in output, Keynes's formal argument and analysis in the *Treatise on Money* itself had the effect of seeming to place the analysis of employment during the adjustment somewhat in the background.

Despite this much remarked upon preoccupation in the *Treatise*, Keynes was perfectly well aware that any shortfall of investment (or excess of savings) had direct and unambiguous consequences for the level of employment: entrepreneurs, he claimed, would "alter the total volume of employment they offer... upwards or downwards" according as desired investment exceeded or fell short of planned saving (1930, p. 136). Indeed, Keynes had deployed exactly this aspect of the analysis in his earlier polemic against the return to the gold standard. Reverting to figure 14.1, we see that this amounts to recognizing that, as the economy moves through states other than those represented by the point *A*, the level of employment should be expected to vary. At a point like *C*, there would be involuntary unemployment owing to a (temporary) failure of the market mechanism to ensure the mutual compatibility of the buying and selling plans of individual agents (on this point, see Keynes, 1930, pp. 132, 184). Since this involves, in turn, no more than the eminently practical observation that the traditional model of markets need not necessarily imply continuous market-clearing outcomes (that is, false trading may occur), it is hardly surprising that Keynes and others placed so much emphasis on the length of the short run in this initial phase of the interwar controversies in the theory of employment.

Quite apart from whether an optimistic or a pessimistic stand was taken on this particular question, what is clear is just how intimately connected with the traditional theory of markets and price determination all these early controversies in the theory of employment actually were. Since the whole of the debate up to this time presupposes the existence of a market-clearing equilibrium, it is based on the model of markets provided by the theories of price determination of Walras and Marshall.

If the above adequately depicts the stage that the old controversies in the theory of employment had reached by 1936, the question immediately arises as to what, if anything, is essentially novel about the contribution to the debate contained in the *General Theory*. It seems that this question is all the more interesting, given the fact that the very kinds of developments we have so far been discussing are, in many quarters, felt to be intimately associated with that book, rather than with its predecessors.

It does not seem inappropriate to start with Keynes's own opinion on the matter: "the novelty in my treatment of saving and investment," he claimed, consisted "in the proposition that it is, not the rate of interest, but the level of incomes which...ensures their equality" (1973, 14:211). Elsewhere, he says: "I should admit [that there are] forces which one might fairly well call 'automatic' which operate under any normal monetary system in the direction of restoring a long-period equilibrium between saving and investment. The point on which I cast doubt...is whether these 'automatic forces' will...tend to bring about not only an equilibrium between saving and investment but also an optimum level of production" (1973, 13:395).

If this claim is to be taken literally, then an interpretation of the essential novelty *General Theory* suggests itself almost immediately: since the earlier argument established its conclusions as to the characteristics of a long-period equilibrium between saving and investment (in particular, the full-employment condition of that equilibrium) as part of a more general analysis that embodied a causal nexus between the determination of relative prices and the determination of offers and demands (of both commodities and factor services), this nexus must be broken by Keynes. To put it another way, in 1936, Keynes clearly claimed that he was joining the debate over the theory of employment, not in connection with the specification of the frictions and rigidities that interfere with the normal operation of the economic machine but, rather, on the characterization of the forces that act to determine equilibrium itself. It is here, it seems to me, that we witness what is at once the most powerful, and the most problematic, of the contributions to the analysis of employment that emerged in the course of these old controversies.

The power of the argument that voluntary savings are maintained in long-run equality with desired investment by alterations in the level of activity rests on the fact that it does not rely on any theory concerning the joint determination of equilibrium relative prices and quantities of the kind envisaged, say, by Marshall or by Walras. Indeed, the principle of effective demand, if applied to a long-period analysis of employment, appears to be quite incompatible with the joint determination of prices and quantities in that particular sense. Keynes's introduction of the propensity to consume as the link between expenditure and output replaces an adjustment process that, under an earlier argument, had been supposed to rely on price flexibility (and, in particular, on interest-rate flexibility) to underwrite full employment. Thus, under appropriate assumptions about the magnitude of the propensity to consume, this alternative adjustment process could be expected to converge toward a stable equilibrium level of output that was not necessarily associated with the full employment of labor. The old-fashioned presumption that there would always be forces at work tending to move output toward its full-employment level would then have no place at all in Keynes's new scheme. Of course, these remarks apply to an analysis of employment based solely on an application of the principle of effective demand to long-period considerations—but what they do make clear is that for the first time in these early controversies in the theory of employment, one can clearly isolate a direct challenge to the model of markets and price determination of the neoclassical school that does not rely on the presence of imperfections.

However, by presenting the analysis of investment and saving in this way, Keynes immediately opened up two matters that had been dealt with at one blow by earlier theory: the determination of the volume of investment and of the rate of interest. These newly created "empty boxes" were filled, of course, by the marginal efficiency of capital and the liquidity preference theory. And here is the problem: if one retains, as Keynes actually did, these quite orthodox explanations of investment demand and of the market rate of interest, the only fully consistent explanation of unemployment is one that stresses its disequilibrium character. The presence in the *General Theory* of such orthodox elements, side by side with more radical ones, is the source from which derives the contemporary opinion that there is a fundamental continuity between its arguments and those of the 1920s. It is also the source of the opinion, which runs counter to that derived by concentrating on the long-run aspects of the theory of effective demand, that no fundamental challenge was launched in the *General Theory* against the existing theory of markets and price determination.

Interestingly, another place in which these counteracting tendencies are manifest is in some of Keynes's more speculative remarks concerning the general role of the state in the conduct of social and economic policy, and also of its relationship to civil society. In certain instances, these also change character rather dramatically between the position Keynes took up in the 1920s and that which he was advocating by 1936. The final chapter of the *General Theory*, for example, is given over to reflections on the social philosophy toward which the theory of effective demand might lead; and prominent among the elements of this is "the vital importance of establishing certain central controls in matters which are now left in the main to individual initiative" (1936, pp. 377–78). In particular, Keynes concluded that "a somewhat comprehensive socialisation of investment will prove the only means of securing an approximation to full employment" (p. 378). What in 1926 Keynes had seen as a relatively straightforward matter of improving "the technique of modern capitalism by the agency of collective action" (1931, p. 319) seems to have become a rather more thoroughgoing requirement for a kind of planning.

In the earlier framework, while the mechanism of competitive capitalism driven by individual initiative could be relied upon to secure the "best" allocation and degree of utilization of society's resources, the state might be required to underwrite the fairness, justice, or equity of its unregulated operation and to ensure stability in the external monetary environment. In Keynes's new argument, however, the state seems to be required to take responsibility for ensuring the appropriate allocation of resources. The radical divide that this sets up between the doctrines of the *General Theory* and those of the existing ideology of welfarism is the essential ingredient in Keynes's contribution to the political culture of the postwar world.

Welfarism grew out of grafting onto the nineteenth-century concern with efficiency an additional concern for justice and stability. By itself, it is not attributable to Keynes. More to the point, it does not represent the basic message of the *General Theory*. According to the welfarist position, while the competitive-market mechanism was seen to be capable of generating efficiency (largely unassisted by the state), the requirements of social justice and stability introduced scope for collective action. Keynes had already arrived at this position by the middle of the 1920s. In his well-known essay "Am I a Liberal?" of 1925, he set out the new ideology in the following terms: "In the economic field ... we must find new policies and new instruments to adapt and control the working of economic forces, so that they do not intolerably interfere with contemporary ideas as to what is fit and proper in the interests of social stability and social justice" (1931, p. 337). If this were the entire legacy of Keynesianism, as many seem still to maintain, then one does not even require the *General Theory* to understand it. To appreciate this, it is necessary to proceed to the *General Theory* itself.

One will not find there an argument where primary emphasis is given to the abovementioned matters. In the first place, Keynes seems to direct our attention away from the concern with stability, arguing instead that "an outstanding characteristic of the economic system in which we live [is that] it is not violently unstable" (1936, p. 249). Second, questions of distributive justice are placed in the background, and nothing is said of them until the very last chapter of the book. More important, however, the role of collective action now becomes relevant to the allocation process itself. Notice that statecraft now entails "securing the optimum employment of the system's entire resources" (1936, p. 340). The task of securing this objective—the efficient use of resources—defines the role of the state.

The New Controversies

Upon encountering an example of the modern species of controversy in the theory of employment, one might be forgiven for failing at first to discern any significant resemblance at all between it and the ancestor we have just been describing. For instance, take the development of the economic theory of labor contracts, where a significant proportion of debate in the theory of employment has taken place.[5]

Since its introduction into the modern literature, the efficiency-wage hypothesis has been offered as a means of providing a reason not only for why firms might be willing to enter into labor contracts under which they pay more to workers than the Walrasian market-clearing (real) wage but also why they will not wish to alter that wage in the face of movements in product demand (thereby also explaining why it is that unemployed workers are unable to compete away the excess of the equilibrium efficiency wage, w^*, over the market-clearing wage). The shared characteristic of the first generation of explanations of efficiency-wage contracts was the idea that labor productivity depended not just on the amount of labor hired but also upon the real wage: $q = f[\varphi(w)L]$.

If f exhibits the usual properties ($f' > 0$, and $f'' < 0$), if $\varphi(w)$—the function relating work effort (productivity) to the real wage—is convex ($\varphi'(w) > 0$), if there exists a minimum wage below which a worker will choose not to offer labor services (w_{MIN}), then a profit-maximizing employer who is unconstrained as to how much labor he can obtain at all real-wage rates $w \geq w_{MIN}$, will offer an efficiency-wage w^* that satisfies the condition that $w\varphi'(w)/\varphi(w) = 1$. If we denote the market-clearing (Walrasian auction contract) wage as $w°$, then if $w^* > w_{MIN} \geq w°$ there will be involuntary unemployment and no incentive for agents to alter the efficiency-wage w^*. All of this is well known, and the situation of involuntary unemployment it describes is depicted in figure 14.2. On the surface, at least, much appears to have altered.

The really crucial question for the analysis of unemployment is why the equation $q = f[\varphi(w)L]$ is a plausible hypothesis. It is here that some of the old actors reappear in new costumes. One way of answering this question has been to argue that workers have a propensity to shirk—that in the case of labor, what you see is not necessarily what you get—so that firms may have to pay a premium ($w^* > w^\circ$) to cover themselves against the moral hazard inherent in the hiring of labor services.[6] Another response has been to argue that employment contracts are "incomplete" in the sense that they do not (and cannot) specify productivity requirements in anything like the detail demanded by the Walrasian auction-market contract; this may be due to problems of bounded rationality, high costs of supervision and monitoring, the difficulty of actually measuring on-the-job effort, and the like. Still another rationale involves the argument that real-wage rates higher than those associated with market-clearing offer employers a method of disciplining workers, in that they have the effect of raising the costs of job loss.

Perhaps the most striking thing about this line of argument is the fact that all the hallmarks of the old controversies regarding the theory of employment, as they stood prior to the *General Theory*, seem to have survived pretty much intact. Indeed, the imperfectionist character of efficiency-wage arguments is readily apparent—the chief differences between the old and the new arguments seem to concern points of detail rather than ones of real substance. There is, however, one particular alteration of detail that is worth noticing. Borrowing the language of the interwar controversies for a moment, the efficiency-wage literature might be said to provide models of what was then called wage rigidity.

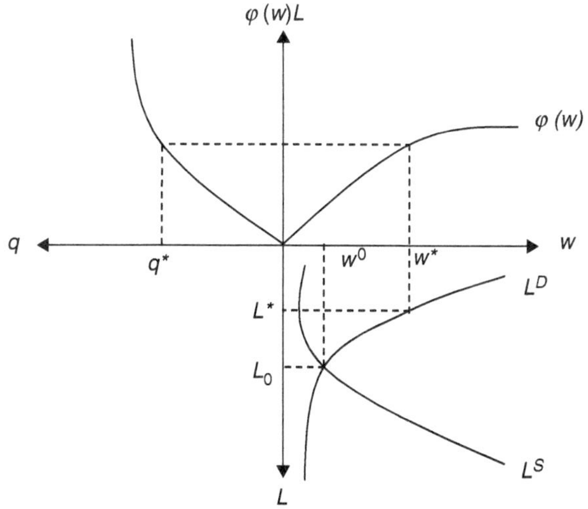

Figure 14.2

Yet it does this without recourse to the additional argument, so prevalent between the wars, that the blame for the problem of unemployment must be placed squarely on the shoulders of the organizations that workers form to secure collectively what is in the individual interest of each. That is, while efficiency wages are sticky in the face of variations in the conditions of labor supply (which are considered as being external to the firm), this is not a consequence of trade-union resistance to (real) wage reductions that employers would otherwise wish to institute. In the efficiency-wage argument, not only are (real) wage rates settled by a contract between individual workers and individual employers, but those employers also have no desire to change them.

The significance of this alteration in the content of the imperfectionist analysis of unemployment is not so much that it forces us to be more careful in specifying just what we mean by sticky wages (though this is an important matter in itself) but, rather, that in this version of it, it is not to the insistence of associations of workers on maintaining "a real rate of wages above the economic level" (Pigou, 1932, p.704) that we must look for an explanation of "an abnormal volume of unemployment." The supplementary claim often advanced on behalf of the efficiency-wage hypothesis—that it provides an account of equilibrium involuntary unemployment—we shall return to below.

Much more in line with both the character and the content of the old debates over the theory of employment in an imperfectionist mold is the fact that, in the new framework, there does not seem to be any formal criterion that might be applied as an aid in choosing among the array of possibilities available for generating efficiency-wage models of unemployment. Instead, everything appears to hinge on factors like personal preference, or views as to the degree of congruence between the particular route taken and the actual case at hand, or (if one is interested in ascribing this kind of approach to some theorist of an earlier generation) the extent of the resemblance of the particular justification for utilizing the efficiency-wage hypothesis to the corpus of that theorist's work—or, of course, some combination of all three.

In a like manner, the traditional conception of labor markets remains in place under the efficiency-wage hypothesis. As in the old debates, two things are simultaneously established by labor contracts: the (real) wage rate and the amount of employment. As we have already mentioned, this conception is simply an extension to the market for labor services of the vision of price-quantity determination in commodity markets that is at the heart of the works of Marshall and Walras. Somewhat surprisingly, however, the new analysis of unemployment is said in certain circles to depart as well even from this aspect of the old-fashioned view: labor services, it has been argued, "are not auctioned off in quite the same way as fresh fruit is" (Azariadis, 1975, p.1185). The fact that one way of thinking about the results produced by efficiency-wage models is to conceive of them as the consequence of introducing a quantity/quality problem for the case of labor services led some to claim that a new conception of labor markets was thereby adopted.. But when it is recognized that all one actually requires to achieve these results is the existence of asymmetric information, the essential equivalence between labor markets and commodity markets is revealed never to have vanished at all.

Efficiency-wage models constitute just one species of a whole class of implicit contract models of the labor market. Another is represented by those who suggest that risk-averse workers may be able to shift the risk associated with an uncertain stream of future income onto the employer. For their part, workers will certainly wish to do this whenever they are imperfectly informed as to the demand for labor services in the future (as when futures markets for labor services fail to exist, or when the economic system is subject to unpredictable fluctuations between good and bad times). For their part, employers will be willing to accept the offer of a risk-shifting (or partial risk-sharing) arrangement whenever the costs of monitoring, enforcement, or screening are nonnegligible—and as long as the probability of bankruptcy is negligible. As in the case of efficiency-wage contracts, implicit contracts of this variety may often be written for a wage that is too high for market clearing.[7] Indeed, in every essential respect, it would seem, these particular arguments are the bearers of all the family traits of the old imperfectionist analyses of unemployment that are present in efficiency-wage models.

With these remarks in mind, it is possible to proceed to another, seemingly distinctive feature of the contemporary debate: that part of the old controversy over long-run versus short-run accounts of unemployment (that is to say, controversy over the equilibrium or disequilibrium status of the theory of unemployment) is apparently absent from contemporary debate. Indeed, one of the more interesting conclusions of the theory of labor contracts that I have just been discussing is said to be precisely that it suggests that certain transactions in the labor market may be mutually agreed upon between individual agents in a price-quantity regime where that market fails to clear—and yet no agent will find it in his or her interest to alter the terms of the transaction. In this sense, or so it is argued, one may observe equilibrium involuntary unemployment (see, for example, Hahn, 1987, pp. 8–9). Debate is then joined over the question of whether the familiar Walrasian (or, more properly, Arrow-Debreu) model is applicable to actual existing conditions or not: "if a description of the economy is best approximated by [an Arrow-Debreu] equilibrium not only is the whole Keynesian opus irrelevant but... unemployment is also problematical" (Hahn, 1987, p. 1).

The lack of symmetry between these new arguments and the old on this count, however, seems to be rather more apparent than real. It arises because of recent developments in the notion of equilibrium itself—developments that have had the effect of transforming into equilibrium models the models that, in the past, would have been deemed to be disequilibrium in character. In brief, the change has come about by reinterpreting equilibrium as a solution concept for any model that specifies the strategies of the actors involved; the external environment (including not only endowments and preferences, but also the information set of the relevant actors) in which they find themselves; and the rules of the game in which they put their strategies into effect. Thus, while clearly not referring to either the Marshallian equilibrium of long-run normal demand and supply or to the Walrasian auction-market equilibrium (which in the old meaning of the term had been the only equilibrium cases admitted), implicit contract models of all varieties may be said to yield an equilibrium structure of labor contracts in the newer sense of the term.

Why the practical consequence of these developments in the definition and theoretical status of the notion of equilibrium has been to obscure the issues that are actually at stake in present controversies in the theory of employment should now be reasonably clear. The old controversies presented the choices in the analysis of unemployment quite unambiguously: one could introduce an imperfectionist hypothesis to construct a short-run disequilibrium account of unemployment (and debate which particular imperfectionist hypothesis best matched the prevailing circumstances); or one could issue a direct challenge to the prevailing long-run equilibrium analysis of employment from which imperfectionist analyses derive. But when the Walrasian auction-market equilibrium is viewed as just another solution concept (in the sense that *all* solutions to *all* models for which solutions exist are of equal analytical status), and the Walrasian competitive market is regarded as just another model of *one* possible actual case (rather than an abstract characterization of *all* possible cases)—and this is the backdrop of contemporary controversies—the choices in the analysis of employment appeared to alter.

However, the analytical procedure and the ultimate choices actually remain the same: begin with the Walrasian auction-market model (or, though this is now a much less favored course than it was in the interwar years, the Marshallian partial-equilibrium model of long-run normal demand and supply), introduce some imperfections, and delineate the characteristics of the solution to this modified model. One then chooses between differing imperfectionist models on the grounds of which provides a significant result—that is, as von Neumann and Morgenstern put it, select that model whose solution is most "similar to reality in those respects which are essential in the investigation at hand" (1944, p. 32). This, of course, serves only further to highlight the connection between the analysis of value and distribution and the analysis of employment—a feature that seems to typify the landscape of the contemporary debate just as much as it did that of its predecessor.

Concluding Remarks

A point has been reached where it is possible to draw together some of the threads of the foregoing argument so as to restate its basic conclusions in much more straightforward terms. Should those arguments prove to be at all accurate, then it seems hardly possible to dispute the claim that, in the mainstream of economic theory, there is an indissoluble link between the explanation of value and distribution (that is, of output and input prices, respectively) and the analysis of unemployment; and that this link is at the very heart of both the old and new controversies in the theory of employment. Indeed, the general nature of this link is itself quite direct and is to be found preserved in the most elementary piece of economic reasoning in which we instruct our students—namely, the argument that, in a competitive economy, the price of a commodity is determined by the relationship between demand and supply.

As it is customarily presented, equilibrium is said to be established at the intersection of a curve relating price to quantity demanded and another relating price to quantity supplied—this intersection is associated with market clearing. When this account of price determination is applied to the economic system as a whole, equilibrium is characterized by a set of nonnegative prices and associated quantities (of commodity outputs and levels of factor utilization) such that the markets for all commodities and all factors of production clear. In particular, the labor market clears at the equilibrium level of the wage (relative to the set of equilibrium prices). There is no involuntary unemployment—in competitive equilibrium, no offers, be they of factor services or of commodities, will ever be turned down. The case for full employment is clinched, so to speak, by drawing demand and supply curves in a way that seems naturally to suggest that any imbalance between demand and supply will automatically set in motion variations in relative prices so as to restore equilibrium. There is, of course, much more to it than this, but one usually draws back from immediately providing the details of the theoretical basis that these "curves" have in the rational action of individual agents; and the fact the even competitive equilibria are often unstable is not usually emphasized.

This appealing vision of the simultaneous determination of prices and quantities, the refined pleasure of contemplating the many in the one, and its underlying conception of how the market mechanism works, immediately opens up an avenue for tackling the problem of unemployment. Any inhibition to the tendency of prices and quantities to find their equilibrium levels will expose the economic system to the possibility of resource misallocation or underutilization. If I may borrow a phrase from Adam Smith (and use it out of context), the moral philosophy that lies behind the imperfectionist analysis of unemployment is that of the best head joined to the best heart: while the economy *would* be self-regulating in the best of all possible worlds (the tendency toward the full employment of labor would be realized relatively swiftly), the market mechanism is prevented from securing its objective by virtue of the presence of a wide variety of imperfections.

The overwhelming majority of modern controversies in the theory of employment are about whether the existence of imperfections ought to temper the application of our most basic vision of the market mechanism to everyday situations. If this is correct, then there is no ultimate theoretical principle at stake in most of the debates that have occupied the pages of our professional journals and the columns of our newspapers over the past two decades or so. It all becomes a matter of degree. Among those who feel that it is impossible to ignore imperfections, controversy in the theory of employment is exclusively over the question of exactly which of the many possible imperfections is, practically speaking, the most important. This was precisely the state of play in the older controversies in the theory of employment during the interwar period until Keynes's *General Theory* appeared on the scene in 1936.

According to what might be called received opinion, the *General Theory* is directly descendent from the above kind of argument—though, perhaps, with a somewhat greater emphasis on the importance of disequilibrium (and on the frictions and rigidities that give rise to it). But this is just one way of reconstructing the argument of that book. Another is to develop the more radical aspects already examined above. In this light, the theoretical choices available in the analysis of unemployment are at least rendered particularly clear.

It is worth emphasizing that these controversies in the analysis of employment are not simply niceties of an arcane theoretical discourse; they are of the most pressing practical concern. The design of policies to eliminate unemployment, and the hotly contested political debate over whether employment policies are necessary or even within the competence of government at all, depend in the final analysis on an accurate diagnosis of its causes.

If unemployment is a matter of the degree to which imperfections make their presence felt, then the superiority of a policy of fiscal expansion over a thoroughgoing social policy designed to eradicate those imperfections is not at all apparent. Indeed, if there is a powerful market mechanism at work—one that would tend to promote full employment—it seems a little perverse not to attempt to activate it. The only plausible reason that might be advanced for not doing so seems, in fact, to be the one invoked by Keynes in the 1920s: the social costs of, say, unsticking the wage might be too great. Even the single imperfection against which, on this account of unemployment, social legislation is not likely to be possible—that of incomplete or imperfect information—seems also to offer a rather precarious platform from which to advocate Keynesian fiscal measures. Since the rational action of individual agents underlies the imperfectionist policy position on unemployment as much as it does that of the laissez-faire school (by virtue of their shared theory of value and distribution), it is difficult to see why rational agents do not adjust their expectations in ways that ensure that their intentions are not systematically and consistently thwarted by the market—and if they do, then the case for laissez-faire is restored.

Notes

This chapter is a newly revised version of a paper by Murray Milgate that appeared originally in *Contributions to Political Economy* (1983)

1. In limiting the comparison to the controversies of the interwar years and those of more recent times, we would not wish it to be thought that we are suggesting that even older controversies in the theory of employment are irrelevant to our contemporary concerns. Indeed, the well-known controversy between

Ricardo and Malthus on overproduction (joined by Sismondi and later Marx), the debate on the effects of the introduction of machinery on employment, and the debates in England in 1819 (and again in 1844) over specific monetary policy measures reveal many of the same issues to have been at stake then as now. But to discuss them all here would occupy far too much space—an account (though by no means an exhaustive one) of some of those parallels may be found in Milgate (1982).

2. Exemplary of these features—or, at least, the first three of them—was the argument of Robert Solow's (1980) Presidential Address before the American Economic Association.

3. Current consumption and current investment will differ from z and k, respectively, as changes occur in inventories of consumption goods or investment goods (that is, as δq_z and δq_k, respectively, differ from zero). Assuming with Keynes that the price level of investment goods (Ω) is determined independently of the price level of consumption goods, then $\Omega = \pi - p$.

4. This particular formulation has the great advantage of rendering transparent the fact that there is nothing in the quantity theory of money that requires one to assume away the possibility of interaction between so-called monetary and real forces—so long as one restricts that interaction to short run situations.

5. In singling out labor contract theory here, we suggest it not be forgotten that the theory of job search also occupies a rather prominent place in debates over the analysis of employment. Yet its basic similarity to the analysis of what Pigou or Keynes would have called frictional unemployment in the old controversies appears to be so pronounced that it does seem necessary to dwell upon it at any length here. This is not to deny the fact that recent contributions have taken the formal analysis of search processes beyond anything that would have been imaginable in the 1920s and 1930s.

6. Of course, a whole class of adverse-selection models has been developed on the basis of the "what you see is not necessarily what you get" doctrine, and these do not rely on the existence of a propensity to shirk—but the only difference between these two answers concerns the extent to which one wishes to emphasize the incentive effects of real-wage rates over their screening effects.

7. Unlike efficiency-wage contracts, however, risk-sharing contracts may equally well be written for a real-wage rate that is too low.

15

Is the International Monetary Fund Past its Sell-by Date?

The international financial system has undergone profound changes since the architecture of the International Monetary Fund (IMF) was determined at Bretton Woods in 1944 and since the Fund commenced its formal operations in March 1947. A combination of the well-known effects of the passing of time, institutional inertia, mission creep, and new international monetary and financial arrangements has given rise to an increased questioning of the adequacy of the Fund as it is presently constituted to secure a tolerable degree of stability in the international financial system. The Fund appears to be becoming increasingly irrelevant, impotent, and incapable of either preventing or resolving the difficulties and uncertainties that confront us today.

These weaknesses are not new. They have been rather starkly revealed in the series of crises that have shaken the international financial system since the collapse of the Bretton Woods arrangements in the 1970s: the Mexican debt crisis of 1982, the Asian crisis of 1997, the Russian and Brazilian debt crises of the late 1998–99, the Argentinean debt crisis of 2001–02, and the 2008 credit crunch and global financial crisis, to name but a few. In each of these crises, and in the many others since the 1970s, the IMF invariably attributed the cause of the problem to the financial practices and policies of the individual economies involved; it imposed upon those authorities mandatory contractionary measures in return for its support (and it refused that support to those countries that would not conform); it found the scale of these crises increasingly large in relation to the scale of its available resources.

More important, the IMF has failed to contemplate what one might have thought would have been apparent to even the casual observer of these crises—namely, the possibility that the problem might reside not in local or national financial policies and practices but in the very nature of the international financial system over which the Fund is meant to preside. It is time for change, and since times of crisis are probably the best times to make the kind of large changes that seem to be called for, that time seems to be now. Even the Fund itself, following upon the meeting of the G20 in London in April 2009, has embarked upon a program of reform.

The IMF—Then and Now

The Fund was one of the two principal institutions set up at the International Monetary and Financial Conference at the Bretton Woods Conference in 1944 (the World Bank being the other). The Bretton Woods system, as it came to be known, had three principal features and three principal aims: (1) to fix exchange rates (with an adjustable peg) in order to prevent competitive devaluations; (2) to regulate the flow of financial capital across the foreign exchanges in order to prevent capital flight; and (3) to provide a mechanism to assist economies facing balance-of-payments difficulties to prevent local deflationary policies that might otherwise be deployed from becoming contagious (as they are wont to do). The Fund, in short, was established to manage, oversee, and underwrite the stability of the international financial system by promoting international monetary cooperation, exchange-rate stability, and orderly foreign exchange arrangements among its members, and by providing short-term funds to members in balance-of-payments difficulties. This last function is especially to be noted; it is for which the Fund had very little to do during its first twenty-five years of operation, and it is for which it has been found most wanting in its second twenty-five years. Yet this function of the IMF is perhaps its foremost objective to be secured.

All of this was summed up in the original Articles of Agreement that were drafted in 1944 at Bretton Woods and ratified by the original twenty-nine members in December 1945:

> *Article I (iii)*: To promote exchange stability, to maintain orderly exchange arrangements among members, and to avoid competitive exchange depreciation.[1]

> *Article VI (i)(a)*: A member may not make net use of the Fund's resources to meet a large or sustained outflow of capital, and the Fund may request a member to exercise controls to prevent such use of the resources of the Fund. If, after receiving such a request, a member fails to exercise appropriate controls, the Fund may declare the member ineligible to use the resources of the Fund.
>
> *Article I (v & vi)*: To give confidence to members by making the general resources of the Fund temporarily available to them under adequate safeguards, thus providing them with opportunity to correct maladjustments in their balance of payments without resorting to measures destructive of national or international prosperity. In accordance with the above, to shorten the duration and lessen the degree of disequilibrium in the international balances of payments of members. (IMF, 1944)

For twenty-five years after the Second World War, under the Bretton Woods system, the international economy witnessed a golden age of uninterrupted growth and prosperity. The original Articles of Agreement have been amended three times—in 1969, 1978, and 1992. The second of these amendments brought into effect a resolution of the Fund's board, taken in 1976, that marks—*de jure,* so to speak—the formal end of the Bretton Woods system (it had ended de facto, when the United States announced suspension of the dollar's convertibility to gold, on August 15, 1971). The second amendment took effect, not without a degree of irony, on April Fool's Day, 1978. The global financial system was cut loose from its moorings and the exchange-rate and capital-account liberalization proceeded apace. Two and a half decades of growth and stability in the global economy were replaced by three decades of exchange-rate volatility, increasingly frequent and severe international financial crises, and generally slower world growth. In this new global financial order, here is what the Fund says it does today:

The work of the IMF is of three main types. Surveillance involves the monitoring of economic and financial developments, and the provision of policy advice, aimed especially at crisis-prevention. The IMF also lends to countries with balance of payments difficulties, to provide temporary financing and to support policies aimed at correcting the underlying problems; loans to low-income countries are also aimed especially at poverty reduction. Third, the IMF provides countries with technical assistance and training in its areas of expertise. Supporting all three of these activities is IMF work in economic research and statistics. In recent years, as part of its efforts to strengthen the international financial system, and to enhance its effectiveness at preventing and resolving crises, the IMF has applied both its surveillance and technical assistance work to the development of standards and codes of good practice in its areas of responsibility, and to the strengthening of financial sectors. (IMF, 2009, italics omitted)

When viewed against the backdrop of our present financial woes, this might better be interpreted as a wish list than a realistic statement of the Fund's actual function.

The IMF in the Bretton Woods Era

Given the manifest successes of the international economy in the golden age after the Second World War—with low inflation, high growth, low unemployment, and international monetary stability the order of the day—it is tempting to conclude that the IMF worked during the era of Bretton Woods. But this opinion needs somewhat careful scrutiny. While on some occasions the Fund did step in to assist members with balance-of-payments problems (for example, the UK in 1967), most of the lending to deficit economies in this era was undertaken by the United States. In these years, it was not so much the Fund that provided economies facing balance-of-payments difficulties with the "opportunity to correct maladjustments in their balance of payments without resorting to measures destructive of national or international prosperity" (as it was established to do), but the international lending practices of the United States.

Two features of the actual working of the Bretton Woods system deserve special notice. The first was that lending from member states in balance-of-payments surplus to member states in balance-of-payments deficit was not primarily channeled through the IMF. Instead, that process took place as a direct result of extensive U.S. lending abroad. These capital outflows from the United States were able to continue on a large scale until the U.S. current account began to fall into semi-permanent deficit in the late 1960s. The second feature of the Bretton Woods system, thus supported by capital outflows from the United States, was that individual economies were allowed to follow conventional expansionary policies to ensure full employment and growth at home—without fear of capital flight or sanctions from the principal international lender. During these years, the major industrial economies not only put into place fiscal and monetary measures to expand domestic demand when they felt that to be desirable, but they also were able to resort to the orderly regulation of trade (often on a large scale). The formation and development of the European Economic Community, and the policies of Japan's Ministry of International Trade and Industry, are indicative of just how far protectionism was the norm.

In this sense, the IMF was far less influential over the policies of individual economies during the Bretton Woods era than it is today—if only because it had to act less extensively and frequently. The success of the global economy in those years took place largely because the international lending position adopted by the United States allowed members to pursue their own domestic policies *as if* they were insulated from the vagaries of international financial flows, rather than because of any fundamental contribution made by the IMF.

Not surprisingly, the Bretton Woods system broke down when the United States was unable to perform its role as the primary financier of the current-account deficits of others—namely, when the convertibility of the dollar to gold was abandoned in March 1973 (the gold window having been closed in August 1971). However, it would be too simplistic to conclude from this that the success of the international economy (and its constituent parts) during the Bretton Woods era was only the consequence of the operation of this de facto mechanism whereby the United States voluntarily redistributed its current account surpluses through the export of capital abroad. Some such mechanism, to be sure, was essential if individual economies were to be relieved of the necessity of engineering a domestic contraction whenever they faced current account deficits. At the Bretton Woods meetings, Keynes had realized this. But he had also realized that it was necessary as well to ensure that national authorities enjoyed the same degree of freedom in the pursuit of full employment at home if that need arose from causes other than current account imbalances (for example, a negative shock to domestic demand).

The IMF in the Era of International Financial Liberalization

With the move to floating exchange rates in the early 1970s, and the successive abandonment of capital controls thereafter, the Bretton Woods system was at an end. Unfortunately, since the opposite was supposed to be the case, this new world order saw individual national economies becoming *more* rather than *less* susceptible to the vagaries of volatile exchange rates and international financial flows. This increasing dependence of national decision makers on the volatility and size of international financial flows might have been mitigated by international monetary arrangements capable imparting a tolerable degree of financial stability to the system—the constitutional objective of the IMF.

But all the evidence seems to suggest that this has not happened. If anything, the world economy has become, both potentially and actually, more subject to crisis and instability than at any time since the Second World War. In its thirty-odd years of operation, this new world economic order has experienced a number of systemic financial crises in which the role of the IMF has been severely tested—and in which it has been found to be wanting. In three of these episodes—the Mexican debt crisis of 1982, the Asian crisis of 1997, and the credit crunch of 2008—the need for a reform of the IMF is the most palpable and pressing lesson to be drawn. Although the context of each of these crises was different, the lessons were the same.

The Mexican Debt Crisis of 1982

The first years of international financial liberalization after the collapse of the Bretton Woods system were associated with the creation of international indebtedness on a scale that, within less than a decade, saw the quadrupling of Latin America's average external debt (see table 15.1 for the experience in selected economies). But not only was the scale of external debt growing exponentially, its structure was also changing. In the 1960s, the vast majority of the lending flowing into Latin American economies was to sovereign governments. Furthermore, it originated either from international agencies like the World Bank and the IMF or from the sovereign governments of the industrial economies, especially the United States. In the 1960s, about two-thirds of Latin America's external indebtedness was to this category of lender. It involved long-term, low-interest capital inflows principally from governments and the international agencies.

By the early 1980s, everything had changed. Capital was now flowing just as rapidly into the Latin American private sector as it was into its public sector. The share of that debt originating in lending from governments and the international agencies had fallen to about 10%. The vast majority of lending into Latin America was now from private commercial

Table 15.1 Gross lending into selected Latin American economies (*Millions of U.S. dollars*)

	A: 1970	B: 1979	B/A
Argentina	487	3,018	6.2
Brazil	882	8,760	9.9
Chile	397	1,315	3.3
Mexico	772	10,667	13.9

Source: World Bank, World Development Report 1981.

banks in the industrial economies, especially those in the United States. It was short- to medium-term, high-interest, principally private lending. This altered scale and structure of Latin America's external debt was a direct consequence of the liberalization of the international financial markets and the vast supply of funds in Western commercial banks placed there by OPEC economies seeking outlets for their huge petro-dollar earnings from the oil price rises of the mid-1970s.

In this situation, all economies were at risk, but the Mexican economy was particularly vulnerable. Although an oil exporter, and so a beneficiary of the oil price rises of the 1970s,[2] throughout this period Mexican non-oil exports were in sharp decline, imports were growing at better than 30% per year, and the real exchange rate was appreciating. In the early 1980s, when oil prices fell back and the Mexican current-account position became increasingly unsustainable, the peso came under severe pressure on international currency markets. A now familiar mechanism swung into operation: the combination of expected exchange-rate depreciation and expected declines in the dollar value of Mexican returns led to capital flight—and so to expectations of further exchange-rate depreciation, of further falls in prospective dollar returns to Mexican holdings, additional capital flight, and so on. A process of cumulative causation was set in motion.

In the case of Mexico, the peso lost nearly half of its value against the dollar in early 1982 and, to make matters worse, as much as half of the huge Mexican external debt was due either for repayment or for rescheduling within the year (see Boughton, 2001, pp. 283–84). But commercial banks refused to renew their lending, and in August 1982, the Mexican authorities announced their inability to finance debt obligations. What would have then been the largest debt default in modern times loomed.

What is worth noting about this episode is the immediate solution that emerged. To that solution, the IMF itself contributed only a small part of the financial assistance needed to avoid immediate default and the international financial crisis that threatened. Instead, it was direct action by individual industrial economies (especially the United States) that prevented that imminent international financial crisis from emerging. Nearly half of that immediate assistance came directly from the United States and commercial banks (see table 15.2), with less than one-third coming from the IMF. In short, most of the financial assistance received by the debt-ridden economies of Latin America was a result of

Table 15.2 Financial assistance to Mexico, August–December 1982 (*Millions of U.S. dollars**)

Source	Type	Date	Amount
	Federal Reserve swap lines 90-day credit	August 4	700
United States	BIS-linked, short term	August 28	325
Strategic petroleum reserve	advance payment for imports	August 24	1,000
Department of Agriculture	credit guarantees	August 15	1,000
US Treasury (Exchange Stabilization Fund)	line of credit:	August 15	
	commitment		1,000
	drawn	(repaid August 24)	(825)
	BIS-linked credit	August 28	600
Bank for International Settlements#	short-term credit	August 28	925
Other bilateral (France, Israel, Spain)	swap lines	August	550
IMF	first credit tranche (immediate)	December 23	220
	extended arrangement (three-year commitment)		3,750
	initial drawing		(110)
Commercial banks lending	medium-term concerted	December 23	5,000

Source: Boughton, 2001. Silent revolution: The International Monetary Fund 1979–1989. Washington, DC: International Monetary Fund, p. 293.

* IMF assistance denominated in SDRs; amounts converted to dollars at market exchange rate.

Non-U.S. G-10 central banks, plus those of Switzerland and Spain.

direct concessions by sovereign lenders (principally the United States) or of the pressure those sovereign lenders put on their own financial institutions to reschedule private debt.

But the IMF was active in all the negotiations surrounding these rescue measures, and it continued to be active for the better part of the next decade. In the case of Mexico, that activity was centered on design of the conditions that the Mexican authorities would be expected to satisfy in return for international support and the monitoring of their adherence to them. This saw the IMF act in two main ways: it imposed severely contractionary domestic fiscal policies on the Mexican authorities as some of the conditions for international assistance, and it would be the arbiter of Mexican credit worthiness for international lenders.

The 1982 Mexican debt crisis had, thus, been "solved" by lenders agreeing to provide bridging finance and to reschedule Mexico's external debt—and then by the IMF's insisting on fiscal measures that involved deep cuts in Mexican social spending and on permanently lower growth rates. In the case of Mexico, these conditions were actually so damaging to its domestic economic activity that they proved economically and politically unsustainable; and the whole crisis simply repeated itself in 1989. This was hardly surprising, since instead of providing the Mexican authorities with the "opportunity to correct maladjustments in their balance of payments *without resorting to measures destructive of national or international prosperity*" (1944, italics added) in 1982, the Fund had apparently forgotten this part of its Articles of Agreement and had done exactly the opposite.[3]

The Asian Crisis of 1997

The crisis that struck the Asian Tiger economies in 1997 bears many of the hallmarks of the Mexican episode. As international financial liberalization had proceeded apace in the 1980s and the early 1990s, short-term capital had flooded into Asian economies. These emerging markets, growing at historically unprecedented rates, offered unparalleled profit-making opportunities to international investors. The weakening economic returns for investors in the major industrialized economies (especially Europe and Japan), growing pools of investible funds seeking outlets, and unregulated international capital markets had their inevitable consequence. International lenders pumped vast quantities of short-term capital into the Asian Tiger economies without much thought to their disbursement or destination—a perfectly rational action, after all, since it was on short-term placement and could be withdrawn at almost a moment's notice. In the Asian Tiger economies, these funds were largely deployed by borrowers to long-term projects. When international investors failed to roll over their short-term lending to Thailand in the first half of 1997,[4] however, the scale of baht selling on the foreign exchanges (as borrowers and lenders sought to convert repayments) triggered a cumulative process that led inexorably to crisis in both currency and asset markets.

As the volume of foreign-exchange transactions increased, expectations of devaluation were triggered. Short selling of the baht by currency speculators only acted to fuel those expectations. But, of course, heightening expectations of devaluation quickly fed expectations of declining returns from assets denominated in baht. As international investors divested themselves of Thai assets (and converted the proceeds into dollars), asset prices fell and expectations of devaluation increased further. The relatively fixed exchange rate held this cumulative process in check, but only briefly. The currency crisis that would have happened almost instantaneously under floating exchange rates happened just a little more slowly—and the stock market collapse accompanied it, with the Thai stock exchange losing nearly three-quarters of its value. The adjustable peg collapsed in July 1997, and the crisis in Thailand rapidly spread to other Asian Tiger economies, which experienced roughly the same cumulative process; collectively, and quickly, the Asian Tiger debt obligations denominated in foreign currencies became unsustainable.

The excess supply of investible funds in industrial economies that flowed without hindrance into Southeast Asia, the failure of lenders adequately to manage the risk inherent in their emerging-market portfolios, and the unregulated nature of international capital markets made the crisis and contagion possible. However, perhaps not surprisingly, the IMF viewed the whole thing differently. According to the Fund, the problem resided in local financial practices and local government mismanagement. Here is how the Fund viewed it:

> [T]he difficulties that the East Asian countries face are not primarily the result of macroeconomic imbalances. Rather, they stemmed from weaknesses in financial systems and, to a lesser extent, governance. A combination of inadequate financial sector supervision, poor assessment and management of financial risk, and the maintenance of relatively fixed exchange rates led banks and corporations to borrow large amounts of international capital, much of it short-term, denominated in foreign currency, and unhedged. (IMF, 1999)

Notice the analysis: borrowers borrowed too recklessly (rather than lenders having lent too recklessly); the local financial sector was inadequately regulated (rather than the global financial sector being inadequately regulated); and finally, to cap it off, borrowers did not engage in hedging (another word for currency speculation). It is an example of the familiar proclivity of Fund staff to look in only one direction (usually the wrong one) to unearth the causes of crises. Indeed, the Fund seems only to have two things right. It was certainly true that there were no fundamental "macroeconomic imbalances" in the Asian Tiger economies, and "relatively fixed exchange rates" certainly played their part in the process, but not in quite the way the Fund staff seem to think they did.

The six months from July 1997 saw the fund commit over $100 billion in loan assistance to the Philippines, Indonesia, Thailand, and South Korea. With its resources thus stretched to the limit, further assistance to these and other Asian economies came instead from a mixture of G7 packages, bilateral assistance, and commercially negotiated debt swaps, rollovers, and restructurings. These amounted to at least as much again as the IMF had pledged.[5]

The price of IMF assistance, once again, was not small. Interpreting its mandate to seek "adequate safeguards" as requiring budgetary cuts and financial reform packages in ailing economies, the IMF went to work with its customary zeal. It insisted on the closure of local banks and financial institutions (over fifty in Thailand and over thirty in Indonesia). On the fiscal front, the Fund's approach almost takes one breath away. Despite the fact that most of the Asian Tiger economies had been running budget surpluses throughout most of the 1990s—and the fact that the rather misleading indicator of fiscal probity (but nonetheless often quoted by Fund staff), the ratio of public debt to GDP, had been falling—the Fund still managed to find scope for fiscal "adjustment." And why? Because, in the eyes of the Fund's staff, a "wider fiscal deficit, if financed domestically, could crowd out financing to the private sector" and "the costs of financial sector restructuring needed to be met" (Lane et al., 1999, p. 56). In short, the Fund insisted on what it called "government savings" (that is, reductions in existing spending areas) to cover financial-sector recapitalizations (bailouts of foreign investors) and any other crisis-induced additional spending. It would seem that among the ranks of the Fund's staff, ways could always be found for legitimating cuts in existing expenditure regardless of the circumstances.[6]

Across Southeast Asia, GDP collapsed, unemployment skyrocketed, business insolvencies reached record levels, and popular opposition led to violence—and in Indonesia, to death on the streets. Governments tumbled in Indonesia, Thailand, and South Korea. Convinced of its good sense, throughout all of this the Fund remained largely unmoved. In April 1998, its deputy director, Stanley Fischer, declared the worst of the crisis to be over. Only Joseph Stiglitz, the (then) chief economist at the World Bank, questioned the veracity of this Washington consensus. The Asian Tigers had become victims of their own success. It took five years for the Asian Tigers to return to stable growth—and even then it was at lower levels than they had once enjoyed (see figure 15.1).

The scale of the Asian crisis had revealed beyond any remaining doubt that the Fund was inadequately resourced to address the crisis. More important, it displayed the Fund's unchanging propensity to blame the patient for the ailment. Talk of bailouts became fashionable. But it is worth remembering just who it was who was being bailed out. It was certainly not the local financial firms, nor governments, as was often thought to be the case. They collapsed. Instead, it was the international lenders into these economies who stood heavily exposed to a full-scale financial collapse, who were bailed out. The whole experience was redolent of what had happened in Mexico not many years before. It revealed a familiar formula: force into insolvency local financial firms and impose policies of monetary and fiscal austerity upon the recipients of assistance from the Fund.

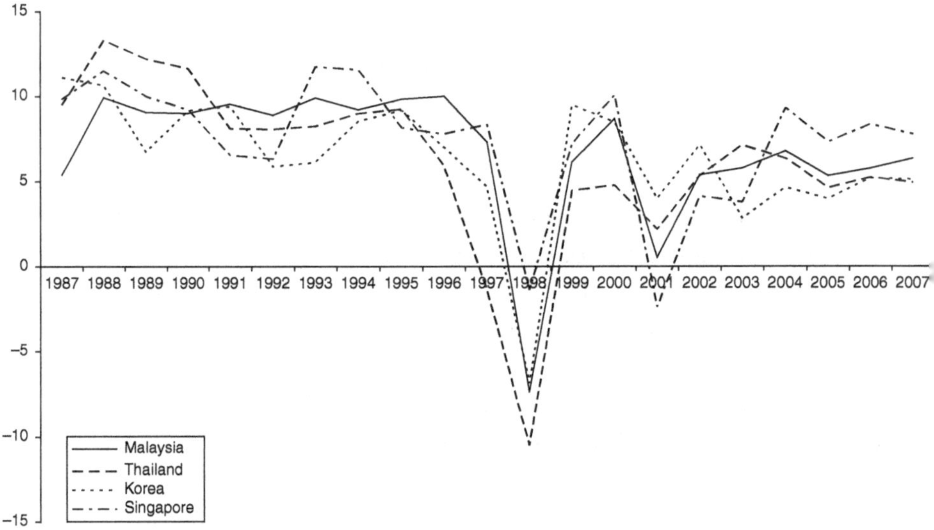

Figure 15.1 GDP at constant prices (annual percentage change): 1987–2007
Source: IMF, *World Economic Outlook*, April 2009).

In the aftermath of the Asian crisis, the idea of precommitment, of the Fund's acting as a lender of last resort, became fashionable for a time. But nothing came of it. This is hardly surprising. The one thing that the whole of modern monetary history makes clear is that monetary authorities become credible lenders of last resort only when they have been able to develop extensive powers of microeconomic supervision and prudential management of the financial institutions in the system—and when they have been able to demonstrate a record of tolerable competence in such regulation. The Fund was hardly in a position to fulfill either of those conditions.

The Credit Crunch of 2008

When the next crisis struck the international financial system in 2008, this time the epicenter was not the developing or emerging markets of Latin America or Asia but the major industrial economies themselves. Its effects were to be wider, deeper, and more prolonged than anything that the international economy had experienced since the Second World War. Given the scale of the assistance that was required, the Fund was in no position to cope (table 15.3). In April 2009, the G20 Summit in London supported a dramatic increase in the Fund's resources to help combat the crisis. They agreed to triple the Fund's lending capacity to $750 billion and to enable the Fund to inject extra liquidity into the world economy via a $250 billion allocation of Special Drawing Rights. Moreover, an immediate doubling of the Fund's resources (from about $250 billion) was to come from bilateral pledges (including $100 billion each from Japan and the European Union). Though substantial, these resources were as nothing when measured against the trillions of dollars that were required worldwide (table 15.4 and chapter appendix).

Fortunately, the Fund was not called upon to act on such a large scale. National governments took the lead instead—and they acted in ways quite different from anything the Fund had done in the past. Most significantly, rather than insisting on fiscal and monetary stringency as the price of state assistance, governments across the world embarked upon programs of fiscal stimulus and monetary expansion. Recognizing the likely scale of the effects of the financial crisis on business investment, economic growth, and unemployment—feedback effects between the so-called money and real economy that the Fund had consistently ignored in imposing its conditions—these largely uncoordinated national responses turned out to furnish something almost resembling a coordinated response to the crisis.

Table 15.3 IMF lending resources: one-year forward commitment (*All figures in SDR billions unless otherwise indicated*)

	2007	2008	April 2009 SDRs	April 2009 US $b
1. Total resources	224.6	224.1	224.1	335.7
Members' currencies	209.6	209.8	209.6	314.0
SDR holdings	2.6	2.0	2.1	3.2
Gold holdings	5.9	5.9	5.9	8.8
Other assets	6.6	6.5	6.5	9.8
2. Less: Nonusable resources	59.3	71.7	70.0	104.9
Of which: Credit outstanding	6.0	17.5	20.4	30.6
3. Equals: Usable resources	165.4	152.5	154.1	230.8
4. Less: Undrawn balances under GRA arrangements	3.1	20.3	51.8	77.6
5. Equals: Uncommitted usable resources	162.3	132.1	102.3	153.3
6. Plus: Repurchases one-year forward	0.3	0.1	0.1	0.1
7. Less: Prudential balance	34.9	34.7	35.7	53.5
8. Equals: One-year forward commitment capacity (FCC)	**127.7**	**97.6**	**66.7**	**99.9**

Source: IMF. *Financial Resources and Liquidity Position*: 2007–*April* 2009.

Table 15.4 Selected financial support packages to October 2008 (*All figures in billions of units of the applicable national currency*)

	Guarantee of banks' wholesale liabilities	Capital injections	Purchase of assets	Other
United Kingdom	£250	£50	£200	£149
United States	$1,400	$250	$450	$198
France		€41		€320
Germany	€400	€130		
Netherlands	€200	€46.8		
Spain	€100	€50		

Source: Bank of England, *Financial Stability Report*, October 2008.

The story was very different, however, in those economies that had to rely on the Fund for assistance, rather than using their own fiscal resources. In these cases, fiscal and monetary stimulus was severely curtailed. Here is how the Fund itself characterized their imposed conditions:

"the average fiscal impulse in the current program is less restrictive than in past crises, although it is tighter than in current non-program cases" (IMF, 2009, pp. 23–24). Tighter, indeed, it was. The examples of Latvia, Hungary, and Ireland spring to mind, but the Greek debt crisis provides further evidence, if any more were needed, of some of the key inadequacies of international responses to financial turmoil.

An EU–IMF support package for Greece worth about 110 billion euros was announced in April 2010. Of the total, 80 billion euros came from the EU and only 30 billion euros from the IMF (as a three-year SDR). Characteristically, the patient was held responsible for its problems—this time correctly, but for the wrong reasons.[7] The Greek fiscal position was mostly due to government inaction on the revenue side of its balance sheets, not to government action on the expenditure side, as claimed by the EU–IMF. The failure of successive Greek administrations to do anything about the size of an untaxed shadow economy that accounted for over one-fourth of GDP (Schneider and Buehn, 2009), and the massive cost of this in terms of tax revenue foregone, is what the Greeks had done wrong—rather than spending "too much" on public-sector pay and pensions. Moreover, even some of what the Greeks had supposedly done wrong on the expenditure side was massively overstated. Greek pension entitlements, for example, were characterized as "extravagant." Tales were told of retirement at age forty-five, as if this were the rule rather than the exception. In fact, Greek provisions differed little, and were sometimes less generous, than entitlements across the rest of the EU. The standard retirement age for men and women (sixty-five and sixty, respectively) in Greece was the same as in Britain and Austria (and less generous than in France and Italy); and full entitlement required thirty-seven years of employee contributions (more than the thirty-five contribution-years required in Italy and the thirty contribution-years required in Britain). Under the conditions imposed by the EU–IMF, the Greek rules would change to require forty contribution-years for men and women retiring at age sixty-five. The cost of the Greek pension provision seems to have had more to do with the combined effects of a rapidly aging Greek population and the failure of many Greek employers to make their statutory contributions to the state scheme than the putative "extravagance" of its entitlements.[8]

Nevertheless, with an inaccurate (or, at best, incomplete) diagnosis of the problem, the patient was prescribed a savage and compulsory dose of fiscal austerity. Quite apart from the fact that the Greek crisis might have been avoided had the EU taken immediately convincing steps to underwrite Greek sovereign debt the moment that servicing difficulties had become apparent (rather than trying to make do with half-hearted words of support for the fiscal measures already under way in Greece), it should not be forgotten that, in being coerced by the EU–IMF into even more severe fiscal austerity than the newly elected Greek government had planned for itself, the citizens of Greece were being asked to bear someone else's burden.

The package was described as a Greek "bailout." Clearly, however, the EU–IMF bailout was to the benefit of everyone but the Greeks. The single largest set of beneficiaries was the holders of Greek sovereign debt. In this case, that was mostly European financial institutions, and especially French and German banks. According to the *Financial Times*, the Belgian financial firms Fortis and Dexia had, respectively, an estimated 3.8 billion and 3 billion euros of holdings in Greek bonds and they faced "exposures proportional to their tangible net asset value of 64% and 35%, respectively." The *Financial Times*, on April 30, 2010, further reported exposures as follows: (1) of the French banks, Crédit Agricole, was "most exposed to lending to Greece through its ownership of Emporiki, the loss-making bank with a 28.4 billion euro balance sheet, but *Société Générale (which owned Geniki)* had a 3 billion euro exposure and BNP Paribas had a 5 billion euro exposure; (2) Hypo Real Estate ("nationalized by the German government") had "8 billion euros of Greek exposure"; and (3) "a regional government minister in Stuttgart said yesterday that LBBW, the local Landesbank, had about 2 billion euro exposure."

With these levels of exposure, it should have been glaringly obvious that a Greek default could quickly have turned into a European banking crisis as bond prices fell, the price of credit-default swaps rose, and the liquidity position of exposed European financial institutions deteriorated. Yet, the unhelpful German attitude toward the Greek crisis suggests a failure to comprehend this possibility. It is difficult to ascribe the manifest German reluctance to provide support for Greece to anything other than economic incompetence. That attitude must bear much of the blame for the costly and catastrophic outcome of the whole episode. Almost as inevitably as day follows night, the EU and the Fund were quickly forced to announce an even larger package, this one worth about 750 billion euros (of which the Fund's contribution was 250 billion euros) to underwrite *all* EU sovereign debt—at least in the short run.[9]

However, what should have been done in the Greek case—and was grudgingly done in the end for the whole euro zone—should have been done in the first place, for none of it was of much benefit to solve either the Greek situation or to strengthen the euro on the foreign exchanges. It seems that bold actions need to be taken at the outset if pressures on the bond markets are to be relieved. Even if the steps are taken eventually, stumbling toward the solution, and complaining all the way, appears to ensure their ineffectiveness. But even if all of these actions did nothing to make things any better, their fiscal accoutrements made matters worse. For, as Greece joined Ireland and embarked upon making swinging cuts in public expenditures—and was quickly joined in this by Italy, Spain, Portugal, and Britain—the bond markets (rather than the policymakers) correctly assessed the consequences in terms of a curtailment in effective demand and a further dampening of economic growth—and they responded accordingly.

To see how Greek prospects might compare to the prospects for other economies—one an IMF program and the other a non-IMF solution—it is instructive to consider the Latvian and the Argentine crises of 2008 and 2002, respectively. In 2008, Latvia entered into an IMF agreement and implemented its austerity requirements. Having grown at a healthy trend rate above 7% since the beginning of the century, in 2009 the Latvian GDP immediately plummeted by 18%. Even optimistic IMF forward predictions (for as far out as 2015) do not suggest a recovery to anything like the previous trend rates (IMF, 2010). This is both a short-run and a long-run catastrophe for Latvia. In 2002, Argentina declined to accept the conditions that the IMF was insisting on and defaulted on its sovereign debt repayments, and offered a take-it-or-leave-it debt-restructuring package instead. Its GDP having fallen by over 4% in 2001, Argentina saw its GDP fall by a further 10.8% in 2002 (IMF, 2010). However, within eighteen months, Argentina had returned to its precrisis growth rates; and between 2004 and 2009, the Argentine economy grew at an impressive average annual rate of 8.5%. Even the pronounced impact of the global recession in 2009 has been less severe in Argentina than it has been in similar economies. Compared to Latvia, Argentina suffered a less severe short-run shock and a far superior long-run outcome.

There is a message here for the effectiveness of the IMF: what the Fund calls "program countries" often do worse than "nonprogram countries" when it comes to both short-run and long-run growth consequences (see IMF, 2009, p.10). Accordingly, the "program countries" do a little worse on the unemployment front, too. It is difficult to reach any conclusion other than that the default/restructure option taken by Argentina in 2002 offers a better course of action than having to resort to the Fund's "help."

Concluding Remarks

These instances of the Fund's responses to crises of various kinds reveal a seemingly unalterable instinct of Fund staff to do the nearly the exact opposite of what is required. Faced with crisis, the Fund blames the patient for the malaise and seeks solutions in terms of monetary and fiscal austerity. That the problem might reside in the nature (and regulatory framework) of international monetary and financial arrangements seems never to pass through the minds of the Fund's staff. The one time it has appeared to be doing so, although at the behest of the G20 in response to the global financial crisis of 2008, the prospect for real change at the IMF looked decidedly bleak. All the talk is still of "funding" bailouts, "containing" fiscal deficits, "reforming" domestic financial markets (meaning more liberalization), "consolidating" public finances, dealing with "structural" deficits, and promoting greater "transparency."

That the Fund's resources are stretched beyond limit is apparent to all—yet the task is to obviate the need for bailouts, not to find ways of funding them. Moreover, the possibility that fiscal austerity might have effects that are the opposite of those envisaged by the Fund also appears to be unthinkable to its staff. This is despite the fact that all of the evidence of experience seems to suggest that, after a visitation by the Fund, and after austerity has done its worst, economies find themselves on permanently lower growth paths than before (and often with the same old "problems"). It is pretty clear that such approaches have passed their sell-by date; and whether the Fund in its present form can open up new policy horizons is an open question.

Notes

This is a revised version of a lecture delivered by Murray Milgate at Osaka, Japan, in January 2010.

1. The original Article IV Section (v) then read: "A member shall not propose a change in the par value of its currency except to correct a fundamental disequilibrium. A change in the par value of a member's currency may be made only on the proposal of the member and only after consultation with the Fund" (IMF, 1944).

2. This was part of the reason that Mexico was viewed by the commercial banks of the industrial economies as being a low-risk borrower. Together with their newfound ability to move large sums across the newly liberalizing foreign exchanges, and the plentiful supply of petrodollars to be recycled, their lending proceeded apace.

3. This institutional memory lapse persisted: the solution in 1989 was simply to insist on the same old conditions first, before agreeing to any bridging finance or debt rescheduling.

4. Initially, it seems, Japanese financial banks led the way. They were major lenders to Thailand, but by the middle of the 1990s they were facing extreme pressure to restructure their internal books in the face of the many nonperforming loans left behind from the bubble economy. To achieve this, repatriation of short-term foreign placements formed part of their strategy.

5. In January 1998, South Korea arranged a swap of short-term debt with commercial lenders that was worth about $24 billion. In September, Japan announced a $30 billion package of assistance for Asian economies.

6. Far from seeing this strategy as *continuing* along the same lines as in the past, the Fund actually heralded this as a *change*: "Forceful, far-reaching structural reforms are at the heart of all the programs, marking an evolution in emphasis from many of the programs that the IMF has supported in the past, where the underlying country problem was imbalances reflecting inappropriate macroeconomic policies" (IMF, 1999).

7. The role of large private financial institutions in the Greek crisis—both as advisers and as active participants in bond markets—is a story that remains to be told. There seems to be a deal of circumstantial evidence to suggest that it was extensive and unhelpful.

8. Another example of the inaccurate reporting of Greek economic circumstances was of its supposedly "bloated" public sector. Thus, according to *The Guardian* (May 7, 2010), "around one million Greeks are employed in the wider public sector with the vast majority holding jobs from which constitutionally they can never be fired." In fact, at the time there were just a little over 5 million workers in Greece, so even if there had been "one million" in the public sector as reported, that would have amounted to about 20% of the Greek workforce. In the UK at the time, public-sector employees accounted for about 22% of the workforce; in France and Holland, about 20%; and in Sweden, about 30%. Their wages and salaries accounted for 26% of government expenditure in Greece—the same as in Britain and only just above France and Belgium at 25% each (OECD, 2008, p. 13). It seems that Greece had no monopoly on "bloated" public sectors. Furthermore, a quick glance at the Greek Constitution reveals that it contains no provision that prevented the dismissal of "the vast majority" of public-sector workers.

9. The European Central Bank was also forced to enter the bond market as a purchaser of EU-denominated debt—something it had embarrassingly asserted it would not do just days before.

Chapter Appendix

Table 15A Consolidated financial-sector support packages: U.S., 2008–2010

Program Name	Gross Outlay *$b*	Net Outlay *$b*	Guarantee *$b*
Troubled Asset Relief Program	**894.2**	**330.7**	**0.0**
Capital Purchase Program	204.9	69.1	
Public-Private Investment Program	40.0	39.6	
Systemically Significant Failing Institutions program	69.8	69.8	
Making Home Affordable	50.0	50.0	
Targeted Investment Program	40.0	0.0	
Automotive Industry Financing Program	80.7	77.1	
Asset Guarantee Program	5.0	0.0	
Auto Suppliers Support Program	3.5	3.1	
Auto Warranty Commitment Program	0.6	0.0	
Unlocking Credit for Small Businesses	1.0	1.0	
Term Asset-backed Securities Loan Facility	20.0	20.0	
Community Development Capital Initiative	1.0	1.0	
Small Business Lending Fund	30.0	0.0	
New Programs, or Funds Remaining for Existing Programs	347.7	0.0	
US Treasury	**0.0**	**0.0**	**1,653.0**
Money Market Mutual Fund Program			600.0
Government-Sponsored Enterprise (GSE) Preferred Stock Purchase Agreements			400.0
GSE MBS Purchase Program			314.0
Student Loan Purchases			195.0
GSE Credit Facility Program			25.0
Other HERA/Treasury (Tax Benefits and CDBG)			19.0
Potential International Fund Liabilities			100.0
Federal Reserve Board	**3,221.3**	**3,221.3**	**1,829.8**
Commercial Paper Funding Facility			1,800.0
Purchase of GSE Guaranteed Mortgage-backed Securities	1,250.0	1,250.0	
Term Auction Facility	900.0	900.0	
Money Market Investor Funding Facility			
Purchase of Treasury Securities	300.0	300.0	
Term Securities Lending Facility	250.0	250.0	
Purchase of Fannie/Freddie bonds	200.0	200.0	
Credit to AIG, purchase of AIG assets	175.3	175.3	

Table 15A (*Continued*)

Program Name	Gross Outlay *$b*	Net Outlay *$b*	Guarantee *$b*
Asset-backed Commercial Paper Money Market Mutual Fund Liquidity Facility	146.0	146.0	
Bear Stearns guarantees to purchaser JPMorgan Chase			29.8
Federal Deposit Insurance Corporation	**0.0**	**0.0**	**1,384.0**
Temporary Liquidity Guarantee Program—Debt Guarantees			
Enhanced Deposit Insurance			700.0
Temporary Liquidity Guarantee Program - Transaction Account Guarantee Program			684.0
Other	**0.0**	**0.0**	**7,139.9**
FHFA—Fannie Mae/Freddie Mac Conservatorship			5,500.0
Federal Home Loan Bank guarantees			1,300.0
NCUA—Temporary Corporate Credit Union Liquidity Guarantee Program			15.2
NCUA—Homeowners Affordability Relief Program and Credit Union System Investment Program (CU SIP)			41.0
Government National Mortgage Association (GNMA) guarantees			149.2
Federal Housing Agency (FHA) guarantees			134.5
Total Exposure	**4,115.5**	**3,552.0**	**16,312.3**

Source: Special Inspector General for TARP: *Quarterly Report to Congress* (April 2010 & July 2009); *TARP Exposure Chart*; consolidated at *www.usfederalbailout.com*.

Part Four

Historical

16

Keynes's *General Theory*

If one were to isolate from the many interpretations of Keynes's *General Theory* those that might be said to have dominated the discipline, including the writings of his theoretical adversaries and his advocates, one characteristic feature would be present in all of them. This is the idea that the *General Theory* is an examination of the disequilibrium behavior of a market system. Of course, to its proponents, the *General Theory* not only provides what the classical economists or Marshall might have referred to as an analysis of the temporary effects of particular changes; it also offers a rationale for viewing these changes as of paramount importance in how we conduct our daily lives. The *General Theory,* it is sometimes said, draws our attention to the fact that the underlying forces working toward the establishment of equilibrium, while ever present, are often only weakly felt. The simple and appealing notion behind this view is that a market economy may become stuck, so to speak, in a situation where certain frictions and rigidities (sometimes of formidable dimensions) prevent the more persistent forces from producing their permanent effects. At the risk of some oversimplification, one may classify those readings of the *General Theory* that view its concern with disequilibrium as falling within the compass of received opinion. One consequence of received opinion has been that debate over the significance of the book is frequently played out in the arenas of empirical argument and practical affairs.

Leaving to one side, for the moment at least, Keynes's *General Theory* itself, the received opinion may be traced back to certain sympathetic views expressed as to its importance (mainly by younger economists of the day) that followed immediately upon its appearance in February 1936. The assessments of James Meade and of Roy Harrod (1937) come to mind. Yet probably best known, since they were subsequently to be incorporated into textbooks as the Keynesian model, and in an important sense are typical of the genre, are the interpretations advanced by Hicks (1937) and by Modigliani (1944). It is not, of course, in the details of these arguments that one finds unanimity; rather, it is in the general tenor of the assessment that the common theme emerges. What matters is not whether the actual obstacle to the attainment of equilibrium arises from, say, money-wage rigidity, or the presence of a liquidity trap, or the operation of the monetary system, or the behavior of trade unions, or any other imperfection. What matters is that the common theme is the question of disequilibrium.

Paul Samuelson, himself swept up by the Keynesian revolution in the 1930s, commented subsequently on the reception of the *General Theory* in terms that loudly echo this theme. Speaking of Schumpeter's negative reaction to the book, for example, Samuelson commented: "[Schumpeter's] instinct—not incorrect but not usefully relevant to policy dilemmas in, say, 1938—was to look for some price rigidity in the scenario and, having located it, to shrug off the phenomenon with the remark: 'Of course, if you introduce rigidities in your system, you can fabricate involuntary deviations from full employment for it" (Samuelson, 1981, p. 16).

Samuelson's remark that the instinct was "not incorrect" is evidence of the presence of received opinion. To be noted also, of course, is the idea that the reception of the *General Theory* depended on the view taken as to its practical relevance: Oskar Lange was later to incorporate what he saw as the high probability for the appearance of such disequilibria in market economics as part of his well-known argument favoring socialist planning (Lange, 1987).

Interestingly, the same theme that defines received opinion also dominated the thinking of Keynes's less sympathetic readers at the time. Thus, for example, Pigou (1936) had held the book to be about disequilibrium and, correctly if abruptly, dismissed any claim that this realm of analysis might have for being general: "we have watched an artist firing arrows at the moon," he reflected, and "while we may all admire his virtuosity, we must question his marksmanship" (Pigou, 1936, p. 132). A decade and a half later, in his self-styled reconciliation with Keynes,

Pigou simply attributed to Keynes a more reachable target. He now held that Keynes's purpose was to deal with "fluctuations over short periods" as distinct from questions of "ultimate equilibrium" (1950, pp. 3–4). A similar case is provided by Schumpeter, whose review of the *General Theory* concluded with the remark: "the whole *theoretical* case...collapses, and we are *practically* left with friction, or 'stickiness,' institutional inhibitions and the like...which prevent the whole of [the] equilibrating mechanism from functioning adequately" (1936, p. 794, italics added).

In his *History of Economic Analysis*, Schumpeter restated essentially the same conclusion. It would have been better, he argued, if Keynes had not objected to the tendency toward equilibrium (at full employment); he claimed, "just as we do not object to the law of gravitation on the ground that the earth does not fall into the sun," rather Keynes really meant that though the tendency stated is correct, its operation "is impeded by certain facts" (1954, p. 624). To the list of critics whose arguments fit this broad pattern might be added the names of Dennis Robertson, Ralph Hawtrey, and Harry Johnson.

The received opinion—that Keynes's *General Theory* is a contribution to disequilibrium analysis—was stamped indelibly on the collective consciousness of the economics profession at an early date, by critics and converts alike. The theme is prevalent also in more recent readings of the *General Theory*. Among the supporters of Keynes, one may single out, for example, the arguments of Leijonhufvud. Though his comments are presented as a criticism of certain details of earlier interpretations, the essential ingredient of the old position is present: "Of course, Leijonhufvud writes, "Keynes used the term unemployment equilibrium...[but] it is not an equilibrium in the strict sense at all. It is preferable to use some more neutral term which does not carry the connotation that no equilibrating forces at all are at work. The real question is why...the forces tending to bring the system back...are so weak" (1969, p. 22, n. 1). Similarly, in his analysis of Keynes's monetary thought, Patinkin has concluded that Keynes's general theory is not "strictly speaking" one of "unemployment equilibrium" (1976, p. 114ff). Following the same line of argument, James Tobin has argued that Keynes showed that "disequilibrium can be protracted and stubborn" (1980, p. 19).

The same theme is everywhere apparent in what is today commonly referred to a New Keynesian Macroeconomics, which derives its macroeconomic conclusions from an imperfectly competitive microeconomics. These newer readings in an old framework are paralleled by the readings of a new generation of detractors who, like their forebears, though skeptical of the lasting value of Keynesian theory, remain agreed that the *General Theory* deals in disequilibrium. Milton Friedman exemplifies this group.

The above typology, of course, is fine enough only to filter out the essential ingredient of received opinion. At this level, the category of disequilibrium has proved to be sufficiently definite to suit its purpose. In fact, it reveals an important feature of received opinion that warrants repeating: its borders do not correspond to those that separate Keynes's critics from his champions. Just where one might have expected to unearth something essential about Keynes's *General Theory*, at the boundary between opposing sides in the Keynesian debate, one actually finds agreement. However, the idea of disequilibrium can itself be subjected to an internal partition that, when taken into account, renders our typology capable of generating a somewhat finer description of received opinion than that which it has secured thus far.

The notion of disequilibrium is dependent on the abstract concept of equilibrium to which it is attached and by which it is defined and constructed. There is one species of received opinion in which the Keynesian disequilibrium is taken as a deviation from the long-priced equilibrium of the system. There is another that considers it to be connected with the possible failure of the market to achieve full intertemporal equilibrium. These two types of equilibrium are species of received opinion. The second and more modern view, based on the notion of intertemporal equilibrium and the related idea of "temporary equilibrium," finds its earliest advocate in Hick's *Value and Capital* (1939). It is necessary to distinguish this category of Keynes reading from others; this is not because Keynes is no longer read as a disequilibrium theorist but because, to the extent that Keynesian cases appear where full intertemporal equilibrium fails to emerge, they are no different from the cases where long-period equilibrium is not achieved. The distinction is introduced only to highlight the differing conceptions of equilibrium being employed.

A warning is in order: in the newer mode of analysis, the familiar terminology of equilibrium and disequilibrium is sometimes put aside in favor of denoting the solution to any model as an equilibrium. Temporary equilibrium, rationed equilibrium, conjectural equilibrium, non-Walrasian equilibrium, and the like are all examples of this trend. It needs to be noted, however, that everything that has been said above could be recast in these terms—but only at the cost of much circumlocution and loss of clarity, at least as far as this subject is concerned.

Given these characteristics of received opinion on Keynes's *General Theory*, much of the Keynesian debate has been concerned with the empirical relevance of different kinds of disequilibrium situations. Exegetical debate has likewise focused on determining which particular case of disequilibrium most accurately reflects Keynes's actual argument. Here, of course, the received opinion has any number of ways of generating the result it is after; the number of frictions and rigidities that might be invoked is limited only by the investigator. These details need not detain us here, yet passing mention needs to be made of the perplexing propensity of some writers to present the dispute as a battle over fundamental or ultimate theoretical principles. It goes without saying that all such claims are entirely without foundation, and that in attempting to sustain them, certain "Keynesians" have been roundly defeated. There is evidence of this singularly unproductive approach in some attacks on the quantity theory of money, monetarism, and rational expectations theory that arose in the 1970s and 1980s.

Before turning to the *General Theory* itself, so as to trace the basis of the received opinion to its sources in that book, we need to consider the familiar idea that the essence of Keynes's work is its macroeconomic character, as distinct from the predominantly microeconomic character of his predecessors. Initially, at least, the differences between these two departments of economic analysis were invoked to account for Keynes's conclusions that seemingly differed so much from preexisting arguments—that is, the possibility of prolonged bouts of unemployment. Though the actual literature that proceeded along these lines appears to be quite different from that already discussed, this perspective on Keynes's general theory is nothing more than an example of received opinion in a slightly different guise. In contrasting the conclusions of equilibrium microeconomics with those of Keynes, it became apparent —first in regard to the aggregation problem and subsequently to the relationship between macroeconomics and microeconomics—that the only way of explaining the Keynesian macroeconomic conclusions was by grounding them in disequilibrium, or an imperfectly competitive microeconomics.

To understand correctly the basis of received opinion in the *General Theory* itself, or of any other opinion on the subject, it is necessary to recognize the composite character of Keynes's argument. First, there are what he regularly referred to as the constructive versus the critical parts of the book. Then, within both, there are the theoretical as opposed to the more polemical pages and passages. There are the inevitable asides targeted at the debates of the day (familiar, perhaps, at the time, but often lost on the modern reader); excursions into historical reconstruction, conjoined with ever-present observations and commentary on the social and political philosophies of other economic writers (and even that of the *General Theory* itself); the original arguments; and the remnants of earlier orthodoxy. Finally, there is the sustained attack (which at few points in the book is far from the surface) on the quantity theory of money. What matters here is that not all of these arguments and points are mutually compatible.

The whole of Keynes's theoretical argument is, of course, built on the idea that reconciliation of otherwise incompatible investment decisions and savings plans is ensured by variations in the level of income (output). This process determines the aggregate level of employment—Keynes dubbed it the "principle of effective demand." So far as can be determined, despite the intensity of Keynesian controversy, there has been no disagreement over this point.

This argument of Keynes departed from what had hitherto been the traditional view—that the mutual compatibility of decisions to save and decisions to invest was secured by relative price adjustments (or, in the language of the Marshallian partial equilibrium framework of the day, by changes in the rate of interest). By relocating the analysis of saving and investment, however, Keynes's argument immediately opened up three topics that had been dealt with simultaneously, so to speak, in the earlier theory: determination of the level of savings, volume of investment, and rate of interest. (He also reopened the topics of wage and price determination, but these are left to one side for the moment.) The marginal propensity to consume, the marginal efficiency of capital, and the liquidity preference were used by Keynes to fill his newly created toolbox. These matters are pretty much uniformly agreed upon.

Armed with this theoretical toolbox, Keynes made his celebrated claim for the principle of effective demand in relation to earlier theory:

> the postulates of classical theory are applicable to a special case only and not to the general case, the situation which it assumes being the limiting point of the possible positions of equilibrium. Moreover, the characteristics of the special case assumed by classical theory happen not to be those of the economic society in which we actually live, with the result that its teaching is misleading and disastrous if we attempt to apply it to the facts of experience. (1936, p. 3)

With the usual warning as to Keynes's singular use of the term "classical," this claim, together with the basic theoretical tools already listed, help to explain how received opinion can find some succour in the *General Theory* itself.

If one retains, as Keynes did, two of the basic postulates of earlier theory— the interest-elastic demand schedule for investment (expressed in the marginal efficiency of capital schedule), and the relationship between the marginal productivity of labor and the real wage (expressed in the usual demand schedule for labor)—the only fully consistent theoretical basis for the idea that unemployment was impossible (and that if it should appear, then it could well be of long duration) had to be based on the argument that the effective demand mechanism would come into play in disequilibrium (arising, say, in the simplest kinds of cases, from interest-rate or wage-rate inflexibility). In these circumstances, aggregate income (output) would not be at its full-employment level, and so everything that Keynes seemed to be saying, whether about the theory of employment and the price level, or about the effectiveness of government deficit spending as a remedy for unemployment, held good.

But not quite everything. The claim that this would be a general theory of employment—at least in the formal sense of being a theory about the full equilibrium of a market system—just could not stand. However, as is quite apparent in the passage where Keynes made this claim, there is a feasible avenue of interpretation open to received opinion, even given this claim. The second sentence of the passage cited above, where Keynes remarked that "classical" theory did not accurately describe the world in which we live, was enough to confirm for the received opinion that perhaps what Keynes was driving at was simply that his theory was more generally applicable to concrete cases than was that of his predecessors. Received opinion thus translated Keynes's claim (see the first sentence of the passage cited above) as a general theory that could be defended as general only on the grounds of its practical relevance. This had the added advantage of keeping intact the preexisting modes of analysis.

This last factor is, in many respects, the single most notable feature of received opinion. Though perhaps is not precisely in the same way, it reasserts the theory of Keynes's predecessors—not, of course, as a theory that necessarily applies to every situation, but as the only claimant to being a general theory in the formal sense of that term. Keynesian cases are, as it were, embedded in the disequilibrium possibilities of traditional equilibrium analysis. It should be said, however, that to its advocates, Keynes's analysis of unemployment highlights cases that are more prevalent and problematic than any considered before his time. After all, deviations from equilibrium were in themselves nothing new. But deviations in which the tendency toward full employment is so weak—as it is in most disequilibrium versions of the principle of effective demand, and where a more direct remedy is available to policymakers than tampering with price mechanisms—had not previously been brought to the notice of the profession. Indeed, much of Keynes's practical appeal stems from the optimistic prospect he offers for a measure of collective action to eliminate unemployment.

Minority opinions regarding Keynes's *General Theory* are more heterogeneous in nature. They have in common little more than what appears to be a shared starting point, in that they attempt to build on Keynes's claim to have completely replaced the traditional analysis of employment. To put it another way, the very claim of generality that received opinion transliterates into a claim of practical relevance is one that the minority opinions take seriously. There are two lines of argument here.

The first argument owes much to the later work of Joan Robinson. It calls into question the whole idea of equilibrium argumentation in economics. Its usual appeal is to the fact of uncertainty and the consequent disappointment of expectations upon which, or so it is argued, Keynes's entire argument is based. Essentially, it says that these features of the economic environment render otiose any vision that sees market economics as operationally stable in any significant sense. This is not, or so its adherents claim, to be mistaken for just another variety of the frictions and rigidities story, even if in many instances it is difficult to see how this claim could be made to stand up.

The second argument takes a quite different track. It focuses its attention on the nature of the market mechanism and the theoretical explanation for its operation. Instead of maintaining (as is customary under received opinion) that Keynes shared with his predecessors their theoretical characterization of the mechanisms through which market economies operate and that he differed only in showing that these mechanisms were not uniformly as beneficent in the actual world as they were in theory, it holds that Keynes's general theory requires replacement of that theory in its entirety. Rather than arguing that the market mechanism *tends* to produce full employment in the absence of frictions and rigidities, as even received opinion would admit, this statement of tendency is put aside.

This particular reading of the *General Theory*, though consistent with many of the claims Keynes himself made for the book, opens up a whole field of new and difficult problems. If the principle of effective demand is to be used as an explanation of what Marshall might have called the long-run normal levels of output and employment, rather than just their disequilibrium or short-run levels, then the question immediately arises as to what explains the rate of interest, the real wage, the level of investment, and not least, the relative prices of commodities. These are all questions that previous equilibrium theory had dealt with in a single blow by conceiving of capitalist society as a world regulated by the maximizing behavior of agents given the preferences of individuals, the available techniques of production, and the initial endowments of the system. These new questions cannot, however, be answered by the theories Keynes himself selected; with the exception of the idea of the marginal propensity to consume, these must be largely left behind, at least as far as long-period theory is concerned.

The resolution proposed is that one might return to the vision of the market mechanism furnished by the classical economists, from Smith through to Ricardo, and by Marx. This may, perhaps, seem paradoxical, given Keynes's own undisguised hostility to both Ricardo and Marx (though probably no more so than the route taken by received opinion that returns to the theory of still orders, for whom Keynes had little regard). According to this line of argument, the market mechanism as a structural feature of capitalist society is activated not by the wills of individuals but independent of them, as Quesnay might have said. This suggests that markets exist to ensure the continued economic and social reproduction of the system. Therefore, the prices determined in these markets need to satisfy the distributional requirements of reproduction. The owners of the means of production must, in the long run, receive the customary rate of profit on the best-practice techniques in whatever lines of production they are engaged, and the real wage must conform to the historical, institutional, and customary norms of the society. However, only a tentative start seems to have been made in this direction.

There are, however, two claims for recasting economic theory along these lines. One concerns theory proper and the other is in the realm of practical affairs. According to the first claim, there would now be no longer any necessity to regard the market mechanism as inherently efficient, save for its potential to become stuck in disequilibrium. That is, if the long-run tendency of the market mechanism is to produce general results like unemployment, then the analytical bases of many pre-Keynesian doctrines vanish. Perhaps principal among these is the old-fashioned quantity theory of money. Moreover, the optimality of the mechanisms of competitive capitalism, so central to the general theory of Keynes's predecessors (and present also in received opinion), is fundamentally called into question. The argument places in the hands of its practitioners reasons to agree with, rather than to dismiss, some of Keynes's most provocative and telling claims made on behalf of the theory of effective demand:

> there are...forces which one might fairly well call "automatic" which operate under any normal monetary system in the direction of restoring a long-period equilibrium between saving and investment. The point on which I cast doubt—though the contrary is generally believed—is whether these "automatic forces" will...tend to bring about not only an equilibrium between saving and investment but also an optimum level of production. (1973, 13:395)

At the level of practical affairs, the argument holds out the prospect that a measure of collective control over the investment and industrial processes of market economies will render possible the achievement of goals like full employment and improved standards of living, which for a long time (and still in certain circles today) had been thought to be beyond the reach of human intervention and control.

Nevertheless, from a work that has captured the attention of leading economists of the twentieth century, it would be foolhardy to draw fixed conclusions. The preceding discussion lays claim only to having drawn what seem to be some broad contours that typify the landscape of Keynesian debate. Elsewhere are to be found many accounts of its specific features. The typology set out here may prove to be fruitful for those wanting to examine existing arguments; how relevant it might prove to be in the future is more difficult to determine.

Note

This chapter was written by Murray Milgate, and was published under its present title in the original *New Palgrave Dictionary of Economics.*

17

Keynesian Economic Theory and European Society

The influence of economic theory on the intellectual, political, and social history of Europe has been extensive. For at least the last two hundred years, the course of events in Europe has moved in channels analyzed, delineated, and not infrequently constructed by economic theory. In part, the influence of economic theory derives from the increasing extent to which economic factors have come to pervade the political, social, and cultural dimensions of modern society. It is not necessary to revert to a crude economic determinism to understand that many features of nineteenth- and twentieth-century European history—the development of the division of labor through technological change and capital accumulation, the extension of the market, the conflicts between labor and capital, the complex relations between the state and the economy, colonial and imperial expansion into Africa, Asia, and the Pacific, and the like—have been issues that at once have shaped and molded the character of contemporary European society and towards which economics has made most of the relevant contributions.

Since these features of the European experience are essentially economic in nature, few would disagree with the claim that economic theory has something to say about them. However, what is more interesting and less widely appreciated is the fact that economic theory has often also been decisive in establishing the character and content of the discourse within which the practical and political reactions to these events have been played out. It has done this quite independently of whether the economic theory itself was abstract, or misleading, or even wrong.

Thus, for example, it would be difficult to imagine an account of nineteenth-century liberalism that omitted mention of the economic theories of Adam Smith, John Stuart Mill, and the Manchester School as crucial to an explanation of its development in Britain. In nineteenth-century France, liberal ideology and practice could hardly be addressed without looking at J. B. Say and de Tracy, and later Bastiat, Cheysson, and Molinari, among others.[1] Understanding the political and economic character of prerevolutionary France without knowledge of the physiocratic system of economic analysis would be quite impossible.[2]

Even if the concern is more particularist—say, the political history of England between 1819 and 1848—economic theory provides the backdrop against which events unfolded, and the content of much of the political dialogue (not to mention the action) draws directly upon it. "Peterloo" and the machinery question, the first Reform Bill, the Chartist movement,[3] the Anti-Corn Law League, the debates over the Poor law Amendment Act and later the Factory Acts, and Peel's Bank Charter Act appear hardly to be explicable without a rather precise understanding of both Smith's and Ricardo's economics. The same can be said of the criticisms of Ricardian theory by Malthus, Bailey, and Senior; of the position of Ricardo's defenders like James Mill or McCulloch; of the work on currency by Tooke, Fullarton, and Overstone; and even of the radical applications of Ricardo made by members of that school of socialists that in England bears his name—for example, writers like Thomas Hodgskin. It seems hardly necessary to cite the impact of Marx's economics on European society to further reinforce the point.

Both In the middle of the twentieth century and more recently, it is to the work of John Maynard Keynes and the subsequent emergence of Keynesianism that one can turn to appreciate just how decisive the impact of economic theory on European thought and society has been and continues to be. Although it would be wrong to attribute to this influence all of the tendencies that have been at work in the postwar period, nevertheless it does appear to be the case that many of them bear the indelible stamp of Keynes and Keynesianism. The rise and fall of the Western European social democratic consensus, together with the swings in the fortunes of the various political parties in Europe (including the recent rise of a new conservatism in Britain, West Germany, and France) can, at least in part, be traced to this source. The varied fortunes of the welfare state, the changing face of European trade unionism, the sequence of economic prosperity giving way to stagnation and industrial decline, and the demise in public popularity during the 1970s and 1980s of democratic socialist and labor philosophies are also susceptible to an explanation of this kind.

The aim of this chapter is to highlight some of the ways economic theory has exerted its influence and to indicate how a recognition of this fact may be of help in explaining both the past course and future prospects of certain aspects of European society. Since the subject matter of such an investigation is large, we propose to narrow our focus a little and to concentrate on three points. To begin with, we will attempt to chart the role that Keynes, and more particularly Keynesianism, has played in setting the agenda of social democracy in Europe, in determining the boundaries and ground rules of political discourse and in influencing the course of social democracy itself. Next, we will attempt to trace, by using the example of indicators of national economic performance and well-being by politicians, the general public, and interest groups, how Keynesian ideas have penetrated the popular consciousness of Europe to such an extent that even the revival of pre-Keynesian doctrines in the last decade or so has failed to erase the Keynesian stamp. Lastly, we will venture into some speculations about whether this influence has now been spent or whether, on the contrary, the immediate prospects for Western Europe remain likely to be influenced by Keynes's contributions to economic theory.

Keynes and Social Democracy

When Keynes suggested in 1926 that people had changed their philosophy of economic life, he was doing no more than highlighting the altered demands being made by individuals (and organized groups) on the economic system within which they conducted their daily lives. In the nineteenth century, the familiar catch phrase of "economic progress" had been traditionally qualified with little more than a narrow utilitarian conception of justice, even by the more sophisticated liberals of Europe. Broader notions of social justice and considerations about greater equality in social conditions (as opposed to the liberal's equality of opportunity), though they had intermittently surfaced as part of the political programs of workers or radical intellectuals, had been largely swept aside.

The twin pillars of liberal politics in the second half of the nineteenth century were individual liberty and economic efficiency. The case was simple and convenient: it held that fostering conditions that minimized government restrictions on individual liberty (and especially restrictions on the freedom of economic action) was sufficient to ensure social optimality and economic efficiency. In England, Gladstone was the embodiment of this liberal philosophy. Leaving aside his role in the extension of the franchise, his crusade was for laissez-faire, against what he saw as excessive government interference in industry and wasteful government expenditures. His practical political view of the public purse was that, except in the most compelling of cases, it should be kept firmly closed. The corollary of this view—that the government should seek to keep its economic house in order by balancing expenditures against revenues—he pursued with vigor. Gladstone's liberalism was of the classical kind:

> The essence of the whole thing is, that the spirit of self-reliance, the spirit of true and genuine manly independence, should be preserved in the minds of the people.... If he loses his self-reliance, if he learns to live in a craven dependence upon wealthier people rather than upon himself, you may depend upon it that he incurs mischiefs for which no compensation can be made. (Gladstone, 1892, p. 132)

Such arguments were, in reality, little more than the rhetorical adornments of economic theory designed to render the latter more suitable for public consumption. This was not, it should be stressed, the economic theory of the old classical economists (from Smith to Ricardo), which had provided the basis of the position of the so-called philosophical radicals of earlier decades of the nineteenth century. Rather, it was the economic theory of the marginalist school—of writers like Jevons, Walras, Marshall, and later Pareto and Edgeworth. The economic theory was a straightforward extension of the late utilitarian political theory of J. S. Mill to the problem of the allocation of resources.

The argument becomes very clear in the work of Pareto. Economic theory, argues Pareto, is "concerned only with certain relations between objective facts and subjective facts, principally the tastes of men" (1897, p. 103). Thus, the abstract object of economic theory becomes a market equilibrium determined by "the opposition between men's tastes and the obstacles to satisfying them" (p. 106). These tastes express both the level of satisfaction to be obtained in different situations and how satisfaction is increased or diminished as external market conditions (prices) alter. Taking tastes and initial endowments as given, and assuming that individuals attempt to maximize their satisfaction subject to these constraints, it is possible to show that an equilibrium will be produced under competitive conditions that is optimal in the sense that no one person could be made better off without making someone else worse off. This utilitarian economic theory was freely invoked in support of the doctrine of laissez-faire upon the grounds of the allocative efficiency of the market mechanism. In view of this economic argument, it was perhaps no accident that Lord Rosebury, a prominent British liberal, declared in 1901 that the liberal's watchword was *efficiency*.

The question of greater equality in the distribution of income was, of course, one that was left largely unanswered by neoclassical theory. It was a question, too, that had often troubled the consciences of some liberals. Although the theory did suggest that all the factors of production would be rewarded with payments equal to their marginal contributions to output—hence, the doctrine that "what a social class gets is what it contributes to production"—it was clear that the idea of a given initial endowment was in a certain sense arbitrary. Any change in the initial endowments of individuals (achieved, say, by redistributing the total endowment in a different manner among members of society) would not interfere with the ability of competitive markets to secure economic efficiency—but the distributional properties of this outcome would be quite different from that of the original situation. Policies of income redistribution were, thus, on the agenda in a way that did not appear at the time to conflict with efficiency criteria. Provided society was prepared to make some collective decisions about the initial distribution, the market mechanism would take care of economic efficiency. J. S. Mill's assertion that the distribution was a human institution and as such could be changed (1897, p. 595) was for the first time given an apparently sound basis in economic theory.

Liberal political philosophy was very nearly ready to take this on board. In 1885, Joseph Chamberlain (on the radical wing of the British Liberal Party) had declared that "the great evil with which we have to deal is excessive inequality in the distribution of riches" (1885, p. 3). Of course, in the first decades of the twentieth century, the party in Britain that was to champion redistribution was that of Labour, but nevertheless, the items on any liberal agenda could no longer exclude a dose (however mild) of redistribution.

The interwar years saw this classical liberalism give way across Europe to its twentieth-century successor, social democracy. In Germany, Max Weber's criticisms of capitalism had already been tempered with a guarded optimism about a social democratic future for politics; and in the third French Republic, the opponents of monarchism and Spencerian individualism, like Emile Durkheim, had seen the possibilities for a state (admittedly corporatist) dedicated to eliminating the abnormal effects of the division of labor in society. The scope for collective action in the economic sphere, which had been narrowed systematically by the economic theorists of the second half of the nineteenth century, was being progressively widened by their successors. Although the economic consequences of World War I did much to shake Europe's faith in the ability of the free play of market forces to create and sustain prosperity, it is important to remember that economists had already begun to lay down the basis of an economic argument that would support this new liberalism.[4]

But what was the economic theory of social democracy as it stood in the 1920s? It was, as Keynes himself remarked on many occasions in the 1920s but failed to articulate in clear terms, the old orthodoxy modified to take into account that actual conditions might rarely if ever correspond to the ideal conditions of equilibrium upon which the theorists of an earlier generation (like Jevons, Walras, and Marshall) had so heavily relied. It is to a discussion of some of its more salient features that we now wish to turn.

At the turn of the century, Knut Wicksell, working in Sweden, had exposed flaws in the traditional dogma that nonintervention in the monetary system could be counted on to guarantee price stability—even under the supposedly self-regulating gold standard. In particular, Wicksell had indicated that without intervention by the authorities to activate adjustment in money rates of interest, the institutional structure of the banking system on its own could lead to cumulative processes of inflation or deflation. Quite independently, in England, some of the younger followers of Marshall had hit upon essentially the same argument; but they had taken it a step further. They had noticed that such dislocations in monetary conditions would have serious consequences in other areas. In his *Good and Bad Trade,* R. G. Hawtrey had observed that the importance of gaining a proper understanding of the effects of monetary fluctuations was "on account of their bearing on the unemployed problem" (1913, p. 3). In *Industrial Fluctuations,* Dennis Robertson (1911), a close collaborator of Keynes until their positions diverged in the early 1930s, had presented a similar case.

These considerations moved very rapidly from the realms of economic theory to the vocabulary of daily politics in the immediate post-War War I years, when Britain was faced with the hotly debated question of whether to return to the gold standard and, if so, at what parity. Only A. C. Pigou, Marshall's successor at Cambridge and economic adviser to successive Conservative governments, stuck fast to the old orthodoxy.[5] The important point is that the parameters of the debate had altered irreversibly. This was despite the fact that the orthodox theory was still at the base of the newer arguments and that, under Churchill's term at the Exchequer, the old orthodoxy won the day when Britain returned to the gold standard. Theoretical debate in economics, and practical debate about the desirability of a measure of collective action to improve economic stability, could no longer be conducted without Keynes's jibe, "in the long run we are all dead," sounding loudly in the background.

The ideas of Keynes and the social democrats in the 1920s are, thus, relatively easy to summarize. The creation of monetary stability was to be achieved through the management of the domestic currency using active monetary policies (intervention in money markets to achieve target levels for interest rates), and the free play of market forces within this more stable environment would be relied upon to secure material prosperity. There was also a role for intervention to reduce socially undesirable disparities in the distribution of income, though this was either a narrow or wide domain for government action depending on whether one spoke to the representatives of Liberal or Labour constituencies. The basic theme in economic theory and political philosophy of the time was that the market would work if it was free from the effects of disturbances that had their origin in the presence of institutional frictions and rigidities in the system.

When Keynes published the *General Theory* in 1936, he changed the whole basis of the economic argument favoring the management of economic affairs by the state. The theory of effective demand was designed to prove that the natural tendencies in an economic system acted generally to produce, not full employment as the earlier theory had argued, but (involuntary) unemployment (see 1936, p. 254). "If this is accepted," wrote Keynes, my "reasoning shows how 'wasteful' loan expenditure may nevertheless enrich the community on balance" (1936, pp. 128–29).

Economic Categories and Modern Political Discourse

The idea that the economy itself could and should be managed by governments, that the market mechanism did not operate to ensure full employment, is the completely new element added by Keynes to the vocabulary of social democracy in the 1930s. It differs dramatically from the already entrenched social democratic concern with social reform and equality. It differs also from the policy of a managed currency that Keynes and others had advocated in the 1920s as a means of securing a stable domestic and international monetary order within which private enterprise would operate to ensure optimal output. Collective action was now required not just (or even mainly) to balance considerations of economic efficiency with those of social justice and to promote monetary stability; it was also needed to determine the levels of annual production and resource utilization themselves. This was to be achieved through the management of investment and consumption by the state. Of course, this theoretical perspective was sufficiently broad to admit a variety of interpretations, ranging from those that held that economic management should be conducted indirectly, by setting taxes and interest rates and government expenditures to stimulate or dampen aggregate activity as the case required, to those who read into the *General Theory* the basis of a manifesto for more direct action along the lines of a thoroughgoing attempt at economic planning. While the tendency that prevailed in Europe in the post-World War II period was the former, we shall call it Keynesianism, the fact remains that the economic theory of effective demand introduced a whole new set of ideas and concerns into the political arena.

This new kind of economic management was put to the test in Britain with the experience of the war economy. Commencing with Kingsley Wood's budget of 1941, the economy was run on essentially Keynesian principles. Of course, the management of social production, of domestic spending and prices, and of national resource utilization under the exigencies of war were not exclusively a British problem; in the United States, Germany, Italy, and Japan, similar responsibilities for social and economic management were assumed by those governments. Indeed, in some cases, these duties had been taken on well before the war. Nevertheless, the opening sentence of the British government's White Paper of 1944, *Employment Policy,* heralded the most important change in the economic philosophy underlying British politics since the abolition of the Corn Laws nearly a century earlier: "the government accept as one of their primary aims and responsibilities the maintenance of a high and stable level of employment after the War." This philosophy set the parameters of political and economic discourse in Western Europe in the postwar period.

The strength of Keynesianism derived from three factors: first, the fact that the ideas, although powerful and new, were susceptible to expression in quasi-orthodox form; second, the experience of the 1930s and of wartime economic management discredited the notion that the organization of the economy could be left safely to the operation of free-market forces—economic management was on the political agenda; third, although an intensely theoretical book, the *General Theory* was composed in very practical terms, in categories that could be measured and that would become both the vocabulary of policy information and the substance of policy implementation.

The key issue in the debate that followed the publication of the *General Theory* was the degree to which Keynes's ideas were a special case of economic orthodoxy—expressed in vigorous and practical terms perhaps, but nonetheless not fundamentally hostile to the existing structure of economic ideas. The stumbling block was Keynes's insistence that there is, in a market economy, no tendency for the labor market to clear—that is, for there to be work available for all those seeking it at an equilibrium level of the wage.

The solution to this dilemma was to argue that Keynes's theory rested not on the denial of orthodox analysis but on the observation that the price mechanism might work imperfectly, that errors and rigidities introduced by the institutions of a modern economy and by the effects of uncertainty on decision making would prevent the supply-and-demand mechanism from guiding prices to their equilibrium levels. Keynes's theory then amounted to recognition of the importance of these practical qualifications to the orthodox story.

The presentation of Keynes's ideas as practical special cases of orthodox pre-Keynesian theory, arising because of the presence of certain imperfections, facilitated their widespread acceptance. Differences over the role of the state in the economy could be presented as arising either from disagreements over the empirical significance of policy measures or from political and social prejudices. The theory of social democracy had been strengthened, but classical liberalism had not thereby been rendered obsolete. Hence, the absorption of Keynes's analysis into orthodoxy both eased the acceptance of Keynesian policy and, by setting the intellectual foundations of orthodoxy in Keynesian aspic, preserved the ideas that today threaten Keynesianism.

The impact of Keynesian ideas on economic policy was not uniform throughout Europe. It was probably greatest in Britain, not just because Keynes was British but also because there was no strong tradition of economic management. In Germany, where the economic role of the state had always been greater than in Britain, the institutions for management and the rationale of management had already been established on quite different grounds. Economic management in Germany had, since the 1870s, been directed toward the structural transformation of the economy. Now, in the postwar era, a new structural transformation was necessary and traditional methods could be employed, so demand management of the Keynesian variety played only a limited role. The situation was similar in France, where the postwar planning apparatus was devoted to overcoming the constraints to the modernization of the French economy.

Yet in both cases, Keynesian methods formed a backdrop for enactment of structural reform, and Keynesian principles provided some of the vocabulary of the plot. The ubiquity of Keynesianism derived from the fact that the structure of national income accounting was based on Keynesian principles. And it was those accounting categories that established the terms by which economic performance was measured, discussed, and economic policy implemented.

Measurements of the national product, its size, composition, and distribution, had existed before the 1930s; early attempts at measurement may be found in the seventeenth century. The peculiarity of the national income accounting procedures devised by Richard Stone in the early days of the second world war, however, was in its categories explicitly derived from Keynesian theory. Each expenditure category included in the enumeration of national income was associated with employment. Hence, the national income as conventionally measured was not intended to estimate national well-being in a general sense. Activities that contribute to that well-being still are not associated with employment (such as services rendered within the family) and are not included.

The empirical strength of Keynesianism went beyond accounting, however. The fact that Keynesian categories are almost all measurable (in contrast to the key orthodox category of utility) stimulated statistical analyses of the economy, both by means of statistical inference and by the construction of empirical models capable of replicating the behavior of key economic variables—and thereby could be used to forecast their future scale and direction.

These empirical elements have left an indelible mark not only on economic debate but also on the social services in general. Yet they have not proved sufficient either to sustain a distinctively Keynesian economics or to form the basis of a broad social philosophy. Those tasks require a comprehensive body of theory. The decline of Keynesianism suggests that this comprehensive body is lacking.

The Decline of Keynesianism

The last quarter of the twentieth century witnessed a sharp decline both in Keynesian theorizing and in the use of Keynesian ideas in the formulation of economic policy. The orthodox propositions that had lived, cuckoo-like, in the Keynesian nest for the over fifty years had expelled their protectors. This decline of Keynesian thinking was due to both failings with Keynesian theory itself (failings that led to the accommodation of orthodox ideas rather than their elimination) and the failure of social democratic thinking to renew and strengthen itself. The theoretical failings can be rectified; it is the wider problems of social democracy that pose the greater difficulty.

Keynes's economic ideas could be only a small part of the broad intellectual foundations of social democracy. They provided the rationale for state intervention in economic management and some of the tools necessary to do the job effectively, but that was all. Social democracy also required an adaptive and adapting body of ideas that would provide the framework for policy across the entire range of social and economic issues. The strength of social democracy after the war derived from the fusion of the collective philosophy of the welfare state (a philosophy of redistribution) with Keynesian economic management.

In the early 1970s, the simultaneous appearance of economic difficulties that Keynesian management seemed to be incapable of resolving and a growing disenchantment with collective provision resulted in a sharp decline in the popularity of social democracy and the rise of the "new right" (more accurately, the resuscitation of the old social doctrines of laissez-faire). Orthodox economics was reestablished, in the form of monetarism, as the basis of policymaking, together with the (orthodox) economics of health, of the law, of housing, and so on. The new policy of removing collective provision in order to enhance choice and individual freedom fits well with the economic individualism of orthodox theory.

A major deficiency in social democracy has been the failure to modernize the proposition that individual freedom derives from collective provision, and to link that proposition to an analysis of the economic role of the state in the process of accumulation and modernization. The relative economic success of France and Germany, and the relative failure of the United Kingdom in the 1970s and 1980s, stemmed in large part from the failure of the United Kingdom to develop institutions that could guide and mold the process of accumulation in a market economy. The British eschewed the structural approach to economic policy, relying on the market to direct accumulation into appropriate paths—a task that the market, as an essentially short-run institution, is peculiarly ill-equipped to perform.

The essence of such a structural approach to economic management is to guide choice in the most economically and socially efficient direction without inhibiting more than is necessary the stimulus of market competition. If interventionist strategies are successful, the range of economic opportunity is widened *even though the range of actions open to the individual is restricted in the process*. In other words, without collective provision and with entirely "free" choice, the total range of opportunities may be identical to the set of choices open to the individual. With collective provision, the total set of opportunities is expanded but the set of choices open to the individual is no longer identical with it. The argument for collective provision rests on the proposition that, for the majority of individuals (it would not be credible to argue that this is true for all individuals), the choice set is greater in the second case. This proposition embodies the essential dilemma of collective provision, for even if collective provision is successful in the above sense, some individuals will still see it to be in their own best interests to foreswear collective provision if they desire (and can thereby attain) access to more existing resources. Social democracy, by its very nature, nurtures the cuckoo of liberalism.

Notes

This is a newly revised version of a paper that Murray Milgate and John Eatwell originally wrote for the History of European Ideas.

1. A recent study of the role of the French ideologues in the making of French liberalism in the first decades of the nineteenth century (Welch, 1984) establishes this point very clearly (see esp. pp. 70–96).

2. This contention is hardly novel. In his study of the *ancien régime* and the French Revolution, Alexis de Tocqueville noted: "Though the Economists figure less prominently than our philosophers in the histories of the period and perhaps did less than they in bringing about the Revolution, I am inclined to think that it is from their writings that we learn most of its true character" (1856/1972, p. 158).

3. As an example of the direct influence of economic history theory in this somewhat unlikely area, we note that, in a pamphlet published by the Kettering

Radical Association in 1839 (and signed by G. T. Green, "brushmaker" and J. A. Leatherland, "silkweaver"), the very first sentence from Smith's *Wealth of Nations* is quoted and invoked in support of the People's Charter, p.108).

4. It is not uninteresting to note that, at the end of the essay from which the remarks of Keynes quoted at the beginning of this section are taken, he left his audience with the question: "Am I a Liberal?"

5. This debate is examined in more detail in Milgate (1983).

18

The Gold Standard and Monetary Theory

It is somewhat strange to find that, in the voluminous secondary literature given over to the study of the activities of economists in Cambridge during the interwar period, little attention has been devoted to the exchanges of comment and criticism that passed between Keynes and Pigou, both on practical matters of economic policy and on the theory of money and the theory of employment. The apparent neglect of this material is all the more perplexing, given that it encapsulates in miniature, so to speak, many of the more important issues that were at stake in Keynes's challenge to what he dubbed the classical theory of money and employment. Indeed, since according to Keynes, Pigou was the chief representative of that very school of thought,[1] the comment and criticism directed by each toward the work of the other warrants serious attention.

Although the material that forms the basis of the analysis of the debates between Keynes and Pigou took different forms,[2] the controversy between them in the interwar years may conveniently be divided into four stages. The first stage covers the period leading up to and immediately following Britain's return to the gold standard in 1925. The second stage covers the period of the *Treatise on Money*. The third and fourth stages overlap—the former relates to Keynes's reactions to Pigou's *Theory of Unemployment*, the latter to Pigou's reactions to the *General Theory*. The purpose here to examine the first two stages the better to highlight the issues at stake in the debates by which they were characterized.

It will be appreciated that such an investigation is of interest from more than a purely historical point of view. There appears to exist today a climate of opinion favoring an interpretation of these first two stages that shows Keynes's position closely resembling that which he subsequently took in the *General Theory;* and how useful that position might prove to be in constructing a thoroughgoing critique of modern revivals of pre-Keynesian ideas. But it will be argued here that, as far as these first two stages are concerned, there was never any ultimate theoretical principle at stake in the Keynes-Pigou debates, nor was Keynes at that time developing an alternative theoretical framework to the old-fashioned quantity theory of money—even though he was to advocate markedly different policy measures from those suggested by Pigou. I do not claim that same conclusion can be applied to the last of the two stages mentioned above; these stages are another matter entirely.

The Gold Standard

Although by far the most important disputes that were to arise between Keynes and Pigou were those subsequent to publication of the *Treatise on Money*, there are some earlier matters on which Keynes and Pigou took differing positions, and these are of interest inasmuch as they highlight the changes that occurred in Keynes's later position with the publication of the *General Theory.*

One of these matters relates to the *First Interim Report on Currency and Foreign Exchanges After the War* of 1918 (*Cmnd.* 9182), otherwise known as the Cunliffe Report; and the *Report of the Committee on the Currency and the Bank of England Note Issues* of 1925 (*Cmnd.* 2392). Students of Keynes's work will be aware that, in the June number of the *Economic Journal* for 1925, Keynes reviewed the latter document, describing it as "indolent and jejune" (Keynes, 1973, 19:378) and charging its members with a lack of "intellectual interest in their subject" (p. 372). They will also be aware that the Cuncliffe Report itself provided the blueprint for Britain's return to the gold standard in 1925 at the prewar parity—an act that Keynes was to describe as a "crazy policy" (p. 263). Indeed, writing in *The Nation and Athenaeum* in July 1923, Keynes described the Cunliffe doctrine as "narrow and obsolete" (1973, 19:103), since the report did not contain "a single reference to stability of prices and employment" (p.100). The members of the Cunliffe Committee dwelt, according to Keynes, in an "imaginary academic world" (1973, 9:213).

Chief among the academic members of the Cunliffe Committee was Pigou. In fact, Pigou was not only a member of that committee (set up in 1918) but also the only academic economist on the Chamberlain-Bradbury Committee (set up in 1924), which produced the second of the two reports mentioned in the preceding paragraph. It was the report of this committee in 1925, reinforcing in a more positive and optimistic tone the conclusions of the Cunliffe Report, upon which then-Chancellor of the Exchequer Winston Churchill based the decision to return to the gold standard at the prewar parity.[3]

The arguments of the Cunliffe Committee, and those of the Chamberlain-Bradbury Committee, were based on a fairly straightforward application of the quantity theory of money. Given that it was the presumption of both committees that the prewar parity was in some sense the right one (see, for example, Moggridge, 1972, p. 18, 230–31); given also that the possibility of shifting to a pure paper currency was rejected; and given, finally, the conviction that prices and costs had risen in Britain relative to the rest of the world (and, in particular, relative to those in the United States), the traditional quantity-theory doctrine suggested only one monetary policy option: a deflation of domestic costs and prices to restore internal and external balance at the prewar parity. This would be achieved by raising Bank Rate and reducing money wages. Pigou's assessment ran entirely along these lines:

> It is obvious that ultimately unless we are prepared to loose all our gold and go upon a pure paper currency, discount rates here will have to be raised sufficiently to stop the tendency of gold to be drained abroad. The raising of discount rates required for this purpose will involve a contraction of credits [and] a fall of prices...and equilibrium will be established with a discount rate and a level of prices more or less equivalent to the world gold level. (1918–19, pp. 98–99, italics omitted)

Of course, no one was unmindful of the upheavals such a policy would produce in the domestic economy. Indeed, an awareness of these problems, especially in the immediate postwar years, partly explains why the Cunliffe Report remained uncommitted on the matter of how quickly the return to gold should be effected. Pigou himself recommended caution: "It is arguable," he reported to the Cunliffe Committee, "that the present policy of postponing the return to equilibrium should be continued for some little time after the war ends" (1918–19, pp. 98–99). As

Hawtrey later observed, "[t]o start peace time with a trade depression seemed an appalling prospect" (1930, p. 407).

By the time Pigou began working on the drafts of the report for the Chamberlain-Bradbury Committee in 1924, however, his initial caution had lapsed somewhat. As Moggridge has pointed out, although Pigou's draft report argued that there was no "immediate and pressing urgency" for a return to gold, his covering letter to that same draft stated that he was "only just on balance in favour of a 'wait and see' policy" (Pigou, quoted in Moggridge, 1972, pp. 48, 49). On two occasions subsequently, Pigou restated this position. In his evidence before the Macmillan Committee, Pigou reported that the argument in 1924–25 for an immediate return to gold was this: "You have to take the plunge, the water is not terribly cold now; it is a gamble whether it will be colder later on. Get it over" (Pigou, 1931a, p. 54). In a similar vein, Pigou wrote in 1947 that "the mistake of the British authorities, if it was a mistake, was not one of technical analysis but one of broad policy...[o]nce that decision [to return to gold at the pre-war parity] was taken...to allow the monetary slump to become profound, in spite of the damage thereby done to industry and employment, was a necessary means to accepted end" (Pigou, 1947, p. 197).

In contrast, Keynes felt the plunge to be entirely unnecessary. His alternative position consisted essentially of two dimensions—both of which were in opposition to the Cunliffe doctrine and to the practical policy measure of returning to gold in 1925. However, in neither case was there any fundamental nor general theoretical doctrine at stake.

In the first place, Keynes suggested a markedly different policy to that recommended by the Cunliffe Committee and subsequently enacted in 1925. This was the proposal for the management of the supply of the currency in an effort to secure stability in the domestic price level and, therefore, according to the quantity theory of money upon which Keynes grounded his argument,[4] prosperity and full employment. For Keynes the argument was obvious: "Currency reform has two objects: to remedy the credit cycle and to mitigate unemployment...and to link the monetary standard to what matters, namely, the value of staple articles of consumption, instead of to an object of oriental splendour" (1973, 19:167).

These ideas, expressed in *The Nation and Athenaeum* in February 1924, were no more than a repetition of the proposals that Keynes advanced in the *Tract on Monetary Reform* only a few months earlier, where he had insisted that "a sound constructive scheme must provide...[a] method of regulating the supply of currency and credit with a view to maintaining... the stability of the internal price level" (1973, 4:141).

This proposal had implications for foreign-exchange policy that departed from the Cunliffe position. In essence, apart from exchange controls designed to minimize seasonal and other temporary fluctuations in the external value of the currency (1973, 4:141), Keynes's alternative policy amounted to a freely fluctuating exchange-rate regime where the external value of the currency was allowed to find its own level (p. 126). Indeed, Keynes reported to the Chamberlain-Bradbury Committee that exchange-rate fluctuation was to be preferred over instituting the deliberate policy of deflation that exchange-rate stability at the prewar parity would require (see Keynes, 1973, 19:259).

It is interesting to note that, while the exact level of the sterling–dollar parity was not especially relevant under Keynes's proposal, on more than one occasion Keynes suggested that under his scheme, overseas inflation, especially in the United States, might be such as to establish an exchange rate not very far removed from that which existed before the First World War (see Keynes, 1973, 19:213, 214). It may be that these arguments, based on little other than intuition, were designed to win over those who, as Keynes put it, "for reasons of national pride," had supported the restoration of the prewar parity. Of course, these arguments have no theoretical basis and are not essential to the case for a managed currency. Nor, it seems, were they particularly successful in convincing the audience to which they were directed.

As to the theoretical basis for each of the alternative policies under discussion, little need be said. It is perfectly apparent that both views derive from the same theoretical framework—that provided by the quantity theory of money. Thus, in defending his proposal at a League of Nations–sponsored conference in 1924 (against criticism from Edwin Cannan), Keynes argued that those who dispute altogether "the relation between the volumes of purchasing power and the level of prices will be impressed no more by [my proposal]... than by any other argument on the subject of money... [b]ut those who agree on the fundamentals of monetary theory with Professor Cannan and myself... can hardly doubt... that contracting and expanding the... volume of purchasing power... must have its effect on prices" (Keynes, 1973, 19:191). It is necessary, therefore, to look to matters other than pure theory to unearth the grounds upon which Keynes launched his critique of the Cunliffe proposals.

This brings us to the other dimension of Keynes's opposition to that position. Parallel to his proposal for securing price stability, Keynes launched a series of attacks directed at the practical effects likely to follow from a return to gold at the prewar parity. Starting from the premise (which Keynes's acceptance of the quantity theory enforced) that, in the long run, both policies would ensure equilibrium,[5] Keynes argued that the short-run consequences of the measures to be carried through in order to restore the prewar parity would be disastrous in their consequences for domestic activity and employment over that short run. Like Pigou, Keynes agreed that the Cunliffe proposal required a deflation of domestic costs and prices, and that "once you have reached your equilibrium it is all over" (19:64–65).[6] However, since it was nevertheless the case that during the period of adjustment toward this final equilibrium there would be a "deliberate intensification of unemployment," (19:218), Keynes held that the Cunliffe policy was one "from which any humane or judicious person must shrink" (p. 218). He castigated the members of what he called the "gold party" for believing, quite incorrectly as it was to transpire, that such adjustments would occur relatively swiftly and harmlessly (see, for example, Keynes, 1973, 9: 214–18, 224; 19: 64–65, 67). Furthermore, Keynes maintained that even were the policy to be carried through to that final equilibrium, it would leave "much injustice behind it on account of the inequality of the changes it will effect, the stronger groups gaining at the expense of the weaker" (9:224).

Keynes did not leave it at that. In addition to outlining the rather harsh practical realities of any deflation policy, he was swift to point out that, even according to the conventional wisdom of the quantity theory, such a policy was best able to check an "incipient boom." It was not a remedy for depression—at least insofar as any reduction in wages that it might ultimately entail would have first to be engineering by increasing unemployment. That is, it was a policy to aggravate a depression (9:220). And if current economic conditions indicated that depression of trade rather than incipient boom was under way, which Keynes felt to be the case in 1924, then any negative effects of transitional adjustment to a gold standard at the prewar parity would be greatly intensified.

In perhaps a final effort to forestall what must have seemed by 1924 to be inevitable, Keynes mustered a further argument against the Cunliffe proposal. Since that proposal required for its success an all-round reduction in money wages, what would happen if money wages were sticky, in the sense that workers (and more particularly trade unions) resisted any move toward a reduction in their earnings? (Keynes, 1973, 19:393, 423, 426). To Keynes, the answer was clear. In such a situation the consequence of any attempt to reduce wages would be increased industrial disputes (strikes and lockouts) and the social disruption and injustice with which these are inevitably associated. In *The Economics Consequences of Mr Churchill,* this argument is summed up as follows: "No section of labour will readily accept lower wages merely in response to sentimental speeches... [w]e are depending for the reduction of wages on the pressure of unemployment and of strikes and lock-outs" (1973, 9:220).

Indeed, so resolute might be worker resistance to money-wage cuts that Keynes felt that it could prove to be "politically impossible" (1973, 19:246) to carry through the required measures in any case. Nowhere are these opinions better captured than in Keynes's evidence (delivered verbally) before the Chamberlain-Bradbury Committee in 1924: "I believe that deflation... is contrary to the public interest, and I go further than that and I say that even if it were desirable, deflation at a rapid rate would probably prove socially and politically impossible in the present conditions" (p.242). Pigou, a member of this committee, was absent from this session of its deliberations.

At the heart of the difference between Keynes and Pigou on the recommendations of the Cunliffe Report and their subsequent enactment in 1925 lies no matter upon which there could be said to have been ultimate theoretical principle at stake. Unlike the differences that were to separate the two in their debates in the 1930s, on this particular matter the difference was one of emphasis and not one of analysis. This point is of vital importance. To understand it properly, it is necessary only to realize that it was the traditional theory of money that provided the two alternatives under discussion.

That theory of money suggested two possible policies. On the one hand, the authorities could act to fix the exchange rate (as in the case of a gold-standard system) and allow the domestic price level to adjust to an equilibrium relative to overseas prices via periodic expansions and contractions of domestic activity. Any departure of the domestic price level from its equilibrium position at the given (and fixed) exchange rate would require alterations in domestic interest rates (to curtail inflows and outflows of gold) and an alteration of money-wage rate. These alterations would be accompanied by upswings and downswings in domestic activity and employment (see, for example, Hawtrey, 1927, pp. 83–84; and Pigou, 1933, pp. 215–22). On the other hand, it was though still entirely within the framework of the quantity theory of money, the authorities could act to secure domestic price stability (say, through management of the supply of money or, as Keynes was to propose subsequently in the

Treatise on Money, through Bank Rate policy) and leave the exchange rate to find its own level (see Hawtrey, 1927, pp. 102–06).[7]

Pigou quite clearly had chosen hesitantly the first alternative—though he was not unaware of the short-period dislocation to industry that this would entail. Furthermore, Keynes's opposition to the general thrust of the Cunliffe Report, as well to the 1925 decision, can also be summed up in terms of these two alternatives. Initially, he had argued for the second of the two, offering as sop to the advocates of the return to gold the possibility that U.S. inflation might act on its own to return the pound to its prewar parity against the dollar, in any case. Subsequently, when matters came to a head in 1924 and 1925, and the Bank of England and the UK Treasury seemed to be proceeding apace with the first option, Keynes chose a more direct attack: the prewar parity was too high in current circumstances, the extent of the domestic contraction required to sustain it was socially and politically unacceptable (especially given that unemployment in Britain was already high), and workers would not, in any case, acquiesce to the cut in money-wages that it required.

If there was a difference between Keynes and Pigou here, it was a difference in emphasis on the importance of these short-period problems. Keynes was really saying no more than he had said in the *Tract on Monetary Reform*, when he had observed that "economists set themselves too easy, too useless a task if in tempestuous seasons they can only tell us that when the storm is past the ocean is flat again" (1973, 4:65). An impression of just how orthodox was the argument that the required fall in money wages might not come about (which Keynes had mustered in *The Economic Consequences of Mr. Churchill*) can be gained by comparing it with remarks that Keynes was later to make in the *General Theory*: "[a] classical economist may sympathise with labour in refusing to accept a cut in its money-wage, and he will admit that it may not be wise to make it to meet conditions which are temporary; but scientific integrity forces him to declare that this refusal is, nevertheless, at the bottom of the trouble" (1973, 7:16). This description of a classical economist fits Keynes in 1926 very well.[8]

There is one final point relating to this episode that deserves to be mentioned. It concerns the attitudes taken by Keynes and Pigou, respectively, toward the role of the economist as economic adviser. These attitudes are clearly revealed in Keynes's arduous questioning of Pigou before the Macmillan Committee about the return to the gold standard. It is apparent that Pigou seemed to have felt that the adviser's role was to operate within the constraints of the policy options suggested by the politicians. Thus, for Pigou, the question upon which he had to report was: "Are we to go back to gold now, or are we to go back to gold later? (Pigou, 1931a, p. 54). This was despite the fact that, at least according to his remarks before the Macmillan Committee, he had been "a stabiliser long before" (p. 54)—that is, despite the fact that as an economist he did not (at least according to these statements in 1930) support any return to gold at all. This perhaps helps explain Pigou's claim, quoted earlier, that the error of 1925 was one of broad policy, not one of the quality of expert advice.

Not surprisingly, Keynes was startled by this position. In reply to the abovementioned remarks (after checking with Pigou that there was nothing in the terms of reference of the Chamberlain-Bradbury Committee thus restricting its deliberations), Keynes asked pointedly: "Was it not for the expert economic advisers to say what should be done and leave to the politicians to say whether they would do it?" (Keynes, 1931, p. 54). Taking this view, it is easy to see why Keynes laid the blame for the 1925 decision squarely on the shoulders of the expert economic advisers.

Pigou on the *Treatise on Money*

On Pigou's reaction to Keynes's *Treatise on Money,* there is little to say. In his published work, Pigou referred to the *Treatise* only infrequently—and even then, mainly on practical matters rather than on matters of theory.[9] However, we do know that Pigou read and commented on the proofs of the *Treatise* (see Keynes, 1973, 13:138) and that he reviewed the book for *The Nation and Athenaeum* in January 1831.

Unfortunately, of the exchange between Keynes and Pigou over the proofs of the *Treatise,* only a few fragments survive (see Keynes, 1973, 13:214–18; 29: 4–6). The single fact worth noting about the contents of this material is that Pigou explicitly pointed out in his comments in the autumn of 1929 that the *Treatise* analysis (using the Fundamental Equations) of the effects of a discrepancy between planned saving and planned investment involved a presumption of unchanging output (see 29:5). It is also clear that Keynes had seen these comments before sending the revised proofs back to the printer.[10] This point deserves mention if only because commentators on this period have previously attributed this discovery of a fixed output assumption either to Hawtrey or to the famous Cambridge Circus, and they have dated Keynes's recognition of the fact to the period immediately after the publication of the *Treatise on Money* (see Moggridge, 1980, pp. 92–93). On the evidence available, this judgment seems to require revision.

Pigou's letter to Keynes ran as follows: "[D]oes what you argue imply... that changes in Bank rate cannot affect E [real income] or O [output]. I don't see why they shouldn't... Anyway ought there not to be some argument to show that E/O stands unaffected? What happens if O alters?" (Keynes, 1973, 29:5). It is very interesting, especially in light of all the publicity that has been given to the supposed crucial importance of this discovery in liberating Keynes from classical modes of thought (see Milgate, 1983) to find that Pigou—Keynes's archetype of the classical economist— did not see any reason variations in the level of output should not be taken into account. But this is as it should be, since orthodox classical economists found no difficulty in allowing for output changes in a disequilibrium process as long as it was maintained that, in the long run, variations in the rate of interest (whether they ensued naturally or had to be induced by conscious acts of monetary policy) were required to restore an equilibrium between full-employment saving and planned investment whenever the two were unequal. Just how traditional this idea was is illustrated by the fact that all the participants in the debate over the gold standard took such output changes into account. Indeed, it has already been shown that it was the probably magnitude of this effect that formed the very basis of Keynes's own objections to the decision to return to gold in 1925, and also accounted for Pigou's caution over the timing of such a return in 1918.

In his review of the *Treatise on Money* (1931b), Pigou concedes the work to be important and "a great advance on anything that has been accomplished hitherto" (p. 544). Yet Pigou only partly subscribes to Keynes's claim that the use of the Fundamental Equations is an advance over the old-fashioned quantity theory equations for the problem of studying the short-period or disequilibrium behavior of the system. For while Pigou does state that their use in the account of the modus operandi of Bank Rate is "much superior... to previous discussions" (1931b, p. 544), he goes on to claim that "the relation of falling prices to industrial activity can be studied more effectively on the lines made more familiar by Professor Irving Fisher than those that... are followed by Mr Keynes" (p. 544). Since, however, Keynes had himself conceded in the *Treatise* that his Fundamental Equations were really no more than an adaptation of the familiar quantity theory equations (Keynes, 1973, 5:120, 135) designed to give a better account of the "causal process by which the price is determined, and the method of transition from one position of equilibrium to another" (p.120), it would seem best to interpret the difference between Keynes and Pigou on this matter as being one related to the manner of development of the same theory.

There is one further aspect of Pigou's review of the *Treatise* that should be recorded; for it was to become a characteristic feature of Pigou's criticism of Keynes after the publication of the *General Theory*. Pigou was uneasy, perhaps even offended, by Keynes's propensity to deprecate the work of others in a manner that made his own contribution seem far superior to anything that had gone before. It is quite clear, for example, that Pigou was most displeased when the earlier writer in question was Marshall. An indication of just how vexed Pigou could become over Keynes's style of controversy is to be seen in the very first paragraph of his review:

> There is too much carping at "current economic theory"—whatever precisely that may be; too much adverse comment on classes of persons...and so on, names not specified; too many naively patronising remarks. It was, perhaps, a fault of Marshall that he discovered more truth in the writing of others than was in fact there, and unduly depreciated his own contributions. There is no fault of that kind in Mr Keynes. (1931b, p. 544)

Notes

This chapter was written by Murray Milgate and appeared originally in *Contributions to Political Economy*.

1. Thus, in writing to Gottfried Haberler in April 1938, Keynes remarked that Pigou "was certainly a classical economist up to last year; though whether he still is today would not be quite easy to say" (1973, 29:270). In his unsigned review of Haberler's "Prosperity and Depression" for the *Economic Journal* of September 1939, Keynes challenged Harberler's assertion to the contrary with the observation that "this part of the discussion is rather lacking...in precise references" (p. 275). This provides clear evidence (if any more were needed beyond the first footnote of the *General Theory*) of Keynes's assessment of Pigou's position.

2. For example, there are direct criticisms, of which Keynes's attack on Pigou's *Theory of Unemployment* in the *General Theory* and Pigou's review of the latter book for *Economica* are two cases in point. Then there are what might be called indirect criticisms, where both authors contributed to a matter of theory or to a topic of contemporary debate and took opposing positions. For both men, such contributions often were little more than thinly disguised attacks on the views of the other. Finally, there are exchanges of correspondence either directly between the two or with a third party.

3. An indication of the extent to which economists in Cambridge held Pigou responsible for the return to gold is captured in the following remarks

of Joan Robinson: "It was an eminent economist [Pigou] who persuaded the authorities that restoring the mere mechanism of the gold standard would restore the harmonious international financial relations in which it had been able to operate" (1951–73, 4:3).

4. The quantity theory basis of the argument is well-known (see, for example, Keynes, 1973, 4:37; 19:191, where Keynes states explicitly his general agreement with this theory).

5. The likelihood of the continued stability of this final equilibrium was also a matter for debate. Keynes was insistent that the Cunliffe proposal would be inherently unstable (see, for example, Keynes, 1973, 19:388) and so unlikely to secure that degree of domestic price stability (and therefore that degree of domestic prosperity) that his own proposal would ensure (see, for example, 4:125–40; 19:106).

6. Thus, Keynes writes: "when the process was complete we should each of us have nearly the same real income as before" (1973, 9:213).

7. The policy would not only establish monetary stability but also facilitate the maintenance of full employment. This is just a consequence of the orthodox belief that in the absence of frictions and rigidities (such as, in this instance, monetary disturbances) the real forces of demand and supply will act automatically to restore equilibrium and so full employment. A clear exposition of this argument can be found in Friedman (1953, p. 157 et seq.).

8. It is interesting to compare Keynes's 1926 arguments on this issue with an analysis of the same question by Joan Robinson (1951–73, 1:184–86), an article written with *General Theory* arguments in mind. In that article, the question was not whether money wages would fall or not but, rather, whether this fall could increase employment as the "classical" doctrine (and Keynes in 1926) presumed. In this light, it is somewhat perplexing to find arguments taken from *Economic Consequences of Mr. Churchill* being used by some Keynesians in an attempt to challenge the contemporary revival of pre-Keynesian doctrines at a theoretical level. In fact, no such theoretical challenge is contained in that pamphlet.

9. Thus, in the *Theory of Unemployment* (Pigou, 1933), there are only three references to the *Treatise on Money* (p. 82; pp. 196–97; see also Pigou, 1941/1949, p. 206, n. 1.). In the *Economics of Welfare,* there is only one reference, and that is to the index number problem (1952, pp. 67–68). In *Aspects of British Economic History,* the only references are to the more applied second volume (1947, p. 163, n; p. 180, n).

10. See the editorial comments in Keynes, 1973, 29:4 to this effect.

19

The Economic Possibilities of Capitalism

John Maynard Keynes and Joseph Schumpeter were in many ways the most influential academic economists of the twentieth century. During what is customarily regarded as a crucial period of innovation, criticism, and transition in economic theory, each of the discipline's two great centers of teaching in the English-speaking world, Cambridge and Harvard, was dominated by a single and powerful intellectual influence. They were both engaged in an attempt to bring the contributions of the masters of late nineteenth-century economic theory up to date so as to arrive at a better understanding of the conditions that industrialized market economies were beginning to encounter.

Although Keynes was rather more critical of his own theoretical upbringing than was Schumpeter,[1] in one key way they took up strikingly similar positions with respect to their predecessors. Each seems to have been driven by a desire to qualify, with a degree of realism previously neglected in orthodox circles, the rather too optimistic conclusions they felt earlier theorists had drawn concerning the probable futurity and long-run efficacy of the system of free-market capitalism. This involved them in a project of reform and revision that was carried forward on two fronts—in theoretical writings, and in social and political criticism—and this feature brings out a connection between the two of some importance. Keynes and Schumpeter occupy prominent positions in the history of that broad tendency that emerged in the first half of the twentieth century that was to culminate in the replacement of nineteenth-century liberalism with twentieth-century social democracy.

In considering the similarities and differences in the roles each played in this transformation, we will be occupied with three questions from economic analysis proper and two from social philosophy, so to speak. Into the first category enter the economists' conceptualizations of the economic tendencies of modern industrial societies and the means through which to analyze them; their studies of the relationship between the monetary conditions of modern capitalism and the real activity that it is capable of generating (that is, the connection between the monetary mechanism and long-run economic performance); and their visions of the role of private investment in economic progress. Into the second category enters the question of the scope for collective action in modern industrial society vis-à-vis the role of individual initiative, and the rather more complicated matter of the economic and cultural potentialities of capitalism and socialism.

The Economic Machine

Schumpeter often claimed that any comprehensive economic analysis would be found to be composed of two closely related yet distinct dimensions. He called them "vision" and "theory" (or, sometimes, "technique"), and these dimensions corresponded roughly to the creative (or intuitive) and analytical elements of an argument. Keynes's vision of the modern world, or so Schumpeter claimed, was a vision of stagnation (1951b, p. 268); his own might justifiably be called a vision of resigned acceptance of the prospect of a future of "specialists without spirit." But no matter how one might characterize the social vision behind each man's argument, those visions are undeniably different; there will be cause to return to them later.

However, Keynes and Schumpeter are a little less at odds with each other in one particular aspect of their "technique of theorizing":— the view that economic relationships in market societies form an interconnected *system*. In this respect, Keynes and Schumpeter were following a path mapped out by the physiocrats and Adam Smith. Like them, they took the view that the economy was a law-governed process, characterized by the presence of systematic and persistent forces, or uniformities, that if unimpeded in their operation would tend to produce determinate outcomes. The whole of Schumpeter's theory of economic growth, and of Keynes's theory of effective demand, is premised on this simple idea. As Schumpeter once said of Cantillon, the problems dealt with are "permeated by uniform principles" (1912, p. 29).

The familiar eighteenth-century analogy that captured the idea that economic processes were law governed, that the market is like a machine, appeared in Schumpeter's *Theory of Economic Development* as a metaphor for the process of economic life (1926, p. 5). In his *Capitalism, Socialism and Democracy,* the related phrase "the capitalist engine" is used repeatedly. Indeed, Schumpeter was fond of speaking of "the mechanism of economic life" that "it is the task of economic theory to explain" (1951a, p. 62). The original metaphor of the economic machine was invoked by Keynes in the *General Theory* as a description of the adjustment process set in motion in the face of a change in long-period conditions (1936, p. 50).

This analogy is the vehicle on which is transmitted something more than just an opinion about the nature of economic relations. It serves also to legitimize and to propagate a particular way of conducting economic inquiry—what is often called the "scientific" or "abstract" approach to economic analysis. If the economy is a vast interconnected system, then it is amendable to "systematic" analysis in the sense in which that idea is used by methodologists. Thus, for example, one finds Keynes advocating the methodological premise that "the object of our analysis is... to provide ourselves with an organised and orderly method of thinking out particular problems" (1936, p. 297).

Of course, the way the economic machine actually worked, and the kinds of results it had a tendency to produce, differed between the two writers. Yet neither subscribed to the notion (which has its origin in the work of those for whom the twin ideas of system and law governed meant "natural" and "good") that the economic machine was likely to generate an order that was essentially sustainable or optimal. It is always possible, Schumpeter claimed, to separate scientific analysis from arguments to the effect that the results of that analysis represented the best possible order of things (1912, p. 47). Although it is quite clear that if a balance sheet of capitalism's achievements were to be drawn up Schumpeter's books would contain rather more credits than those of Keynes, it would not be on account of the presence of any idea of "natural" or "spontaneous" order in the work of Schumpeter; a fact which has escaped the attention of certain neo-Austrian theorists.

Of equal significance is the rejection by Keynes and Schumpeter of the idea of a smoothly functioning economic machine, this not only at any given point in time a possibility admitted by earlier theorists under the heading "frictions" and "rigidities" or market imperfections—but also over time. In this sense, their views bear a family resemblance to those of Marx. But this "instability of capitalism," to borrow the title given by Schumpeter to the first appearance in English of his theory of economic development, in the pages of the *Economic Journal* for 1928, needs to be understood rather precisely, since it means quite different things in each case.

For Schumpeter, instability has a double character: in the first sense, it is endogenous; in the second, it an engine of prosperity.[2] The formal argument is straightforward. Whenever a disturbance of equilibrium occurs, establishing the prospect of windfall profits in certain industries, a process of creative destruction is set in motion (provided the financial system backs those heroic entrepreneurs, of whom more will be said later) that "alters and displaces the equilibrium state previously existing" (1926, p. 64). From the present point of view, this last factor is the key: the disequilibrium-adjustment process is itself capable of altering the underlying position toward which the economic system is adjusting. Were it not for this factor, the process would be no more than that which occurs whenever "one of the many classes of friction" is brought into account (1951a, p. 66). This is the essential novelty of the Schumpeterian conception of the operation of the economic machine: "economic life changes... partly because of changes in the data, to which it tends to adapt itself. But... there is another... kind of change arising from *within the system which so displaces its equilibrium point that the new one cannot be reached from the old one by infinitesimal steps*" (1926, p. 64, n, italics in original).

Schumpeterian instability, then, does not refer to the familiar problems with proving the stability of competitive equilibrium in, say, the Walrasian model (see, for example, 1939, p. 47; 1951a, pp. 50–51)—indeed, Schumpeter seems to have felt that Walrasian equilibrium was likely to be rather more "stable" (in the familiar meaning of *stability*) than many contemporary theorists would be prepared to admit. Nor is Schumpetarian instability an issue of maladjustment in the short period owing to frictions, like the stickiness or rigidity of prices, the presence of lags, or the existence of uncertain expectations (1939, pp. 49–56). To borrow Schumpeter's rather Durkheimian terminology, instability is an economic fact *sui generis*.

A correct understanding of this point should not be thought to imply any inconsistency between it and another important element of Schumpeter's argument: that "the instabilities which arise from the process of innovation tend to right themselves and do not go on accumulating" (1951a, p. 70). This argument simply holds that the instability consequent upon Schumpeter's "gale of creative destruction," while a perennial feature of the operation of the capitalist system, is not in itself a threat to the institutional existence of capitalism: "there is, though instability of the *system*, no economic instability of the *order*" (1951a, p. 70, italics added). We shall defer consideration of the prospects for the institutional survival of the capitalist order until later, when we turn to Schumpeter's social and political philosophy.

It is worth emphasizing, too, that the process of creative destruction is one of competition, selection, and evolution. However, this competition operates not just in the traditional Walrasian sphere of prices but in the sphere of innovation, as well. Thus, the usual picture of the process of selection under competitive conditions that the pure price-competition model suggests—that firms rise and fall depending on their ability to pursue profit-maximizing/cost-minimizing strategies effectively—is supplemented with a condition requiring successful innovation and adoption of new technologies. According to Schumpeter, this provides a more accurate description of "the situations we actually observe in surveying capitalist evolution" (1939, p. 96):

> In a society with private property and competition, this process is the necessary complement of the continual emergence of new economic and social forms and of continually rising real incomes of all social strata.... These changes are theoretically and practically, economically and culturally, much more important than the economic stability upon which all analytical attention has been concentrated for so long. (1926, p. 255)

This theme of the evolutionary character of capitalist development, which runs throughout the argument, colors Schumpeter's view of the nature of progress in economic life. In this framework, it is hardly surprising that Schumpeter's view of the historical record of capitalism should have led him to the opinion that the "past social costs of capitalist achievement"—he mentions child labor, sixteen-hour work days, and the like— "are not necessarily relevant to the balance of alternatives for the future' (1942, p. 70). Nor is it remarkable that he should have been so taken with the complex pattern of capitalist development that emerges from the simultaneous operation of Kitchin, Juglar, Kuznets, and Kondratieff cycles.

Yet there remains a certain ambiguity in Schumpeter's conceptual apparatus that seems to compromise his own view of the formal connection between his work and that of his predecessors. The argument sets out from a quite traditional analytical conception: one takes certain data (in Schumpeter's case, the data of Walrasian theory—endowments, preferences, and technology), and from this derives the equilibrium configuration of the system. The idea behind this procedure is that, compared to the dependent variables that these data are used to determine (relative prices, the distribution of income, the structure, and level of output, and so on), the forces that act to determine the data are both more slowly moving and exogenous. In the Walras-Pareto conception, the data are actually determined by noneconomic factors (thus giving rise to the charge of reductionism sometimes leveled against it in certain circles). Another way of putting it is to say that the process that determines equilibrium is separate from the processes that determine the data themselves.

But Schumpeter jettisoned this last idea, arguing instead that the process of equilibration will itself change the data. The problem is that, if this possibility is admitted, then the data no longer meet the requirements set for them in the Walras-Pareto conception— that is, it is no longer admissible to classify them as being either more slow to change or exogenously determined. A theorist is certainly free to do this—to construct a kind of closed-loop theory—but it is hardly appropriate that he continue to consider this an extension of earlier analysis, as Schumpeter seems to have done. The idea that "there is no difficulty in inserting all this" (1951a, p. 69) into the traditional method of analysis seems problematic.

The problem can be put in another way. To the extent that Schumpeter's argument models the process of economic change as one where actual conditions are constantly chasing a shifting theoretical norm, then a difficulty arises if changes in the theoretical norm are induced by the chase-process itself (a proposition Schumpeter also maintains). For, then, the theoretical norm is deprived of its analytical content and status, and it takes on the character of a will-o'-the-wisp.

The position that Keynes took on the question of the operation of the economic machine can be understood with the aid of the familiar analytical framework whose application in Schumpeter's hands we have just been examining. Keynes called into question the orthodox idea that the economic machine was essentially a smoothly functioning device, with the simple-sounding claim that market society "seems capable of remaining in a chronic condition of sub-normal activity for a considerable period without any marked tendency ... towards recovery" (Keynes, 1936, p. 249). But just what it is that Keynes might have meant by this, and how his argument stands in relation to that of Schumpeter, is a rather more complicated (and controversial) matter.

One line of argument, perhaps the dominant opinion in the profession today, holds that the Keynesian problem of effective demand (and, consequently, of unemployment) arises owing to the presence of certain frictions and rigidities (of formidable proportions) that inhibit the smooth operation of the economic machine. There are many species of argument that fall into this genus. Some attribute the problem of unemployment to sticky prices (often a downward rigidity in money wages); others attribute it to institutional factors (sometimes the monetary system is called into play; on other occasions it is monopolistic price setting); and yet others hold it to be attributable to the manner in which uncertainty holds the forces of demand and supply at bay. These are the "obstacles to full employment" readings of the *General Theory*, and we have referred to them elsewhere as imperfectionist theories of unemployment.

These readings seem to have a firmer basis in Keynes's pre-*General theory* arguments than in the *General Theory*. For example, the popular imperfectionist view that the forces of demand and supply might be held at bay by the effects of uncertainty and disappointed expectations is prominent in Keynes's 1926 essay on the "End of Laissez-faire": "[T]he greatest economic evils of our time are the fruits of risk, uncertainty and ignorance...these same factors are also the cause of Unemployment of Labour" (1931, pp. 317–18).

The imperfectionist character of this early argument is further illustrated by Keynes's proposed solutions: the underwriting of stability in the "external" environment by the management of currency and credit, and the dissemination of information by central authorities. Similar kinds of arguments, though the particular "frictions and rigidities" differ, are evident in Keynes's position in the debate over the return to the gold standard in the mid-1920s, where the now familiar imperfectionist case of a downward rigidity of money-wages plays its part in the argument.

Any instability of the market mechanism that might be said to arise in these contexts is not the same as the idea that underpins Schumpeter's argument. Nor, more important, is it actually at all novel when considered against the backdrop of earlier opinion. It may be, as some who propound this reading have actually argued, that Keynes's obstacles are rather more intractable than had hitherto been admitted to be possible, or even that they are more immediately relevant to practical affairs than any that had been examined before him, but this would hardly render his analysis especially profound. Or it may be that the policy suggestions of the *General Theory* were more appealing than the idea of legislating against uncertainty. However, to all intents and purposes, such views would render it equivalent to preexisting conceptions of the operation of the economic machine—where "essentially smoothly functioning" was always qualified with the proviso "in the absence of frictions and rigidities."

Interestingly, this is the very species of argument to which Schumpeter assigned the theory of effective demand when he came to assess what he felt Keynes's contribution amounted to: "[T]he whole *theoretical* case...collapses, and we are *practically* left with friction, or 'stickiness,' institutional inhibitions and the like, which in particular may prevent the...equilibrating mechanism from functioning adequately" (Schumpeter, 1951a, p. 156). Not surprisingly, it is here that we encounter one of the reasons for Schumpeter's hostility toward Keynes, a point to which we shall return later.

The obvious problem with this rendering of the *General Theory* is that it fails to accord with the central claim Keynes was making for the book—namely, that it provided a "general" theory of employment, at least in the formal sense of its being a theory about the full equilibrium of the economic system. In short, Schumpeter's assessment of the weight of Keynes's argument would be correct (though his dismissal of its relevance would be open to question). A second argument, which claims to be rather different from the previous one, holds that the *General Theory* should be read as saying that the predominating influence of uncertainty is sufficient to remove the traditional idea that the economic machine has any tendency to produce sustainable states at all. The characteristic that renders this a different species of argument from the one just mentioned is the idea that the chaos consequent upon the existence of uncertainty is capable, endogenously so to speak, of altering the theoretical norm toward which the economic system is tending at any given time. Minsky's financial instability hypothesis provides a good example of this line of thinking: "[E]very reference to equilibrium is best interpreted as a reference to a *transitory* set of system variables, towards which the system is tending: but, in contrast to Marshall, as the economy moves toward such a set of system variables, endogenously determined changes occur which affect the set of system variables towards which the economy tends" (Minsky, 1976, p. 71).

Of course, if no distinction can be made between changes in the data and changes in the dependent variables of the system, then there can be no equilibrium (not even a transitory one), despite Minsky's statement to the contrary. There is just no difference between dependent and independent variables in such a world. This line of approach derives ultimately from certain later arguments of Joan Robinson against equilibrium analysis itself. Though for quite different reasons, it should be fairly obvious that if this is to be taken as the correct rendering of the basic Keynesian conception of the economic machine, then it is essentially the same as that of Schumpeter—and it would, of course, be subject to exactly the same analytical ambiguities that have already been found to be present for that concept.

Moreover, it is difficult to reconcile this kind of argument with Keynes's own view of his theory, where equilibrium does not seem to be the essential point at issue. Keynes was quite emphatic about this:

> There are... forces which one might fairly well call "automatic" which operate under any normal monetary system in the direction of restoring a long-period equilibrium between saving and investment. The point upon which I cast doubt—though the contrary is generally believed—is whether these "automatic forces" will... tend to bring about not only an equilibrium between saving and investment, but also an optimum level of production. (Keynes, 1973, 13:395)

The issue Keynes focuses on here is quite clearly the *theory* that is used to explain equilibrium—for it is that theory that establishes the outcomes (like full employment or unemployment) of the operation of the economic machine.

Developing this observation, we see that there is a third argument that holds neither that effective demand is a problem stemming from inhibitions to the operation of the economic machine, nor that there are no systematic tendencies at work in market economies at all but, rather, that the economic machine operates systematically to produce inefficient states. The theoretical norm, to stay within the confines of the traditional terminology, is characterized by unemployment. The upshot of this rendering of Keynes's basic argument is of some importance in the present context, since it is neither the same as preexisting arguments nor the same as that of Schumpeter. Instead, one is left with Keynes's basic proposition that "we oscillate... round an intermediate position appreciably below full employment," a mean position determined by "natural tendencies" (1936, p. 254). All the elements of the traditional conception of the economic machine remain intact here—the difference relates to the outcomes that emerge from its operation. What all of this makes quite apparent is that, in the last analysis, it is to the account of the operation of the economic machine, and the results it has a tendency to produce, that one must turn.

Money and Economic Activity

Ever since Adam Smith's harsh jibes at the obscurantist arguments that he claimed were adduced in support of the mercantilist maxim "heap up gold and silver," orthodox economic opinion had tended to the view that money is a veil behind which real forces act independently to determine economic activity. However, during the nineteenth century, a growing band of economic heretics had begun to question this conventional wisdom. The reasons for the increasing skepticism that surrounded the received opinion were many and various, and need not be detailed here. But a recurring critical theme was that wile monetary conditions could readily be observed in practice to impinge, in one way or another, on almost all of the economic relations that are established between individuals and institutions in market economies; from a theoretical point of view, they were supposed to be essentially ephemeral. By the early decades of the twentieth century, and particularly during the interwar years, the heretical tendencies had assumed the dimensions of a groundswell of heterodox opinion opposing the traditional doctrine.

To this chorus of opposition, Keynes and Schumpeter lent their not insignificant voices. They did so by installing the monetary mechanism at center stage in their respective theoretical arguments. In consequence, the notion that the operation of the economic machine could be understood satisfactorily without having recourse to monetary conditions—that money is like a lubricant, to use the analogy of J-B Say—was abandoned. Instead of arguing that monetary conditions exerted no effect on real economic activity in the long run,[3] Keynes and Schumpeter constructed a fundamental connection between the behavior of the monetary system and the real conditions of economic prosperity.

Yet despite this broad agreement, the conservative versus radical inclinations of our two subjects come out very clearly when we consider the uses to which this idea was put when confronted with the traditional dogma of the quantity theory of money. However, before proceeding to that matter, there remain other interesting parallels between the two arguments that stem from Keynes's and Schumpeter's broad agreement on the importance of monetary conditions. Some of these concern points of detail.

In the first place, the definition of money alters in their hands. The old-fashioned view that it is possible to draw clear lines of demarcation between "money proper" and other kinds monetary and financial instruments (often referred to as "credit" by the quantity theorists), which can be traced at least as far back as the Bullionist Controversy and the Currency School–Banking School debates of the nineteenth century, was called into question.

In this sense, the same procedure—that no meaningful distinction can be drawn between money and credit—that had allowed sympathetic critics of the quantity theory like Tooke, Fullarton, and later Wicksell to modify its conclusions for purposes of short-period analysis, was applied more generally by Keynes and Schumpeter. But while the variability in the velocity of circulation consequent upon a breach in the nexus of the classical dichotomy for short-period analysis was formally admissible, the general application of essentially the same idea altered that nexus entirely.

The conclusion that Keynes drew from his analysis was that the quantity theory of money was untrue even in long-period equilibrium. The conclusion that Schumpeter drew from his was that, while scientifically correct, the quantity theory of money was relevant only to conditions of equilibrium. Of course, to the extent that Schumpeterian evolution rendered equilibrium a less and less practically significant state of affairs, the domain of applicability of the quantity theory was drastically circumscribed. But it remained on the books. Keynes's theory of effective demand, on the other hand, erased it entirely.

As to the particular relationship between the monetary mechanism and economic activity, while there is a superficial similarity between their two arguments, the positions are actually quite different in character and content. The similarity arises from the fact that both men agree that the process of extending credit at any existing interest rate can generate self-sustaining expansion. This can be thought of as arguing that the initial provision of finance for new investment, rather than prior and voluntary acts of individual saving, is the principal channel though which the monetary system exerts its effects on economic activity. And these effects are likely to be lasting ones. Both men, therefore, moved away from the forced-saving doctrine so prevalent at the time.

The forced-saving doctrine had held that even though it might be possible for such action by the financial system to generate real effects for short periods, the process would be brought to a halt when the supply of voluntary savings forthcoming was insufficient to cover the outstanding commitments of financial institutions. In the long run, then, interest rates would have to return to the equilibrium level, and any change in the volume of investment that might have occurred beforehand would have to be reversed. The consequences of this kind of stoppage might be significant—as can be seen, for example, in overinvestment theories of crisis like that of Hayek.

The forced saving case is illustrated in figure 19.1. Assuming that the conditions of production, the preferences of agents, and the initial endowments of the system are all given, equilibrium will be established at some rate of interest (i^* in the diagram) where voluntary saving just matches planned investment. Now, suppose that owing to some exogenous shock, the prevailing market interest rate (represented as i_A) falls below the equilibrium rate. Saving will be retarded and investment stimulated. In the normal course of events, according to the argument, this excess demand for investible funds would immediately drive up the rate of interest until the system returned to the original equilibrium at i^*. This will occur as long as the function $g[I(i) - S(i)]$ is continuous and decreasing, and as long as the data remain the same.

However, suppose that instead the banking system were simply to meet all demands for investible funds at the lower rate $i_{A.}$ Investment would then actually exceed voluntary saving, and at least in the first instance, there need be no pressure for interest rates to rise. Since these additional amounts of investible will be competing for resources that were already fully utilized (the original position was one of equilibrium), a

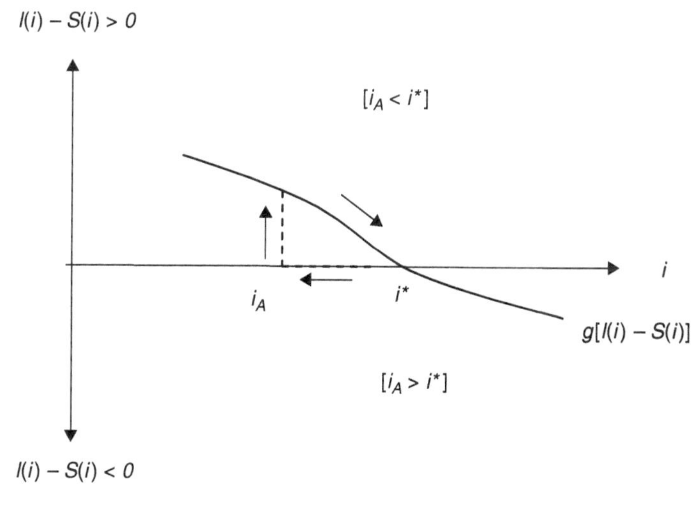

Figure 19.1

process of rising *nominal* incomes (but with constant *real* incomes) would be set in motion. The ensuing inflation would generate forced saving and close *artificially* the gap between voluntary saving and investment. But this would only be temporary. Either the banking system will run up against reserve requirements, and so be forced to alter the terms upon which advances are being made (interest rate rises), or agents (customarily savers, but this restriction is not essential to the case) will eventually correctly perceive that there has been no alteration in the underlying real conditions (given by preferences, technology, and endowments) and readjust their actions accordingly (in this way bring back into motion an adjustment of the prevailing rate of interest).

In the case of Schumpeter, the problem of forced saving is sidestepped, thanks to the argument that investment (no matter how it might be financed) changes and enhances technological possibilities. The Schumpeterian process commences from the same point as the forced saving argument: financial institutions make loans to entrepreneurs at prevailing interest rates, even when these are below the equilibrium rate. As Schumpeter puts it, the possibility of windfall profits arises whenever there is a discrepancy between prevailing and equilibrium interest-rate regimes. In this eventuality, investors approach financial institutions for advances. However, unlike the forced-saving argument, the funds advanced in this way are used to finance changes in production functions (technology), and not simply increases in the volume of investment in available technologies. It is precisely this endogenous change in technology that allows Schumpeter to avoid having to conclude that the system needs to collapse back to the old equilibrium.

In the case of Keynes, the problem of forced saving is eliminated, courtesy of the operation of the effective demand mechanism, whereby additional investment generates higher levels of aggregate income (and so more voluntary savings, under the assumption that the propensity to consume is less than one). It is the operation of this effective demand mechanism that allows Keynes to conclude that the new position is one of equilibrium between voluntary saving and investment, and so to deny the idea of having to return to the original position. His argument against the forced-saving idea is worth quoting:

> [T]he notion that the creation of credit by the banking system allows investment to take place to which "no genuine saving" corresponds can only be the result of isolating one of the consequences of increased bank-credit to the exclusion of the others. If

> the grant of bank credit to an entrepreneur allows him to make an addition to current investment...incomes will necessarily b e increased...the public will exercise "a free choice"...to increase their savings. Moreover, the savings which result from this decision are just as genuine as any other savings. (Keynes, 1936, p. 85)

Notice that, unlike the Schumpeterian case, this argument does not require that new investment generate changes in productivity conditions or, for that matter, the rate of interest.

The matter can be put another way. For Schumpeter, investment generates changes in the given production possibilities of the forced-saving case, so *moving* the equilibrium (though that equilibrium is determined along exactly the same lines as in the forced-saving case). For Keynes, investment generates increases in aggregate income, so *determining* a new equilibrium (in a manner that differs from the forced-saving case). It is essential to observe that if private investment did not embody the Schumpeterian property, then his argument would reduce to that of the forced-saving school. The analysis of private investment in the two cases is, therefore, vital to their respective arguments.

Private Investment

By common consent, Keynes's emphasis on the twin elements of aggregate effective demand (consumption and investment) constitutes one of the more important insights in the *General Theory.* One fairly obvious implication of this concept—that a high level of investment is a precondition for sustaining economic prosperity—which in itself is of little novelty, was also a view to which Schumpeter attached considerable weight. But here again, a superficial similarity masks some quite fundamental differences of opinion.

Keynes was primarily interested in investment as one of the determinants of effective demand; Schumpeter was interested in it essentially as a determinant of the rate of technological progress. On Keynes's argument, the normal situation was that investment activity, when left solely to the discretion of individual agents, could act as a drag on prosperity; whereas for Schumpeter, investment activity would act in normal situations as an engine promoting prosperity.

According to Keynes, the received opinion that the volume of investment was "self-adjusting at the optimal level" was inadequate

(1936, p. 339). On the contrary, private investment could not be relied on to reach automatically or naturally a level that would secure full employment. The basic argument is simple enough. Defining investment so as to include net additions to existing kinds of capital assets (whether fixed or circulating capital goods, or inventories), and considering the amount of investment to be the outcome of the "collective behaviour of individual entrepreneurs" (1936, p. 63), Keynes said these latter decisions depend on two factors: animal spirits and the rate of interest.

In these two factors there is nothing to lead one to expect that conditions might be established that would normally produce a level of investment compatible with full employment. Of animal spirits (or spontaneous optimism), little could be expected—not so much because, as some have argued, expectations are violently unstable or subject to waves of irrational psychology but, rather, because they are based on conventional practice and opinion, which offer no guarantees of prosperity. Of the rate of interest, upon which in normal circumstances everything therefore depends (1936, p. 164), the level that would be established in money markets need not be that which, other things being equal, would produce a full-employment level of investment.

According to Schumpeter, on the other hand, unregulated private investment is the prime mover of the economic machine. Investment is the vehicle through which new technologies are put in place. It is not so much the volume of investment that matters (Keynes's point) as the technological characteristics of that investment. The striking difference between this and what Schumpeter took to be Keynes's theory of investment is well captured in a simple analogy Schumpeter drew: "add successively as many mail coaches as you please, you will never get a railway thereby" (1926, p. 64, n). By characterizing Keynes's theory as one that relied on a falling inducement to invest, Schumpeter found Keynes's analysis of private investment altogether unconvincing:

> Since Mr. Keynes eliminates the most powerful propeller of investment, the financing of changes in production functions, the investment process in his theoretical world has hardly anything to do with the investment process in the actual world, and any proof, even if successful, that (absolutely or relatively) falling "Inducement to Invest" will produce under-employment would have no greater practical importance than a proof that motor cars cannot run in the absence of fuel. (1951a, p. 156)

The problem is that, even if one were to add an element of embodied technological change to Keynes's theory of investment, the resulting accumulation path need not guarantee full employment—so long, of course, as the effective demand mechanism operates in the long run. Secular changes in technology would, on this argument, certainly improve the level of employment established in equilibrium over longer periods of time (as, indeed, would net accumulation of capital). But since that level of employment was determined by the level of effective demand, and here the volume of investment is what matters most, equilibrium unemployment of labor would not be avoided, even if equilibrium moved slowly over time. There would be, as Joan Robinson pointed out long ago, the real possibility of ending up in a "bastard golden age."

An indication of the difference in the positions taken by Keynes and Schumpeter in this area is provided by the very language they employed in their respective discussions of the investment process. Schumpeter speaks in terms of "heroic entrepreneurs," Keynes in terms of "animal spirits." These opposing positions are revealed even more in their respective discussions of individual initiative versus collective action, to which we may now turn.

Individual Initiative and Collective Action

The final chapter of the *General Theory* is given over to reflections on the social philosophy toward which the theory of effective demand might lead. Prominent among the elements of this is "the vital importance of establishing certain central controls in matters which are now left in the main to individual initiative" (1936, pp. 377–78). In particular, Keynes concluded that "a somewhat comprehensive socialisation of investment will prove the only means of securing an approximation to full employment" (1936, p. 378). Clearly, what in 1926 Keynes had seen as a relatively straightforward matter of improving "the technique of modern capitalism by the agency of collective action" (1931, p. 319) had become a more thoroughgoing requirement for a kind of planning.

In the earlier framework, while the mechanism of competitive capitalism driven by individual initiative could be relied on to secure the best allocation (and degree of utilization) of society's resources, the state might be required to underwrite the fairness, justice, or equity of its unregulated operation and to ensure stability in the external and monetary environments. In Keynes's subsequent argument, however, the state would be required to take on the responsibility for ensuring appropriate allocation of resources. The radical divide that sets up between the doctrines of the *General Theory* and those of the existing ideology of welfarism—a point scarcely appreciated by commentators who pay insufficient attention to the economic arguments that lie beneath the two positions—is the essential ingredient in Keynes's contribution to the political culture of the postwar world.

The ideology of welfarism, of twentieth-century liberalism, so to speak, grew out of grafting onto the nineteenth-century concern with efficiency an additional concern for justice and stability. This ideology, by itself, is not attributable to Keynes. More to the point, it does not represent the basic message of the *General Theory*. According to the welfarist position, while the competitive market mechanism was seen to be capable of generating efficiency (largely unassisted by the state), the requirements of social justice and stability introduced scope for collective action. The problem of justice had been set out, though not placed immediately on the practical political agenda, by John Stuart Mill. And in the last decade of the nineteenth century, the Swedish economist Knut Wicksell seems to have been among the first to introduce the stability problem as an arena for action.[4] Wicksell's analysis of the monetary mechanism, and the cumulative processes of inflation and deflation that it was inclined to generate if unregulated, provided solid ground for an argument that held it to be the responsibility of the state (through the intermediation of its monetary authorities) to underwrite a stable monetary climate.

Keynes had arrived independently at this position by the middle of the 1920s. In his well-known essay "Am I a Liberal?" of 1925, he set out the new ideology in the following terms: "In the economic field...we must find new policies and new instruments to adapt and control the working of economic forces, so that they do not intolerably interfere with contemporary ideas as to what is fit and proper in the interests of social stability and social justice" (1931, p. 337).

But this is only a part of the legacy left to us by Keynes. It is necessary only to proceed to the *General Theory* to see how much richer that legacy turns out to be. One will not find there an argument where primary emphasis is given to the abovementioned matters. In the first place, Keynes directs attention away from the concern with stability, arguing instead that "an outstanding characteristic of the economic system in which we live [is that] it is not violently unstable" (1936, p. 249). Second, questions of distributive justice are placed in the background, and nothing is said of them until the very last chapter of the book. More important, however, the role of collective action now becomes relevant to the allocation process itself. Notice that "statecraft" now entails "securing the optimum employment of the system's entire resources" (1939, p. 340). The task of "securing" this objective—the efficient use of resources—defines the role of the state. This is the essential novelty of the *General Theory*. It is not the same as arguing (as previously) that the state take on the task of ensuring the "right" conditions within which the market mechanism can be counted on to guarantee efficiency. This, of course, is nothing more than a consequence of the appearance of the theory of effective demand presented in the *General Theory*—an argument entirely missing in the 1920s.

In short, collective action becomes a necessity in the very sphere where individual initiative had previously been left unchallenged. We shall return to this point in the following section.

To appreciate Schumpeter's views on the question of collective action, it is necessary to remember that he was in the habit of drawing distinctions between what he called "competitive" capitalism and "trustified" capitalism. The differences between them are "great enough to serve as the water-shed between two epochs in the social history of capitalism" (1926, p. 67). This was a convenient distinction, for it allowed Schumpeter to introduce the idea that a certain later (that is, "trustified") stage of capitalist development would witness a slowing down of economic growth—a proposition that forms an essential part of his historical argument about the decline of capitalism and the rise of socialism.[5] But it is a distinction that also serves to highlight just how positively Schumpeter viewed the role of private initiative in the sphere of investment activity.

When one finds Schumpeter speaking of the spirit of the industrial bourgeoisie and its "schema of motivation" (1939, p. 145), it is no surprise that he is led into giving glowing praise. After all, the "rise to leadership of new men" (1939, p. 96) was for him a necessary condition for innovation, and this in turn called for as free a hand as possible given to individual initiative. In fact, interference with this freedom of individual action is used by Schumpeter not only to describe but also to explain (in part) the final stage of capitalist development: its trustified stage.

There is more than a note of criticism of those "intellectuals" who carp at the system and undermine the social function of entrepreneurship. There is little doubt that Schumpeter saw Keynes as one such gainsaying intellectual. An indictment of this kind can be found in a late essay from Schumpeter's pen entitled "English Economists and the State-managed Economy" in 1949 (see, 1951a, pp. 296ff), and it is everywhere apparent in the eighth chapter of *Capitalism, Socialism and Democracy*.

Capitalism and Socialism

The attitudes of Keynes and Schumpeter toward capitalism and socialism are somewhat paradoxical. Schumpeter argued that socialism was a historical inevitability, yet the tone of his discussion of the demise of capitalism is tinged with regret at its passing. Keynes argued that many of the ingredients of capitalism might be retained, yet his policy prescriptions in some of their more radical forms seem effectively to eliminate the conditions necessary for its continued existence.

Keynes's general opinions on this subject were, however, less subject to the kind of evolution that we have seen at work in other areas. Before the emergence of the *General Theory*, in drawing a distinction between capitalism as a "way of life" and capitalism as an "efficient" economic system, Keynes declared his colors in 1926 with these words: "For my part, I think that capitalism, wisely managed, can probably be made more efficient for attaining economic ends than any alternative system yet in sight, but that in itself it is in any alternative system yet in sight, but that in itself it is in many ways extremely objectionable" (1931, p. 321).

Here, of course, is the platform for modern liberalism—though when he enunciated it in the 1920s, Keynes could still ask his readers "Am I a Liberal?" and not be entirely sure of their answer. It is the kind of remark that might have come from a Liberal Party (or social democratic) politician in Britain today, or from a member of the liberal wing of the Democratic Party of the United States. Its program is remarkably similar to that actually adopted in most of the industrialized West after the Second World War, under the banner of Keynesianism. It is easy enough to appreciate, even at an abstract level, that this position presents no threat to the continued existence of capitalism. This becomes especially obvious when it is recognized that its practical application for better than a quarter of the twentieth century, has left the essential features of the capitalist system unaltered. Not only should capitalism be allowed to survive, provided it was well managed, but the competing claims of socialism were not to be taken seriously.

Of course, part of Keynes's position on this subject derived from his attitude toward Marx—from whom, so he claimed in the *General Theory*, one could learn less than from Silvio Gesell. And this attitude was of long standing. In the mid-1920s, it gained expression in Keynes's sketch of Soviet Russia: "How can I accept a doctrine which sets up as its bible, above and beyond criticism, an obsolete economic textbook which I know to be not only scientifically erroneous but without interest or application for the modern world" (1931, p. 300). Another part of the explanation for his hostility to socialism is to be found in his own particular brand of social and cultural elitism (so favorable to rule by intellectuals), which clashed with what he saw as the essence of socialist politics—both as it was practiced overseas and as it was promised by the socialists of the British leftists of the day. What is interesting about Keynes is that he retains pretty much exactly this early vision of reformed capitalism and a contempt for socialism in the *General Theory*, despite the fact that his own economic analysis of capitalism is quite different in that book from what it had been beforehand.

It is hardly surprising that some readers of the *General Theory* saw it as being quite radical in its implications. Certain of Keynes's own statements even give cause to wonder at the future of private enterprise.

> The State will have to exercise a guiding influence on the propensity to consume through its scheme of taxation, partly by fixing the rate of interest, and partly, perhaps, in other ways. Furthermore, it seems unlikely that the influence of banking policy on the rate of interest will be sufficient by itself to determine an optimum rate of investment. I conceive, therefore, that a somewhat comprehensive socialisation of investment will prove the only means of securing an approximation to full employment. (1936, p. 378)

To the extent that it is the process of private investment that ensures the ownership of the means of production remains in private hands, to the extent that Keynes's new program involves rather more than "wisely-managed capitalism," it is difficult to see how the proposed "comprehensive socialisation" of investment activity would perpetuate private ownership. Yet Keynes himself, true to his earlier inclinations (if not entirely to his new theory), maintained that it could be so. As if to emphasize the paradox, in the political culture of the postwar world in Britain, it was the Labour Party that took more congenially to Keynes's message. It did not, of course, carry through its democratic socialist program, for the practical political agenda seems to have adopted fine-tuning rather than "comprehensive socialisation" as the basis of received political discourse.

Interestingly, writing after the war, Schumpeter reached the opposite conclusion to that which Keynes had drawn from his own theory, and he represented Keynes as a signpost on the road to socialism. Not just practically, in the sense that Schumpeter read Keynes as placing in the public sphere control over investment and production (part of his working definition of socialism), but also historically, in the sense that Keynes was part of the "hostile intellectual environment" that undermined capitalism. Indeed, Schumpeter spoke of the existing "degree of propensity to socialize" as a good measure of the "degree of decay of capitalist society" (1951a, p. 298).

Yet Schumpeter's view of socialist society, though he saw it lurking just around the corner, is not at all a positive one. There is little reason to believe, he argued, that socialism "will mean the advent of the civilization of which orthodox socialists dream"; instead, "it is much more likely to present fascist features" (1942, p. 375). "As a matter of practical necessity," he claimed, "socialist democracy may eventually turn out to be more of a sham than capitalist democracy ever was" (1942, p. 302).

While Schumpeter might be said to have contributed to socialist thought an argument suggesting the historical inevitability of socialism (which differed from that of Marx), it was Keynes who provided criticism of the capitalist system that extended to its core (which was also different from that of Marx). It is scarcely surprising, therefore, that Keynes's ideas have proved in general to be rather more amendable to democratic socialists in the West, while Schumpeter's have been championed (increasingly so in recent years) by the prophets of unregulated capitalism. Schumpeter himself was never enthusiastic about the decline of capitalism, though his own argument suggested its likelihood. Keynes was never enthusiastic about the economic possibilities of the capitalist system, though the practical application of moderate doses of Keynesianism has helped to sustain its existence.

Notes

This is a newly revised version of a paper by Murray Milgate and published as "Schumpeter e Keynes sobre as Possibilidades Economicas do Capitalismo," in Edward J. Amadeo's book *John Maynard Keynes: cinquenta anos da Teoria Geral* (Rio de Janeiro: INPS/IPEA). It has not previously appeared in English.

1. Keynes was always anxious to highlight the errors of his teachers, while Schumpeter was concerned to stress the continuing value of his work. Nothing remotely similar to the kind of criticisms that Keynes directed at Marshall in the *Treatise on Money* and the *General Theory,* for example, is to be found in Schumpeter. On the contrary, more often than not, he conveyed the distinct

impression that he believed that Walras and Böhm-Bawerk could do no wrong—even if, in some cases, there was more to do. Yet, perhaps paradoxically, there is a richness and a credibility about Keynes's sketches of the lives of his teachers that strikes one as stemming from a genuine admiration for their intellectual achievements. This seems to be altogether missing in anything that Schumpeter ever wrote, as anyone who has read through Keynes's *Essays in Biography* and Schumpeter's *Ten Great Economists* may begin to appreciate. Of course, to what extent this is a simple and direct reflection of their outward characters or, more accurately, of those characters that one's mind's eye constructs for them from the reports that have been left by others, is impossible to judge.

2. We are speaking here of what Schumpeter called the instability of the capitalist system—that is, "something akin to what business men call the stability or instability of business conditions" (1951a, p. 49). We are not referring to the question of the institutional survival of capitalism. Schumpeter called the latter the capitalist order, and for the present we do not wish to address this matter.

3. Temporarily, in short periods, this neutrality doctrine was often modified to allow for a purely transitory influence of monetary variables on real variables (witness the doctrines of forced savings and hoarding). But these modifications were at a secondary level of approximation and represented transient situations only (on this point, see Milgate, 1982, ch. 5).

4. The explanation for the lateness of the appearance on the scene of the issue of stability is complicated. Nevertheless, it seems clear that one part of it has to be with the fact that earlier in the nineteenth century, cyclical fluctuations, monetary disturbances, and crises were regarded as essentially short lived and noncumulative in their operation—a view that can be traced to Ricardo. Later in the nineteenth century, it would hardly have done for "liberals" to dwell on the issue, since it was among the primary charges leveled at the system of laissez-faire capitalism by their socialist adversaries. When this is recognized, it is less difficult to understand the convergence of certain socialist views and "liberal" views in the second and third decades of the twentieth century.

5. From a purely analytical point of view, it needs to be emphasized that this aging hypothesis is produced much in the way as a magician produces a rabbit from a hat. The rabbit might be real enough (a question that will occupy us in the next section), but there is nothing in the economic theory itself that could have produced it. It is an exogenous factor that Schumpeter invokes in order to render plausible his broader arguments about the institutional survival of capitalism. There is nothing in his formal economic analysis of the dynamics of capitalist development that warrants the conclusion that it will necessarily falter.

References

Abbreviations used in author-date citations in the text:

BIS Bank for International Settlements
BCBS Basel Committee on Baking Supervision
EBRD European Bank for Reconstruction and Development
FSA Financial Services Authority
GB HMSO
IAIS International Association of Insurance Supervisors
IMF International Monetary Fund
OECD Organization for Economic Cooperation and Development
UN United Nations
WIDER World Institute for Development Economics Research

Adrian, T., and H. S. Shin. 2007. Liquidity and leverage. Working Paper. Federal Reserve Bank and Princeton University.

———. 2008. Liquidity, monetary policy and financial cycles. *Current Issues in Economics and Finance, 14*(1).

Alesina, Alberto, Vittorio Grilli, and Gian Maria Milesi-Ferretti. 1994. The political economy of capital controls. In *Capital mobility: the impact on consumption, investment and growth,* eds. L. Leiderman and A. Razin, Cambridge: Cambridge University Press.

Alexander, K., J. Eatwell, A. Persaud, and R. Reoch. 2007. Financial supervision and crisis management in the EU. Document IP/A/ECON/IC/2007-069, Policy Department: Economic and Scientific Policy, European Parliament, Brussels.

Allen, F., and D. Gale. 1999. Bubbles, crises, and policy. *Oxford Review of Economic Policy, 15*(3): 9–18.

———. 2000. Bubbles and crises. *Economic Journal,* 110: 236–55.

Allen, F., S. Morris, and H. S. Shin. 2003. Beauty contests, bubbles and iterated expectations in asset markets, Cowles Foundation Discussion Paper no.1406, Cowles Foundation. Yale University.

———. 2006. Beauty contests and iterated expectations in asset markets, *Review of Financial Studies.*

Amsden, Alice. 1989. *Asia's next giant: South Korea and late industrialisation.* Oxford: Oxford University Press.

Arrow, Kenneth J., and Gerard Debreu. 1954. Existence of an equilibrium of a competitive economy. *Econometrica, 22*: 265–90.

Arrow, K. and F. H. Hahn. 1971. *General competitive analysis.* Edinburgh: Oliver and Boyd.

Ashton, T. S. 1948. *The industrial revolution, 1760-1830.* Oxford: Oxford University Press.

Azariadis, C. 1975. Implicit contracts and underemployment equilibria. *Journal of Political Economy, 83*(6): 1183–202.

Azariadis, C., and J. Stiglitz. 1983. Implicit contracts and fixed price equilibria. *Quarterly Journal of Economics, 98* (Suppl.): 1–22.

Bank for International Settlements (BIS). 1992. 62nd annual report. Basle.

———. 1993. Survey of Foreign Exchange Activity in April 1992. Basle.

———. 1995. 65th annual report. Basle.

———. 1996. Central Bank survey of foreign exchange and derivatives market activity, *1995.* Basle.

———. 1998. 68th annual report. Basle.

———. 2004. Credit risk transfer. Committee on Banking Supervision, Joint Forum, Basle.

Bank of England. 2001. Risk transfer between banks, insurance companies and the capital market. www.bankofengland.co.uk.

Barker, T. 1980. The economic consequences of monetarism: A Keynesian view of the British economy 1980-1990. *Cambridge Journal of Economics, 4*: 319–36.

Barro, Robert. 1974. Are government bonds net wealth? *Journal of Political Economy, 82(6)*:1095–117.

Basel Committee on Banking Supervision (BCBS). 2004. Credit risk transfer. Bank for International Settlements, Basle.

Baxter, Marianne, and Alan C. Stockman. 1989. Business cycles and the exchange-rate regime: Some international evidence. *Journal of Monetary Economics, 23*(3): 377–400.

Bayoumi, Tamim. 1990. Saving-investment correlations: Immobile capital, government policy, or endogenous behaviour. *IMF Staff Papers,* 37(2): 360–87.

Bayoumi, Tamim, and Barry Eichengreen. 1994. Macroeconomic adjustment under Bretton Woods and the post-Bretton Woods float: An impulse-response analysis. *Economic Journal, 104*(425): 813–27.

Bayoumi, Tamim, and Ronald MacDonald. 1995. Consumption, income, and international capital market integration. *IMF Staff Papers, 42*(3): 552–76.

Bayoumi, Tamim, and Andrew Rose. 1993. Domestic savings and intra-national capital flows. *European Economic Review, 37*(6): 1197–202.

Binswanger, M. 1999. *Stock markets, speculative bubbles and economic growth.* Aldershot: Edward Elgar.

Black, Stanley. 1987. International monetary institutions. In *The new Palgrave: A dictionary of economics,* eds. John Eatwell, Murray Milgate, and Peter Newman, London: Macmillan.

Blanchard, Olivier. 1987. Crowding out. In *The new Palgrave: A dictionary of economics,* eds. John Eatwell, Murray Milgate, and Peter Newman, London: Macmillan.

———. 2008. The state of macro. NBER Working Paper no. 14259, Cambridge, Massachusetts.

Blanchard, Olivier J., and M. W. Watson. 1982. Bubbles, rational expectations and speculative markets. In *Crisis in economic and financial structure: Bubbles, bursts and shocks,* ed. P. Wachtel, Lexington, MA: Lexington Books.

Blinder, A. S. 1999. High clouds, no storm in sight. *New York Times,* August 24, A15.

Blundell-Wignall, Adrian, and Frank Browne. 1991. Macroeconomic consequences of financial liberalisation: A summary report. OECD Department of Economics and Statistics Working Paper no. 98.

Bohm, Peter. 1987. Second best. In *The new Palgrave: A dictionary of economics,* eds. John Eatwell, Murray Milgate, and Peter Newman, London: Macmillan.

Boughton, James M. 2001. *Silent revolution: The International Monetary Fund 1979–1989.* Washington, DC: International Monetary Fund.

Bryant, Ralph. 1987. *International financial intermediation.* Washington, DC: Brookings Institution.

Buiter, W. 1980. The economics of Dr Pangloss: A critical survey of the new classical economics. *Economic Journal, 90*: 34–50.

———. 2010. The unfortunate uselessness of most "state of the art" academic monetary economics. *Financial Times,* March 3.

Caballero, R. J., and A. Krishnamurthy. 2006. Flight to quality and collective risk management. NBER Working Paper no. 12136, Cambridge, Massachusetts.

Camdessus, Michel. 1994. The way forward for the international monetary system: 50 years after Bretton Woods. An address delivered at Fundacion Ramon Areces, Madrid, 9 May 1994, and excerpted in *IMF Survey,* May 30.

Chamberlain, Joseph. 1885. *The radical platform.* London.

Cho, Yoon-Je, and Deena Khatkhate. 1989. Financial liberalisation: Issues and evidence. *Economic and Political Weekly,* May 20.

Clifton, J. A. 1977. Competition and the evolution of the capitalist mode of production. *Cambridge Journal of Economics, 1*(2): 137–51.

Clower, R. A. 1965. The Keynesian counter-revolution: A theoretical appraisal. In *The theory of interest rates,* eds. F. H. Hahn and F. Brechling, London: Macmillan.

Coakley, Jerry, Farida Kulasi, and Ron Smith. 1995. The Feldstein-Horioka puzzle and capital mobility. Birkbeck College Discussion Papers in Economics no. 6/95.

Cohen, B. and H. S. Shin. 2003. Positive feedback trading under stress: Evidence from the US Treasuries securities market. *London School of Economics: Working Paper.* June.

Commission of the European Communities. 1977. Report of the Study Group on the Role of Public Finance in European Integration. (MacDougall Report). Economic and Financial Series no. 13, vols. 1 and 2, Luxembourg..

Corbett, Jenny, and Tim Jenkinson. 1994. The financing of industry 1970-89: An international comparison. Discussion Paper no. 948, Centre for Economic Policy Research, London.

Coutts, Ken, Wynne Godley, and William Nordhaus. 1978. *Industrial pricing in the United Kingdom.* Cambridge: Cambridge University Press.

Crockett, Andrew. 1984. Exchange rate volatility and world trade. IMF Occasional Paper no. 28. Washington, DC.

———. 1993. Monetary policy implications of increased capital flows. *Symposium*. Federal Reserve Bank of Kansas City.

Culp, Christopher, and Merton Miller. 1995. Metallgesellschaft and the economics of synthetic storage. *Journal of Applied Corporate Finance, 7*(4): 62–76.

Davies, H. 2002. A toxic financial shock: General insurance companies may be taking on risks that are hard to quantify. *Financial Times*, January 30.

De Grauwe, Paul. 1987. International monetary policy. In *The new Palgrave: A dictionary of economics*, eds. John Eatwell, Murray Milgate, and Peter Newman, London: Macmillan.

Debreu, G. 1959. *Theory of value: An axiomatic analysis of economic equilibrium*. New Haven and London: Yale University Press.

Devlin, Robert, Ricardo Ffrench-Davis, and Stephany Griffith-Jones, eds. 1995. *Coping with capital surges: The return of finance to Latin America*, Boulder and London: Lynne Reinner.

Domar, Evsey D. 1944. The "burden of the debt" and the national income. *American Economic Review, 34*(4): 798–827.

Dutt, A. K., and E. Amadeo. 1990. *Keynes's third alternative? The Neoricardian Keynesians and the post Keynesians*. Aldershot: Edward Elgar.

Eatwell, John. 1976. Irving Fisher's rate of return over cost and the rate of profit in a capitalistic economy. In *Essays in modern capital theory*, eds. Murray Brown *et al.*, Amsterdam: North-Holland.

———. 1977. The irrelevance of returns to scale in Sraffa's analysis. *Journal of Economic Literature, 15*(1): 61–68.

———. 1982. *Whatever happened to Britain? The economics of decline*. London: Duckworth.

———. 1994a. The co-ordination of macroeconomic policy in the European Community. In *Unemployment in Europe*, eds. Jonathan Michie and J. Grieve Smith, London: Academic Press.

———. 1994b. Co-ordination failure. *New Economy*, Issue 3, September.

———.1995a. A recovery faltering through lack of investment. *The Observer*, August 27.

———.1995b. Disguised unemployment: The G7 experience, *UNCTAD Review*, 67–90, Number 106, October.

———. 1996. Unemployment on a world scale. In *Global unemployment: Loss of jobs in the '90s*, ed. John Eatwell, Armonk, NY: M.E. Sharpe.

———.1997. International financial liberalisation: The impact on world development. ODS Discussion Paper Series no.12. UNDP, New York.

Eatwell, John, Michael Ellman, Mats Karlsson, D.Mario Nuti, and Judith Shapiro. 1995. *Transformation and integration: Shaping the future of Central and Eastern Europe*. London: IPPR.

Eatwell, John, and Murray Milgate, eds. 1983. *Keynes's economics and the theory of value and distribution*. London & New York: Duckworth & Oxford

Eatwell, John, and Lance Taylor. 2000. *Global finance at risk: The case for international regulation*. New York: New Press.

Edey, Malcolm, and Ketil Hviding. 1995. An assessment of financial reform in OECD countries, OECD Economics Department Working Paper no. 154.

Edwards, Franklin. 1993. Financial markets in transition—or the decline of commercial banking. *Symposium*. Federal Reserve Bank of Kansas City.

Eichengreen, Barry. 1993. Epilogue. In *A retrospective on the Bretton Woods system*, eds. Michael Bordo and Barry Eichengreen, Chicago: University of Chicago Press.

———. 1996. *Globalizing capital: A history of the international monetary system.* Princeton, NJ: Princeton University Press.

European Bank for Reconstruction and Development (EBRD). 1995. Transition Report Update. London.

Fazzari, Stephen, R.Glenn Hubbard, and Bruce Petersen. 1988. Financing constraints and corporate investment, Brookings Papers on Economic Activity, 2387, 141–95.

Federal Reserve Bank of Kansas City. 1988. *Financial market volatility. A symposium.*

———. 1993. *Changing capital markets: Implications for monetary policy. A Symposium.*

Feldman, Allan. 1987. Welfare economics. In *The new Palgrave: A dictionary of economics*, eds. John Eatwell, Murray Milgate, and Peter Newman, London: Macmillan.

Feldstein, Martin. 1994. Tax policy and international capital flows. *Weltwirtschaftliches Archiv, 130*(4): 675–97.

Feldstein, Martin, and Philippe Bacchetta. 1991. National saving and international investment. In *National saving and economic performance*, eds. John Shoven and Douglas Bernheim, Chicago: University of Chicago Press.

Feldstein, Martin, and Charles Horioka. 1980. Domestic saving and international capital flows. *Economic Journal, 90*(358): 314–29.

Felix, David. 1995. Financial globalization versus free trade: The case for the Tobin tax. UNCTAD Discussion Paper no. 108.

Financial Services Authority (FSA). 2002. *Cross-sector risk transfer.* London.

Financial Stability Forum. 2008. *Report on enhancing market and institutional resilience.* www.fsforum.org/publications/r_0804.pdf.

Fisher, F. 1969. The existence of aggregate production functions. *Econometrica, 37*(4): 553–77.

———. 1983. *Disequilibrium foundations of equilibrium economics.* Cambridge: Cambridge University Press.

Fisher, Irving. 1930. *The theory of interest.* New York: Macmillan.

Frank, Julian, and Colin Mayer. 1990. Takeovers, capital markets and corporate control: A study of France, Germany and the UK. *Economic Policy,* 10: 189–231.

Frankel, Jeffrey A. 1992. Measuring international capital mobility: A review. *American Economic Review, 82*(2): 197–202.

Fridson, M. S. 1995. *Confusions and delusions: Tulipmania, the South Sea bubble and the madness of crowds.* New York: Wiley.

Friedman, Milton. 1953. *Essays in positive economics.* Chicago: University of Chicago Press.

———. 1968. The role of monetary policy. *American Economic Review, 58*(1): 1–17.

———. 1974a. A theoretical framework for monetary analysis. In *Milton Friedman's monetary framework*, ed. Robert Gordon, Chicago: University of Chicago Press.

———. 1974b. Comments on the critics. In *Milton Friedman's monetary framework*, ed. Robert Gordon, Chicago: University of Chicago Press.

———. 1980. *Memorandum of evidence.* London: House of Commons Treasury and Civil Services Committee. GB HMSO.

Gagnon, Joseph E. 1993. Exchange rate variability and the level of international trade. *Journal of International Economics, 34*(3-4): 269–87.

Galbraith, John Kenneth. 1954/1968. *The great crash, 1929.* Harmondsworth: Penguin.

———. 2000. Keynes's impact on America: FDR and the New Deal. Interview. Transcript at http://www.pbs.org/wgbh/commandingheights/shared/minitextlo/int_johnkennethgalbraith.html#1.

Garber, P. M. 1989. Tulipmania. *Journal of Political Economy, 97*: 535–60.

———. 1990. Famous first bubbles. *Journal of Economic Perspectives, 4* (Spring): 35–54.

Garegnani, Pierangelo. 1960. *Il Capitale nelle Teorie della Distribuzione.* Milan: Giuffre.

———. 1970. Heterogeneous capital, the production function and the theory of distribution. *Review of Economic Studies, 37*: 407–36.

———. 1976. On a change in the notion of equilibrium in recent work on value and distribution. In *Essays in modern capital theory,* ed. Murray Brown et al., Amsterdam: North-Holland.

———. 1978-79. Notes on consumption, investment and effective demand: Parts I & II. *Cambridge Journal of Economics, 2: 335–53 & 3: 63–82.*

GB HMSO. 1919. Final report of the Committee on Currency and Foreign Exchanges After the War (Cunliffe), Cmnd. 464. London.

———. 1925. Report of the Committee on the Currency and the Bank of England Note Issue (Chamberlain-Bradbury), Cmnd. 2392, London.

———. 1931a. Report of the Committee on Finance and Industry (Macmillan), Cmnd. 3897, London.

———. 1931b. *Minutes of evidence taken before the Committee on Finance and Industry.* 2 vols. London.

———. 1944. Employment Policy. White Paper.

Gerschenkron, Alexander. 1962. *Economic backwardness in historical perspective.* Cambridge, MA: Harvard University Press.

Gertler, Mark, and R. Glenn Hubbard. 1988. Financial factors in business fluctuations. *Symposium.* Federal Reserve Bank of Kansas City.

Giovanetti, Giorgia. 1991. Exchange rate volatility, prices and trade flows. *Revue d'Economie Industrielle, 55*: 25–38.

Glyn, Andrew, Alan Hughes, Alain Lipietz, and Ajit Singh. 1990. The rise and fall of the golden age. In *The golden age of capitalism: Reinterpreting the postwar experience,* eds. Stephen Marglin and Juliet Schor, pp. 39–125, Oxford: Clarendon Press.

Godley, Wynne. 1995. A critical imbalance in U.S. trade: The U.S. balance of payments, international indebtedness, and economic policy. Jerome Levy Economics Institute Public Policy Brief no. 23.

Godley, Wynne, and William Nordhaus. 1972. Pricing in the trade cycle. *Economic Journal, 82*: 853–82.

Goldberg, Linda S. 1993. Exchange rates and investment in United States industry. *Review of Economics and Statistics, 75*(4): 575–88.

Goodhart, Charles and Avinash Persaud. 2008. A party pooper's guide to financial stability. *Financial Times,* June 4.

Gordon, David. 1987. Six-percent unemployment ain't natural: Demystifying the idea of a rising "natural rate of unemployment." *Social Research, 54*(2): 223–46.

Graaff, Jan de Villiers. 1957. *Theoretical welfare economics.* Cambridge: Cambridge University Press.

Green, Roy. 1982. Money, output and inflation in classical economics. *Contributions to Political Economy, 1*: 59–85.

Grilli, Vittorio, and Gian Maria Milesi-Ferretti. 1995. Economic effects and structural determinants of capital controls. *IMF Staff Papers, 42*(3): 517–51.

Group of Ten. 2001. Report on Consolidation in the Financial Sector. Basel: Bank for International Settlements.

Haberler, G. 1958. *Prosperity and depression*, 4th edn. London: Allen and Unwin.

Hahn, F. H. 1973a. *On the notion of equilibrium in economics*. Cambridge: Cambridge University Press.

———. 1977. Keynesian economics and general equilibrium theory; reflections of some current debates. In *The microfoundations of macroeconomics*, ed. G. C. Harcourt, London: Macmillan.

———. 1978. On non-Walrasian equilibria. *Review of Economic Studies, 45*(1): 1–17.

———. 1980. Monetarism and economic theory. *Economica, 47*(185): 1–17.

———. 1987. On involuntary unemployment. *Economic Journal, 97* (Suppl.): 1–16.

Hahn, F. H. and R. R. Neild. 1980. Monetarism: Why Mrs Thatcher should beware. *The Times*, London, 25 February.

Harberler, G. 1939. *Prosperity and depression*. London: Allen and Unwin.

Harrod, R. F. 1937. Mr. Keynes and traditional theory. *Econometrica, 5*(1): 74–86.

———. 1948. *Towards a Dynamic Economics*. London: Macmillan.

Hawtrey, R. 1913/1970. *Good and bad trade*. Reprint. New York: Augustus M. Kelley.

———. 1927. *The gold standard in theory and practice*. London: Longmans and Green.

———. 1930. *Currency and credit*, London: Longmans and Green.

Hayek, Friedrich A. 1931. *Prices and production*. 2nd ed. (1935). London: Routledge.

———. 1932b. Money and capital: A reply. *Economic Journal, 42*: 237–49.

Helleiner, Eric. 1994. *States and the re-emergence of global finance: From Bretton Woods to the 1990s*. Ithaca, NY: Cornell University Press.

Hendricks, D., J. Kambhu, and P. Mosser. 2006. *Systemic risk and the financial system*. New York: Federal Reserve Bank of New York.

———. 1937. Mr. Keynes and the "classics": A suggested interpretation. *Econometrica, 5* (April): 147–59.

———. 1939/1946. *Value and capital*, 2nd ed. Oxford: Clarendon Press.

Hicks, J. R. 1974. *The crisis of Keynesian economics*. Oxford: Basil Blackwell.

Huizinga, John. 1994. Exchange rate volatility, uncertainty, and investment. In *Capital mobility: The impact on consumption, investment and growth*, eds. L. Leiderman and A. Razin. Cambridge: Cambridge University Press.

International Monetary Fund (IMF). 1999. The IMF's response to the Asian crisis. Factsheet. www.imf.org/external/np/exr/facts/asia.HTM

———. 2004a. *Financial sector regulation: Issues and gaps*. Washington, DC: International Monetary Fund.

———. 2004b. *Financial sector regulation: Issues and gaps—Background paper.* Washington, DC: International Monetary Fund.

———. 2009. *Review of recent crisis programs*. Washington, DC: International Monetary Fund.

———. 2010. *World economic outlook*. Washington, DC: International Monetary Fund.

Kaldor, Nicholas. 1939. Speculation and economic stability. *Review of Economic Studies*, 7(1):1–27.
———. 1959/1964. Economic growth and the problem of inflation. *Essays on Economic Policy*, vol. 1. London: Duckworth.
Kalecki, Michael. 1937. The principle of increasing risk. *Economica* 4 (New Series), pp. 440–447.
———. 1939. *Essays in the theory of economic fluctuations*. London: Allen and Unwin.
———. 1971. *Essays on the dynamics of the capitalist economy*. Cambridge: Cambridge University Press.
Kay, John. 2009. "Too big to fail" is too dumb to keep. *Financial Times*, December 15.
Keating, Giles, and Jonathan Wilmot. 1992. *Prosperity or decline*. London: Credit Suisse First Boston.
Kennedy, John F. 1962. Commencement address. Yale University, June 11.
Kenway, Peter. 1980. Marx, Keynes and the possibility of crisis. *Cambridge Journal of Economics, 4:* 23–36.
Keohane, Robert, and Helen Milner, eds. 1996. *Internationalization and domestic policies*. Cambridge: Cambridge University Press.
Keynes, J. M. 1930. *A Treatise on money*. 2 vols. London: Macmillan.
———. 1931. *Essays in persuasion*. London: Macmillan.
———. 1933. *Essays in biography*. London: Macmillan.
———. 1936. *The general theory of employment, interest and money*. London, Macmillan.
———. 1937. Alternative theories of the rate of interest. *Economic Journal, 47*: 241–52.
———. 1937a. The general theory of employment. *Quarterly Journal of Economics, 51*(2): 209–23.
———. 1940. *How to pay for the war*. London: Macmillan.
———. 1971. *Economic consequences of the peace*. London: Macmillan (1st edn: 1919).
———. 1973–. *The collected writings of John Maynard Keynes*. Mult. vols. London: Macmillan.
Kindleberger, Charles P. 1973/1986. The world in depression, 1929–1939. Rev. ed. Berkeley: University California Press.
———. 1978/1996. *Manias, panics and crashes: A history of financial crises*. Basingstoke: Palgrave.
———. 2002. *Manias, crashes and panics: A history of financial crises*. 4th ed. London: Palgrave.
Kindleberger, Charles P. and Robert Z. Aliber. 2005. Manias, panics and crashes: A history of financial crises. 5th ed. London: Palgrave Macmillan.
King, Mervyn. 1995. Credibility and monetary policy. *Scottish Journal of Political Economy, 42*(1): 1–19.
King, Mervyn, and Sunil Wadhwani. 1988. Transmission of volatility between stock markets. LSE Financial Markets Group Working Paper no. 48. London: London School of Economics.
Kitson, M. and Jonathan Michie. 1994. Fixed exchange rates and deflation: The Gold Standard and the ERM. *Economics and Business Education, 2*(I:5): 11–16.
Krugman, Paul. 1993. Comment on Marston. In *A retrospective on the Bretton Woods system,* eds. Michael Bordo and Barry Eichengreen, Chicago: University of Chicago Press.

———. 2000. How complicated does the model have to be? *Oxford Review of Economic Policy, 16:* 33–42.

———. 2008. *The return of depression economics and the crisis of 2008.* London: Penguin.

———. 2009a. Review of Robert Skidelsky's *Keynes: The return of the master. The Guardian,* August 30.

Lagana, M., M. Peoina, I. von Koppen-Mertes, and A. Persaud. 2006. Implications for liquidity from innovation and transparency in the European corporate bond market. Occasional Paper Series no. 50. Frankfurt: European Central Bank.

Lane, Timothy, Atish Ghosh, Javier Hamann, Steven Phillips, Marianne Schulze-Ghattas, and Tsidi Tsikata. 1999. IMF-supported programs in Indonesia, Korea, and Thailand: A preliminary assessment. IMF Occasional Paper no. 178. Washington, DC: International Monetary Fund.

Lange, O. 1987. The economic operation of a socialist society. Lectures delivered at University of Chicago, May 1942. Reprinted in *Contributions to Political Economy, 6*: 3–12.

Layard, R., S. Nickell, and R. Jackman. 1991. *Unemployment.* Oxford: Oxford University Press.

Leijonhufvud, A. 1968. *On Keynesian economics and the economics of Keynes.* New York: Oxford University Press.

———. 1969. *Keynes and the classics.* London: Institute for Economic Affairs.

———.1971. *Keynes and the classics.* London: Institute of Economic Affairs.

Lipsey, Richard, and Kelvin Lancaster. 1956. The general theory of second best. *Review of Economic Studies, 24*(1):11–32.

Lucas, R. 1972a. Expectations and the neutrality of money. *Journal of Economic Theory, 4*(2): 102–24.

———. 1972b. Econometric testing of the natural rate hypothesis. In *The econometrics of price determination,* ed. Otto Eckstein, Washington: Federal Reserve.

Lucas, R. E. 2003. Macroeconomic priorities. *American Economic Review, 93*(1): 1–14.

Malinvaud, E. 1977. *The theory of unemployment reconsidered.* Oxford: Basil Blackwell.

Malkiel, Burton. 1987. Efficient market hypothesis. In *The new Palgrave: A dictionary of economics,* eds. John Eatwell, Murray Milgate, and Peter Newman, London: Macmillan.

Mankiw, N. Gregory. 2006. The macroeconomist as scientist and engineer. *Journal of Economic Perspectives, 20*(4): 29–46.

Markovitz, H. M. 1952. Portfolio selection. *Journal of Finance, 7*(1): 77–91.

Marshall, Alfred. 1923. *Money, credit and commerce.* Reprint. New York: Augustus M. Kelley.

———. *Principles of economics,* 9th (Variorum) Edition. London: Macmillan.

Marston, Richard. 1993. Interest differentials under Bretton Woods and the post-Bretton Woods float: The effects of capital controls and exchange risk. In *A retrospective on the Bretton Woods system,* eds. Michael Bordo and Barry Eichengreen, Chicago: University of Chicago Press.

Marx, K. 1967. *Capital.* Volume Three. New York: International Publishers.

Mas-Collell, Andreu, Mike Whinston, and Jerry Green.1995. *Microeconomic theory.* New York: Oxford University Press.

Mathias, Peter. 1969/. *The first industrial nation.* London: Routledge.

McGee, Susan. 1995. Volatility is making hedges grow. *Wall Street Journal*, June 12.

Mello, A., and J. Parsons. 1995. Maturity structure of a hedge matters: Lessons from the Metallgesellschaft debacle. *Journal of Applied Corporate Finance*, *8*(1): 106–20.

Merton, R. C. 1973. The theory of rational option pricing. *Bell Journal of Economics and Management Science*, 4, no: 1(Spring): 141–183.

Milgate, Murray. 1977. Keynes on the 'classical theory' of interest. *Cambridge Journal of Economics*, *1*(3): 307–15.

———. 1979. On the origin of the notion of "intertemporal equilibrium." *Economica*, *47*: 1–11.

———. 1982. *Capital and employment: A study of Keynes's economics*. London and New York: Academic Press.

———. 1983. Keynes and Pigou on the gold standard and monetary theory. *Contributions to Political Economy*, *2*: 39–48.

Mill, John Stuart. 1897. *The principles of political economy*. 7th ed. London: Longmans.

———. 1945. Notes on Nassau Senior's Political Economy. *Economica*, *12*(147): 134–39.

Minsky, H. P. 1957. Central banking and money market changes. *Quarterly Journal of Economics*, *23*(2): 171–87.

———. 1975. *John Maynard Keynes*. London: Macmillan.

———. 1976. *John Maynard Keynes*. New York: Columbia University Press.

Modigliani, Franco. 1944. Liquidity preference and the theory of interest and money. *Econometrica*, *12*: 45–88.

———. 1977. The monetarist counter-revolution, or should we forsake stabilization policies. *American Economic Review*, *67*: 1–19.

Moggridge, Donald. 1972. *British monetary policy, 1924-1931*. Cambridge: Cambridge University Press.

———. 1980. *Keynes*. 2nd ed. London: Macmillan.

Morris, S., and H. Y. Shin. 2002. The social value of public information. *American Economic Review*, 92: 1521–1534.

Mussa, Michael, and Morris Goldstein. 1993. The integration of world capital markets. *Symposium, Federal Reserve Bank of Kansas* City.

Muth, J. 1961. Rational expectations and the theory of price movements. *Econometrica*, 29: 315–35.

Naples, Michele, and Arben Arifaj. 1995. Measuring business failures for policy purposes: The 1983-84 data discontinuity and creation of a consistent series. Mimeo, Trenton State College, New Jersey.

Nield, R. R. 1963. *Pricing and employment in the trade cycle*. Cambridge: Cambridge University Press.

Obstfeld, Maurice. 1986. Rational and self-fulfilling balance of payments crises. *American Economic Review*, *76*(1): 72–81.

———. 1993. International capital mobility in the 1990s. NBER Working Paper no. 4534.

Olivier, J. 2000. Growth-enhancing bubbles. *International Economic Review*, *41*(1): 133–51.

Organization for Economic Cooperation and Development (OECD). 1994a. *The OECD jobs study: Facts, analysis, strategies*. Paris: OECD.

———. 1994b. *The OECD jobs study: Evidence and explanations. Part I: Labour market trends and underlying forces of change*. Paris: OECD.

———. 1994c. *The OECD jobs study: Evidence and explanations. Part II: The adjustment potential of the labour market*. Paris: OECD.
———. 2009a. *Economic outlook: Interim report*. Paris: OECD.
Orr, Adrian, Malcolm Edey, and Michael Kennedy. 1995. The determinants of real long-term interest rates. OECD Department of Economics and Statistics Working Paper no. 155.
Pareto, Vilfredo. 1897. *Manual of political economy*. Reprint. New York: Augustus M. Kelley.
Parker, H. M. D. 1957. *Manpower*. London: HMSO.
Parkin, Michael. 1987. Inflation. In *The new Palgrave: A dictionary of economics*, eds. John Eatwell, Murray Milgate, and Peter Newman, London: Macmillan.
Patinkin, D. 1974. Friedman on the quantity theory and Keynesian economics. In *Milton Friedman's monetary framework*, ed. Robert Gordon, Chicago: University of Chicago Press.
———. 1976. *Keynes' monetary thought*. Durham, NC: Duke University Press.
Persaud, A. 2000. *Sending the herd off the cliff edge: The dangerous interaction between modern risk management practices and investor behaviour*. Washington, DC: Institute of International Finance.
———. 2003. Market liquidity and risk management. In *Liquidity black holes: Understanding, quantifying and managing financial liquidity risk*, ed. A. Persaud, London: Risk Books.
———. 2004. Credit derivatives, insurance companies and liquidity black holes. *Geneva Papers on Risk and Insurance, Issues and Practice, 29* (April): 300–12.
Pesaran, M. H. 1982. A critique of the proposed tests of the natural rate-rational expectations hypothesis. *Economic Journal*, 92: 529–54.
Phelps, E. 1967. Phillips curves, inflationary expectations and optimal employment over time. *Economica, 34*: 254–81.
———. 1968. Money wage dynamics and labor market equilibrium. *Journal of Political Economy, 76*(4): 678–711.
———. 1970. Monet wage dynamics and labor market equilibrium. In his *Microeconomic foundations of employment and inflation theory*. New York: Norton.
Pigou, A. C. 1918-19. Memorandum. In *proceedings of the Committee on Currency and Foreign Exchanges After the War*, quoted in *British monetary policy, 1924–1931*, by Donald Moggridge, Cambridge: Cambridge University Press.
———. 1931a. Evidence before the Macmillan Committee. In [G.B. H.M.S.O. (1931*b*).]
———. 1932. *The Economics of Welfare*. London: Macmillan (1st edn, 1920).
———. 1933. *The theory of unemployment*, London: Macmillan.
———. 1936. Mr. J. M. Keynes' general theory of employment, interest and money. *Economica, 310* (May):115–32.
———. 1941/1949. *Employment and equilibrium*. 2nd ed. London: Macmillan.
———. 1947. *Aspects of British economic history 1918-1925*. London: Macmillan.
———. 1950. *Keynes's general theory*. London: Macmillan.
———. 1952. *Essays in economics*. London: Macmillan.
———. 1954. *Lapses from full employment*. London: Macmillan.
Pollin, Robert. 1995. Financial structures and egalitarian economic policy. *New Left Review, 214*: 26–61.
Posthumus, N. W. 1929. The tulip mania in Holland in the years 1636–37. *Journal of Economic and Business History, 1* (May): 434–55.

Reinhart, C. M., and K. S. Rogoff. 2009. *This time is different: Eight centuries of financial folly.* Princeton, NJ: Princeton University Press.

Ricardo, David. 1951–73. *The works and correspondence of David Ricardo.* 11 vols. Edited by Piero Sraffa, with Maurice H. Dobb. Cambridge: Cambridge University Press.

Rizvi, S. A. T. 1994. The microfoundations project in general equilibrium theory. *Cambridge Journal of Economics,* 18: 357–377.

Roberts, D. 2001. Glorious hopes on a trillion dollar scrap heap. *Financial Times,* September 6, p. 12.

Roberts, J. and H. Sonnenschein. 1977. On the foundations of the theory of monopolistic competition. *Econometrica,* 45: 101–13.

Robertson, Dennis. 1911. *Industrial fluctuations.* London: LSE reprint series.

Robinson, Joan. 1937. Disguised unemployment. In her *Essays in the theory of employment.* London: Macmillan.

———. 1951. *The rate of interest and other essays.* London: Macmillan.

———. 1951-73. *Collected economic papers.* 6 vols. Oxford: Blackwell.

———. 1953. The production function and the theory of capital. *Review of Economic Studies, 21*: 81–106.

———. 1978. *Contributions to modern economics.* Oxford: Basil Blackwell.

Rowthorn, Robert. 1977. Conflict, inflation and money. *Cambridge Journal of Economics, 1*(3): 215–39.

———. 1995. Capital formation and unemployment. *Oxford Review of Economic Policy, 11*(1): 26–39.

Sampson, M. 2003. New eras and stock market bubbles. *Structural Change and Economic Dynamics,* 14: 297–315.

Samuelson, Paul A. 1948. *Economics.* New York: McGraw-Hill.

———. 1955. *Economics.* 3rd. ed. New York: McGraw-Hill.

———. 1958. What the classical theory of money really was. *Canadian Journal of Economics, 1*: 1–15.

———. 1981. Schumpeter's Capitalism, Socialism and Democracy. In *Schumpeter's Vision,* ed. A. Heertje, New York: Praeger.

Sargent, T. J. 1973. Rational expectations, the real rate of interest and the natural rate of unemployment. *Brookings Papers on Economic Activity, 2*: 429–72.

Sargent, T. J. and N. Wallace. 1976. Rational expectations and the theory of economic policy. *Journal of Monetary Economics,* 2: 169–83.

Schneider, Friedrich, and Andreas Buehn. 2009. Shadow economies and corruption all over the world: Revised estimates for 120 countries. *Economics, 1*: versions 1, 2.. http:*//www.economics-ejournal.org/economics/journalarticles/2007-9.*

Schumpeter, J. A. 1912. *Economic doctrine and method.* Translated by R. Aris. New York: Oxford University Press.

———. 1926. *The theory of economic development.* Cambridge, MA: Harvard University Press.

———. 1936. Keynes' *General Theory of Employment, Interest and Money* (Review). *Journal of the American Statistical Association, 31* (December): 791–95.

———. 1939. *Business cycles.* 2 vols. New York and London: McGraw-Hill.

———. 1942. *Capitalism, socialism and democracy.* New York: Harper and Row.

———. 1951a. *Essays.* Edited by R. V. Clemence. Cambridge, MA: Addison-Wesley.

———. 1951b. *Ten great economists from Marx to Keynes.* New York: Oxford University Press.

———. 1954. *History of economic analysis*. New York: Oxford University Press.
Schwert, G. William. 1989. Why does stock market volatility change over time, *Journal of Finance*, *44*(5): 1115–53.
Shackle, G. L. S. 1967. *The years of high theory*. Cambridge: Cambridge University Press.
Shaikh, A. 1975. The laws of algebra and the laws of production: The humbug production function. *Review of Economics and Statistics*, *56*(1): 115–20.
Sharpe, W. F. 1963. A simplified model for portfolio analysis. *Management Science*, *9*(2): 277–93.
Shiller, Robert. 1988. Causes of changing financial market volatility. *Symposium*. Federal Reserve Bank of Kansas City.
Shin, H. S. 2008. *Risk and liquidity*. Clarendon Lectures in Finance. Oxford: Oxford University Press.
Shonfield, Andrew. 1965. *Modern capitalism: The changing balance of public and private power*. Oxford: Oxford University Press.
Singh, Ajit. 1993. The stock market and economic development: Should developing countries encourage stock markets? *UNCTAD Review*, 4: 1–28.
———. 1994. Openness and the market-friendly approach to development: Learning the right lessons from development experience. *World Development*, *22*(16): 1811–23.
———. 1995. Pension reform, the stock market, capital formation and economic growth: A critical commentary on the World Bank's proposals. Mimeo, Cambridge University.
Singh, Ajit, and Javed Hamid. 1992. *Corporate financial structures in developing countries*. IFC Technical Paper no.1. Washington, DC: World Bank.
Sinn, Stefan. 1992. Saving-investment correlations and capital mobility. *Economic Journal*, *102*(414): 1162–70.
Skidelsky, Robert. 2000. *John Maynard Keynes: Fighting for Britain 1937-1946*. London: Macmillan.
———. 2009a. How to rebuild a newly shamed subject. *Financial Times*, December 15.
Smith, Adam. 1776/1961. *An inquiry into the nature and causes of the wealth of nations*. 2 vols. Edited by R. H. Campbell and A. S. Skinner. Oxford: Oxford University Press.
Solow, R. 1970. *Growth theory*. Oxford: Oxford University Press.
Solow, R. A. 1963. *Capital theory and the rate of return*. Amsterdam: North-Holland.
———. 1967. The interest rate and the transition between techniques. In *Capitalism, socialism and economic growth*, ed. Charles Feinstein, Cambridge: Cambridge University Press.
Solow, R. M. 1980. On theories of unemployment. *American Economic Review*, *70* (1): 1–11.
———. 1990. *The labor market as a social institution*. Oxford: Blackwell.
———. 2008. The state of macroeconomics. Unpublished Paper.
Sraffa, P. 1932a. Dr. Hayek on money and capital. *Economic Journal*, *42:* 42–53.
———. 1932b. A rejoinder. *Economic Journal*, *42:* 249–51.
———. 1960. *Production of commodities by means of commodities*. Cambridge: Cambridge University Press.
Stewart, Dugald. 1854–60. *Collected works*. 11 vols. Edited by William Hamilton. Edinburgh: Thomas Constable.

Stiglitz, Joseph E. 2010a. Dangers of deficit-cut fetishism. *The Guardian*, March 7.
———. 2010b. The non-existent hand. *London Review of Books*, *32*(8):17–18.
———. 2010c. Reform the euro or bin it. *The Guardian*, May 5.
Strøm, S. and L. Werin. 1978. *Topics in disequilibrium economics*. London: Macmillan.
Sudweeks, Bryan L. 1989. *Equity market development in developing countries*. New York: Praeger.
Symposium. 1966. Paradoxes in capital theory. *Quarterly Journal of Economics*, *80*(4): 503–83.
Taylor, Lance, and Jonathan Schlefer. 1995. Mexico's made-in-USA mess. *Washington Post*, October 8.
Temin, Peter. 1989. *Lessons from the great depression*. Cambridge, MA: MIT Press.
Tobin, James. 1966. Deficit, deficit, who's got the deficit? In *National Economic Policy* by James Tobin, 50–55. New Haven: Yale University Press.
———. 1980. *Asset accumulation and economic activity*. Oxford: Blackwell.
———. 1958. Liquidity preference as behaviour towards risk. *Review of Economic Studies*, *25*(1): 65–86.
Tobin, J. and W. Buiter. 1976. Long-run effects of fiscal and monetary policy on aggregate demand. In *Monetarism*, ed. J. L. Stein, Amsterdam: North-Holland.
Tocqueville, Alexis de. 1856/1972. *The old regime and the French Revolution*. Translated by S. Gilbert. New York: Doubleday-Anchor.
Triffin, Robert. 1960. *Gold and the dollar crisis*. New Haven, CT: Yale University Press.
United Nations (UN). 1993. *World economic survey, 1993*. New York: United Nations.
———. 1995. *World economic and social survey, 1995*. New York: United Nations.
———. 1996. *World economic and social survey, 1996*. New York: United Nations.
Von Neumann, John and Oskar Morgenstern. 1944. *Theory of games and economic behavior*. Princeton: Princeton University Press.
Wadsworth, J. 1994. The terrible waste. *New Economy*, *1*(1): 25–27.
Wagner, W., and I. Marsh. 2004. *Credit risk transfer and financial sector performance*. Working Paper no.13, CERF, University of Cambridge.
Wald, A. 1939. On some systems of equations in mathematical economics. *Econometrica*, *19*: 368–403.
Walters, A. 1971. Consistent expectations, distributed lags, and the quantity theory. *Economic Journal*, *81*: 273–81.
Ward, J. 2002. The supervisory approach: A critique. Mimeo, ESRC Centre for Business Research, University of Cambridge.
Welch, Cheryl B. 1984. *Liberty and utility: The French ideologues and the transformation of liberalism*. New York: Columbia University Press.
Wicksell, Knut. 1935. *Lectures on political economy*. Vol. 2. London: Routledge.
Winch, Donald, Stephan Collini, and John Burrow. 1982. *That noble science of politics*. Cambridge: Cambridge University Press.
Wolf, Martin. 2009. Narrow banking alone is not the answer. *Financial Times*, December 15.
Wood, Adrian. 1994. *North-south trade, employment and inequality: Changing fortunes in a skill-driven world*. Oxford: Clarendon Press.
Woodall, Pamela. 1995. The world economy: Financial markets, a survey. *The Economist*, October 7.

Woodford, Michael. 2009. Convergence in macroeconomics: Elements of the new synthesis. *American Economic Journal: Macroeconomics*, *1*(1): 267–79.

World Bank. 1994. *Averting the old age crisis: Policies to protect the old and promote growth.* New York: Oxford University Press.

World Institute for Development Economics Research (WIDER). 1990. *Foreign portfolio investment in emerging equity markets.* Helsinki: United Nations.

Index